A SIEGEL FILM

an autobiography

Don Siegel

FOREWORD BY
Clint Eastwood

faber and faber
LONDON · BOSTON

To my wife, Carol

I thank you for your love,
for your hard work,
and for putting up with me –
which ain't easy,

Your Don

First published in 1993 by
Faber and Faber Limited
3 Queen Square London WC1N 3AU
This paperback edition first published in 1996

Photoset by Wilmaset Ltd, Wirral
Printed in England by Clays Ltd, St Ives plc

Don Siegel is hereby identified as author of this work
in accordance with Section 77 of the Copyright,
Designs and Patents Act 1988

A CIP record for this book
is available from the British Library

ISBN 0–571–17831–6

2 4 6 8 10 9 7 5 3 1

Contents

Illustrations

Foreword

He encouraged me to direct and I encouraged him to act . . . those are two of the most positive aspects that came from a working relationship which had the strangest of beginnings, to say the least.

I had signed with Universal Pictures to do a film called *Coogan's Bluff*. This was to be my second American film after coming in off the plains of Spain. The studio had recommended a director by the name of Alex Segal, who had come from back East and had several plays, television shows, and movies to his credit. Alex Segal proceeded to have some personal problem which precluded him from doing this film and he withdrew. Then the studio came up with the suggestion, 'How about Don Siegel?' Now in a business in which nepotism runs rampant, I began to think, 'Hold on just a minute, what relationship do these two have and how many more Siegels are we going to go through before we get this picture on the road?' I didn't know much about Don but, as a courtesy to the studio, I ran some of his work before I began looking for another director. While running his films, I began to see that this man was extremely underrated; and although he had done more pictures than I had, he was from a similar background – always having to exist with low to moderate budgets at best and never being allowed the luxury of some of the high spending which frequents the movie industry today. Upon viewing *Invasion of the Body Snatchers* (which is probably one of the two or three finest B movies ever made), I realized that this was a man who could do an awful lot with very little. *Coogan's Bluff* was a modest-budget picture, but perhaps we could get a lot more on the screen for the dollar and push the film on to a higher echelon of 'look'. So I said, 'Yes, let's go with Don Siegel.'

Now of course the big catch was that Don Siegel wasn't familiar with *my* work – he had never seen any of the *Dollar* films and maybe had seen a minimal amount of *Rawhides*. He certainly wasn't aware of anything I was doing at that particular time. So Don would have to look at my films, which he did, and he felt the same sympathy for the Leone pictures, which looked a lot stronger than they actually were from a financial standpoint.

We fenced back and forth on the script and finally overcame various disagreements, but when the first day of shooting came I realized I was not working with just an ordinary person. Don kicked off so fast and so furiously in his shooting that this was clearly not a game of guessing – he had a solid concept in his mind and this was true film directing at its best. Maybe as a result of his background in the montage department, and working under Jack L. Warner, he came in completely prepared and the film went easily under schedule, as did the ensuing films we made together over the years. I think if there is one thing I learned from Don Siegel, it's to know what you want to shoot and to know what you're seeing when you see it – and that's something I haven't seen a lot of over the years.

We went on to make *Two Mules for Sister Sara*, *The Beguiled*, *Dirty Harry* and *Escape from Alcatraz*. All of these films were modest budget at best. Several became big stepping stones in both our careers. *The Beguiled* showed that Don could direct highly unusual, off-beat material with a very sensitive touch, and *Dirty Harry* showed he could handle the detective genre as well as anybody around.

Don Siegel had the greatest memory for events that happened in his life. I think you will be extremely entertained by his droll, acidic humour and the constant fight against the bureaucracy of studio mechanics. He may have more intelligent information to transmit to young film-makers than any working director today.

Clint Eastwood

Preface

Most people write books, scripts or poems because they like the subject matter, the form, their fellow writers, the prestige and, of course, the chance to make money. I don't deny their motives are worthy. But that is not my reason for attempting to write this book.

I'm not a writer. I'm a director/producer, in that order. Fellow directors, writers, young, middle-aged and elderly people interested in films ask me thousands of questions: 'How did you get your first feature to direct?' 'What's your favourite film you've directed?' 'Of all the films ever made, which is your favourite?' . . . Producers and executives rarely ask anything except, 'Can you make the budget?' 'Can you make the schedule?'

The list of film autobiographies runs well into the hundreds. Almost all the authors love their work, the people they work with and the people they work for. They adore their stars. The moguls can, at least in print, do no wrong.

Well, I'm going to try to be honest and tell the truth. This is not a book of hate. There is a great deal of love and fun in it. I wish I could erase the disappointments, the lies, the cruelties, the stupidities, the dark side of making pictures. I hope you lovers of film, you would-be directors, you army of questioners, benefit from my mistakes. I trust you will learn something. I didn't.

DON SIEGEL

Acknowledgements

My sincerest appreciation to Dr Howard B. Gotlieb, Director of Special Collections of the Mugar Memorial Library at Boston University, for having a collection of Siegel memorabilia: a compilation of hundreds of manuscripts, screenplays, reviews, interviews, correspondence, notes and photographs. Without Dr Gotlieb's generosity in sending them to me, I would never have been able to write my memoirs.

I am immensely grateful for the assistance given to me by Leith Adams of the Warner Brothers Archives at the University of Southern California Library. Leith is a most knowledgeable film buff and his unfailing enthusiasm for my memoirs, in addition to his constant encouragement, helped me enormously. I thank him for caring and for the many favours.

My grateful acknowledgement to Curtis Hanson, writer, director and editor of *Cinema*. Curtis's interview with me after the release of *Madigan* created a sensation. He has the mysterious knack of making the person he is interviewing completely relaxed. In my case, the result was a great interview. I apologize for having re-edited his interview here, because I had used similar material earlier in my memoirs. I am very proud of his directorial achievements and was happy that I was able to open a few doors to help Curtis get his well-deserved chance. Many thanks for his belief in my work.

My grateful acknowledgement to Stephen L. Karpf, writer, producer and professor in the Department of Cinema at the University of Southern California. Stephen's interview, 'Speaking Frankly', proved most interesting and entertaining. I thank him for allowing me to use it in my memoirs and apologize for the need for some re-editing. I greatly appreciate Stephen's interest in my work.

My grateful acknowledgement to Stuart Kaminsky. Certain passages from his book, *Don Siegel: Director*, have been paraphrased and the synopsis of *The Beguiled* has been extracted from his book.

Stills appear courtesy of BFI Stills, Posters and Designs. Copyright in the films is held by Warner Brothers (*Star in the Night, Hitler Lives, The Verdict, Night Unto Night, Dirty Harry*); Paramount (*Hell Is for Heroes, The Shootist, Escape from Alcatraz, Rough Cut*); RKO (*The Big Steal*); Allied Artists (*Riot in Cell Block 11, Invasion of the Body Snatchers*); Twentieth Century Fox (*Flaming Star*); Universal (*The Killers, Madigan, Coogan's Bluff, Two Mules for Sister Sara, The Beguiled, Charley Varrick, The Black Windmill*); MGM (*Telefon*); United Artists (*Jinxed*).

The Shootist

1976

Dino De Laurentis
presents
a Frankovitch/Self Production

JOHN WAYNE
LAUREN BACALL

A Siegel Film

And then come more credits, ending with 'Directed by Don Siegel'. It's exhausting just reading them. The only way to judge a picture is by seeing it, preferably on a large theatre screen.

I wasn't sure what Dino De Laurentis actually did. I believe he supplied the necessary dollars or liras. I do know that Paramount distributed the film in America and that CIC distributed it throughout the rest of the world. We shot all that was possible at the Burbank Studios, including the main streets of Carson City.

Mike Frankovitch was definitely the producer. The only contact I had with his partner, Bill Self, was when he gave me, on three separate sheets of paper, his criticisms of the writer's (Miles Hood Swarthout's) first script. Self was very successful for years as head of TV at Twentieth Century Fox. His pages looked like a combination of CBS, NBC and ABC censor notes. Most of his criticisms had to do with profanity, cancer, violence, etc. There were a few ideas, or suggestions on how to fix the script. Frankovitch had some other ideas and considerable enthusiasm. He was also incredibly good at casting suggestions.

One remarkable fact was clear from the start: no one in the world could play the leading role of J. B. Books but John Wayne. At the beginning of the picture, before the credits on the main title appeared, we saw shots of the younger Duke, in sepia, plying his trade as a shootist, gradually growing older. We also used 61 feet of the Duke from *Red River*, shot in 1948; 9 feet of the Duke from *Hondo* (1953); 13 feet of the Duke from

Rio Bravo (1959); two 13-foot sequences of the Duke from *El Dorado* (1967).

Even more remarkable than their parallel careers as shootists was that the credo of J. B. Books was exactly the same as that of John Wayne.

WAYNE: (*Voice over the early shots of him*) I won't be wronged. I won't be insulted. I won't be laid a hand on. I don't do these things to others, and I require the same from them.

John Wayne *was* J. B. Books. They both suffered from an incurable cancer. They were as one in bravery, temper, sense of humour, short-temperedness, and kindness to those who proved worthy of their kindness.

*

Mike Frankovitch drove me to Wayne's home in Newport and introduced me to the Duke.

DUKE: (*Wrapping his hand around mine twice*) Well, it's about time.
ME: (*Because I can't keep my mouth shut*) Actually, we met twice, in the late forties.
DUKE: Hey, sit down over here. (*Yells off stage.*) Bring some coffee! (*Looks at me closely.*) Where'd we meet?
ME: At a party. You were with Bo Roos and feeling no pain.
DUKE: That son of a bitch!
FRANKOVITCH: (*Thinking there might be trouble*) Hey, let's start talking about the script.
ME: It was either late in the evening or early in the morning. You came over to me and somebody introduced me to you as Don Siegel. You turned to Bo Roos.
DUKE: (*Disbelievingly*) But *this* is Don Siegel.
ME: You turned to me, stuck out your hand and said, 'Kid, I owe you an apology.' Looking up at you, not having the slightest idea – and I still don't – why the apology was necessary, I said in my very best Western accent, 'I reckon ya better.'
DUKE: I remember that somebody gave you a bad rap; said you were a Commie. A case of mistaken identity. I apologize.
(*His servant appears with a large tray bearing a pot of coffee and three large mugs with 'DUKE' written on them.*)
DUKE: Now, how about some coffee?
(*He starts pouring hot coffee into the mugs.*)
FRANKOVITCH: Let's cut out all this bullshit and get on with it.
DUKE: (*Quietly*) What changes have you made in that profane book?

2

FRANKOVITCH: (*Conciliatory*) I'm making all the changes you suggested. No dirty words, practically no mention of cancer. I spoke with the writer and you'll get the script exactly the way you want it.

DUKE: (*To me*) Is that the way you feel about it?

ME: I hope I can agree with all your changes, but I doubt it.

FRANKOVITCH: (*Angrily*) What the hell are you talking about?

ME: I'm not referring to dialogue that needs censoring. I'm talking about the construction of the screenplay, the continuity. The script as now written feels cold. I want, yes, in a Western, tears in the eyes of the audience. I want moments of love between the Duke and Bacall, but I'm not talking about sex. I want tenderness between Ron Howard and Duke.

FRANKOVITCH: (*Standing up*) I think you've flipped your wig.

DUKE: Sit down and stop interrupting.

(*I realize there is considerable tension between Frankovitch and Wayne.*)

DUKE: (*Turning to me*) I like your way of thinking. Have you talked with this kid writer, what's his name?

ME: Miles Hood Swarthout, and I didn't make it up.

DUKE: What do you think of him?

ME: I like his dad, who wrote the book. I have about seventy pages of notes, although I feel we will ultimately wind up with an excellent script.

FRANKOVITCH: (*Interrupting*) Stop right there. That's what we all want.

ME: What I was going to say before you interrupted was that I don't believe the kid can cut it. What's more, he's not co-operating, perhaps not wilfully. But I don't basically like his script. I feel we need a new writer who can give us what we want. Remember, Mike, this is his first script ever and he got to write it only because of his old man.

DUKE: (*Looking hard at Mike*) Still playing your usual stupid games. (*Getting up, towering over us.*) If you don't get a new writer that Don approves of, you can count me out.

(*Mike stands up, flashing me a look of hatred.*)

FRANKOVITCH: We came down here to discuss the script and you're quitting before this writer has a chance to carry out our changes.

DUKE: You're a procrastinator and a liar to boot. Quit trying to save pennies. The script is all important to me and should be to you.

FRANKOVITCH: (*Retreating*) What's your dialogue director's name?

3

ME: Scott Hale. He has fixed a number of scripts that I made into pictures.

DUKE: (*To me*) Is he the man you want?

ME: Obviously he's not the only apple in the barrel. But I've known Scott for years and I'm positive you'll like his work.

DUKE: (*Putting his arm around Mike*) Now you be a good fellow and give Don what he wants.

FRANKOVITCH: (*Protecting his position*) We'll read carefully Miles's rewritten script, and to show my good faith we'll hire this Scott Hale so we won't be wasting time. (*Face clouding in anger.*) But I won't pay him more than minimum scale.

On that happy note we left, but not before Wayne seized an opportunity when Mike was out of the room to ask me to talk script with him the next day, alone.

*

I brought the first script written by Miles, plus censor notes by Frankovitch and Bill Self. In addition, I had about seventy pages of my notes for Miles.

While waiting for the Duke to finish his ablutions, I wandered around the house. It had large, beautiful rooms, simply furnished in excellent, masculine taste. He even had a large gun room. The house stood on a peninsula surrounded by the Newport Bay, and he found me staring out across the bay, totally swept up in its beauty.

DUKE: (*Off screen*) Wanna buy it, Don?
(*He walks over to me carrying two cups of hot coffee and hands me one. He is smiling, in good humour.*)

ME: What will you take for it? A good film?

DUKE: It's all I've got left. (*Bitter.*) Two lousy, crooked business managers done me in.

ME: You're kidding.

DUKE: (*Looking down at me, his face set*) I don't kid about things like that. The last bastard that left me broke was my son-in-law. Funny, he was married to the only daughter I liked.
(*He sits down on a patio chair. I join him.*)

ME: He was crooked?

DUKE: Yeah, and stupid too.

ME: Let me get my briefcase. I love it out here.
(*When I return, he is looking across the bay in a pensive mood.*)

DUKE: All I wanted, for all the years I've worked, was to keep the status quo.

ME: (*Opening up my briefcase*) The status quo looks mighty good to me. (*Pulling out papers, scripts, etc.*) I'm sorry to do this to you, but you've got to catch up with me.

DUKE: In what way?

ME: You've got to read all this crap. Then we can talk.

DUKE: (*Sorting through the pages*) Will I like any of this stuff?

ME: You'll enjoy the censor notes by Bill Self and Mike. You'll hate the script by Miles, I hope. I also hope you'll like my notes to Miles on how to fix the script. I'm expecting plenty of comment on them.

DUKE: (*Deliberately starting to read my seventy pages of notes*) I'm many things, but I'm not shy. (*Looking up at me.*) Why don't you give an old fella like me a break? Let me have some time to digest, or throw up over them? We'll meet tomorrow. (*Gets an idea.*) Now why don't you follow me in your car to a building I rent. I want to show you something. After you've seen it, you can leave for LA from there.

(*He gets up and yells for Pat Stacey, his secretary, as I follow him.*)

ME: What kind of a building is it?

DUKE: (*Mysteriously*) It's full of garbage. (*Laughs at my incredulous look.*) I'll explain it all when we get there.

Duke got into his new, specially built Buick station wagon. Because of his huge torso, the roof of the wagon had to be raised. Pat came rushing out and got in beside him. She yelled to me as I got into my car.

PAT: Keep your eyes peeled. He's tough to follow.

She wasn't kidding. He screeched out of the driveway, catching me unaware. I drove a 300 SEL 4.5 1972 Mercedes and, despite the fact that his car was brand new, I felt certain that if I didn't lose him right now I could keep up with him.

He drove and acted like a kid. For a while I was worried about getting a ticket for speeding. I could only assume that cops in Newport would never give Duke Wayne a ticket – but what if I was pulled over?

It took everything I had, plus a lot of luck, finally to catch him. I pushed down on the throttle and slowly passed him; then, braking hard for an approaching red signal, I looked over at him questioningly. He grinned back at me. The moment the signal started changing, he tore off, but he couldn't get away from me. Finally, we reached an inconspicuous grey, one-storey, factory-like building. I pulled up behind him. Duke and Pat got out of his wagon.

DUKE: Lucky for you that Pat was with me, or I'd have creamed you.

5

ME: Thank you, Pat. You saved our lives.

I followed them inside. A maze of galvanized pipes ran throughout the otherwise empty building. It looked exactly like a complicated Rube Goldberg invention. In the background a man in overalls slowly made his way towards us.

DUKE: (*Looking around proudly*) What do you think, Don?
ME: It's a Communist plot to do us in.
DUKE: (*Turning to the man in overalls*) Genius, meet Don.
  (*The man wipes his hand on a soiled rag he is carrying. We shake hands. I notice a strong odour of garbage and a very faint smell of oil.*)
INVENTOR: Had a small problem this morning. Couldn't get the goddamn contraption to run. But I think I can get it started now.

We followed him back to where he had first appeared. Before us was a large, open bin filled with garbage. He picked up several small bottles of colourless chemicals and sprinkled them over the garbage. Faint wisps of smoke began to rise from the bin. He then picked up some heavy lead weights, the kind that are used on motion-picture booms, and piled them on top of the garbage. I guessed the pressure would force the garbage through a large pipe at the bottom of the bin. The chemicals now smelled worse than the garbage. But it was much more complicated than that. When he finally got the small engine started, puffing and wheezing, he pulled a switch which started a noisy vacuum, which sucked the garbage into the pipe.

We all followed Duke as he walked excitedly beneath the pipes as the garbage went through. At one point another motor started, which began to pulverize the garbage into pulp. At another point steam suddenly shot out of overhead vents. Finally we reached the end of the last pipe, which had a large spigot turned to the off position.

DUKE: Don, it's unbelievable. You saw the garbage in the bin. Well, when I turn the spigot on, oil will flow, my friend . . . oil will flow.
  (*The inventor pulls a large barrel underneath the spigot.*)
INVENTOR: Turn on the gusher!

Duke, his face wreathed in optimism, turned the spigot on. Nothing happened. Both men looked baffled. Then a couple of drops of blackish liquid appeared and dripped into the barrel. Then nothing at all. Duke stared at the spigot for a long moment. He looked disgusted and about to explode. I was in an awkward position, because if I opened my mouth I'd put my foot in it. I wanted that oil to gush out. Duke was like a kid who had had his lollipop taken away from him.

Suddenly, he let off steam with the longest string of profanity known to man. I took the 'chicken' route. Yelling 'See you tomorrow!', I rushed out of the building, jumped into my Mercedes and careered down the street towards what I hoped was the road to LA.

*

When I saw Duke the next day, he liked my notes on Miles's script. He wanted to know what was happening with my dialogue director.

ME: It's unbelievable, but Mike is trying to get Scott Hale to write for the same salary he gets for being the dialogue director — a difference of fifty bucks a week.

DUKE: Mike's a pompous ass. Just tell this Scott fella to hang in.

ME: Mike's a good guy, but a puzzler. He's generous to a fault, but will fight to the death over pennies.

DUKE: Well, he ain't gonna win this fight, I promise you.
(*Smiles.*) On your notes. I might surprise you with a few of my own.

Duke's idea of 'a few of my own' rapidly developed into an avalanche of ideas. Some I liked, some sparked me into new channels of thought, some I plain didn't like. Duke may be many things, but he's no fool. We liked and respected each other. I enjoyed working with him. It was fun.

When we quit for lunch, we were joined by his grandchildren. Duke asked me why Clint Eastwood made such violent pictures with such profane language.

ME: There's very little gratuitous violence, sex or bad language in an Eastwood film.

DUKE: (*Exploding*) Bullshit! His films are full of fucking, goddamn obscenities. It's a bad image to paint himself into. A fucking shame.
(*I notice his grandchildren busily eating, paying no attention to the foul language being bruited about by Grandpa. Apparently he is unaware that his tongue is full of profanities.*)

ME: I'll tell you something you might not know. Clint would like to make a picture with you. He admires you.

DUKE: Well — I didn't say he was a bad guy.
(*He fills his mouth with food and stops talking.*)

*

The next time I saw Duke, I brought Scott Hale with me, even though his deal was still not set. Scott and Duke got along well. We worked for a few hours, Scott taking copious notes and making excellent suggestions about continuity and dialogue. He was definitely the writer. When the question arose of how many guns a 'shootist' would carry on his person and on his horse, Duke got up.

DUKE: I've got a few items I've picked up over the years. Follow me.

He took us into his huge gun room and showed us a gleaming carbine, made at the beginning of the nineteenth century, with a holster, which would be on the horse. He got down on his knees in front of a large closet, slid the door open and started cursing. It was filled with revolver holsters, stirrups and God knows what else. Finally he found the holster he wanted and handed it to me. It looked well worn, but clean.

When he started to get up, Duke began cursing again. His breathing became heavy. For a moment, it looked as if he wouldn't make it. Scott made his first mistake

SCOTT: (*Offering his hand*) May I?
DUKE: (*Grunting with effort*) No! Goddamnit!

When he got to his feet, his face red with effort, he lurched over to a glass cabinet attached to the wall. There were about ten pistols on display. He opened the cabinet door, surprisingly unlocked. Reaching in, he removed a pearl-handled forty-five. He handed it to Scott.

DUKE: Every gun is loaded.
    (*Scott, startled, holds it gingerly.*)
DUKE: Never keep an unloaded gun. That's how you can get hurt. The kids damn well know it.

He went over to a desk, opened the top drawer and lifted a small wooden gun case, which he set on the desk top and opened to reveal a derringer. He lifted it out and weighed it in his hand. No longer breathing heavily, he smiled at us.

DUKE: Betcha you never figured I'd use a derringer.
SCOTT: I would never have thought of it.
ME: Where do you carry it?
DUKE: (*Pleased*) Up my sleeve. You know in the beginning of the picture, in the middle of nowhere, when the robber character holds me up? When I throw him my wallet, at the same time I shoot him with this little sweetheart.
ME: I always saw it as a quick draw with your revolver.

8

DUKE: (*Concerned*) You mean you don't like the scene with the derringer?

ME: Not at all. It's great.
(*With a straight face.*) I'm glad I thought of it.

DUKE: (*Relieved and amused*) Well, I'm glad you thought of it too.

ME: I'm genuinely glad that you're not wearing, *à la* William S. Hart, two revolvers, one on each hip.

DUKE: That two-gun shit went out with William S. Hart.
(*Duke puts everything away and leads us back to the room where we had been working. We all sit down at the table. Scott immediately starts writing notes about the various guns.*)

ME: Before I forget, I have to pick locations and do a million other things, so Scott will be working every day with you, if that's all right?

DUKE: (*Grinning evilly*) I'm glad I thought of it.

ME: Touché. (*Looking closely at Duke.*) Why not, for a change, wear a moustache and small Vandyke?

DUKE: Because I can't grow the fucking hair to make the moustache and Vandyke. And I'm not going to wear any wigs. (*Smiles.*) Excepting for the top of my head. What the hell are we doing growing old?

ME: Before I answer that one, how about letting it grow before the picture starts? We'll see how it looks. If *you* don't like it, shave it off. No arguments, period.

DUKE: (*Thinks for a moment*) I'm taking my boat out for a two-week cruise as soon as I finish with Scott, so I'll give it a whirl.

ME: Thanks, Duke. Now, to answer your question about growing old. It's God's evil design, being brought into this disturbed world as a weeping, screaming, peeing baby. My idea is much better. You appear on earth in perfect health, around eighty-five, give or take a year, successful and happy. Then, with all of your knowledge, you work your way backward and when you reach the age of, say, six months, you're kicked off this peaceful, tranquil, lovely earth – and that's that.

DUKE: (*Staring at me*) Do you feel OK? How about some golden tequila?

ME: Back to the drawing board. Scott, for Christ's sake, quit making notes about guns and join our little group.

We got back to the script discussions as the sun sank in the beautiful west . . .

*

Russ Saunders, an all-American, barrel-chested half-back from the University of Southern California, worked as the production manager for producer Mike Frankovitch, a strong all-American guard for the University of California at Los Angeles. This didn't necessarily make them good location managers.

Russ, who has been in the business even longer than I (I first met him in 1934 at Warners when he was a first assistant director), scouted locations with Robert Boyle, winner of four Academy Award nominations, who was an excellent location manager. They came back from a short location trip without finding a suitable town, circa 1901.

RUSS: We found several places that might work: Prescott, New Mexico. There . . .

BOB: (*Breaking in*) They definitely won't work. Prescott doesn't fit our town and Las Vegas and New Mexico are too high in altitude for Wayne. However, we found a great period house in Carson City for the character Mrs Bond Rogers.

ME: Good. I think Mike's trying to work out a deal for Lauren Bacall, who'd be sensational. (*To Russ.*) What else did you find?

RUSS: A great place on a lake very near Carson City for the scene when J. B. Books takes Mrs Rogers for a ride in the buggy. Another great place up in the mountains, near Carson City. Full of snow, absolutely beautiful and accessible. That's for the main titles and for the robbery sequence immediately following.

BOB: But Russ, didn't you tell me that because it's 6,000 feet high Wayne might not be able to take the altitude?

RUSS: Well, we found that other place at about 3,000 feet which would work. Beautiful snow-capped mountains in the background.

BOB: But practically no snow on the ground. There's no comparison between the two spots.

ME: (*To Russ*) We'll set up a recce, or location trip if you prefer to call it that, as soon as possible. What worries me is the town. Obviously if the locations, like the house . . .

BOB: (*Interrupting*) We can only use the exterior of the house. The interior is hopeless. We definitely will have to build the interior.

ME: That all right with you, Russ?

RUSS: Absolutely. In addition, in the back of the house is a barn that you could use for the scene between Books and Gillom, which takes place in a barn, exterior and interior.

ME: Hey, that sounds good.

RUSS: What will sound even better is that the background of snow-

10

capped mountains is exactly the same mountains we see at the three-thousand-foot location in the beginning of the picture.

ME: With all these locations it sure looks like the town is Carson City. However, where do we find the town that we'll call Carson City?

RUSS: When I discovered how difficult it is to find the town, I realized that if we're to find the right place you've got to be with us. Otherwise, to use Bob's favourite word, it will be 'hopeless'.

ME: You get the OK from Mike – and by that I mean the money for an extensive trip – and we're off.

BOB: I know how you hate the backlot, but I think you ought to take a look at it.

ME: First things first, Bob. I know the Warner backlot as well as the palm of my hand. I spent fourteen straight years at Warners and still have the scars on my back to prove it. Universal has a much better kept-up backlot than Warners' – and I hate it . . . If we fail to find the town . . . you know we don't have much time before we're supposed to start shooting. I'll look at anything you want me to see. (*Standing up*.) Gentlemen, I'll see you both in Carson City.

*

After a couple of days of going seriously into our casting problems with Mike (he had the excellent idea of casting as many stars or well-known actors as he could get), I took off for Carson City with Russ and Bob.

Everything worked better than I had anticipated, but we still faced the same problem – we couldn't find a town that even began to work. Before setting out for distant locations with no guarantee that we would find anything, I caved in. I agreed to look at the Warner backlot. The pressure of an early start date scared me. Mike was already making tentative commitments with such luminaries as Lauren Bacall, James Stewart (I didn't think Mike would get him as the part was too small), Hugh O'Brian, Scatman Crothers, Richard Boone and God knows how many others. So I had good cause to return to Hollywood.

I took a cruise of the backlot with Bob Boyle alone, because I had great respect for his talent. Also, I knew he would level with me.

The street that we were interested in for the main street of Carson City was badly run down as a whole. I found it depressing.

ME: As if I had to ask, what do you think?

BOB: There are possibilities, providing we get two things . . .

ME: I know: time and money.

BOB: Exactly. I think for many reasons we'll get both. For one thing, it will cost less in the long run. We don't have to pay for the usual costs of locations, transportation, living expenses for cast, crew and animals. We also will have to build certain structures, no matter where we go. Secondly, if you stick to your guns, and I mean really stick to them, this ugly, unkempt, nothing street can be transformed into a street much better than anything we could possibly find.

ME: (*Pointing*) What about those scrubby hills?

BOB: You know better than I do. A couple of matte shots and you're really in Carson City. (*Pointing*.) We'll see distant mountains covered with snow.

ME: What about the bars, particularly the Metropole, where at the end of the picture Duke has the big shoot-out?

BOB: You're standing right in front of it.

(*All I can see is a run-down drapery-store front.*)

BOB: (*Smiling*) I'll not only give you the best-looking exterior, but you'll be able to walk into the interior of the best-looking and biggest saloon west of the Rockies.

ME: What about Dr Hostetler's residence, exterior and interior?

BOB: (*Pointing*) You're blind.

(*I stare at an empty space and start laughing.*)

ME: OK. You win. But before we see Mike, I need two long-shot sketches of the street, one in each direction.

BOB: (*Pleased*) One picture is . . .

ME: (*Relentless*) Two sketches . . .

BOB: Two sketches are better than a thousand words.

*

Duke sent me a postcard from a Mexican seaport town telling me that he was feeling great. There was also an enclosure: a polaroid photo of him sporting two weeks' growth of moustache and Vandyke. He had scrawled on the polaroid, 'I can't believe it. Duke.'

*

Bob walked in carrying one large colour sketch of the Carson City main street, circa 1901. A mule-driven street car was making a turn in the immediate foreground. Decipherable on its side was 'Carson City Traction'. Iron rails ran down the centre of the cobbled street. Wagons, rigs and buckboards moved along in front of two- and three-storey buildings. There was a bank, hotel, two saloons, including the Metropole, a barber's shop and a small opera house. Pedestrians were shopping, crossing the street. Tall poles strung with lines for telephones and electricity ran along the sidewalk. In the distance, a steam-driven engine was crossing the street. In the far distance were those snow-covered mountains.

ME: I truly didn't think it was possible. Congratulations and many thanks.

BOB: Wait till Mike and Russ see it. Their eyes will look like blinking cash registers.

ME: (*Picking up the phone*) Keep the faith.
(*Mike answers the phone. Unusual for him, as he has two secretaries.*)

ME: You busy, Mike?

MIKE: Skipped lunch. Didn't have time for a sandwich.

ME: Could you sandwich in a meeting with Bob and me on the Warner backlot street in, say, thirty minutes?

MIKE: You bet your bottom buck I could.

ME: Would you please bring Russ?

MIKE: Sure. See you in half an hour.
(*We hang up.*)

ME: Let's work it this way. Hide your sketch. We'll stumble through the street before we show him the sketch. Has Russ seen it?

BOB: I never show anything to anyone before the director.

ME: (*Getting up, putting my arm around Bob and going to the door*) He could have stuck his head in the drafting room and seen you working on it.

BOB: (*Pleased*) No chance. Three flights of stairs.

Mike Frankovitch and Russ Saunders found us waiting in the Warner street; the sketch, showing the incredible transformation into Carson City's main street, was well hidden.

As we walked down the street, I kept up a running commentary of my intense dislike for it: how shabby it was; how it had nothing remotely usable for *The Shootist*; how it had been used endless times for TV series; how the California background of hills covered with dry grass and a few small, dead-looking oaks would destroy the believability of the excellent locations we had already found.

MIKE: (*Concerned*) First, I want to thank you for at least taking a good look at the street. Isn't there something you could do with it?

ME: Burn it to the ground and rebuild it.

MIKE: You're completely satisfied that a street on location can't be found?

ME: Ask Russ.

RUSS: Of course a street can be found, although we don't have much time before the start date. But even if we found something, Mike, we would have to fix it up to fit our story. Considering the location costs, I doubt that it would cost less than whatever you build here.

MIKE: (*Bitterly, looking around*) They sure let it run down. What the hell can we do? I agree with Don – it stinks.

BOB: (*Taking over, according to our plan*) Well, I don't agree with you, or Don. Sure, the street is bad; but architecturally speaking, there's a great deal that can be saved.

MIKE: Thank God. Though I don't see how without spending a fortune.

BOB: I'm not saying it's not going to cost money – a lot of it. But I agree with Russ – it's the only ball game in town.

MIKE: Give me a ball-park figure.

BOB: It's stupid to guess. First, we have to find out if Don will buy it.

MIKE: How about it, Don?

ME: (*Looking around slowly*) Well, I never thought I'd be faced with this miserable decision. (*Looking Mike square in the eye.*) But if you promise, on your word of honour, that you won't chisel, scrimp – oh hell, that you'll let Bob and me build a street that will be as good or better than anything in the picture, I'm enthusiastically for it.

MIKE: (*Solemnly*) I promise.

RUSS: That's a wise decision, Mike.

ME: I believe, Bob, you have something to tell us.

BOB: (*Enjoying everything*) *One* sketch is worth a thousand words. Follow me.

We all trudged through the dust-heavy street. When we reached the top, Bob suddenly disappeared into the darkness of a store front and quickly emerged with the large sketch. Quietly, he handed it over to Mike. Wide-eyed, Mike stared at it. Russ peered over his shoulder. Bob had the audacity to give me a quick wink.

MIKE: (*To Bob and me*) You sons of bitches! It's the goddamndest best-looking street I've ever seen. Everything's in it. Oh, my God, I promised to build it.

BOB: (*Quickly*) Russ and I can give you an honest budget in a couple of days. It's not going to cost as much as you think.

MIKE: Can I keep the sketch?

BOB: After we show you the budget.

MIKE: You and Russ, drop everything and get right on it. (*Turning to me.*) All right, smart ass, let's walk back to my office. My heart's pounding wih excitement.

ME: (*Calling after Bob and Russ, who are walking back to Bob's office in the opposite direction*) Good luck! (*Putting my arm around Mike.*) I'm happy and will thank you by shooting a picture we'll all be very proud of.

*

Everything progressed smoothly. Bob Boyle showed me various prints of the street, which looked very good to me. I initialled my OK, as did Mike. Russ hesitated a bit, trying to cut down the cost, but Bob and I held firm. The budget for the street was under $300,000. I thought that was very reasonable, although Mike and Russ moaned. But that's what they're there for, to moan. I wasn't sure Bob would bring it in on budget, but he felt cocky that he'd be close.

I received another polaroid from Duke. He looked great. His moustache and Vandyke were distinctly visible. He had scrawled on the back of the polaroid, 'I'm beginning to like it. Hope it's not catching. Been working on the script. Will send you some ideas. Hope all's well with you and Scott. Duke.'

Mike was absolutely fantastic with casting. He now had commitments

1   *The Shootist*: Bob Boyle's sketch of the main street

15

2   *The Shootist*: the main street

– though they were somewhat loose, to protect us in case we got screwed up on our start date – from Lauren Bacall, Ron Howard, James Stewart (believe it or not), Richard Boone, John Carradine, Scatman Crothers, Harry Morgan, Sheree North, Hugh O'Brian, Richard Lenz and others. A truly great cast, headed of course by the Duke.

I finally got Bruce Surtees as my cinematographer; Doug Stewart as my film editor; Scott Hale, eventually, as the writer; and Al Overton as the sound mixer. All these men were the best in their field and Mike was difficult about all their salaries. Needlessly so.

I got a letter from Duke, sent from La Paz, Mexico, with his script ideas. I thought they made a lot of sense. I hastened to give them to Scott, who had practically finished the script, which I liked. Scott is a bit defensive about making changes on anyone's suggestions, including mine; however, he made them.

We decided to shoot the beginning of the picture and the attempted robbery at the 3,500-foot location. Duke's doctor refused to take any responsibility if we went over 3,000 feet, so Boyle tacked on a tree, 'Altitude exactly 3,000 feet'.

The day started well. When Duke began to mount his horse, the photographer started shooting stills. Duke let out a bellow of rage and had his horse lash out a kick at the stillman, knocking him down. I rushed in and helped the poor man to his feet, telling him that he had done no wrong but advising him not to shoot any stills that day.

I discovered that Wayne had his own photographer and refused to have anyone else. All this was explained in a loud, profane tirade to Frankovitch. Mike immediately capitulated: Duke's stillman would be on the set tomorrow morning; Mike had made a stupid mistake in not hiring Duke's man. As it later turned out, Duke's stillman, Dave Sutton, spent 95 per cent of his time playing chess with Duke.

We finally made the main title shot, on which I was allowed to yell 'Action' and 'Cut'. But when we came to the sequence where the burly robber holds a rifle on Duke while attempting to get his wallet, Duke took over the picture. He didn't do too badly. He used the derringer to wound the robber, said a few parting words of his own to the sprawling robber and rode off. This took all day. I wasn't welcome to have anything to do with it.

I felt that Duke had every right to have his own stillman, although I disliked him and thought him untalented. But he did play chess, and lost consistently and peacefully to Duke. But what about the director? If Duke was going to direct *The Shootist*, what about my beautiful title, 'A Siegel Film', in script immediately above the main title? I was completely discombobulated . . . and getting a teeny weeny bit angry. I made no comment about the situation to Duke, Mike or Russ. As we finished working I couldn't resist announcing calmly, though I was seething, 'We will commence shooting here tomorrow morning. We lost half a day.'

I left without saying goodbye to anyone. I was embarrassed and despondent. In addition, I was truly surprised.

*

Next morning, around 6 o'clock, I was having breakfast with my associate Carol Rydall. Carol was a symphony violinist, and thus excellent at using music in post-production work. Not only was she a diligent and alert dialogue director, but to my surprise she was also most helpful in working on the script. Her ideas were original. Most people are unaware that she worked for Clint Eastwood for eight years, running his office. She learned a great deal from Clint and I made good use of it when she worked for me. I had just finished telling her that I was going to have it

17

out with Duke, in his trailer at the location, when the phone rang. I picked it up. It was Duke.

DUKE: Can I see you up in my suite before you leave for the location?
ME: Your timing's perfect. I was just telling Carol that I was going to see you in your trailer as soon as I got to the location. I'll be right up. (*Hanging up and turning to Carol.*) I'll be back in a few minutes.
CAROL: Please don't lose your temper. It's not good for you. (*Kissing me.*) Good luck.
ME: I'll need it.

Duke opened the door to his suite and immediately yelled at Pat Stacey and her girlfriend, who were having breakfast.

DUKE: (*Full of anger*) I told you both to get your asses out of here. I want to speak to Mr Siegel alone.
(*They scurry out of the room. As I enter, a loud knock is heard at the door.*)
DUKE: (*Opening the door again*) What the hell do you want?
(*It is Dave Grayson, Duke's make-up man.*)
DAVE: I'm here to make you beautiful.
DUKE: I'll see you in the trailer on location.
DAVE: But Duke, we agreed yesterday that it would be easier for *you* if I did your make up in your room.
DUKE: (*Livid*) Goddamn your miserable soul, when I tell you something, do it!

He spun him round and pushed him hard down the corridor. The ebullient Dave disappeared without further protest. Duke slammed the door, still totally ignoring me, and noticed a door to his right slightly ajar.

DUKE: Luster! You miserable eavesdropping bastard! Close that door or I'll wrap you in your wardrobe and throw you out the window!

The door closed silently. At last we were alone together. I confess my adrenalin was racing. Duke came over to me, put his arms around me and started to cry.

DUKE: I don't know what came over me yesterday. I'm sorry. It will never happen again. I swear to you . . .
ME: (*Disentangling myself*) It wasn't as bad as all that. You had many good ideas. (*Finally catching his eye, which is full of tears.*) The trouble is simply this. I have to work loose, or I'm no good.

18

DUKE: I know, I know.

ME: You're very knowledgeable, Duke. You know a great deal about directing.

(*Because I have diarrhoea of the mouth and can't leave a winner, I continued.*)

ME: I've even seen every picture you've directed, and I didn't like any of them.

Duke took it like a man. He embraced me once more, saw me to the door and thanked me for coming up to see him. I left bewildered, bewitched and bothered.

When I appeared on the location, Duke embraced me once more. I noticed Mike, Russ, the camera crew, in fact everybody watching, their mouths agape.

DUKE: (*Loudly*) Mr Siegel, there's one director on this picture and thank God it's you. What's your pleasure?

ME: Give me a few minutes with my cameraman. I'm going to break up . . .

(*Smiling at him.*) . . . what you shot yesterday.

Throughout the day's shooting, Duke asked my permission for every action or idea he had.

DUKE: (*Calling out*) Mr Siegel, is it all right that I look more startled but not fearful of the 'robber'? . . . Sir! Sorry to bother you. Can I, sir, throw the 'robber' in that icy pond as I ride off? . . .

This politeness and respect went on all day. The cast and crew, plus the executive staff, couldn't believe their ears and eyes. I felt great and confident once more. This euphoria lasted for three days.

The dailies looked excellent. I was a bit surprised that Duke didn't attend. Not that I was looking for trouble. Actually, I preferred actors *not* to see the dailies. Generally, if they got up and left the projection room without a word, you were ahead of the game.

Work continued smoothly until the day beside the lake and snow. Duke drove a horse and buggy with Bacall by his side. After several shots, which worked fine and looked wonderful in the crisp air, with sunshine peeking through the denuded limbs of the sycamore trees, Bruce was overseeing the laying of a dolly, which was being pushed with great difficulty by the grips and labourers. Suddenly, without warning, Duke appeared and exploded.

DUKE: (*To Bruce*) What the hell are you doing? (*Not waiting for a reply.*) You'd do a damn sight better if you concentrated on the lighting instead of fucking around with dollies, making the cast look like zombies.
(*I leap off the bank and race up to Duke.*)
ME: You should be ashamed of yourself criticizing Bruce for his photography. You haven't seen *one foot* of film and you dare to open your big mouth.
(*Duke starts to say something, but I continue heatedly.*)
ME: I want to see you as soon as you can get to the projection room at the hotel. It will be interesting to hear your criticisms *after* you've seen the film. (*Turning away from him to Bruce and the crew.*) That's a wrap! (*To Bruce.*) Tear that dolly track up. You and your key grip and gaffer go down to the lake where the big tree is. Tomorrow we'll make a stationary shot of Bacall and Duke in the buggy. Give them a full shot set-up. That way you can shoot pretty postcard pictures. I'll rustle up the editors and get all the dailies we have to the projection room. Maybe the new ones have arrived. Be in the projection room as soon as you can.

I strode off, my mind awhirl. I was worried about what Duke would think of the dailies. The latest ones – the scene with Ron Howard and Duke in the barn – had arrived and were already on the projector, and the projection room was already partly full when I got there. Word had apparently spread. My sensitive cameraman arrived with his crew. Bruce looked pale, and I'm sure I didn't look any better. Finally, the Duke, freshly washed and dressed, entered the projection room. He sat quietly in a chair behind Bruce. I waved to Judi Dolan, our projectionist, to start. The shades were drawn, the lights turned off. The noisy machine started, the light from the projector hitting the screen. The show was on.

God, we were lucky. Not only did the scene between Ron Howard and Duke play well, but Bruce's photography was superb. Duke's face lined with feeling. It was exactly what I wanted. When it was over there was complete silence, broken only by the pulling up of the shades. The lights went on. I got up and faced Duke. Tears were streaming down his face. He grabbed Bruce.

DUKE: (*Incoherently, with much emotion*) Damnit, kid, that's the best damn film of me I've ever seen. I love yuh and hope you'll forgive me.
(*Bruce is so overcome with emotion and embarrassment that he can't talk, and I break in to help him.*)

ME: Duke, we couldn't be happier. Let's all get to the bar. Drinks on me.
   (*As we straggle out, everyone talking animatedly, I manage to get behind Bruce and whisper in his ear.*)
ME: You're good for about three days.

Bruce nodded contentedly. However, I was wrong. We completed all our location work without further incident.

*

One Sunday Duke graciously invited Carol and me up to his suite to share his new-found treasure – fresh clams. A friend of his from Seattle flew in on his own jet early on Sunday morning to give a load of iced fresh clams to Wayne. He was so excited, I didn't have the heart to tell him that I had never eaten clams before. The thought of them made me sick. However, when he served us at the bar, with a chaser of golden tequila, I found to my surprise that I liked the clams. Maybe it was the tequila. It was a memorable afternoon, what I remember of it, with his friends from Seattle, his secretary and a most gracious Duke.

We gathered in front of the television set to watch a football game, eating clams and drinking tequila. Duke stuck his head in the room. The hubbub subsided. He didn't look well.

DUKE: Put your money on the Steelers. They're too tough for Dallas.
   I'm a little under the weather. Sorry I can't be with you.

He closed the door to his bedroom. It took the edge off the game. Frankly, we were all worried about the extent of his illness. This was the first indication we had had that anything was wrong with Duke, although most of us knew that he had half a lung, that he had had a bout with cancer which, apparently, he had won. We had only a week's more work on location before returning to Burbank Studio. Thank God, there was nothing strenuous for Duke to do. Knowing him, if he could get up on his feet, he'd kill himself rather than not perform. Each day he was always the first member of cast on the set. I crossed my fingers.

He looked a little wan early on Monday morning on location. I went over the week's work with him, and he declared it 'a snap'. I urged him to let me know the minute he felt tired. I could easily shoot around him.

DUKE: Thanks for your consideration. If there's one thing I hate, it's people worrying about me. It makes me sick, so cut it out.

Duke finished the week's location work not only on schedule, but his performance was up to his usual high standard.

*

21

We all travelled back to LA on Sunday. We were to begin studio work the next day, first on the stages, then on the street. On Monday morning, early, before going to Stage 14, the interior of Dr Hostetler's (James Stewart's) office, I rushed over to the Carson City street. Even though it appeared that a lot of work was still needed to complete it, it looked great – better than my expectations. I thanked Bob for his hard work.

He and I looked over the Hostetler set together, discussing how I was going to shoot it, and then I stuck my head into Duke's trailer. He was being made up.

DUKE: Belasco, the famous stage producer, once said, 'Twenty-five per cent for the set, twenty-five per cent for the story, *fifty per cent* for the *cast*.'

ME: No, he didn't. He said, 'Twenty-five per cent for the set, twenty-five per cent for the cast and *fifty per cent* for *the story*.'

DUKE: Tell me something. How come you don't park your car next to the stage door?

ME: You saw the parking signs: Frankovitch–Wayne–Siegel.

DUKE: A director *always* parks next to the stage door.

ME: I know. I can't help it if Frankovitch and Russ are ignorant. (*I rush over to Jimmy Stewart's trailer, knock and enter. He is made up and dressed. We shake hands.*)

JIMMY: How's the Duke feeling? I heard a couple of things.

ME: He had one bad spell – but he arranged for it to happen on a Sunday. It didn't affect his work or the schedule.

JIMMY: It never has and never will. He's too ornery, in spite of which he's one of my best friends.

ME: Let's take a walk to your set. There are a couple of things I'd like to talk to you about.

JIMMY: (*Leading the way to the trailer door*) I already sneaked a look. The set decorator knows the period and the story. (*As we walk over to the set.*) I like to be with the director before Duke gets to him. That way maybe I can get all the best angles.

ME: When you two scene stealers get together, all hell breaks loose. Let's waltz through it.

I told Jimmy that he would open the door for Duke, who would enter his office; then I'd pull back with the two of them, Duke sitting on a sofa and Jimmy pulling up a chair.

JIMMY: You're shooting the left side of my face?

ME: Yes. Anything wrong?

JIMMY: Nope.

ME: Do you have a 'better' side?

JIMMY: Nope. (*Smiles.*) To tell you the truth, whichever side the camera points at is my best side.

(*Duke walks on to the set and embraces his old buddy.*)

DUKE: (*To Jimmy*) Quit holding up rehearsals. Where do you want us, Don?

ME: Before we stumble through a rehearsal, there's one thing I'd like to discuss with you two inexperienced actors. These scenes are very poignant and touching. I hope you agree that we should play against that. If you don't allow any sentimentality to creep in, if indeed you play the scene somewhat matter-of-factly, the pain, the suffering, the pathos will all be there.

(*They look at me, then at each other.*)

ME: Gentlemen, I rest my case.

DUKE: (*To Jimmy*) Don't you hate it when the director plays the scene exactly the way you intend to do it?

JIMMY: Exactly the way I feel.

Needless to say, they played their scenes as only Duke and Jimmy could play them – perfectly. It was very interesting to watch these two old pros working together in complete harmony and accord. They knew that I knew that they knew what they were doing. Just about all I did was direct traffic.

I did learn one thing from Duke about Jimmy. Jimmy was outside the door waiting for his action cue to come in. I gave him the cue – nothing happened. I gave it to him again, louder. There was no movement outside the door. Duke leaned down to my ear and whispered, 'He's slightly deaf.' I yelled my action cue and all went smoothly and well.

On location we had finished all the exteriors of Mrs Roger's (Lauren Bacall's) house. On Stage 14 were the complete interiors of the house. Even as one entered the porch, steps and path leading to a backing, all exactly matched what was actually shot in Carson City. The set was so cleverly designed that in one continuous shot I showed Bacall and Duke entering the house; her pointing out the parlour, the dining room, the pantry; the two of them walking past the kitchen, which could be seen in the background, the bathroom, and into a bedroom, which he rented. The remarkable thing was that no audience could possibly tell when we were shooting in Carson City or at the studio. Our set decorator, Art Parker, also did a sensational job. The period was absolutely correct and in perfect taste.

On the set, I was asked if I could see Miss Bacall in her dressing room. Betty (as she was known) looked lovely, as usual, when I arrived, but there was fire in her eyes as she paced up and down.

BETTY: If that big slob spits on my hemline once more, I'll crack his head wide open with a two-by-four.

ME: (*Stalling*) Mind if I sit down? I promise not to spit.

BETTY: Don't get funny with me. I'm in no mood to banter words with you.

ME: (*Still stalling*) Please accept my apologies. I don't believe you ever knew that Jack Warner, as a punishment, took off my mantle of director and made me a tenth assistant director. He placed me on the *To Have and Have Not* set. There was a young, beautiful girl playing opposite Humphrey Bogart. She and he fell deeply and for ever in love. From my observation post, I fell in love with you too.

BETTY: (*Collapsing on a couch*) What the hell this has to do with 'spit', bewilders me.

ME: Know anything about baseball?

BETTY: What *is* this? A quiz show?

ME: Patience, Betty. Please. There is a point somewhere.

BETTY: Well, you're throwing a hell of a long curve getting to it.

ME: (*Clear and crisp*) Baseball is our national sport. Skipping past all its good qualities, it is the filthiest, most unsanitary game played anywhere. Every ball player and manager spits. On the field and in the dugouts, there is an unending stream of spit. Spit that not only soils, but is contagious. Suppose one has a strep throat, or tuberculosis, or God knows what – anybody can catch it. Yet it is accepted as the norm by the American public at large.

BETTY: (*Bursting out laughing*) That's the damndest defence I ever heard. (*Pulling herself together.*) But it won't work with me. You know, you're crazy.

ME: It helps. Seriously, Duke doesn't know he's doing it. He'll feel ashamed when I tell him. I promise *not* that he won't spit, but that he won't spit on you or near you.

BETTY: Thank you – finally. Just so you're not the only one who remembers, do you recall having drinks with Bogie at his house? You were with Peter Lorre.

ME: (*Getting up to leave*) Well, at least I didn't show up with a stunning doll. (*Singing.*) 'I'm off to face the spitter . . .'
(*I close the door.*)

24

When one is faced with a large, intricate and difficult sequence that is filled with violence and yet at the end brings tears to the audience, one has to be prepared before starting to expose film. I'm astounded and confused at many of my peers who courageously, or stupidly, depending on your point of view, film any sequence with endless set-ups without pre-planning.

The set of the Metropole Saloon was designed and built by Robert Boyle to represent the finest and largest bar and gambling casino west of Chicago. One entered from the busy main street through heavy, ornate wooden doors, then through the swinging doors, which seemed mandatory before entering any saloon.

I shot the last shoot-out in the afternoon. The bar is empty except for the bartender (Charles Martin), lazily cleaning various sized glasses. At the faro table in the rear sits Jack Pulford (Hugh O'Brian), coolly dealing faro to himself. Jay Cobb (William McKinney) is seated at an empty table on the right, near the front, a shot of whiskey before him. The camera enters with Sweeney (Richard Boone) and sees what Boone sees: the bartender behind the empty bar, O'Brian at the faro table, McKinney seated at a near table on his right, glaring at him. The camera follows Boone to the bar, where he orders a whiskey. The bartender pours him a shot. Boone downs it in a gulp and grabs the already corked bottle. He grins at the bartender and starts to cross the room. O'Brian indicates for Boone to play faro with him. Boone snorts his disdain. He crosses to a table against the wall opposite the middle of the bar. He ignores McKinney as he grabs one of the upended chairs on a table and sets it roughly on the floor, sitting on it. He pulls the cork from the bottle with his teeth, spits it out and takes a deep swig. He has a perfect view of the bar, of O'Brian to his right, of McKinney and the half-doors' entrance to his left. He pulls a peacemaker from his belt and lays it in his lap.

That was the end of shooting, as Duke showed up on the set and I discussed with him the way I intended to shoot him entering the saloon. I wanted to see him enter the bar and pan him to the bartender in the centre of the bar, his back to Boone and McKinney. Apparently, he totally ignores the three men seated. But as he orders a shot of whiskey, the camera almost imperceptibly moves behind his head as in the mirror he sees McKinney in the front corner, Boone, directly opposite against the wall lifting his bottle, toasting Duke, and O'Brian behind the faro table in the rear.

That's as far as I got. Duke sized everything up, then walked back and through the half-doors. I followed him.

DUKE: Why don't you shoot behind my head? That's where I'll see the three gunmen and the bartender.

ME: I already made that shot.

DUKE: Huh?

ME: I introduced the positions of O'Brian and McKinney to Boone and the audience by shooting the exact set-up you showed me.

DUKE: (*Displeased*) Well, we'll do it with me.

ME: (*Firmly*) No we won't and I'll tell you why. When I see your *face* as you come through the swinging doors, I don't want you to see the three men. You totally ignore them. Yet when you're at the bar, you clearly see them in the mirror and know exactly what you're up against.

DUKE: I like that Boone shot.

ME: So do I. But for your introduction to the Metropole, I greatly prefer the shot on your face. I'm not talking about the artistry in the mirror shot. I'm talking about your character, your attitude towards three gunmen who are ready, willing and able to gun you down.

DUKE: Well, you seem to have made up your mind. Line it up and let's shoot it. I'll be in the trailer when you're ready.

I knew two things: Duke obviously wasn't happy and I sensed he didn't feel well. So I gave Surtees the set-up and told him to hustle it up a bit; I was expecting trouble with Duke.

We shot Duke's entrance the way I had described it to him without incident. When he drank his whiskey, the bartender left the bar and was out of sight. The mirror shots looked sensational. I told him if I could keep shooting in the same direction, shooting at him when he's shot at by McKinney and pulls himself over the bar, I'd save a hell of a lot of time. Duke agreed, so that's what we did. We continued to shoot Duke returning McKinney's fire and killing him. Duke gets shot by Boone, but fires three shots killing him. Duke, wounded and lying on the floor behind the bar, hears O'Brian approaching. He looks up and sees a shadow crossing the glass he left on the bar. Duke drops his empty revolver on the floor and, with difficulty, draws the second revolver from his waistband. He turns his wounded body painfully, aiming his revolver at the end of the bar near the entrance. I made a reverse on Duke lying stretched out on the floor shooting at O'Brian off scene. I also made a close shot of Duke firing, the flash and smoke from the revolver filling the screen.

DUKE: (*Weakly*) Why not shoot O'Brian getting shot and the insert of the shadow crossing my glass?

26

3   *The Shootist*: John Wayne's last shoot-out

ME: Because frankly, old boy, you look a bit pooped to me. We can always pick up those shots.
DUKE: (*Getting to his feet with difficulty*) I've been waiting for you to wrap the moment I got here.
(*He leaves with his wardrobe man and Dave Grayson, his make-up man*)
DUKE: (*With a farewell gesture*) See you all tomorrow. Don't drink up all the booze.

But when tomorrow inevitably showed up, there was no show on the part of Duke. I was already lined up on the insert of the glass, O'Brian was already dressed to play the 'shadow', when Frankovitch and Saunders rushed in and told me they wanted to talk to me in my trailer. When we got there, the door safely closed, they told me the bad news.

FRANKOVITCH: Duke's sick.
ME: Hope it's nothing serious.

SAUNDERS: We have no idea when or if he'll show up.

FRANKOVITCH: How much stuff can you shoot without him?

ME: Duke won't like it. He likes to be around when I shoot.

FRANKOVITCH: Please answer the question.

ME: I'd want to go over the work with you, Russ . . . But I'd hazard a guess: not shooting Duke, at least a couple of full days. You'll see in today's dailies that I shot most of the film on Duke firing his revolver and getting hit. I didn't make any shots of Boone, O'Brian or McKinney doing any firing.

SAUNDERS: How come?

ME: It's the way I laid it out when I was doing my homework. It's a tough sequence. I thought if I didn't make too many tie-up shots and concentrated on Duke, I would be lighting in one direction. Naturally, I would gain time.

FRANKOVITCH: I appreciate that. Shoot anything you can. We should know more later in the day.

ME: If you talk to Duke, tell him to take it easy. The Metropole bar is always open to him.

(*They open the door to leave.*)

ME: (*To Saunders*) Why don't you come back in a few hours and we'll fix up a temporary schedule?

Saunders, still looking grim, nodded 'yes'. They left the stage. I was worried about Duke. It was difficult to concentrate. I started to shoot the insert of Duke's glass. After we made the shot, which was effective, we made a two-camera set-up on O'Brian sticking his head round the bottom part of the bar. We rigged it so he was literally blown away. His close-up was particularly shocking. O'Brian wasn't supposed to fire back, but he accidentally fired back at the camera operator. We had to send the operator to the hospital. Fortunately, he wasn't too badly injured and came back to work the next day.

We made various shots of O'Brian, with Bruce operating, covering the entire sequence, dropping to the floor at the faro table and firing at Duke. Off scene is Duke emptying his revolver at Boone. Duke is wounded in his left arm and falls behind the bar. The camera now pans O'Brian scurrying to the bar, pistol in hand. He hesitates, then bends over low to the floor, passes the glass on the bar and crosses swiftly and silently to the end of the bar near the entrance of the swinging doors. He disappears around the bar from the shot.

We now reversed ourselves to finish off McKinney throughout the sequence. We made shots of him loosening his gun flaps, leaping to his feet, drawing his right gun and shooting at the back of Duke off scene. When Duke fires back off scene, we see McKinney shot in the stomach. He curls up in pain and tries to make it to the swinging doors, his back to Duke off scene. He is hit in the back and killed by a bullet from Duke's gun.

Before shooting and killing Boone, I went over his action with him. (All action except Boone's was off scene.) He drops to the floor immediately after Duke kills McKinney, and fires, the bullet creasing Duke in his right shoulder, causing him to crash into bottles and glasses in front of the mirrors, which splinter. Duke fires back instantly, wounding Boone in his right shoulder. Then I had Boone lift the table like a shield, using the table as a battering ram as he charges towards Duke. Duke fires three shots through the table top, and Boone staggers towards the bar and drops the table. Blood flows from three wounds in his chest. He stands for a moment, then crashes to the floor. Boone loved the concept. He wanted to add one thing. After he dropped the table, he would say, 'And I'll tell you . . . that was for Albert' – Albert being his dead brother, killed in a gun fight with Duke. I thought it would work well.

I got the table rigged for three holes in the top. Then I had Boone's chest rigged for three corresponding holes, gushing blood as the table falls to the floor. During the time it took to light and rig the table top and Boone, I had an opportunity to talk to Russ, who had been hanging around for about half an hour. We sat in my trailer.

RUSS: I don't know if there's much use in rescheduling. It doesn't look too good.
ME: What precisely do you mean by that?
RUSS: There's talk about shutting down. Duke might not be coming back.
ME: (*Getting up and pacing about*) I don't like to hear that kind of talk.
RUSS: We have to face up to the truth, whether we like it or not.
ME: Russ, I always face up to the truth. Until we know the truth, I'm not accepting conjectures. Are you making out a new schedule?
RUSS: No.
ME: Good. I never pay any attention to them anyway. I'm going to keep on shooting until I run into work that involves Duke. Make yourself comfortable.

I left the trailer and went back to work. I kept my mouth shut about Duke. The following day, I had about two days' work that didn't involve Duke, but, there were shots of Ron Howard, James Stewart and Charles Martin that I needed to rehearse with Duke. My problems were compounded by receiving a letter from Shootist Productions Limited, informing me that, with immediate effect, my employment was suspended due to the illness of John Wayne. So I had to tell my cast and crew that, because of Duke's illness, regretfully we were shutting down for an indefinite period. The next day Frankovitch called me for a private chat with him in his office. He came right to the point.

FRANKOVITCH: I don't know why you were placed on immediate suspension. At least they could have let you finish everything possible without Duke.

ME: I must confess I was a bit surprised. But the only important thing is that Duke comes back, strong and healthy, to finish the picture.

MIKE: Of course. That's the only solution, and we all want it. But off the record, I do have a question. I hate even to think this way, but supposing Duke is so ill he can't come back? Does that mean that all the film we've shot goes down the drain?

ME: That's a decision for the moguls.

MIKE: I'm not going to beat about the bush. They've already talked to me. They want to know if you can finish the picture without Duke.

ME: If we try to do that, it will ruin the picture.

MIKE: But at least the picture can be released. Some of the money spent can be recouped.

ME: I don't want to think about it. Supposing, just supposing, I started using doubles to complete the shooting. What happens when Duke reappears, which with all my heart I pray for? He'll be pissed off, and I can't blame him. He'll walk off the picture and I'll be walking with him.

MIKE: The sixty-four-dollar question: can you complete the picture without Duke?

ME: Anything can be done. But I'm not sure it'll be worth a damn.

MIKE: Naturally, the suspension will be lifted.

ME: Naturally.

(*Mike leans forward, his face set and hard.*)

MIKE: Give me a straight answer. I have to face the leeches.

ME: I'll have to think it over. I don't want to do it, but I'll talk with my agent and lawyer. I'll give you an answer tomorrow morning. (*Getting up and leaving the room.*) After all, I might as well enjoy my suspension.

*

My agent, Lenny Hirshan, and my attorney, Arnold Burk, agreed that contractually I was obligated to finish the picture. From what they had heard, there was little chance that John Wayne would return in the immediate future. So I started shooting everything in the last shoot-out at the Metropole that I could think of.

We, the cast and crew, felt downhearted and downcast as we went about our work. I, and the others I'm sure, felt embarrassed at using the double for Duke. I keenly missed his presence. Although the ending would cut together, the picture would suffer without his face being seen, particularly in his dying scene with Ron, when Duke shows on his face his approval of Ron's throwing away the revolver after killing the bartender. When Duke dies, one knows that he approves and is happy that Ron is *not* going to become a shootist. To me, that was the most important element of *The Shootist*. Unfortunately we didn't have it.

When Duke, thank God, eventually appeared on the set, we were overjoyed. He looked a bit wan, but make-up would fix that. He had the same inimitable walk, the same charisma, the same presence. However, when he asked what we had been doing while he was ill, I knew I was in trouble.

We went to his trailer and I asked everyone there to leave, as I wanted to talk privately with Duke. I explained as well as I could the position the front office took. I was sure he knew all this, but he never let on. I showed him the list of shots I had made with his double. I pointed out that when he was shot in the back by the bartender, it would be stupid to do those kind of shots with him, as it would be too much of a strain for him and totally unnecessary. He said nothing. I went on describing how I, reluctantly, had shot the dying scene between Ron and himself. His eyes sparkled angrily, but he still said nothing.

ME: I would like to re-shoot that entire sequence. It obviously doesn't work without you.
DUKE: (*Taking his time*) Really?
ME: I would appreciate your seeing all the film I shot while you were ill. Anything you don't like, we'll re-shoot with you.
(*He still doesn't react, so I decide to get it settled once and for all.*)
ME: Surely you knew what we were doing. There was no secret about it.
DUKE: (*His voice strained*) That's not true. There was no publicity about your finishing the picture without me.
ME: That's true, and I was pleased about it, as I was sure you would be. I told Frankovitch that I didn't want to shoot anything while you were ill. The front office notified me that I was on immediate suspension. My agent and lawyer said that, legally and

31

contractually, I had to shoot whatever they wanted me to. I wasn't happy about it and longed for you to return.

Duke looked at me long and hard. I felt terrible about the whole embarrassing mess.

ME: Would you prefer another director?
DUKE: (*Ignoring the question*) Let's shoot the dying scene first. I'll go over this list of shots you've made and make up my mind what we should re-shoot.

I left, certainly not on the best of terms with Duke, for which I didn't blame him, but pleased that at least we were re-shooting the dying scene.

It was complicated redoing the sequence, mainly because I not only had to explain exactly what happened in the first shot, but also because the wardrobe and make-up men had to explain in detail every drop of blood, every tear in the clothing. But the scene was brilliantly acted by Duke and Ron. There was no comparison between what I had done originally with the double and what was portrayed by Duke. I felt great respect not only for his acting ability, but for his courage in subjecting himself to a great deal of discomfort, and undoubtedly some pain.

All went well, though slowly, until Duke asked me how I had shot McKinney's death. By now I was able to 'read' Duke: I realized that someone had told him exactly how McKinney was killed. I felt no guilt. In fact, I liked the way McKinney was gunned down. I suggested we go to my trailer, where I carefully explained that McKinney, without warning, shot first while Duke was at the bar, his *back* to McKinney. When Duke's *double* dived over the bar, McKinney's bullet cut a furrow across the top of the bar, barely missing him. Duke fired back two shots at McKinney, one in the stomach and, as McKinney tried to escape through the swinging doors, his back naturally exposed to Duke, Duke fired again, this time killing him. Duke exploded.

DUKE: You mean you had me shoot him in the back?
ME: Of course. His first shot tried to kill you in the back.
DUKE: Whatever the cause, I would never shoot anyone in the back. It's unthinkable for my image.
ME: I see nothing wrong with your image. You've shot a man once in the stomach. He struggles towards the door; his back is now naturally towards you. If you don't shoot, he may escape. Are you going to let him escape by not shooting him in the back because of your image?

DUKE: You're damn right. I spent many years in this business building up my image.

ME: I've never asked you for a favour. I am now. You direct McKinney anyway you want to.

DUKE: No, goddamnit. You fix it!

ME: OK, I'll re-shoot it, but I'll tell you this. I think your image in this instance is ridiculous and senseless.

I stormed out and set up to re-shoot the scene. McKinney didn't believe me. He said it didn't make any sense after taking a shot in his gut and struggling desperately to get out. The last thing he would do was turn back to Duke so that he could get shot again in the belly. What's more, he was going to tell Duke that. I hastily advised him against it. Duke was so image-conscious, at least on film, that he would never give in.

ME: But I've a simple solution. After you've heard it, if you don't like it, go to Duke, with my blessings.

MCKINNEY: OK.

ME: (*Demonstrating*) When you're curled up here clutching your belly, you half crawl, half stagger towards the exit. You stumble, half turning back towards the bar. Voilà! Duke shoots you again, killing you.

MCKINNEY: A genius. Fire away.

We shot the McKinney sequence and started to clean up and finish everything else that Duke wanted re-shot, more or less. I guessed about two more days' work. We were rehearsing to shoot Duke in the foreground as he pulls himself up to his feet behind the bar. In the background, the bartender appears, carrying a shotgun, when, again, Duke erupted. This time at Bruce, my sweet, sensitive and talented cameraman.

DUKE: (*To Bruce*) You don't know your ass from a hole in the ground. I've never looked worse.

BRUCE: (*Finally breaking*) If your make-up didn't make you look like a Red Indian, I might do better.
(*Before Duke has a chance to yell a string of expletives, I enter the fray.*)

ME: Stay right where you are. We're ready to shoot.

To my astonishment, Duke didn't utter another word of protest. I was about to make probably the worst mistake of my career. I went over to Bruce and whispered in his ear.

ME: I'll get my crew together. You get your boys. We'll leave the Red Indian all on his lonesome behind the bar.

BRUCE: (*Full of anguish*) Oh Don, please don't. We've only got about two more days to go. Let's stick it out.

Thank God for Bruce. I realized at once that he was right. I guess Duke's constant hammering had cost me my senses. We made the shot and in two days we completed the picture – alive, well and happy. So happy that in Duke's trailer we toasted each other and *The Shootist* with his golden tequila.

DUKE: (*At ease, sipping tequila*) How long have you been in the business?

ME: Too long. Since 1934.

DUKE: Hell, you're just a kid. I broke in in 1927. Pappy, John Ford to you, hired me as a labourer/propman. (*Reminiscing.*) I guess because I played football for USC. (*Filling our glasses.*) How'd you break the barrier?

ME: Nepotism.

DUKE: Figures. Pappy gave me some small bit parts in his early films. Finally he introduced me to Raoul Walsh. You knew him, didn't you?

ME: Very well. I shot many second units for him. A great guy.

DUKE: You telling me? He changed my name to John Wayne and gave me my first leading role, way back in 1931 . . . a film called *The Big Trail*.

ME: (*Starting to get drowsy*) My Uncle Jack, God rest his soul, arranged for me to see Hal Wallis at Warner Brothers. I remember being in a large office and Wallis saying to me . . .

The scene slowly blurred to . . .

2
Warner Brothers Era I

First Introduction

WALLIS: Come over here and sit down.

I wasn't out of breath when I reached the desk, but I was becoming increasingly nervous. I studied Mr Wallis: about thirty-five, dark hair, intimidating face. The spell was broken. He looked up and studied me. I realized I didn't have an idea in my head. I wanted to get out of his presence *right now*. But he spoke.

WALLIS: (*With a slight smile*) How's Jack feeling?
ME: I don't know.
WALLIS: (*His smile erased*) You're related to him, aren't you?
ME: He's my Uncle Jack. I've been in Europe since 1928.
WALLIS: Oh. Well that explains why Jack didn't tell you the situation here. (*His face sets.*) Each year in the spring, we sort of close down the studio. Stop making pictures. This means not hiring people, but laying them off.
(*My mind starts clicking: 'Please, Mr Wallis, make it short, sweet and painless.'*)
WALLIS: We've had to let many experienced men go. (*Sharply.*) By the way, how much experience have you had?
(*I figure I'll get it over quickly by telling the truth.*)
ME: I've had exactly the same amount of experience as you've had, Mr Wallis, before you ever started to work.
(*He stares at me for a long moment, then suddenly laughs.*)
WALLIS: On your way out, give my secretary your address and telephone number.
ME: (*Bewildered*) Thank you, Mr Wallis.

But he was already huddled over his desk, totally engrossed and busily writing on his pad.
  Note: When looking for a job, be it in 1934, 1984, or 2004, the

procedure in the motion-picture industry is always the same. There are *no jobs*. If there were, you must have experience. But better than experience is nepotism. If you don't have an Uncle Jack, invent one. Don't hesitate to bluff or lie. The moguls or lesser fry do the same.

The Film Library

I eventually received a telephone call from the production department of Warner Brothers: I was to report immediately to De Leon Anthony, head of Warners' film library. My thanks were abruptly cut off by the phone hanging up. The film library! Thousands of books, periodicals, magazines of all sizes and shapes, crammed with knowledge, technical data and stories galore. I dressed hastily, but with a certain amount of care. What does a film librarian wear? A tie, of course, you idiot.

I stepped into the film library into total shock. There was nothing there but film cans, film reels, some with wound film, others empty. Strips of film hung precariously on thin metal U-shaped hangers, falling into large metal bins, overflowing on to the cement floors. Through this disarray, I became aware of a small elderly man, his eye glued to a little round magnifying glass through which he was running a long strip of film that hung around his neck.

ME: Mr Anthony?
ELDERLY MAN: (*Eye glued to magnifying glass*) In the next room, through the door.

I thanked him as I made my way through the debris to the door. I stood for a moment, gathering myself, then entered.

The second room was, if anything, in worse chaos than the first. Reaching up for a film can on a high rack, loaded with other cans, was a muscular, dark, curly-haired man over six feet tall. All I could think was, 'Not a book in sight.'

ME: Mr Anthony?
ANTHONY: Yeah. What can I do for you?
ME: I'm Don Siegel. I was told . . .
   (*He crosses over to me, shaking my hand in a grip like a vice.*)
ANTHONY: Been expecting you. Hear you're gonna work for us.
   (*He crosses to his desk, carefully placing the film can on top of a stack of others next to the desk. He grabs a stool, straddling it.*)
ANTHONY: Grab a seat, anywhere.
   (*I carefully straddle the stack of film cans.*)
ANTHONY: (*Sizing me up*) Know anything about film?

ME: Not a damn thing.

ANTHONY: Good. (*Sticking his hand out.*) You're hired.
(*I wince as he wraps his paw around my hand.*)

ME: Great. What do I do?

ANTHONY: Get off your ass and carry that stack of film to Projection
Room One, right across the outdoor corridor.

I leapt to my feet and bent over the seven cans of film I was sitting on. I
wiggled my fingers under the bottom can, flexed my knees and pushed up
as hard as I could. With a mighty grunt, I staggered towards the door.
Anthony was already at the door, holding it open for me. As I lurched past
him, he grinned.

ANTHONY: To your right and up the stairs. (*He hears me groan and
starts laughing.*) I didn't think you could make it, kid.

Inside the projection room, I was seated next to Anthony. My muscles
were bent into a pretzel knot, torn and hurting. Anthony's face was
creased with a sardonic smile.

ANTHONY: I'm letting you rest in a comfortable projection-room chair
while I point out the stock shots in the film we're gonna run. The
room will be dark, so you can doze off and get some sleep.

ME: Mr Anthony, what's—

ANTHONY: (*Interrupting*) Kid, call me Lee.

ME: Lee, my name's Don.

LEE: OK, Don. What did you want to ask me?

ME: What's a 'stock shot'?

LEE: (*Pushes buzzer*) Fasten your seat belt. When the lights go out and
the film starts running . . . (*Lights go out and film starts running.*)
. . . it's very complicated. Takes a kid to understand it.
(*The film is in black and white. Lee doesn't speak until a car
appears in the distance.*)

LEE: See that car approaching in the distance? Now's that's a stock
shot. I'll buzz the projectionist. He'll put a small piece of paper in
the reel so we can find it. That car could be used in a new picture
and nobody would be the wiser.
(*The screen now shows a close shot of the car with people talking.*)

LEE: That shot's not usable for stock because the people are
recognizable and are also talking. What we're looking for are long
shots of cities or countrysides, inside machine shops or factories,
with no one identifiable, and no signs. Stock shots save the studio
a ton of money and . . .

As Lee's voice droned on, I had dozed off into a sound slumber.

*

The weeks flew by. I was now making $36 a week, a raise of $6. Not bad for lifting cans and dozing off in projection rooms. I could now afford to bring my parents to Los Angeles and became head of the family, which I've been ever since. My Dad was ill. He was the world's greatest mandolin virtuoso. My Mom was tiny and adorable. Dad called her 'Dearie' and she called him 'Darling'. It was a real love match. Unfortunately, I took after neither of them.

Lee interrupted my reverie.

LEE: (*Sharply*) Get me a bunch of sprocket holes, on the double. You'll probably find some in the paint shop on the backlot.

I darted off. I wondered how much a bunch of sprocket holes weighed. The paint shop had none left. They suggested that I go to the grip department on the other side of the lot. They might have some, or at least know where I could find them. But they were out too. They sent me to the special-effects department on Stage 5. Hours later, grimy and tired, I returned to the film library, without even one sprocket hole. Lee looked me up and down.

LEE: Didn't you try any other places?
ME: (*Dispiritedly*) I criss-crossed the entire lot.
LEE: (*Disarming smile*) I can't even begin to guess how many thousands of sprocket holes you could have found right here. (*Reaching over for a strip of film.*) Each frame of film has two sprocket holes on each side. How many holes does that make?
ME: (*Stony-faced*) Four.
LEE: Excellent. Now the sprocket wheels in the projection machine pull the film through the back-lighted lens at twenty-four frames a second. Any idea how it does it?
ME: The sprockets on the turning wheel fit into the holes.
LEE: Excellent. There's only one thing missing.
ME: (*Face set*) What's that?
LEE: (*Leaving the room*) A sense of humour.

I stared after Lee for a long moment, then slowly smiled. I had figured out my revenge.

Revenge may be sweet, but it can't be stupid. I must top the sprocket-hole safari. In a corner of the room where empty film cans lay scattered about, a family of black widow spiders had made a nest. They liked the coolness and safety around the cans. The female black widow is venomous: its bite is supposed to be as deadly as that of a rattlesnake. The way to tell the poisonous female from the harmless male is to turn the spider on to its back. On the female's abdomen a red hourglass mark can be clearly seen. Good luck.

I had worked out a plan to capture one of these babies without getting bitten – I hoped. I took a plain, clear water glass and covered it with a thin plastic card so that the mouth of the glass was completely closed. Near the glass I placed the bottom part of a film can. Next to the can I put a small piece of thick cloth wrapped around something the size of a marble, handling it gingerly. I picked up the glass and card. The hunt was on. I held the glass in my right hand, the card in my left. Walking slowly towards the corner of the room, I spotted my prey – a black beauty crawling away from me. Moving quickly, I was directly over her. In a flash the glass trapped her. With my left hand I carefully slid the card under the glass and under the wildly excited spider. Eureka! Returning to the open can, I pressed the card firmly as the spider tried to get out. I felt a bit squeamish as I lowered card, spider and glass into the can. At the last moment, I pulled the card free, as the open part of the glass settled on the bottom of the can imprisoning the frantic widow. Trying to climb the sides of the glass, she slipped down on her back. Before she could right herself, I got a brief glimpse of the red hourglass. My pulse quickened as I picked up the small piece of cloth and dumped its contents into the can. It was a piece of dry ice. It appeared to be smoking slightly.

I lifted the glass straight up in the air, prepared to hurl it away if the spider was attached to it. Taking advantage of her new-found freedom, she was scrambling for the side when suddenly she noticed the smoking dry ice and went on the attack, leaping at it to bite. Instantaneously, she was frozen solid, hopefully dead. With a pencil, I flicked her off the ice. She made not the slightest movement. She was perfect in every respect except that of living. My plan had been to pick her up and place her in my open palm, but I didn't have the guts. I pushed her around with the pencil. Eventually, I reached tentatively for the widow. The moment I touched her, my finger jerked back as though from an electric shock. Then, without further ado, I picked her up and placed her on my open left palm. My palm tingled; she felt cold. I heard Lee's voice approaching and got to my feet, left palm outstretched, and went out into the outside corridor to meet him. Lee stopped in shock, his eyes riveted on my outstretched palm.

LEE: What in the hell have you got there?
ME: Isn't she a beauty?
LEE: You stupid son of a bitch, that's a *black widow*!

(*I stick my outstretched hand closer to his face, causing him to recoil in fear.*)

ME: How do you know?

LEE: (*Really angry*) Because, you dumb kid, I caught a flash of red on its tummy, which means it's definitely a black widow.
(*With my right hand I turn her over. The red hourglass is very evident.*)

LEE: You gotta be the craziest kid with the shortest lifespan. (*Deadly.*) Get rid of it!

ME: (*Beguiling*) Gee, Mr Anthony, I must be colour blind. That marking sure looks grey to me.

Lee hit down on my arm hard. The second the black widow touched the ground, Lee's big shoe squashed her. We faced each other. My arm felt numb – plus, he was my boss.

ME: (*Rapid-fire*) I killed the black widow with dry ice. (*Looking down at the remains.*) She was a perfect specimen. I'll trade you the remains for a bunch of sprocket holes. (*I looked at his set face and smiled.*) All that's missing is a sense of humour.

Lee smiled and stuck out his hand. I should have known better. I shook his hand. My hand became numb and remained so for a week.

*

Lee and I became great friends. We fell into a deadly routine. At night we'd go bar-hopping, sometimes with his lovely wife. The next day we'd sleep it off in a projection room, 'searching' for stock shots.

Lee was a great badminton player. He had made a short with the American champion. When he heard that I was a table-tennis champion, he insisted on playing me. I beat him easily. When we played badminton, he murdered me. The games are completely opposite. Badminton is only volleying; table tennis is only ground strokes. Nevertheless, he went to the head of the shorts department and got permission to shoot a test of me playing one of the local champions. It was great fun.

I was fascinated watching Lee editing the test on a movieola.

ME: Do you think I could learn to edit?

LEE: I don't know about editing, but you could certainly cut film.

ME: What's the difference between cutting and editing?

LEE: Cutting is mechanical, editing is cerebral. (*Looking up at me.*) Ask the old man to give you the can with rolls of sunset film. Learn how to use the splicing machine. It's dangerous. Don't cut your fingers off.

The splicing machine works like a guillotine. A sharp blade, put in an overhead position by a left pedal, is released to come crashing down on a piece of film when the right pedal is pressed. There's no such thing as being careless. Wham – and the tip of your finger is gone. Nevertheless, with all ten fingers intact, I finished splicing about ten rolls of sunsets, which I put on a reel.

Seated beside Lee in a projection room, I waited impatiently for him to buzz for the film to start.

LEE: (*Calmly lighting a cigarette*) Have any trouble?
(*I lift all ten fingers unscathed. Lee pushes the buzzer, the lights go out and the film starts. A sunrise appears, followed by another sunrise.*)

LEE: I thought we were to see sun*sets*, not sun*rises*.
(*Finally, the reel of sunrises ends. The lights go on.*)

ME: (*Chagrined*) I don't know what happened.

LEE: Well, you did something remarkable. You turned every sunset into a sunrise.

ME: How'd I do that?

LEE: Magical. You turned every sunset upside down. Voilà! They all became sunrises.

ME: (*Dejected*) I'm sorry.

LEE: Nothing to be sorry about. I'd just as soon have a reel of sunrises as a reel of sunsets. I've been doing a lot of thinking about you. (*He stubs his cigarette and lights another.*) You're twenty-one. Too young to be drinking with me every night, dozing throughout the day, supposedly watching out for stock shots. So I'm gonna get you another job.

ME: I don't want another job.

LEE: That shows how stupid you are. You stay here, maybe in twenty years you'll be head of the film library. Yippee! Ain't that a great future?

ME: As far as I'm concerned, it's the best job.

LEE: (*Sincerely*) Worse thing you can say to a kid is, 'It's for your own good.' Well, you've already got a new job: an assistant cutter. Your boss Warren Lowe, is an excellent editor. (*Sticking his hand out to me.*) Good luck, Don.

Would you believe I could be so forgetful as to shake his hand? As usual, he crushed it. My eyes watered, but not from pain . . .

The Editorial Department

The cubicle was similar in size to the film library. It too had a lot of film in it, but unlike the cluttered mess of the library, the cutting room was immaculate. Every can was carefully marked with grease pencil on white tape. The film was visible and hung so that it spilled into bins, the circular sides and bottom of which were covered with white cloth so the film wouldn't be scratched. On tables were neat rolls of film of varying sizes. Standing up, looking through a movieola, was the editor, Warren Lowe: thickset, tough, ex-marine. He was running the sound track back and forth to match the film. The dialogue sounded ordinary and banal when running forwards. Running backwards, it sounded exciting, like a foreign language.

You might wonder what I did while my editor was busy working. Nothing. The reason, besides my ineptitude, was that Warren did everything himself. He not only edited the film, he hand-spliced each cut. He also cut and hand-spliced the sound track, ordered dissolves and cut them in. He even blooped the cuts in the sound track with wide strokes of black ink, looking like an upside down V. This was done to cover the pop that each cut on the sound track made when running through the projection machine.

Of course, I carried the reels of cut film to the projection rooms. I was also allowed to carry the film back to the cutting room. I became a delivery boy. When Warren had run out of blooping ink, paperclips, grease pencils, lead pencils, etc., I'd go and get them. It wasn't all Warren's fault. I was lazy and soon became the worst assistant cutter on the lot. I didn't have the slightest idea how to cut in sound overlaps. I'm not even sure if I knew what they were. So I got bored and longed to return to Lee in the film library.

Whenever we ran dailies, however, I was fascinated. How did the director know what angles to shoot? Warren's answer was always the same, 'He knows.' How do you know how to cut it together? 'I know.' Obviously I was learning nothing, which in reality was fine with me, I thought.

Late one afternoon, Mr Dieterle, a famous German director, was running yesterday's dailies with us. I have a faint recollection that it was *Satan Met a Lady*, starring Warren William and Bette Davis (an earlier and much inferior version of John Huston's brilliant *Maltese Falcon*). I thought the dailies were poor and whispered as much to Warren. He ignored me. Later, I whispered again that the various takes didn't match and it would be impossible to edit. Surely Dieterle should be told.

42

WARREN: (*Hissing angrily*) You open your mouth again and I'll ram my fist down your throat.

When the lights were turned on after the dailies had finished, Dieterle got up and faced us. He was 6 feet 4 and wore the thin white gloves that editors use in handling film. He wore them constantly so that he wouldn't catch a disease.

DIETERLE: (*With a heavy German accent*) Well boys, what do you think?
WARREN: (*Leaping to his feet*) There's nothing to do but cut the slates off. Very good, Mr Dieterle.

Dieterle looked over at me. Unfortunately, Warren was glaring down at me too. So I silently nodded my head up and down, becoming a member of the largest club at Warner Brothers: the Agreers.

Dieterle and his wife were total believers in astrology. It was common knowledge that the start date of all his pictures was determined by a favourable astrological reading. One day I walked on to his set. He was directing some young children. After each take was completed, he would look at his wife to see if she okayed it; she either shook or nodded her head. He wasn't getting what he wanted. He was trying very hard to be pleasant, but the dam of anger finally broke. He grabbed a child by her arms, swung her up in the air and, screaming in German, forcefully placed her in a new position. He took his hands off the child and she fainted dead away. I left the set wondering what directing was all about. I'm still wondering.

*

Warren Lowe was one of the best editors in the business. When Hal Wallis left Warner Brothers to set up his own production unit at Paramount Studios, the best people went with him. Warren was chosen immediately and he remained with Wallis as his top editor for many years. So there's no doubt of his excellence, nor am I questioning it.

The job of an editor is to get the best out of the film that the director has given him to edit. He must understand the story. He must understand what the director wants his picture to say. He must know what is entertaining and what is not. It is not a mechanical job of cutting. On the contrary, the editor must edit the film so that the finished film is much better than the director's dailies indicated. In doing many films, presenting different and difficult problems, the editor must be intelligent and well educated.

Warren Lowe, as far as I knew, had never been in a museum or an art gallery. So what? He was intelligent, but not well educated. It's a puzzle to understand how he could turn out such beautiful and artistic pictures.

One day, Wallis had gone through an entirely cut picture with Warren and had made many changes in every reel. The trouble was that Wallis had insisted that he run with Warren the next morning at nine o'clock. Warren knew that he would not have time to make all the cuts and hand-splice each one. He told me at 6 p.m. to go to dinner, then come back and machine-splice all the cuts, picture and track. He also told me to bloop the track carefully.

WARREN: (*Worried*) I'm running tomorrow morning with Wallis at nine a.m. in Projection Room Five. Be sure everything's in the projection room by eight thirty in the morning. I've got a dinner date tonight I can't break.

ME: No problem. See you in the morning.

We both left, going our separate ways. Warren didn't know that I was going to meet a glorious new date and had no intention of going back to the studio immediately after dinner. I'd see how the date worked out, play it by ear.

I woke up with a sudden start. My temples throbbed. I felt awful. I became aware that I was in a strange bed. Groggily, I looked over at an alarm clock and dimly made out 3.42. I dressed in the darkness and left without waking, or thanking, my 'glorious new date'.

After finishing the splicing and blooping, I carried all the film back to the cutting room. As it was still dark, I realized I couldn't get into Projection Room 5. I sat down to wait for the projectionist to arrive, when *wham!* – my head hit the table. I didn't move.

WARREN: (*Starting to shake me vigorously*) Holy Mary! Are you dead?

ME: (*Coming to*) Yes.

WARREN: Did you finish all the splicing?

ME: Yes.

WARREN: And the blooping?

ME: (*Now awake*) Of course.

WARREN: (*Slumping down on a stool*) Your elbow was on the table. Your head was resting on your hand. I yelled out 'Don!' I hit your elbow. Your head crashed down on the table. You didn't move. God, I was scared.

ME: I don't feel so good.

WARREN: Get the film over to Room Five. If you've made any mistakes, you'll be dead anyway. I'll see to it.

I got the film out of there as fast as I could move. There must have been no mistakes, because I'm still living.

*

Warren needed some paperclips. He sent me to Thelma Benson, who was not only secretary to Harold McCord, head of the editorial department, but she also ran the whole department with a firm hand. I introduced myself and asked her for paperclips for Warren Lowe.

THELMA: (*Irritated*) What's he do, eat them?
ME: (*Shrugging*) I don't know too much about the business. It's tough to learn.
(*Thelma snorts as she doles out about twenty clips, my palms forming a cup.*)
THELMA: You think your job is tough? You have no idea how difficult things can be with Mr McCord.
(*I proceed to the door.*)
ME: (*In my most casual manner*) Well, it ain't exactly a bed of roses being the illegitimate son of Jack Warner.

As I let the half-glass door close, I caught a fleeting glimpse of Thelma's awestruck face, her mouth agape.

The rumour spread like wildfire. Not that anyone asked me, 'Are you actually Jack Warner's illegitimate son?' They were too frightened of repercussions. But I knew that they knew. In a strange way it affected and probably helped my career at Warners. I'm glad it's not true, for I surely would have killed him long before I left the lot.

It seemed before I even got back to Warren's cutting room, carrying the clips in my cupped hands, people whom I scarcely knew went out of their way to say a few friendly words of greeting. Even Warren looked strange as he picked up the phone.

WARREN: (*Dialling for the operator*) This is Warren Lowe. May I have a Beverly Hills line?
OPERATOR'S VOICE: (*Offstage*) I'm sorry, Mr Lowe, but Mr Warner does not allow any toll or long-distance calls.
(*Warren slowly hangs up. He is about to blow a fuse.*)
ME: (*Getting rid of the clips*) Do you mind if I try?
(*Warren looks at me peculiarly as he hands me the phone. I hesitate a moment. Is it possible that the news about me has spread this quickly?*)
ME: (*Dialling o*) Oh darling, this is Donald Siegel. May I have a line to Beverly Hills?

OPERATOR'S VOICE: (*Offstage*) Certainly, Mr Siegel

The line clicked. I handed the phone to Warren.

*

Lee ran into me on the lot. As usual, I was carrying a load of film to one of the projection rooms.

LEE: (*Smiling*) I don't see much change in your status quo.

ME: Hate to be one of those guys who says, 'That's what I told you', but that's what I said.

LEE: (*Turns to go, turns back*) The shorts department turned your table-tennis test down.

ME: It figured.

LEE: No. They figured you looked like a cross between John Gilbert and Gilbert Roland. They told me Pete Smith's about to make a ping-pong short.

ME: Who the hell is Pete Smith?

LEE: He's the head of the shorts department at MGM. He makes the best in the business. That's what did us in. (*Turning away.*) So long, Gilbert.

By the time I had finished delivering the cans of film, I had an idea. I rushed back to the cutting room. Warren was busy snipping away, but I burst right in on him.

ME: Do you know Pete Smith?

WARREN: If you're referring to the guy who makes shorts at MGM, no.

ME: How can I get in to see him?

WARREN: (*Turning back to his snipping*) I don't know. Call him on the phone and make an appointment, but for Christ's sake don't keep interrupting me.

ME: Sorry. If I need some time off, is that all right with you?

WARREN: Be my guest, but shut up!

I sneaked off before he had a chance to change his mind.

I had my story fairly well worked out by the time I managed to get inside MGM to see Mr Pete Smith. He was a small, middle-aged man with a feisty, no-nonsense attitude.

SMITH: What kind of a con game you trying to pull?

ME: None. I only know that you've got the well-deserved reputation of making the best shorts. You can't make them unless you have the best people.

46

SMITH: (*Exploding*) I've only got the ping-pong champion of America.

ME: That's exactly the point. Ping pong is owned by Parker Brothers, a manufacturer of sports equipment. Table tennis is the official sport throughout the world.

SMITH: Are you telling me you can beat Coleman Clark?

ME: The last time I played him was at the Illinois Athletic Club in Chicago. I beat him easily.

(*Mr Smith is not one to waste time.*)

SMITH: (*Getting up, starting for the door*) Follow me.

He led the way through the busy traffic on Lot 1. When he got halfway into Lot 2, he turned sharp right. There was bald-headed Coleman playing one of the local kids. Smith walked up to Coleman. I was right on his heels. When Coleman saw me, I thought he was going to faint.

SMITH: (*Indicating me*) This young fellow says he can beat you. Play him.

I took the bat from the kid and started to warm up. I thought it stupid of Coleman not to have got in touch with me to play him in the film. I would have been more than willing to have made him look good by losing to him. Now, with immodesty and no compassion, I creamed him 21–12, 21–7.

SMITH: That's good enough for me. Come back to the office with me, Mr Table Tennis, and I'll draw up a deal. You start playing this coming Monday.

As we started back, we passed Mickey Rooney, who was a pretty good junior player. We had played many times.

ROONEY: Shit. I could beat him without working up a sweat.

I rushed back to the cutting room and handed Warren a memo on the deal, signed by Pete Smith. When he got to the part where it stated that I would be paid $600 for five days' work, he let out a whistle of amazement.

ME: You notice that I have to play for five days. Is that all right, my leaving you for five days?

WARREN: Never ask a question if the answer 'No' is going to upset you.

(*My face drops.*)

WARREN: There is one condition. We use some of the six hundred for booze.

ME: As much as you can drink.

WARREN: (*Drily*) Don't put me to the test. (*Back to normal.*) And don't just stand there with your teeth in your mouth. Put away all these trims and mark the cans.

ME: Thanks, Warren.

WARREN: Just be careful not to strain yourself. We need the six hundred.

The table-tennis setting looked good. Grey velour drapes totally encompassed the table. There was about 30 feet of playing area at each end of the table. There was another table made entirely of glass on the other side of the drapes. I met the director, David Miller, who explained to me the two camera set-ups. He took me off to one side.

MILLER: (*Pleasantly*) Play the best you can. Show us a complete variety of strokes, offence and defence. (*Quietly.*) I'll let you know when to lose to the . . . (*Winks at me.*) . . . champion. (*Yells.*) Coleman! How about starting to practise with Don? We're about ready to start shooting.
(*I stick my hand out. Coleman shakes it, limply.*)

ME: Let's give them a good show.
(*Coleman doesn't bother to answer as we begin to play. After a short spell, they start to shoot.*)

ASSISTANT DIRECTOR: Let's have it quiet on the set. All right, roll 'em!

SOUND MIXER: (*After a short delay*) Speed!

MILLER: Keep the rallies going until I yell 'Cut!' OK. Action!

I fed Coleman high lobs to his forehand which he hit from corner to corner. Finally, he wound up and really cracked one deep to my forehand, driving me back to the drapes. I tried to chop the ball back, but my foot hit a two-by-four behind the drapes, severely wrenching my right ankle. I fell heavily to the floor. The very first shot in the picture and I wind up on my back with a wrecked ankle.

Miller yelled 'Cut! Cut!' and ran over to me, followed by the others. They took my sneaker and sock off. The ankle not only looked swollen, it hurt. The first aid arrived, out of breath, carrying a doctor's bag. He barely glanced at the foot, but immediately started wrapping the entire foot and ankle with wide adhesive tape. He put the sock and sneaker back on, lifting me to my feet.

FIRST AID: You're as good as new. Try putting some weight on it.
(*I tentatively step on it and, to my amazement, it doesn't feel too bad.*)

ASSISTANT DIRECTOR: OK. Let's get going.

MILLER: (*To Assistant*) Shut up! (*Turning to me.*) Are you all right, Don?
ME: (*Taking a few steps*) Let's give it a go.
(*On the next shot, after a short rally, I take a step backwards. As I fall to the floor, somehow I get my bat on the ball and return it over the net. Coleman mis-hits the ball into the net.*)
MILLER: Cut! Excellent.
(*Pete Smith, whom I haven't noticed before, rushes over to me and lifts me to my feet.*)
SMITH: That was one hell of a shot.
ME: Now you know the difference between ping pong and table tennis.

Five days later, as scheduled, we finished shooting. Although Coleman officially won the match, I received all the congratulations.

ME: (*To Smith*) When will this picture be out in the theatres?
SMITH: It's the middle of May 1936. We'll have no trouble getting it out in the fall. I'll let you know when we run it.
ME: Thanks, Mr Smith.
SMITH: Have a doctor look at the ankle and send me the bill. Now that you've finished working for me (*smiles*) the name's Pete.

*

Warren and I were sipping our third zombie at Don the Beachcomber. We were feeling no pain. I wanted to toe-dance on the bar.

WARREN: When I was in the Marine Corps, serving time in China, I had the same idea as you, only I slid down the entire bar. I fell off backwards and broke a lot of glassware and bottles. To put it politely, that was the end of my tenure as a marine.
ME: It turned out well, you being an editor and a damn good one.
WARREN: (*Lifting his empty glass to a passing waitress*) Two more of the same. There's something I want to tell you, but I can't remember.
ME: No business tonight.
WARREN: (*Excitedly*) That's it, business. You're a genius, Don.
ME: (*Singing*) No business is my business.
WARREN: Let's face it kid. You're a great ping-pong player. (*Waitress returns with drinks.*) Here's to you, kid.
ME: Here's to you, Sarge.
(*We click glasses and take a long drink. Warren breaks the spell.*)
WARREN: I hope you'll forgive me, but you're the worst assistant I've ever worked with. I wonder why?

ME: (*Euphoric*) Stupid, lazy and bored.

WARREN: Exactly. You ain't gonna change unless you change jobs.

ME: Think I should stick to ping pong?

WARREN: Nope. I ran into Lee the other day. We had a good talk about you.

ME: God help me.

WARREN: Ever hear of special effects?

ME: Sure. Lee sent me to Stage Five to pick up some sprocket holes.

WARREN: (*Grinning*) How many did they give you?

ME: Up yours.

WARREN: (*Serious*) Supposing I told you that Lee and I think we can get you a job on Stage Five?

ME: (*Annoyed*) Hey, what's with you guys wanting to get rid of me?

WARREN: Supposing I told you that you'd find the work not only interesting, but exciting. There are miniatures to shoot, all sorts of inserts to make up and shoot, every kind of thing imaginable to explode – I mean really blow up. Need I say more? There are matte shots, montages, optical . . .

ME: (*Interrupting*) Whoah! I give in. I'm not only interested and excited, but damn grateful too.

WARREN: Let's not get maudlin about it. We'll finish these drinks and get a couple more.

I don't remember the rest of the evening. But in the morning, I gave up drinking for life.

Special Effects

In a plain, small office with only a calendar tacked to the wall, Bobby Agnew, a former child star, was seated behind a small, bare desk.

AGNEW: I'm the unit manager of special effects. We've been so busy on Stage Five that I can no longer be in charge of the insert department. What experience have you had?

ME: I was an assistant to Mr Anthony in the film library and an assistant to Mr Lowe in the editorial department.

AGNEW: Have you had any experience in shooting inserts?

ME: None.

AGNEW: Well, I'll introduce you to Mr Haskin, who is the head of special effects. He makes all the decisions.

Agnew got up and led me out of his office which opened directly on to the floor of Stage 5. It was full of activity, with a number of units working on the large stage. We passed Bette Davis, sitting in a car in front of what appeared to be a transparent screen. A wind machine was blowing at her. Two men, on opposite sides of the car, were jerking two-by-fours vigorously under the car, making it bounce up and down. I wondered if Miss Davis would get car sick.

AGNEW: (*A bit prissily*) Don't stare at Miss Davis. She has a vile temper. Let's not dawdle. The wind machines give me a beastly headache.

Agnew entered Mr Haskin's office, which looked like one. It had various drawings on the walls, several interesting models of aeroplanes and cars. Behind the desk was a corpulent, ruddy-faced man in his late fifties with thinning blond hair. He smiled amiably at me.

AGNEW: Mr Haskin, this is Donald Siegel.
  (*To my surprise, Mr Haskin stands up.*)
HASKIN: (*Sticking out his hand*) Very happy to meet you.
ME: (*Shaking his hand, which is soft*) Thank you, sir.
HASKIN: Sit over here, on the left side, otherwise you'll be looking into the sun. (*To Agnew.*) Take a look-see at the lab and find out when they expect to start printing again.
AGNEW: I'll get right on it and let you know, Bun.
  (*He exits as Haskin slowly sits down, apparently at ease with the world.*)
HASKIN: I understand you want to run the insert department.
ME: I'm afraid I don't know much about running an insert department, but Mr Lowe and Mr Anthony seem to think I could do it.
HASKIN: So they told me. Well, it's no big deal. You'll have plenty of help. A camera operator, an assistant cameraman, a grip and an electrician.
ME: (*Stunned*) You mean I'll have my own crew?
HASKIN: (*Drily*) It might prove difficult to shoot without one. (*Pleasantly.*) Of course, if you fall on your ass, I might have to take the crew away from you.
ME: I've been knocked on my ass before, but I've always managed to get back on my feet.
HASKIN: It's tricky footing, making inserts. Jack Warner says, 'Inserts are made so that you can read them.' Inserts are always close-ups, such as an article in a newspaper, a wrench turning a bolt, an insect crawling out of a crack in a wall. You follow me?
ME: Clear as a bell.

HASKIN: How about joining me in a cup of dreadful coffee while I chatter on?

ME: That's very kind of you.

(*Haskin goes over to an old tin coffee kettle on a single burner and starts to pour. He continues talking without pause.*)

HASKIN: If the director doesn't shoot the insert on the set, the editor sends a snip of film to the insert department and explains what he wants. Are you still with me?

ME: For example, where do I get the tiny insect?

(*He gives me a cup of coffee, takes one back to his desk and sits down.*)

HASKIN: The propman of the picture will supply you with the insect, the ring, the letter being written, etc. For example, if you're going to show Olivia De Havilland writing a letter, you have to get a good-looking young female hand to write it. (*His face lights up.*) That way you'll get to know, hopefully, an interesting young lady.

ME: Sounds great. I know I'm not even on the starting line, but I'm ready to run.

HASKIN: I can see that. But let's finish our coffee while we chat. Stage Five is a complete studio within a studio. We have everything there to make a picture, except sound. If we need sound, we get it. (*Dreamily.*) Every day when we get stars to come to Stage Five for process, I get the feeling I could shoot a complete picture, if I had the co-operation of the stars, without the studio knowing anything about it. (*Laughs.*) Maybe one day I'll do it.

ME: Do it. I'll supply the inserts.

HASKIN: Thanks. Can you help me with process?

ME: I'm afraid you've got me there.

HASKIN: Process is not really complicated, but it's very, very useful. Instead of shooting on location, frequently one can shoot the sequence on the stage. It's a lot cheaper, although it can sometimes be dangerous. In process, the camera shoots an aeroplane, a car, people running, etc., in front of a process screen. Projected on to the screen is film previously shot from a moving insert car, which is specially built for a camera to shoot from the front, back and sides. When you see the finished product, the mystery unravels. The aeroplane, car or whatever is moving, but when it was shot, it was stationary. Simple, isn't it?

ME: Simple it's not, but I kind of get the idea.

(*Haskin stands up and takes me to the door, which he opens.*)

HASKIN: Anything that bothers you, feel free to see me. I'll let you into a little secret. I don't know everything . . . only God does. (*He points to some stairs leading to a large room.*) That's the insert department. The operator's name is Archie Dalzell, a camera operator who's a whiz at shooting inserts. Tell him you're in charge, but you need and will appreciate his help. Good luck.

ME: Thank you.

I started towards the stairs. I didn't realize that those stairs were leading up to the beginning of my career.

Insert Department

Archie Dalzell, a tall, lean man in his thirties, was officially a camera operator. However, he also shot as a first cameraman without the union being aware. We shot hundreds of inserts that the editors were constantly ordering. Anything an editor ordered I would write down immediately in a little notebook so I wouldn't forget. I was in my early twenties and already senile.

For the distinguished picture *Dark Victory*, starring Bette Davis and George Brent, there was a most important insert to be shot. While waiting for the doctor to return to his office, Miss Davis idly turns the pages of her case history which is lying on the doctor's desk. Suddenly her eyes widen in terror. We cut to the insert 'Prognosis negative', which leaves the page (it was written on glass) and fills the screen. It creates a startling, chilling effect. Miss Davis, in a most dramatic way, knows that she is doomed to become blind. I was becoming more aware of the power of film.

When we would go outside and actors or stuntmen were involved, the Cameraman's Union insisted that a first cameraman go along with Dalzell. One day we were shooting two cars pursuing another car along a narrow, winding road next to a small ravine. Ed Dupar, a first cameraman in his early sixties with a twirled moustache, always had a cigarette in his mouth. He was famous for never leaving his camera. Dupar would stand directly behind the camera with Archie operating it. This was very dangerous, for if one of the speeding cars hit the camera, the crew could be seriously injured or killed. It was not necessary for Dupar to stand directly behind the camera. And there was absolutely no rhyme or reason for me to be standing next to Dupar. After all, he was an old man and I was just a kid. But I stood next to him.

The assistant director, safe in the ravine, yelled through the bullhorn: 'Action.' The first car swept into view, went into a slight skid and whipped over very close past the camera. I had one eye on the car and one eye on

53

Dupar, who puffed calmly away. The second car, careening into view, went into a skid, just missing the camera. It took everything I had not to leap down the ravine, but there was Dupar showing no sign of emotion. And then the third car appeared, going much faster than the other two – to my eye, totally out of control. Just as the car skidded right at the camera, it spun violently in a circle, the back end certain to wipe us all out. Both my eyes were on the whirling car and I took off, head over heels into the ravine, thinking, 'I don't want to die.' I turned round and looked up. There was Dupar with what was left of the cigarette dangling from his mouth, looking down at me.

DUPAR: What's the matter, Don? You chicken shit or somethin'?

*

Back at the insert department, I opened a large envelope addressed to me. Enclosed was a page of script with a paragraph circled. A note was attached, instructing me to shoot it as written. On stage, I read the paragraph to my crew.

ME: 'The chicken hesitated in the open doorway. It looked first to the right, then to the left, then back to the right. She cackled, then jumped to her left on a chair, sprung on to a table and fluttered across the room to land on a couch.'
(*Everyone laughs.*)

DAZELL: Great. We'll be here a year.

ME: Put your camera over here and light it exactly the way I read it. If they're stupid enough to write it, we'll shoot it. At least we have a 'star' for the scene.
(*Archie soon shouts out.*)

DAZELL: I'm ready for anything, even eating it.

ME: (*To crew*) Now no laughter, no noise. I'm going to discuss the scene with my actress and I want absolute silence on the set.
(*I walk over to the chicken and bend down. The chicken looks me straight in the eye.*)

ME: (*To chicken*) Now darling, I want you to look this way, then that way. Take a deep breath, enter the room and jump on this chair. (*I stand up and demonstrate.*) From here, my love, jump on top of this table. Then look across the room and flutter your adorable wings to that couch over there. (*To crew.*) OK. Let's have it quiet. Roll the camera. Anytime you're ready, sweetheart.

The chicken looked to her left, then to her right, then back to her left, then entered the room. The silence on the set was mounting. Suddenly, the chicken cackled and jumped on the chair. Then, without further ado, she jumped on to the table. Everyone but my 'star' stopped breathing. But our gal, evidently a trained actress, fluttered across the room and landed on the couch. I fell over backwards, convulsed with laughter and unable even to yell 'cut'. The crew congratulated the star with her director still helpless on the floor.

*

A message came to me that Tenny Wright, the production manager of the studio, wanted to see me, *muy pronto*. I stopped everything and was on my way. A former boxer and a tough guy with a foul tongue, he wasted no time in greeting me.

WRIGHT: Who the fuck ever told you that you could shoot Joan
  Blondell going up the brownstone steps?
ME: I told the director, Lloyd Bacon, that I had a crew and could save
  him some time if I shot it. He said OK.
WRIGHT: Oh he did, did he? Well, I got news for you, you snot-nosed
  punk. I didn't give you the OK. (*Biting off the end of a cigar and
  chewing it.*) Anything that those sons of bitches directors are too
  lazy to shoot automatically becomes an insert. Haskin said he
  didn't know from nuthin'.
ME: All I know is that I saved and am saving Warner Brothers money.
  Isn't it better I shoot film that's cut into the finished picture than
  just sitting on my ass doing nothing?
WRIGHT: If you've nothin' to do, maybe we oughta fire you.
ME: (*Getting up*) Look at any of the film I've shot. If you think it's a
  waste of time, I'm on my way to Bellingham to catch a freighter to
  China as a mess boy.
WRIGHT: You gotta big mouth and one of these days (*lifts his fist*) I'll
  close it. Get the hell outa here.

I disappeared before he had chance to utter another word.
  I immediately told Bun (Haskin) about my brief encounter with Wright.

HASKIN: Well, you won, you idiot. What are you complaining about?
ME: I'm tired of begging directors for work which, by the way, is pretty
  dull. Sometimes worse than inserts.
  (*Bun gets up and shares some of his dreadful coffee with me.*)
HASKIN: I've got an idea that probably won't work, but stands a good
  chance of getting Tenny, even Warner, mad. Interested?
ME: How about setting fire to the studio?

HASKIN: Do you know anything about montage?

ME: It's generally something slapped together for a lapse of time.

HASKIN: True, but it needn't be. The script calls for a lapse of time. The director shoots a few inconsequential shots of principal players, let's say walking. The editor gets some stock close shots of feet walking. They dump the film on one of my optical printers, who mishmashes it into a montage. He doesn't even know what he's supposed to be getting across, and couldn't care less.

ME: Bun, I understand and agree with what you're saying. Maybe it's the dreadful coffee, but what's all that montage chit-chat got to do with me?

HASKIN: Go and see Vorkapitch at MGM. He's very knowledgeable about optics and understands symbolism. Talk to him, see some of his work.

ME: I'm lost. At least that's a good start. How do I get to use this voodoo knowledge?

HASKIN: When you read a script, and you read them all, whenever a montage is called for – like a ten-year lapse of time, a boy and a girl falling in love, a train wreck, etc. – rewrite it and shoot it. Nobody will know what you're doing except yourself and *maybe* me. I'll even let you have Bob Burks, who is fantastic at photographing anything in special effects.

I got up and the wheels of chance began propelling me upwards.

Montage

Slavko Vorkapitch looked like a montage slightly tilted. He was pedantic and took himself and montages very seriously. I listened, looked and absorbed.

VORKAPITCH: Montage literally means the placing of one picture on to another. Eisenstein used it as a form of editing: taut, precise, sometimes a matter of frames. Generally, it gets over a lapse of time. But when one considers that montage is the single section of film that gives the audience credit for creative intelligence, the importance of montage transcends the mundane film as a whole. The use of symbolism stirs the imagination of the viewer. One can show the invisible or intangible by means of visible impressions. The whole film can be made more vivid and given more pace by the proper use of montage technique. (*Pauses.*) I will allow you to look at a reel of some of my montages. Unfortunately, I can't be with you as I have to leave the lot.

Obviously, I was impressed with what I saw, but also somewhat bewildered. Superimpositions were everywhere. The photography was at times exquisite; at other moments, phantasmagoric, somewhat obtuse and confusing. But the overall effect, the quick staccato cuts, was exciting.

When I returned the reel to Vorkapitch's cutting room, no one was there. I noticed large sheets of lined paper filled with markings representing the footage of each shot. I helped myself ('stole' is a more suitable word) to some lined paper without any markings on it and got out quickly, carrying the paper with a feeling of guilt, but also of anticipation.

*

The insert department was getting so busy shooting endless inserts, writing and shooting montages without official approval and surreptitiously picking up second-unit work that I had to get additional help. Jim Leicester, a super assistant editor, joined my crew as the montage editor and my personal assistant. With Jim Leicester and Bob Burks, we grappled with many creative montage problems.

We used the lined sheets I had 'borrowed' from Vorkapitch to make hundreds of sheets for at least 100 montages. Each line of the montage paper represented one foot of film. We carefully drew each shot to show its length clearly. The dissolves going in and out were indicated exactly. We wrote in the different percentages we wanted each shot to be printed. We drew in superimpositions along the shot or shots it was superimposed over. Sometimes the montage sheets were 3 feet wide and 5 feet long. We could read and understand them as a composer reads his musical score. We would give the lined sheet to the optical printer, who would have to do it exactly as drawn on the lined sheet. A simple montage of a man looking for work would look something like that shown on p. 58.

Confessions of a Nazi Spy

In a montage we made for this film, our purpose was to shoot hundreds of Nazi posters fluttering down from a building to the busy Los Angeles street twelve storeys below. The pamphlets bore the Nazi swastika with such charming slogans as 'KILL THE JEWS', 'BURN THE NIGGERS', 'THE NORDIC RACE RULES THE WORLD', ad nauseam. Naturally, when the people below read the various vicious slogans, their reaction might be violent. Certainly street traffic would become disrupted. Did we have a

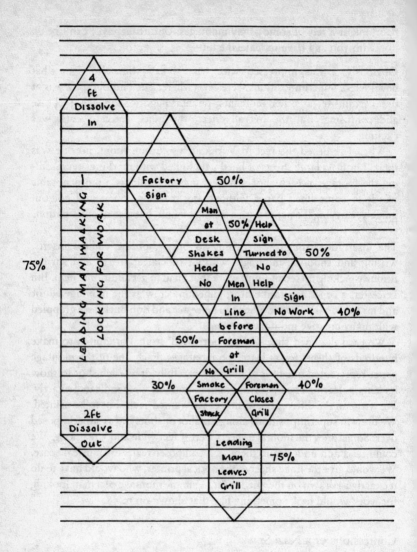

police permit to drop these vile pamphlets on to innocent pedestrians below? No. Did we at least have studio approval? No.

The sequence could have been shot in several cuts, but I insisted on shooting the entire sequence in one shot, which increased the difficulty enormously. I wanted to start on an insert of the pamphlet which would flutter away, revealing hundreds of other pamphlets filling the screen. The people below, who were totally unknown to us, and unpaid by us, would hopefully pick up the pamphlets, look up at us and shake their fists, as traffic came to a halt.

There is a board about 12 feet long known as an airplane board. It's very strong and, with my fingers crossed, I watched the grip, who apparently knew what he was doing, bolt and tie down the wild Mitchell camera, stripped of all unnecessary weight, to the very end of the board so that we could shoot straight down on to the street below. Then the other end of the board was tied down with heavy rope and iron chains to the floor of the roof.

Now it got a bit scary. The grip went out on the board, wrapped his legs around it and pulled himself to the camera to check it. He circled his forefinger and thumb, indicating that everything was OK. He pulled himself back quickly to the roof, got off and smiled at Archie to take his place. Archie wasted no time as he rapidly pulled himself to the camera. He racked it over so he could see the street below, took out a pamphlet and held it under the lense. He changed focus as it fluttered to the street below.

ARCHIE: Looks great. Now when I yell 'Drop', throw all the pamphlets into the air. When the screen's full, I'll let the pamphlet in front of the lens go. (*To me.*) Want to check the set-up, Don?
ME: (*Weakly*) Absolutely.

Archie, without difficulty, returned to the roof and helped me to get on the airplane board. I held on for dear life, frozen. Slowly, I made my way to the camera. I held on so tightly, I was afraid I'd splinter the board. I didn't like the name *airplane* board. Suppose it took off? I could hear the board creaking as I continued towards the camera. I raised myself reluctantly to peer through the eye-piece. I saw absolutely nothing. I raised my circled thumb and forefinger up in the air to indicate that the set-up was OK. Immediately, and ever so slowly, I wiggled my way back to the roof. Archie and the grip grabbed my drenched-in-fear, sweating body and put me down on the roof.

We made the shot in one take, thank God. It worked perfectly. People not only waved their fists at us, they also screamed obscenities vilifying us. We got off that roof as quickly as possible, before they either killed us or had us arrested. To this day, I have no idea whether the camera was racked over so I could see, or whether the crew knew what I knew. I hadn't seen a damn thing.

Every dissolve in the movie was a travelling matte shot of goose-stepping Nazi legs. I was told by Bun, 'A startling innovation.'

An excellent stuntman, Sol Gorse, refused to put on a Nazi uniform. In many of the sequences we had to shoot, we needed uniformed Nazi soldiers. Sol was trembling with rage. I told him this was an anti-Nazi film we were making. I pointed out to him that Warner Brothers, for whom we were working, were Jewish. I was born a Jew and realized the importance of being an American making an anti-Nazi picture. I said what he was doing by refusing to wear a Nazi uniform was sick, stupid and un-American. When he abruptly left the set, I felt sorry for what I had said to him and felt damn lucky he hadn't punched me out.

Roaring Twenties

Roaring Twenties was lustily directed by Raoul Walsh, based on a story by Mark Hellinger. James Cagney and Humphrey Bogart, in their inimitable fashion, pulled the picture along to become a hit.

There were many montages in *Roaring Twenties*, mostly the kind that bore me. Whirling papers, newsreel shots, narration announcing the end of World War I, more of the same about the rise of crime and, finally, the Wall Street crash. I decided, without front office permission but with Haskin's knowledge and support, to do the Wall Street crash using symbolism to get over the disaster; not using newspaper headlines or newsreel shots, and, if possible, no narration.

We built a huge ticker-tape machine, which spewed tape over hordes of people trying to climb steps to reach the machine looming over them. We had wind machines blowing full blast against the sprawling mob, forcing them tumbling, sliding and falling. It was exciting to shoot and somewhat scary too. Haskin pointed out that not only did we not have any money to pay for the shots I was making, but no one, including the director and producer (Wallis and Warner), had the slightest clue what we were doing. But I kept right on shooting.

Finally, Wallis ran the montage and said it was great. Need I add that all his sycophants, plus Walsh and Hellinger, vigorously agreed. It dawned on me that with film properly executed, anything was possible. I walked on air for weeks.

Knute Rockne – All American

This picture starred Pat O'Brien as the Irish coach of Notre Dame, although Knute Rockne was in fact Norwegian. Ronald Reagan played the dying football hero, Gipper. The most famous line in the picture was a passionate plea by O'Brien to his football team: 'Win it for the Gipper.' Gipper died before the team went out to play their most important game. This picture was a combination of Notre Dame football and patriotic waving of American flags. But they could play football better than any other college. It was my job to show how they played and what made them so good.

In the first montage I showed their backfield, famed as the Four Horsemen (James Crowley, Elmer Layden, Donald Miller and Harry Stuhldreher), go through their intricate formations. It was like a ballet: precise movements, speed, grace, splendid blocking and vicious, elusive running. They were quite a team in actuality, and on film. Nick Lukats, who played for Notre Dame much later than the Four Horsemen, was our technical director and actually played the part of James Crowley in the picture.

The second montage was a fascinating one. I had an idea that by using a series of blackouts I could show how proficient they were under actual game conditions. By sticking the football directly into the matte box covering the lens, everything was black. When the ball was thrown away from the camera, it fell into the arms of a running back, who was immediately tackled. I cut to a closer shot of the Notre Dame man who was tackled falling on to a camera which was totally blacked out. From that blackout, I went to the back of one of the Notre Dame players, who was pressed against the matte box, making it black, and as he ran away from the camera it revealed him running towards the goal line. As he ran across the goal line, we saw him fall to the ground and, in a closer shot, fight his way towards another camera, blacking it out.

Then we came to a most difficult shot. From the blackout we saw a close shot of a football boot kicking a ball towards the goalposts. From that, we went on a high parallel behind the goalposts. Below was a Notre Dame player drop-kicking the football over the goalposts and, hopefully, into the matte box, blacking it out. Nick Lukats was famous as a drop-kicker. He kept trying to hit the matte box with his educated toe. Unfortunately, the takes ran up. Soon we were at take ten, then twenty. I was getting uneasy. Then thirty . . . I thought very seriously of giving up, but I needed it. Then forty. Then fifty. I knew I'd have to stop. As a quick director, I had never shot more than five or six takes in my life. Then came fifty-one, fifty-two, fifty-three, fifty-four – everybody thought I was crazy. Fifty-five, fifty-six, fifty-seven – and on the fifty-eighth take, the football hit directly into the lens, blacking out the camera. It was a sensational montage and I was very, very lucky to get it.

Meet John Doe

I received a call from Frank Capra's secretary, saying that he would like to meet me.

SECRETARY: Now that Mr Capra is working on the lot, when would be a convenient time for you to meet him, Mr Siegel?

ME: (*Excitedly*) Anytime.

SECRETARY: (*Laughing*) How about four this afternoon?

ME: Thank you, and please thank Mr Capra. See you at four.

When I met Capra, I was struck by his congeniality and politeness.

CAPRA: I hear you're the bright young man who does all the montages for Warners.

ME: I've done a number that I hope you don't ever see.

CAPRA: Why?

ME: Because they're not too good.

CAPRA: (*Laughs*) Do you think if you did some for me they might be better?

ME: They'd have to be much better, if only because you're the best director in the business.

CAPRA: Well, thank you, young man. I love to hear and read nice things about me.
   (*He reaches behind him and gives me some material on* Meet John Doe.)

CAPRA: Read this material. Where montages are indicated, write them up, just as you would shoot them.

I took the material and thanked Mr Capra for the opportunity to work for him. I was thrilled and determined to please him.

   When I read the pages of *Meet John Doe*, it was clear that Capra wanted to show the media arousing mass hysteria over John Doe – the idealist tramp, played by Gary Cooper, turned into a public idol. A girl reporter (Barbara Stanwyck) and her editor (James Gleason) were most active in starting 'Meet John Doe Clubs'. Posters, newspapers and radio were used somewhat disappointingly. It seemed rather old hat. Capra took the side of the common man (John Doe) with moralistic messages.

   When Capra read the montages, he surprised me. He liked them. However, before I left, he suggested more old-fashioned ideas of whirling posters, emphasizing 'Meet John Doe', dollying quickly into newspaper headlines, 'Meet John Doe'. So I left somewhat puzzled. I rewrote the montages the way I thought he wanted them. They seemed more old-fashioned than ever, more on the nose. But when Capra read the montages, he liked them much better than before. Then he started to want bigger posters and more of them, bigger headlines and more of them.

ME: (*Hesitantly*) Mr Capra, if you don't like my work, I would appreciate it if you would tell me so.

CAPRA: (*Starting to laugh*) Let me ask you something. If I had not criticized your montages when you first showed them to me, would you have worked on them?

ME: (*Reflecting*) No, probably not.

CAPRA: Exactly. Now, when I shoot a picture, the script is never final until the film is shot and in the can. Do you understand what I'm getting at?

ME: I think I do. Yes.

CAPRA: Good. Send the changes back to me. I'll study them and let you know my feelings. I'm sure I'll like them.

ME: (*Getting up to leave*) I'll do my best.

CAPRA: That's all I expect of anyone.

I finished the new montages as quickly as possible. I didn't feel comfortable with them. Nevertheless, I felt the only proper course was to give the man what he wanted. After all, Capra was Capra. His pictures spoke for him. He was indubitably the best. I had the montages delivered to him and kept my fingers crossed.

Two weeks passed with no word from Capra. Then one day an unusually large manilla envelope, addressed simply to the Montage Department, was delivered to me. I opened it to discover two blueprints. I knew I hadn't had anything to do with them. Printed clearly on the top left of both blueprints was 'Meet John Doe'. In the lower right-hand corner was a signature, 'Slavko Vorkapitch'. I put the blueprints down on the table, not examining them further. Obviously Vorkapitch was doing the montages for Capra. There was nothing wrong with that, but I was disturbed that I hadn't heard a word from Capra, nor even from his charming secretary. I knew the business was cruel, but I didn't expect this sort of treatment from Capra. I felt a little sick in my stomach. One never knows.

In 1975 a paperback book was published: *Frank Capra: The Man and His Films*, edited by Richard Glatzer and John Raeburn. The chapter on *Meet John Doe* contains this passage: '. . . one of the saddest things is to find Capra so preoccupied with getting over a message of holy-hokum that he lets in a half a dozen of the worst montage transitions – mumming faces, headlines, wheels and whorls – that have been seen in a major effort since the trick first turned stale.' I must confess that I would not have liked to have read the above about any of my montages. I felt very, very lucky.

Blues in the Night

Richard Whorf, a talented painter and set designer, was relatively inexperienced as an actor when he did Anatole Litvak's *Blues in the Night*. The story was about five musicians who formed a jazz group centred around the piano player, Whorf. Each finger of a hand represented a musician. In montages we showed the 'hand' in split screen, playing their music against a map of the States as the 'hand' travelled across the map. One of the biggest problems was to show clearly that Whorf was losing his ability to play the piano. His fingers couldn't function. It was both physical and mental.

We had a special piano built with a keyboard made of marshmallow. When Whorf struck the keyboard, desperately trying to remember the music, his fingers stuck to the keys. When he tried to free his hands, the marshmallow remained stuck to his fingers, immobilizing them. A horrific shock.

I showed the montages to Haskin, who was very impressed. But his face creased into a deep frown.

HASKIN: We're in trouble.

ME: I thought you said they were terrific.

HASKIN: That, my boy genius, is why we're in trouble.

ME: I don't dig you at all, Bun.

HASKIN: Mr Wallis has an iron-clad rule that he sees the montages before anyone else, excepting, of course, us.

ME: So?

HASKIN: Mr Litvak has in his golden contract that he sees the montages first.

ME: What if we run it with them together?

HASKIN: Not a good idea, because to impress each other with their power they'll change the montages. (*Pauses.*) I think I have the solution for these idiots. We'll make up another print and, at exactly the same time, in different projection rooms, at opposite ends of the lot, I'll run with Wallis in Projection Room Four, while in Projection Room One you run with Litvak.

ME: How do we run it separately with Warner?

HASKIN: We don't. He's sunning himself at Cannes.

ME: You're not only brilliant, you're full of guile.

HASKIN: And also crap.

Two days later, we did just that. Both parties thought the montages were 'out of this world'. Wallis instructed Haskin to have Litvak see the montages as soon as possible. Litvak thought that, when convenient, I should run with Wallis. The extra prints cost money, the extra projection rooms and projectionists cost money, but that's the way the crazy ball bounces in the movie industry.

Later, when Litvak was dubbing the picture, he told me that he was worried about the title song, 'Blues in the Night'.

ME: I wouldn't worry about that. It's the best blues I've ever heard. If I were you, I'd worry about your picture, which is five per cent as good as the song . . .

LITVAK: (*Annoyed*) You think you're pretty good, don't you Don?

ME: (*Fresh as usual*) You said some pretty nice things about the montages.

LITVAK: True, but when you dolly into the poster you could have had someone walk past the poster. And you should have started on that person and ended on the poster. You must always have a reason for your camera movement, be it a dolly or a pan.

And you know something, he was right. He taught me a lesson I used for the rest of my life.

Incidentally, one of the musicians in the jazz group was played by Elia Kazan. I was amused by the way he used to talk vehemently about showing 'them' (presumably the front office) that one day he would make it. I thought he was referring to his acting. No question that he was a good actor, but his face, though full of character, was not the face of a leading man. I had no idea that indeed he would show 'them' his great talent as a director.

They Died With Their Boots On

I directed a number of second units – sequences, stunts or background shots not handled by the main unit – but I received little recognition. For *They Died With Their Boots On*, which consisted mainly of horses falling to the ground, cavalry being killed by arrows and Indians falling dead as they were shot from their horses, we also showed Custer (magnificently played by Errol Flynn) in other victories against the Confederate forces in various short montages. Raoul Walsh directed the picture.

When doing montages and second units, I tried to shoot in the style of the director. Raoul Walsh usually shot from eye-level and didn't move his camera much. He had his actors come up to the camera rather than dolly or pan. Michael Curtiz, on the other hand, dollied in on his actors and did considerable panning. Howard Hawks didn't make many set-ups, nor did he shoot much footage. Anatole Litvak shot endless takes. Sometimes he'd print takes two, seven, fifteen and twenty-six. He was a good editor and made unusual and interesting set-ups, but he sure wasted a lot of footage.

Unlike directors such as Walsh, I pre-planned my shots very carefully. Although the second-unit work was in the genre of the first director, I followed certain rules faithfully. I would explain carefully to the stunt co-ordinator or stuntman exactly what I wanted. Their ideas often differed from mine, mainly over how to execute the stunt. My first rule was that no one was to get hurt. Under no circumstances would we be rushed by anyone, regardless of their title. Rule number two was that the stunt was to be as exciting as possible – but always bearing in mind rule number one.

In the thousands of stunts I have directed, by following the above rules I have never hurt any stuntman or actor. I refuse to continue working overtime if I feel the stuntmen are getting tired. If I feel we've made take one as good as we can, I walk away from the printed first take. I never shoot 'protection' shots. I do use multiple camera set-ups, not only for editing purposes, but so that I'm protected in case of a camera malfunction.

I began to realize that it was stupid of me to imagine that the studio wasn't aware of the enormous amount of work I was doing on inserts, montages and second units. By ignoring my work, which they must have liked or they wouldn't have let me carry on, they chose to ignore my desire to direct features.

So one day I waited for Jack L. Warner. As he left Projection Room 4, he seemed to be in a good mood and actually smiled at me.

ME: I hate to bring up a problem, but you are the only person who can help me.
WARNER: (*Antennae on the alert*) You going to talk about money?
ME: No. I want to direct features.
   (*Warner starts to hurry back to his office, but I keep up with him.*)
ME: Do you know that I have more film in Warner pictures than any other director on the lot?
WARNER: (*Increasing his pace*) No. And I don't believe it.
   (*I stop and let him walk away from me.*)
ME: (*Calling after him*) I apologize for drawing it to your attention. Please check it out.

Warner disappeared from sight. I whirled around in the other direction and started back to Stage 5.

Flight From Destiny

The phone rang at 7.10 a.m. at home. It was Tenny Wright. Vincent Sherman, who was directing *Flight From Destiny*, had just told him that he was sick and unable to report for work. He was about to shoot an important scene in which Thomas Mitchell walks the 'last mile' on his way to pay the penalty for murdering a woman.

ME: Tenny, I don't know the story. Can I call Vincent?

TENNY: No. He's running a high temperature and I don't want it to get any higher when he hears you're directing the last sequence in the picture.
(*Impatiently.*) Quit arguing and get there as soon as possible.

ME: Where's there?

TENNY: Stage fifteen, and thanks.
(*When I get to the stage, unshaven, without breakfast and looking a mess, the first assistant is lying in wait for me. He hands me several pages of script.*)

ME: What the hell is the name of the picture?

ASSISTANT DIRECTOR: *Flight From Destiny.*

ME: Who's in the sequence?

ASSISTANT DIRECTOR: Thomas Mitchell and a bunch of extras.

ME: Where is Mitchell?

ASSISTANT DIRECTOR: As soon as he arrives, I'll take you to his trailer.

ME: Take me to the trailer now. I'll read the pages. Bring me some coffee and a plain doughnut.
(*I am finishing my doughnut when Mitchell arrives. I introduce myself and we shake hands.*)

ME: Mr Mitchell, I'm sorry to inform you that Mr Sherman is sick and unable to work. I'm also sorry to inform you that I've been asked to take over and I don't have the foggiest idea of how to direct the scene.
(*Mitchell starts to change his clothes. The wardrobe man comes in to help. The make-up man enters, ready to paint away. The hairdresser, a lovely girl, sticks her head in to inform Mitchell she will be waiting outside. It is nice and peaceful and quiet for a serious discussion between director and star.*)

MITCHELL: (*Busy*) I don't think we will have any trouble. You must have a lot of friends – I've heard nothing but good things about you.

ME: Thank you, but one thing bothers me. When you're walking the 'last mile', are you thinking of the dreadful woman you murdered? Or are you thinking that you knew you only had a few months to live anyway? Or do you think of Geraldine Fitzgerald or Jeffrey Lynn? And, most important, how do you show who or what you're thinking about as you're on your way to being electrocuted?

MITCHELL: Extraordinary. (*Turning to wardrobe and make-up men.*) Would you be kind enough to give my director and me a few minutes alone?

(*They leave. Mitchell puts on a robe and sits on the sofa next to me. He ponders a moment, then smiles.*)

MITCHELL: When I worked for John Ford on *The Long Voyage Home*, I had a similar problem. I was on a ship, having a glorious fight with certain members of the cast and lots of burly stuntmen when, according to plan, I crashed into the main mast. I was presumably knocked senseless. When I regained consciousness, I was supposed to think of many things that had happened in my life: my brothers and I fighting a gang of toughs, my sweet mother singing a song to my father, who listened while drinking a beer, and so on. (*Pauses, his eyes sparkling with memories.*) So I went to Mr Ford and explained that I had a problem knowing how to portray my wonderful memories. Ford said, 'You don't.' 'Then what do I do, sir?', I asked. 'Nothing,' he replied. 'You don't have a thought in your head. Your mind is blank. If the audience thinks you are thinking of the fight, fine; of your wife, fine; of the joy of sailing the seas, fine. Whatever the audience thinks, fine.' So you see, it's quite simple.

ME: What a brilliant idea!

(*Starting for door.*) See you on the set.

The grips laid the dolly tracks so that the men in the cells on death row could be seen in the background. On either side of Thomas Mitchell were two burly prison guards. Behind him was a Catholic priest carrying an open Bible, his lips moving silently. Mitchell walked slowly but erect. His face showed no overt thought, but obviously his mind was alive with memories. The day's work went very smoothly.

The next day I saw the dailies. I was not surprised when the other people in the projection room thought Mitchell looked wonderful. I agreed with them. Thank you, Mr Mitchell, and thank you, Mr Ford.

Yankee Doodle Dandy

Working with Cagney was electric. He is truly one of the great actors of our time. I worked with him on a number of films, including *Angels with Dirty Faces* (1938), *Each Dawn I Die* (1939), but I didn't really get to know him until we worked together on *Yankee Doodle Dandy* in 1942.

Because of having to be ready to shoot the moment a big star like Cagney arrived on the set, I laid out the shot. I was shooting in a basement set. Through a window could be seen the legs of passers-by. We were prepared to have it snowing outside. The dolly was to follow Cagney when he sat down near the window.

Cagney arrived. I explained what I intended to do and he walked through the scene with the dolly closing in on him as he sat down. He sat for a moment, then got to his feet.

CAGNEY: The way you've lined it up, you'll never see the street.

ME: (*Embarrassed*) Pretty stupid of me.
  (*I immediately give instructions to reset the dolly so that when Cagney sits down, the legs of the passers-by can be seen, the falling snow will be visible.*)

ME: I'll make a hell of a director, Jimmy.

CAGNEY: As long as you keep a pipe in your mouth, at least you'll look like a director.
  (*Aware that I am not happy with myself, he tries to make me feel better.*)

CAGNEY: It's not the usual, if you'll pardon my Latin, modus operandi, to lay out a shot before the actor appears.

ME: That's true, but surely Curtiz, once you're on the set, lays out the shot.

CAGNEY: The only thing Curtiz has to say is (*with Hungarian accent*) 'Don't do it the way I showed you. Do it the way I mean.'
  (*I smile, feeling better. The dolly has been reset, the passers-by are ready to walk, the snow is ready to fall.*)

ME: OK, Mr Cagney, we're ready for a run-through.
  (*Cagney takes his starting place.*)

ME: (*With a lousy Hungarian accent*) Remember, don't do it the way I showed you. Do it the way I mean.
  (*Cagney smiles as I yell 'Action!'*)

The most difficult montage in *Yankee Doodle Dandy* was a continuous dolly shot across the roofs of Broadway, panning down to the various marquees, identifying the theatres on both sides of Broadway. On each marquee, in lights, was the name George M. Cohan, starring in the hit show that was playing at that particular theatre. Over each one, Frances Langford's voice was heard, singing the various hit songs beautifully.

The effect was truly exhilarating. It was accomplished by painting a huge matte shot of the roofs on both sides of Broadway. Each of the lighted marquees was painted in with the names of the shows realistically lit up with real lights. The camera, on a boom, would sweep across the roofs and swoop down to each marquee long enough to read it. There was no way this continuous shot could have been made other than the way we did it.

Frances Langford insisted that when her voice was heard over the various marquess, her face would also be seen. This was totally unacceptable to the studio, but they found a way of getting round that problem. To my dismay, I was instructed to shoot Frances singing the various songs *without any film in the camera.* Under no circumstances was she to have any inkling that we were not photographing her. So an ugly charade was acted out. We went through the business of having Frances's face made up, her hair carefully coiffured, her dress beautifully designed to fit her perfectly, her shoes chosen to match her dress, her accessories picked with taste; her jewellery real and expensive. To make things even more embarrassing, her husband, Jon Hall, was full of suggestions.

The assistant director yelled, 'Roll!' the soundman sang out, 'Speed!' and the empty camera was presumed running. The boom-man had the mike in the correct place for Frances to sing into. 'Anytime you're ready,' I said to her, and she began to sing – beautifully. When she finished, Jon Hall consulted with her about how she had sung, how she had looked, and so on. I think we made five takes. Each one made me feel more guilty. I felt strongly that it was a typical studio dirty trick. Every man on our crew felt the same. But we were paid to obey orders, which we did.

At the sneak preview, which I believe was in Pasadena, I took my seat in the last row of the balcony. The audience, at least around where I was sitting, were young, rowdy and restless. When the Warner Brothers insignia came on, the sound of raspberries was distinctly heard. I muttered to myself, 'We're dead.' But as the picture began playing, the audience quietened down. They started to laugh in the right places; they appeared definitely to be with the picture. At the end, everyone stood up, cheering and clapping and yelling their approval. I was never so thrilled in my life. I noticed Jim Leicester's name and mine during the end titles. I was very proud, though my vision was blurred.

The Adventures of Mark Twain

This picture was directed by Irving Rapper and produced by Jesse Lasky. The picture covers the full seventy-five years of Mark Twain's life and, consequently, included many, many montages to cover the various lapses of time. Two of the montages that I did I felt were interesting, not only because they turned out well, but because the front office had no idea how I did them and were very upset at the possible cost.

For one, I found five camels, took their picture in dozens of poses, printed the pictures, cut them out and mounted them on a camshaft to have them move. Then I set up a scene with Fredric March projected on a miniature screen on a miniature minaret. As the camera pulled back, it picked up the camels and came through a cut-out crowd of Arabs – it looked as though there were thousands of them. The camera stopped at two of the five real actors, who turned to each other and laughed at Mark Twain's joke. When Jack Warner saw the sequence he blew his stack. He thought hundreds of extras had been hired and he blamed me for wasting a fortune.

The second montage apparently took place in London's Albert Hall. I used cut-outs for the audience, which numbered over 1,000 people because the balconies were also filled; and I had a matte made, which in essence means that I had the structure, walls, etc., of the Albert Hall painted in. On the stage stood Fredric March. I made my reverses on his face when he talked, as well as making shots from the stage at the huge audience facing him. Again, it was a fooler, and obviously if I *had* used a thousand people and built a replica of the Albert Hall it would have cost a fortune. Again, Warner was flabbergasted; he had no idea how I did it and I, instead of giving him a straight reply and explanation, sort of shrugged it off as though I *had* actually used thousands of people.

Nevertheless, Warner liked both montages very much and for the time being, at least, he was very friendly. I was sure that when he found out the real costs he would not be angry at all.

Then one day I was called in to Tenny Wright's office. He seemed very upset.

TENNY: You're in a lot of trouble, kid.
ME: Why? What have I done?
TENNY: It's those damn montages you did on *The Adventures of Mark Twain*.
ME: (*Wryly*) Well, I ran with Mr Warner and he liked them very much and said so.
WRIGHT: Well, he doesn't like them now and he wants to know

exactly, day by day, what they cost. Let's start with how many electricians you employed on June twentieth.

ME: (*Somewhat annoyed*) I haven't the foggiest idea, nor do I intend to try to figure out how many electricians I used on June twentieth, or whatever the bloody date was.

WRIGHT: How many grips did you have on July seventeenth?

ME: Forget it, Tenny, I mean forget it and shut up, because you have no control over me – none whatsoever. If Mr Warner liked my montages so much and now I have to go through this rigmarole, I'm quitting, and as of this moment you can tell him to shove it, and be sure to give him my best regards when you tell him to shove it because I'm leaving the lot.

I went over to see Jesse Lasky, a very pleasant, intelligent producer. He was shocked at the trouble I was in. He loved the montages and insisted on calling Jack Warner immediately to find out what the trouble was.

ME: Mr Lasky, I don't want you to call Jack Warner under any circumstances because I really want to leave the lot. I've had it – I don't like it here. I do like you very much, Mr Lasky; it was a pleasure working for you and I'm sure that we'll get together one of these days when you're working at another studio.

LASKY: (*With tears in his eyes*) Believe me, Don, the day that you direct a picture for me will be one of the happiest days for both of us.

I left him. I then went to my office, where I was betrayed by somebody and put on the phone.

WARNER: (*On phone*) What the hell are you so mad about? I told you to your face that I liked the montages.

ME: What annoyed me was the fact that after telling me this you then have Tenny Wright ask me idiotic questions like how many electricians did I have on such and such a date, and how many grips did I have on another date. Anyway, I want to leave the lot. I don't like working under these conditions.

WARNER: (*Firmly*) I never told Tenny to investigate it (*of course, he is lying*) . . . I think your montages are wonderful, and I want you to keep on working.

ME: Well, I'll have to think about it, because I must say I don't find it much fun working here. I'm still not ecstatic about the amount of money I'm making; but I'm in the middle of another montage, so I guess I'd better finish it before I walk off the lot.

That was the end of our conversation and, of course, I stayed on like an idiot.

After attempting to quit Warners and complaining about my salary to Jack Warner, I received an envelope containing two cheques: a regular salary cheque for $150, which was certainly most welcome, and a surprising 'bonus cheque' for $65, which, although it pleased me a great deal, puzzled me because it was called a 'bonus cheque'. Why not add the $65 to the $150 and give me one cheque for $215? I was to discover the reason all too soon – but I'll keep you dangling until it happens.

Mission to Moscow

Mission to Moscow, directed by Michael Curtiz, is a story based on US Ambassador Joseph Davies's dealings with the Russians between 1936 and 1941. In Stuart Kaminsky's book, *Don Siegel: Director*, Kaminsky interviewed Tom Tully, who played an engineer from Texas. In one scene he had to explain the workings of a large Russian machine plant to Davies (Walter Huston): 'Don had erected an enormous machine plant in back of a stairway that led up a treadmill. We walked on the treadmill and the process screen in back of us teemed with action. At a signal from Don, Huston and I started up the real stairs, Don followed us with a camera on a crane. He was sitting right on top of it. At the top of the stairs, the door to what was supposed to be my office was rigged to break away so the camera could follow us right in. I went to the desk and finished my monologue and all Huston did was listen, which I discovered was the best kind of part to have. Anyway, I did the whole scene in one take.' That scene, which was shot in the studio's machine shop, took a great deal of timing and luck. It did look enormous and certainly suggested the power and energy of Russia.

Another scene had Huston speaking from a stage in a large auditorium filled with Russian workers. Huston's speech was filled with technical data, figures, etc. He would break down, start again and break down again. After several agonizing minutes of this, I finally stopped the scene.

ME: Walter, there is no way anyone could possibly learn numerical dialogue like this.

HUSTON: Well, I've had some tough ones in my day, but nothing like this gibberish.

ME: Precisely, and, with your permission, I think I have a solution. Supposing we hang large pieces of framed black cloth in as many sections of the auditorium as we need to cover the speech. We'll

73

letter each section with white dialogue painted on the black cloth.

HUSTON: Hey, that makes sense. We'll hang them up so that I'll say a few words to the centre of the house, to the right side, to the left side, to the front, up to the balcony . . .
(*Scratches his head and smiles.*) Sure glad I thought up this gag. When you get to my age (*chuckles*) you need all these actor tricks.

ME: (*To the propman, standby painter, head grip*) Let's hop on it. You're on report for holding up production.

I couldn't believe the consummate artistry of Huston. While doing the speech, his gaze encompassed the whole auditorium: his eyes focused near and far, up and down. There was no way anyone could tell that he was reading his dialogue. In fact, for the first time since reading the script, the dialogue made sense.

One day, while shooting Huston in a crowd scene, I sensed a certain antipathy against me from the extras and bit players, I guess because it was second unit and I was young. It made me uneasy. I noticed something that Walter was doing. For the life of me, I can't remember what I said to him, except I know it was definitely unimportant.

HUSTON: (*Thumping his forehead with his hand*) Thanks, Don, for pointing it out to me. God, I'm stupid!

Of course, he did this for the benefit of the crowd. I noticed their attitude towards me changed immediately: they were attentive, polite and did whatever I asked them to do. In addition to all of Walter's attributes, he was indeed a kind man.

After the reviews of *Mission to Moscow* came out, which were surprisingly good, I was having lunch in Warner's private dining room when Mike Curtiz came in. Instantly, the entire table of about fifteen people applauded. Mike beamed at all of us as he sat down. Then it started.

JERRY WALD: (*Ignoring Curtiz*) The montages that Siegel did made the picture, I felt.

RANDY MACDOUGALL: Don made more set-ups in the second-unit work than Mike did in the picture.
(*I don't dare look up at Mike as others join in with the teasing. Finally Mike speaks.*)

CURTIZ: When Don shoots, I shoot. After all, he is my protégé.

ME: Thank you, Mike. (*Getting up and leaving the table.*) I owe it all to you.

Passage to Marseilles

Passage to Marseilles was produced by Hal Wallis and directed by Mike Curtiz. A number of people from the very successful *Casablanca*, also produced by Hal Wallis and directed by Mike Curtiz, were put into *Passage to Marseilles*, including such stars as Humphrey Bogart, Sidney Greenstreet, Peter Lorre and Claude Rains. However, the picture didn't turn out anywhere near as well as *Casablanca*, which was sensational. I thought that the trouble with *Passage to Marseilles* was its construction: flashbacks into flashbacks into more flashbacks, etc. I wrote a number of montages that covered those sequences ineptly and I didn't particularly like the picture; but there were two second units that were reasonably well done and in some ways were physically quite difficult.

In the first, Humphrey Bogart leads four of his comrades (Peter Lorre, Helmut Dantine, George Tobias and Philip Dorn) to make an escape from Devil's Island. This meant going through slime and muck and mud and swamp – very difficult physically not only for me, but certainly for the actors. But they didn't complain. Anyway, they make their escape in a canoe, and when we pick them up later they are in really bad shape when a French freighter stops and rescues them. That, more or less, took care of the first second unit.

The second one took place on the French freighter. A mutiny erupts and, in addition, the freighter is attacked by German aircraft. This was quite difficult to do. We had miniature aeroplanes attacking and when the bullets from the planes hit the ship you could see the bullets cutting through the wooden deck, the mast and other areas. I remember one instance when Humphrey Bogart was telling a funny story and everybody was enjoying it. He kept telling it right up to the time when the assistant director yelled 'Roll 'em!' Everybody, with the exception of stupid Helmut Dantine, instantly got back into their roles. Unfortunately, Helmut did not and carried on laughing. The scene was quite dangerous: when I yelled 'Action!' various sailors, all stuntmen of course, were immediately hit by major explosions. As they were shot up into the air, out of camera range, they grabbed on to dangling, heavy rope netting and entwined themselves in it until we let them down.

ME: (*To Helmut*) You stupid son-of-a-bitch. You wrecked the shot. One more idiotic mishap on your part and I'll throw you head first over the side of the ship on to the cement floor. You've got a cement head anyway, so you'll only have a cracked head. (*I hear Bogey laughing and go over to him.*) The only reason we get along, Bogey, is the indisputable fact that you always beat me at chess. You dislike Mike, you hate the picture and you're dying to finish it. However, it will take us the rest of the day to re-rig it.

We were good for about two set-ups a day, if we were lucky. But we finally got the shot and it turned out to be quite exciting. Bogey apologized to me. But he still had his sardonic smile.

Now and then I would run into Mike Curtiz as he directed a love scene in the cabin of the ship between Michèle Morgan and Bogart.

ME: Why don't we swap scenes? You shoot the mutiny on board ship and the escape from Devil's Island, and I shoot the love scenes. (*Pointing out to Mike.*) I'm only thinking of the difficulty in getting the shots.

But Mike was a wily Hungarian whose vocabulary got progressively worse the longer he worked at Warner Brothers and I was unable to get him to consider switching scenes. I was tired of shooting second unit and to work with Michèle Morgan would have been a most welcome change.

Hal Wallis and Michael Curtiz seemed to like what I shot. I put it into a rough cut and added sounds, such as bullets and various other explosions. Wallis asked me to run with Mike my cut film and also what they had in cut form at his house. At 8 that night, Mike and I arrived separately at Wallis's home in the San Fernando Valley. We ran the picture, then the lights went up. Mike and Hal had a rather unpleasant discussion regarding Michael's work in the picture. Then Wallis made the fatal mistake of asking my opinion of what I had seen. I told him flat out that I didn't think the use of constant flashbacks into flashbacks worked and I felt that it was due to poor construction, not necessarily in what Mike shot, but in the script, for which Hal Wallis was obviously responsible. Wallis turned to me and asked me to leave. They had no further use for my opinion on the picture.

The next day, Mike waited while I was shooting, then he would step in and use my crew to shoot some process shots while I waited for him. We did that switching four or five times, and in between shots Mike asked me in more detail what I thought was wrong with the picture and how I felt it should be fixed. So I told him a few things. Then Wallis arrived and I went to say hello to him. He was very unpleasant. I became annoyed at his tirade and pointed out succinctly, and in a surprisingly even tone, that he should never ask me my opinion unless he expected two things: one, that I would answer, and two, that I would answer truthfully. I turned my back on him and when Mike finished his shot I carried on with my next one. Of course, Wallis never forgave me. He told me that he had been thinking about giving me a picture to direct, but that I could forget it. I replied that I was sorry he felt that way. All I was trying to do was to help what I felt was a sick, untidy and rocky passage in *Passage to Marseilles*.

Jack L. Warner

When I received a telephone call to see Jack Warner immediately, I didn't have a clue why. However, I did decide on the way to his office to address him as J.L. Every director on the lot referred to him as J.L. Maybe he'd treat me with more respect.

As I entered his extremely large office, Warner started pacing up and down, really angry with me.

WARNER: Do you think all I have to do is talk to damn actors who sing your praises and say that you'd make (*sarcastic*) a super director?
ME: (*Intrigued*) J.L., I haven't the slightest idea who those 'damn actors' are.
WARNER: Walter Huston for one, and Sidney Greenstreet for another.
ME: Obviously, I didn't ask them to talk to you. Do you think they would have if I had asked them to see you?
WARNER: Well, they were here bothering me.
ME: J.L., why don't you give me a break, directing?
(*Warner, dismisses the thought by turning back to sit in the chair behind his large desk.*)
WARNER: I can get directors a dime a dozen. Where am I going to get someone to do your work?
ME: OK. Pay me what you pay your 'dime a dozen' directors and I'll be happy to go back to my job and quit bothering you.
WARNER: You just quit bothering me right now.
ME: Surely you must know by now that I'm more than qualified to direct features. I think Huston and Greenstreet are decent, talented, kind men.
WARNER: Let me tell you something, kid, and don't ever forget it. Every actor is a shit. (*Reaching for phone.*) Now get your ass out of here. I'm busy.

Inasmuch as many actors were my friends, I was shocked at Warner's crudity. I left depressed at the lack of rapport between us.

*

Although J.L. certainly didn't like me, he frequently had me run film with him in his projection room. One day he was running a dreadful film that had one man, with an unlit cigarette in his mouth, asking a second man if he had any matches.

SECOND MAN: Sure.
    (*He takes a small, plain box of matches from his coat pocket and hands it to the first man.*)
SECOND MAN: I always carry matches.
FIRST MAN: Thanks.
    (*He lights his cigarette and hands the box of matches back to the second man.*)
SECOND MAN: You can keep the matches.
FIRST MAN: Thanks again for the matches.
    (*J.L. breaks in.*)
WARNER: Make an insert of the box of matches.
ME: Why?
WARNER: Because, damnit, I told you to.
ME: But J.L., there's no message on it. It's very clear from what we see and hear that the audience, if there is any, will certainly know what the small, plain box of matches is.
WARNER: (*Edgy*) Whose name is outside the studio?
ME: You and your brothers'.
WARNER: Shoot the box of matches!

I shot the box of matches.

On another occasion J.L. was running a film in which I had shot a title superimposed over Mexican countryside. When the title appeared on the screen, J.L. started reading it aloud.

WARNER: 'The date was December 17, 1818. A ragged Indian boy ran away from home. His name was Juárez.'
    (*He reads it twice more. The title dissolves out.*)
WARNER: Make the title longer.
ME: But J.L., you read the title three times before it disappeared.
WARNER: Make it longer and keep your mouth shut.

I kept my mouth shut. I didn't make it longer because I figured he had read it three times; consequently, he was familiar with the text and would read it faster.

Five days later I ran the supposedly longer title for J.L. He read it three and a half times before it dissolved out.

WARNER: Good. It's exactly the right length.

I smiled to myself, but I was not pleased. If I had any guts, I would have told him that the title was the exact length of the one he had said was too short. I realized then that I had joined the huge army of sycophants who worked for him.

Saratoga Trunk

Saratoga Trunk was produced by Hal Wallis and directed by Sam Wood. There was a large sequence of two trains, one carrying the 'bad guys', headed by Frank Hagney, the other carrying the 'good guys', headed by Gary Cooper. We used 175 stuntmen representing both the good and the bad.

Although the stage was big, the action called for was immense. Two trains were to head towards each other carrying the 175 stuntmen. I went through my usual rigmarole.

ME: (*A bit nervous*) One, nobody gets hurt. Two, I want the stunts to be as good as possible, but always remember that number one is *always* more important than number two.

So we made long shots and close shots of the engines supposedly crashing into each other. We had shots of stuntmen jumping off the moving freight trains, shot from outside up as they jumped. We had shots from inside the moving freight cars from behind the men, showing them jumping off. This posed a new problem for me. When shot from outside the moving freight cars, jumping off, the men were moving camera right to left. Yet when I made the reverse shot of the same men jumping off from inside the freight cars, they were jumping off camera left to right. The script girl, the cameraman and, of course, the assistant director said I couldn't do it; it would never cut together. I was aware of the rule of left to right and right to left. The bad guys' train was moving right to left. The good guys' train was moving left to right. I had the same problems with both trains. But what they were really saying was that one couldn't make reverse shots. That, I felt, was ridiculous. It made for dull shooting.

Actually, when I cut it together, the geography being established, it worked. Larry Butler, at that time a special-effects director, came up with a splendid shot during the mêlée of fighting – and a mêlée of 175 men can be a mess. We set a dolly track right in the middle of them and lined up stuntmen on each side of the dolly tracks. When we quickly pulled back, the instant the camera cleared, the stuntmen threw vicious punches at each other along the entire length of the dolly track.

Although Cooper didn't throw punches particularly well, his face showed the strain of battle excellently. On the other hand, while the stuntmen threw punches well, their faces were expressionless. Despite the many angles I shot, many favouring the bad guys, you probably guessed it correctly: the good guys, fearlessly led by Cooper, won the stirring encounter.

I rarely discussed the sequence with the director, Sam Wood. I was aware of his visiting the set only once. I thought that strange, if for no other reason than that his star, Gary Cooper, was fighting throughout the sequence and obviously might get hurt. I, on the other hand, watched Sam Wood direct Ingrid Bergman and Gary Cooper on his set without being invited to be there. I noticed that in explaining the scene to his stars he seemed almost inarticulate. When he walked back to the camera, Cooper smiled knowingly at Bergman, who smiled back and shrugged helplessly.

Yet Sam Wood directed many fine films. What talent or knowledge did he have that enabled him to be so successful? He had good taste, a requisite for a fine director. He had the patience and the stubbornness not to give up until he got the scene. The front office meant nothing to him. Wood was fearless.

Some weeks later I received a call from Hal Wallis's office to be in Projection Room 5 at 6 p.m. for a running of the rough cut of what had been shot so far. Wood would be there. I was intrigued. Why should I be asked by Wallis to see a partial rough cut? Perhaps in the film that still had to be shot there might be some added second-unit work. Anyway, it should be interesting viewing. I wondered how my work blended into the picture. Maybe Wallis and Wood would gang up on me to destroy my work . . . I calmed down and waited till 6 p.m. There wasn't much else I could do anyway.

At 6 on the dot, Wallis and Wood entered the projection room, followed by Wood's editor. Wallis looked grim as he sat in the back row, next to the projection controls. He indicated for me to sit next to him as Wood and the editor sat halfway down in the centre of the room. The silence was deafening. Wallis pushed the start buzzer. The lights dimmed; the picture started. In this rough cut there were no titles, no dissolves and no music; there was no attempt to balance the picture or the sound. So one really was seeing *Saratoga Trunk* at its worst.

The picture seemed slow, but the acting was excellent. The period sets looked real, the costumes correct. When my second unit came on, I realized I had failed to do what I generally did: shoot in the style of the director of the picture. Inasmuch as the action in the picture seemed quite slow, my second unit seemed too quick. It made Wood's rough cut, naturally enough, need editing. Finally, the picture abruptly ended and the lights came on. This time, the silence seemed unending.

I sneaked a look at Wallis. His first grim visage seemed like a smile. He was now in a blue funk. He stared straight ahead at the back of Wood's head. Finally, Wood turned in his seat and stared back at Wallis. He took his time before speaking, but no one could outwait Wallis.

WOOD: (*Strangely calm*) Any thoughts about the film?

WALLIS: (*Sharply, angry*) No good ones, that's for sure.
(*Wood stands up, still facing Wallis. His editor remains seated, staring straight ahead.*)

WOOD: I take it you don't like it.

WALLIS: It's a disgrace. And you still have about two more weeks to go.

WOOD: More like three or four.

WALLIS: (*His anger mounting*) The hell you have. You're already over budget and we're going to stop that right now.

WOOD: (*Deceptively smooth*) Hal, how much are we over budget?

WALLIS: Too goddamn much for this dull picture to ever show a profit.

WOOD: Really? How much have we spent on the picture up to date?

WALLIS: A little under two million.

WOOD: (*Changing gears*) Do you think you could come up with an exact figure?

WALLIS: To the penny.

WOOD: Well, let's say it's two million. (*Raises his hand to stop Wallis from interrupting.*) I'll buy it.

WALLIS: (*A bit shaken*) You'll what?

WOOD: I'll have my auditor go over the books. I'll also pay for whatever we have to shoot, plus all post-production work.

WALLIS: You're crazy!

WOOD: Maybe. You stand to lose nothing. You won't have any money in the picture and you'll make money because Warners will still have the distribution rights.

Wallis, his face ashen, sat down, indicating for me to leave. I got up immediately and quickly left the room. The voices got louder as I closed the door.

I had made a momentous discovery. Money talks and money wins. What a glorious position for Wood to be in. You don't like my picture? Fine. I'll buy it and you can take your criticism and shove it. Hurrah for America. The land of the free and the bucks.

The Conspirators

There was a message from my secretary (yes, I now had a secretary) that Mr Wallis would like to see me at 3 o'clock in his office. He was most pleasant and cordial. He gave me a book entitled *The Conspirators*, by Frederic Prokosh. It was to be filmed starring Hedy Lamarr. The rest of the supporting cast would be of the same calibre as *Casablanca*.

WALLIS: (*Friendly*) If you like it, get back to me as soon as possible. We'll kick the story around.

ME: (*Picking up the book*) Would tomorrow be too soon?

He laughed. I couldn't get back to my office fast enough. I remembered how on *Passage to Marseilles* he told me he wasn't going to give me a picture. Well, here was the book in my hand – so something good must have happened. I told my secretary to accept no calls. I closed my office door, settled in a comfortable chair and started to read.

The book was in the genre of *Casablanca*, only it was set in Lisbon. Although Hedy had made many pictures, I kept thinking of *Ecstasy*, in which she appeared nude and beautiful. Unfortunately, I found the book dull. Wallis must have liked it or he wouldn't have bought it. The fact that he said 'We'll kick the story around' was dangerous. If I told him what I really thought of the book, I would wind up getting kicked off the project. After all, I knew from past experience that he didn't like to have his judgement questioned.

To be given the opportunity on my first picture to work with Hal Wallis, which made it automatically an A picture, was reason enough to direct it. *The Conspirators* had a nice ring to it, to say nothing of Hedy Lamarr. I decided to let Wallis do all the talking, if possible. I knew he was smart as a whip and would see through me instantly if I said nothing but good things about the project and agreed with everything he said, but I thought I had an angle that might work.

I decided to talk about the weather in my discussion with him.

1   'This sequence seems cold.'

2   'The book needs editing.' Always a safe thing to say to Wallis, who was a crackerjack editor.

3   'The love scenes seem too hot, too humid, too sticky.'

When I ran out of weather, I would use my best lethal weapon. I would use a simple word like 'focus'. I would add on a 're'. The magic word became 'refocusing'.

4   'The second act, though exciting, needs refocusing.'

82

The plan seemed too simple. But 'the best things in life are simple'. So, this simpleton was ready for . . .

5 'We'll kick the story around.'

The story conference went too well to be believed. Wallis liked the weather references. He focused on 'refocusing'. He agreed that it was indeed necessary to refocus on the entire project. I became queasy at that: I might be included in the 'refocusing'. He walked with me to the door. He had never done that before. I still had the book in my hand, which at least he didn't take away from me. He said I would be hearing from Steve Trilling, Jack Warner's assistant. He wished me luck, we shook hands, smiled 'goodbyes' and that was that. I was on my way to fame and fortune – all due to 'weather' and 'refocusing'.

*

About two weeks went by before I heard from Mr Trilling. His secretary asked if 11 a.m. tomorrow would be convenient to meet with him in his office. I wish I could say that I rudely hung up on the innocent secretary, as it would have saved me a lot of grief. But I didn't. I agreed with a cheery lilt in my voice.

Steve Trilling, whose office was next to Jack Warner's, even had a very private door which had direct access to Warner's office and vice-versa. It was a good way to hide from angry employees. I studied him while he read and signed various documents. He was a small, pudgy man in his sixties with a shop-worn, weary face. I'd frequently seen him walking about the lot with Warner, a half-step behind him. They would converse that way.

Trilling carefully put his papers aside. The rest of the desk looked an absolute mess, like mine.

TRILLING: Sorry to keep you waiting. Congratulations.

ME: Thank you, Steve. I was afraid I would have a long grey beard before I became a director.

TRILLING: It is a rare happening for a man who started carrying cans of film to suddenly become a director.

ME: Well, it wasn't all that sudden. Did you know that when I was shooting inserts, montages and second units I had more film in Warner pictures than any other director?

TRILLING: (*A bit sharp*) No I didn't and I don't believe it.

ME: J.L. didn't either. He said what you said. I sent you a note, many months ago, asking to see you. I mentioned that I knew how busy you were, but I was busier. Evidently you didn't believe that note either, for I never heard from you.

TRILLING: (*Very sharply*) Let's get down to business.

(*He hunts through the mess on his desk for a small piece of paper with numbers scribbled on it.*)

TRILLING: Hal wants you to direct a film titled *The Conspirators*, which J.L. has okayed. We have come up with figures for a new seven-year contract.

(*I sit up in my chair, listening attentively.*)

TRILLING: (*Reading from paper*) The first year: $300; second year: $325; third year: $350; fourth year: $375; fifth year: $400; sixth year: $425; seventh year: $500.

I was so shocked, I was speechless. Trilling was aware of my state of mind. He tried to make amends by explaining it to me.

TRILLING: You are very fortunate that you are given a picture to do with Hal as a first directorial assignment. You must appreciate that.

ME: (*As calmly and as lucidly as I can*) I appreciate the opportunity to work on a Hal Wallis production. But I am now making $215 a week.

TRILLING: No you're not. You're making $150 a week, with a bonus of $65 a week. That $65 bonus has nothing to do with your contract. It is on a separate cheque and can be taken away from you at any time.

ME: Steve, if I sign this new contract for seven years and fail to turn out a good picture for Wallis, you obviously will not let me continue directing; and you would be right in doing so.

TRILLING: It's a pleasant change to hear you agreeing.

ME: I have a counter-offer. Why the necessity for a new contract? We have two years to go on my old contract. I didn't ask for a new contract. Let me do the picture according to the terms of my present contract. That way you save money.

TRILLING: J.L. okayed the new contract and so do I.

(*I am losing my calm.*)

ME: That new contract is a disgrace. I doubt if the Screen Directors' Guild, of which I'm a member, would okay it. I know, for a certainty, I won't sign it. (*Getting up to leave.*) You have a nice office here. It's a shame that you have to do such senseless, dirty work in it.

I left, full of angry things to say, full of a deep aching disappointment. Of course, I reported to Wallis all that had happened in Trilling's office. He sat staring at me, growing angrier and angrier.

WALLIS: Don, I can't tell you how sorry I am. Steve and J.L. are dreadful, stupid, evil people. I think you did the right thing in turning down that asinine, absurd contract. If it's any consolation to you, I wouldn't be surprised that the reason for the contract is to get back at me. They know that as soon as my contract has run out, I'm leaving.
(*He gets up, puts an arm around me and sees me to the door.*)
WALLIS: One day your contract will also run out. See me wherever I am. I know I won't be here.
ME: Thank you, Hal, for giving me my start in the business. I can't tell you how sorry I am that I can't do your picture. I hope one day I get another chance.

I left as he slowly closed the door.

The repercussions of my refusing to sign the new director's contract began with Tenny Wright telephoning me.

WRIGHT: Are you serious about not signing the contract to do a picture with Wallis?
ME: Did you read the contract?
WRIGHT: No, but I know the terms.
ME: Did you think the terms were fair?
WRIGHT: It's an enormous break for you.
ME: True. However, there's no point in belabouring the issue. I'm not signing *that* contract.

He hung up. A short time later, Trilling was on the phone.

TRILLING: I felt that I should let you know that J.L. is furious that you refused to sign the new contract.
ME: I'm sorry about that. My decision is unchanged.

He hung up. About an hour later, J.L.'s male secretary called to inform me of a meeting in J.L.'s office at 3 o'clock with Tenny and Steve. I told him I'd be there. I hung up.

When I arrived at 3 sharp at J.L.'s office, I was admitted immediately. J.L. was seated behind his desk, flanked by Steve on one side and Tenny on the other. I walked straight up to the middle of the desk, directly opposite J.L.

J.L.: (*Glowering*) You're a very stupid young man.
ME: (*Turning to Steve*) Did you tell J.L. my counter-offer?
STEVE: Yes.

J.L.: Never mind that bullshit. Are you going to sign the contract or not?

ME: I'm not going to sign that contract.

J.L.: (*Starting to get out of his chair*) I'm going to kick the shit out of you!

I threw a quick glance at Tenny. He cast his eyes down. He was an ex-pro boxer and I wasn't going to be cold-cocked by him. Steve meant nothing. He'd bruise his soft hands swatting at a fly. J.L. got halfway around his desk, Steve stepping back. I knew exactly what I was going to do. I relaxed, one eye on Tenny.

ME: J.L., you couldn't kick the shit out of anyone.
(*He stops, thinks better of getting nearer to me, retreats to his desk and sits down.*)

J.L.: (*Trembling*) You're on suspension, effective *right now*!

ME: (*Turning to leave*) It's all right to lead me, but don't ever try to push me. You almost got hurt.

I left the three of them staring at me. I was trembling too, the adrenalin flowing.

I received verbal and written notice of three months' suspension. They must have prepared the written suspension notice before I was invited to J.L.'s office. J.L. was right about one thing. He did kick the shit out of me.

*

My vacation of three months passed swiftly. I worked out a great deal – played tennis, table tennis, boxed at the Hollywood YMCA, cycled up every canyon on a fixed-spoke bike – and felt physically great. I fell in love with the most beautiful redhead in the world, Kathleen O'Malley. When she and her two red-headed sisters went to church, the whole congregation would turn to stare at their beauty. I read every script I could get my hands on. I read books and magazines avidly. My mind still didn't function. I still thought I had done right in turning down the contract.

After three months I received notice to report to work, only to find out that Warners had taken up my option for one day and promptly laid me off for another three months. I was paid for one day and had six months without pay.

On the imposition of the second three months, I received a call from Mark Hellinger to drop in and see him at the studio, anytime. I didn't know Mark too well. He was the writer/producer of *Roaring Twenties* and apparently had liked the montages I had done on his picture. Although I had no social contact with him, I got to know and like him at work. He was famous for two things: the hundreds of short, short stories that were published each day in the *New York Mirror*, which he wrote every day; and the undisputed fact that he always picked up the cheque. No one, to my knowledge, had ever dared to try to break this claim to fame.

When I walked into Mark's office he seemed genuinely glad to see me.

HELLINGER: God, you look good, you lazy bums who don't work. You've got the world by the tail.

ME: (*Sitting down*) Apart from gaining a little weight, you don't look too bad yourself.

(*Mark picks up a large chequebook, opens it and starts writing.*)

HELLINGER: I gained only six pounds and it's not from overeating. Just drinking. (*He stops writing.*) You're not gonna be stupid and come back to this cesspool.

ME: If I can get out of my contract, I'll sure as hell get out.

HELLINGER: (*Starting to write*) Me too.

ME: Are you in contract trouble too?

HELLINGER: No. My contract's up in a few months. They won't fuck with me. They know I'll write a little story about them. Maybe I will anyway. (*He has finished writing.*) The trouble with you is you've got diarrhoea of the mouth. So shut up and take this. (*Handing me a cheque.*) And shut up!

(*I take the cheque, which is made out to me for $100.*)

HELLINGER: There are some funny things going on here that I don't like. There will be one of those each week you're off salary.

ME: Mark, I can't . . .

HELLINGER: (*Interrupting*) Just keep your mouth shut and get the hell out of here.

ME: (*Speaking with difficulty*) I promise if I need any money, I'll come to you first.

(*I put the cheque back on the table. Hellinger looks at it and at me with great disgust.*)

HELLINGER: You couldn't be a nice guy and let me enjoy getting back at Warner. Get out of here . . . (*I start out.*) . . . and take care of yourself.

I knew hundreds of people better and longer than I had known Hellinger, but he was the only one who offered me a dime. I was very touched. I also walked tall.

*

The second three-month suspension was up and I was assigned to *The Conspirators* as an assistant director, a role I had never had before. This, of course, was the picture I was to have directed for Hal Wallis. I guess Warner or Trilling or Wright felt this manoeuvre would break my spirit. Reggie Callow, who would have been my assistant on the picture, was now the first assistant to Jean Negulesco, who was directing it. The moment he saw me, Reggie came rushing over.

REGGIE: Please, Don, get lost. I'm terribly embarrassed at what happened. That goes for all of us.

On the set, I saw Negulesco turn his back to me. I felt strange that at no time did he express to me any feeling about his taking over what was to have been my picture. He could have at least offered me some condolences. The phrase 'If you have a Romanian for a friend, you don't need an enemy' seemed to be only too true in Jean's case.

One pleasant note. The picture turned out to be a complete failure, both financially and artistically.

To Have and Have Not

My next assignment was *To Have and Have Not*. This picture, an excellent one, was produced and directed by Howard Hawks. It starred Humphrey Bogart and a new, lovely young girl, Lauren Bacall. Hawks handled his stars very differently from Mike Curtiz. Before starting to direct a new sequence, Hawks would have them sit around a large table with himself at the head and would discuss the various important things that he hoped to get over in the sequence. He would seek their input, encourage them to voice their ideas. I noticed, for the first time, that Bogey was happy and full of ideas. If Hawks didn't agree, he would explain very carefully and lucidly why it wouldn't work. If he liked any of their ideas, he thanked them, praised them and used their ideas.

This was all new to me. Curtiz talked to his cast in broken English, which they didn't understand, only when they were rehearsing, with the result that his actors, like Bogey, were unhappy and disgruntled. But Hawks's actors were not only excited to be working with him, they really felt an important part of the picture – not just by acting in it, but by making important contributions in dialogue changes, interpretations of their roles and even changes in the continuity, done with seriousness by all concerned. In addition, they had fun and great respect for each other. I learned, for the first time, how an excellent director got the best out of his cast. So thank you, Mr Warner, for giving me the opportunity to observe and learn what I might never have seen or known.

It was obvious that Bacall and Bogey were very much in love. It was beautiful to watch him help her give a great performance. Remember, this was her very first film.

One day, in the crowded café sequence where Bacall sings, I was asked by a new second assistant to sign the time cards of the extras. As he didn't know me, he must have thought, 'Why not put the bum to work?' All I did was sit in a chair where I wouldn't disturb Hawks or his cast. As the long line of extras handed me their time cards to OK and sign, I gave each one time and a half, or double time. Some of the extras I knew tried to point out the error I was making, but I hustled them on their way. Others, seeing my mistake, would rush off the stage. I had a great time with Warner's money.

The next day, orders came down from a very angry Tenny Wright, very much the head of production. He didn't care what Warner wanted. I was not to be allowed to do any type of work as an assistant director. In fact, he would prefer if I wasn't allowed on the stage. Unfortunately, the new second assistant was fired. I felt badly about that, but there was nothing I could do – I wasn't allowed on the stage. I guess Tenny must have told J.L. what had happened, because I was instructed to see Mr Warner at once. He greeted me with his usual warmth.

WARNER: I see where you fucked up on the *To Have and Have Not* set.
ME: I've never been an assistant director, so I didn't know what I was doing.
WARNER: That'll be the day when you don't know what you're doing.
ME: Why thank you, J.L. That's the first nice thing you've ever said to me.
   (*Warner studies me for a long moment. He actually smiles at me.*)
WARNER: I want you to go back to work.
   (*I immediately start to leave.*)
WARNER: Sit down, Goddamnit! There's been a lot of water under the bridge. I —
ME: (*Interrupting*) Excuse me. What do you mean by that?
WARNER: All right, wise guy, I want you to direct a short.
   (*I quickly get up and start for the door.*)
WARNER: (*Loudly*) You can do any short you want.
   (*That stops me at the door.*)
ME: Let me think it over. If I can come up with an idea, I'll get in touch with you tomorrow.

I came up with an idea for a short that I was sure Warner would hate. A modern parable of the birth of Christ – *Star in the Night*. I figured Warner, who was Jewish, would turn it down. To my surprise and dismay, he okayed the project.

4   *Star in the Night*

Star in the Night (*1945*)

An allegorical tale presents problems. Does one believe the story? Does one tell it as simply as possible? I worked on the script of *Star in the Night* with the writer Saul Elkins, whom I found most amenable to suggestions. In addition, he was a good, solid, knowledgeable writer with lots of experience. Robert Burks, the first cameraman that I had ever worked with, was the cinematographer. This was a great break for me, for we got along with each other extremely well. He was probably the best cameraman I had ever worked with. I know in later life he became Hitchcock's favourite cameraman, winning an Academy Award for *To Catch a Thief*.

The cast was headed by J. Carrol Naish, an old friend of mine with whom I had worked on montages and second units. He was superb. Two other actors, Donald Woods and Anthony Caruso gave excellent performances. The point I'm trying to make is that I had good 'tools' to work with. Apart

90

from the three cowboys and the Magi, whom I thought were awkward in their roles, everything seemed to work well. But when I saw the completed film, I didn't like my work. It was over-sentimental, cloying with syrup and gooey molasses. However, Warner liked it. *Star in the Night* won an Academy Award as the best two-reel short in 1945. It surprised me.

Hitler Lives (1946)

Warner insisted on another short immediately. This time I tried to come up with an idea that he would definitely turn down. Obviously, Warner hated Hitler, so I proposed a documentary short entitled *Hitler Lives*. Again, to my chagrin, Warner okayed the project.

The idea that I was trying to accomplish in this documentary was to show visually that, although Hitler was dead, his evil spirit still lived throughout the world. Saul Elkins wrote the script and the film would

5   *Hitler Lives*

91

consist almost entirely of stock footage. It was full of montages made up of stock that we got from the Warner library and other sources. Saul deserves most of the credit, if indeed there is any. I shot very little footage: a few shots of Hitler, a few shots of Nazis goose-stepping, large maps and newspaper headlines. I felt as if I was back in the insert department.

We were too close to the end of World War II to have any perspective. Everything was overdrawn, overstressed. We showed the normal German race as viciously as we portrayed the Nazis. The narrator, Knox Manning, practically hissed every time he mentioned the Nazis, or the German people. When the narrator spoke of America, or Americans, his voice rang out with approval.

I thought the film was old-fashioned and dull. Nevertheless, Warner liked it and tried to take credit for it, which I gladly gave him.

A quote from Jack Warner's autobiography, *My First Hundred Years in Hollywood*, was shown to me recently. I had never read the book and was angered by this statement of Warner's: 'After the war, I made a tour of Europe as General Eisenhower's guest and it was obvious that Nazism had still not been completely obliterated. I made reams of notes, gathered photographs and documents and converted all this material into a script. I produced a documentary picture called *Hitler Lives* and the industry voted to give us a special Oscar for it. I wish Adolf Hitler, Goebbels and the rest of the Nazi hoods had lived long enough to see the film.'

There was no *special* Oscar. *Hitler Lives* won the Academy Award for the best two-reel documentary short in 1946. As is very well known in the industry, Jack Warner was 'honour crazy'!

Hal Wallis: the Other Side of the Coin

My Warner Brothers contract was running out – a date that I had long waited for. Trilling suggested I do a third short, which I firmly turned down. I told him flatly that I was not interested in any shorts, second units or montages. He and J.L. must have got the message because there were slight overtures about doing a feature. Nothing definite, but they knew that my contract ended in a matter of months and that unless I had a picture to direct I would soon be leaving.

Hal Wallis by now had a very successful production unit in full swing at Paramount Studios. My uncle, Jack Saper, was in charge of production. I decided *not* to involve him in any negotiations with Hal. I called Wallis's associate, Paul Nathan, to set up an appointment to see Mr Wallis. He called me back within the hour and told me that Wallis could see me tomorrow at 11 a.m. So far, so good.

Wallis stood up and shook my hand.

WALLIS: You seem to have weathered the Warner storms. Draw up a chair.

ME: (*Sitting down*) You look ten years younger than the last time I saw you.

WALLIS: (*Beaming*) For the first time in years, I'm enjoying my work. I guess it shows.

ME: Hal, I know how busy you are. I appreciate your seeing me. I'll come right to the point. My contract is up and I'd like to work for you.

WALLIS: I can't say I'm surprised. (*He reaches for a sheet of paper, turned face down.*) You realize that I'm making two pictures at this very moment. In other words, I don't know exactly what you will be doing if you come over here to Paramount.
(*I begin to feel a little uneasy.*)

ME: I hope to direct pictures for you. When I'm not directing, if you wish, I can read scripts. I'd like to be in the projection room when you're verbally editing. You're a fantastic editor.

WALLIS: Thank you. We're a small family out here and I expect everyone to pitch in and help me make the best pictures possible.

ME: I'm your man.

WALLIS: Good – I know that. (*Picks up paper.*) Here's the deal. You start at $300 a week the first year. You'll get yearly rises of $25 each week through the sixth year. During the seventh year you'll get a $75 rise, bringing the total amount to $500 a week.

Of course, I was shattered. It didn't seem possible that after his, to put it mildly, bad reaction to the Warner contract he would now offer me the exact same contract. For all I knew, maybe *he* wrote the Warner contract. But I made up my mind not to argue, or even say a word. There were indeed two sides to the 'Wallis coin'.

WALLIS: Think about it and let me know.

ME: (*Getting up*) I'll sure do that, Hal. Thanks very much for all the time.

I left and went back to Warners. Instead of telling Wallis that I was about to sign a new seven-year contract with Warners, starting at $600 a week and going up to $2,000 in the seventh year, I realized that he would learn about it indirectly. So much for Wallis. Another keen disappointment – but in the motion-picture business you soon learn to slip the punches, or you're not around very long feeling sorry for yourself.

3

Warner Brothers Era II

The Verdict (1946)

The studio gave me a script entitled *The Verdict*, written by Peter Milne, based on the novel *The Big Bow Mystery* by Israel Zangwill. The story took place in London before the turn of the century. I had no choice but to do the picture. I was on a term contract that covered all bases for Warner Brothers and none for Director Siegel. But, having learned my lesson with Steve Trilling and Jack Warner, then with Hal Wallis, I took the picture.

All was not bad. The producer, William Jacobs, though a studio man, was a pleasant person, at least to my face. I wanted Robert Burks as my cameraman. I got Ernest Haller, the most respected cameraman on the lot. The script was, at least to me, dull. I decided to make it move and fill it with excitement and suspense. Jacobs was strictly on the fence. Either he didn't know, or didn't care. Anyway, he was of little help. What was miraculous was getting a first-rate cast: Sidney Greenstreet as the Inspector of Scotland Yard; George Coulouris as Greenstreet's replacement; Peter Lorre, a close friend of Sidney Greenstreet, as a young artist who painted corpses exquisitely; and Joan Loring, who played a tart who sang and danced.

The story is, in capsule form, a Victorian suspense drama. Sidney Greenstreet sends an innocent man to the gallows by mistake. His successor, George Coulouris, feels that there was no excuse for that tragic error. Greenstreet sets about executing the perfect crime, which will implicate Coulouris in the exact set of circumstances that Greenstreet was in, with one exception: Greenstreet has to murder an innocent man, then Coulouris charges an innocent man with the murder Greenstreet has committed. The innocent man is on his way to the gallows when Peter Lorre forces Greenstreet to confess.

There was one more obstacle to clear before I got to start my own feature: my friend Michael Curtiz. Mike ran *Star in the Night* and saw a trick process shot at the beginning behind the credits which was like something he wanted to do in his next picture. I knew he was very happy for me, but he asked me to hold off on it and co-direct his film: Don Siegel and Mike Curtiz. I asked him if it wouldn't be Mike Curtiz and Don Siegel and told him to forget it, but if there was any way I could help him, I would. The next thing I heard was that Warner's assistant Steve Trilling wanted to see me. Trilling told me that Curtiz wanted me to do the second unit on his film. I said, 'Listen, I'm not doing second or first unit on it. I'm doing my picture, *The Verdict*. Let's get that real clear, and tell Mike Curtiz that if I hear any more of this, I'm going to punch him right in the mouth and knock out all his Hungarian teeth.'

Now there was Mike Curtiz, a man who really liked me, who went around saying I was his protégé, a man for whom I had done a tremendous amount of work. But when I got my first break, he thought about one person: Michael Curtiz.

*

Greenstreet and Lorre were a perfect team. Although their approaches to their parts were diametrically opposite, they made a perfect blend. Greenstreet was huge and obese; Lorre was slight and small. Greenstreet studied his lines and knew them; Peter, on the other hand, would walk on the set and politely ask the script clerk what the name of this studio was. Then he would borrow her script, as he had mislaid his somewhere. Now the rehearsals would start. Greenstreet didn't need a script, as all his lines were perfectly memorized. Lorre took his position opposite Greenstreet.

LORRE: (*Holding the script upside down*) I had no idea this script was so fascinating.
    (*I turn the script right-side up.*)
LORRE: Oh, what an improvement.

The cardinal rule was strictly enforced. Greenstreet didn't care what Lorre said or did, just as long as his cue lines remained exactly the same. Lorre always lived up to this rule. Greenstreet rehearsed dead seriously and correctly. Lorre rehearsed with teasing and fun. It did two things; it released whatever tensions were on the set, and made the crew, cast and me laugh. I like working in good humour.

*

On crossing the bridge over what is laughingly known as the Los Angeles river, I saw about two blocks away a large group of people standing in front of the Warner auto gate. They were looking at an overturned car. As I approached the gate, my montage crew yelled, 'Keep moving, Don! The strikers will overturn your car!' Sure enough, a large group of toughs moved towards me. I spun my wheels and careened out of sight. I parked near a drug store, opposite Warners' front entrance, which was being

95

picketed. I went into a telephone booth and dialled the Screen Directors'
Guild. I spoke to Joe Youngerman, who ran the Guild, and explained
what was happening. I asked if I had to go in. He stated emphatically that
the Screen Directors' Guild had a contract with Warner Brothers and that
I had to honour it.

ME: You mean I have to fight my way in?
YOUNGERMAN: No. Call Tenny Wright and tell him you want police
    protection to get you in safely, without getting hurt.
ME: OK, but I'm not staying overnight.

I hung up. I got hold of Tenny Wright on the phone, explained my
predicament and told him where I was. He said to stay inside the drug
store. Police cars and motorcycles would be there in less than a minute.
Sure enough, two squad cars and two motorcycles showed up. I began to

6 The strike at Warner Brothers

tingle with excitement. One of the motorcycle cops told me to get into my car and drive slowly – they would surround me. We approached the gate, the sirens suddenly blaring and the red lights flashing. The angry crowd of strikers gave way slowly, shouting obscenities. Faintly, I heard my montage group cheering in the distance.

On the stage where we had worked the day before was a skeleton crew. There was no one who knew how to load the camera. I waved at a couple of bit players and extras; there were no stars. Bill McGann, a former director, was now head of the camera department. I told the gaffer (head electrician) to call McGann and have him come to the stage immediately. In the meantime, I tried to figure out what I was going to shoot and came up zilch. McGann bustled in.

MCGANN: What's the trouble, Don?
ME: I guess, Bill, just about everything, including your camera.
MCGANN: What's wrong with it?
ME: Well, for one thing, none of us knows how to load it.
  (*McGann goes over to the camera and opens it up, then takes a can of unexposed film and starts to open it.*)
GAFFER: (*Drily*) You better take that into the darkroom over there.
MCGANN: (*Looking a bit unsettled, then pulling himself together*)
  Somebody bring the camera into the darkroom.

McGann disappeared into the darkroom, followed by the gaffer, with the camera and 'know nothing' me. I must say McGann tried. The fact that there was only a single dim red light on may have been the reason that he couldn't load the camera. His face grew red with anger. He was a big man. I decided not to open my mouth for two reasons: we had nothing to shoot and he was a big man.

May I add that on this day, the strikers won. We were the only picture in production and we didn't make a shot.

Next day, 5 a.m. Every non-striking employee, with the exception of producers and executives, met across the street from the gate. We were going to fight our way in. I was with my cousin, Marco Meyer, an ex-master sergeant marine, who now worked in the insert department. Not a cop was in sight, but the strikers were three deep in front of the auto gate.

The fire department tried a stupid stunt. They turned the hoses, full force, at the strikers. On the roof of a restaurant behind us on the opposite side of the street, a left-handed striker, who was one hell of a pitcher, fired coke bottle after coke bottle, which came skidding on the cement and splintering against the gushing canvas hose. Ultimately, holes appeared in the hose and water shot out in all directions. A great cheer went up from the strikers as the firemen retreated and turned off the water. The strikers turned to face us, ready. They wore hard hats with the tip filed down to a cutting edge. The word was passed from man to man: we were to charge and fight our way into the studio through the main auto gate. Also passed along was the wonderful news that a hospital had been set up on Stage 6, the first stage on our right. I wondered about two things: why am I fighting for Warner Brothers, and why am I fighting against the strikers? I didn't even know what the strikers were fighting for: 'Ours not to reason why. Ours but to do or die.'

At 6 a.m. a whistle sounded. We surged into the fray. It happened so quickly, I didn't get hit, hurt, or even scared or angry. I dodged several swinging fists, swung at someone who ducked out of the way, then I was inside, Marco by my side. Others were not so lucky. We helped carry several bleeding 'Warnerites' into Stage 6. First aid people hustled them off. Marco, breathing hard, smiled.

MARCO: I saw more action this morning than I saw in the entire war.
    (*His knuckles are bleeding.*)
ME: You must have run interference for me. Let's get to work.

We made several shots of Greenstreet and Lorre walking slowly through the streets to the prison. I had to lay in heavy fog for almost all the exteriors to hide the obvious fact that the various buildings, visible in the background, were circa 1945. *Not* in the mid-Victorian period. The general public accepted the fog as the norm for weather in London. I felt it was quite ridiculous, but there was really little I could do about it.

*

Sidney Greenstreet came down with pneumonia. We were informed by the legal department that we were on lay-off, without pay, for at least two weeks. I tried to get hold of Sidney, but wasn't allowed to speak with him.

Peter came up and asked if I would like to go to Palm Springs for the 'holidays'. We skiddled-skattled out of the studio and found ourselves in sunny, warm Palm Springs within four hours. We stayed at the B-Bar-H Ranch on the outskirts of town – a dude ranch with all the trimmings. We immediately headed for the bar and drank a toast to Sidney and thanked him. Then Peter wanted to go horseback riding.

ME: I don't know how to ride.
PETER: I'll teach you.
ME: You're too effete to ride.
PETER: (*Proudly*) All Hungarians ride horses and women.

I put on a pair of blue jeans, sports shirt and sneakers. Peter had jodhpurs,

7 *The Verdict*: Don Siegel (centre) with Peter Lorre and Sidney Greenstreet

boots, Western hat and a big buckle attached to his hand-carved belt. He helped me mount and, small as he was, he mounted with professional ease. My horse started moving.

PETER: Pull back your reins, easy like.
   (*My horse becomes stationary.*)
PETER: You're a good student.
ME: Does that go for women, too?
PETER: Of course. Listen carefully. Whatever the horse wants to do, you make him do the opposite.
ME: What if I want to get down?
PETER: You're being stupid. You can always fall off.
ME: I never thought of that.
PETER: (*Speaking slowly*) If the horse wants to go left, make him go right. If he wants to stop, make him move forwards. If he wants to go forwards, make him stop. It's that simple.

99

Believe it or not, it worked. In half an hour I was in control of the horse. Peter rode superbly. I never saw him with a woman. I imagine he excelled there too. There was one thing Peter didn't tell me. I was sore for days. But I never had more fun.

That night we had dinner with Alice Faye and Phil Harris. When Phil laughed, which was all the time, his body moved, while sitting down, as though he were walking. I've never seen anyone enjoy laughing more than Phil. Right in the middle of our hysterical laughter, pausing only to down our drinks, Jack Warner entered the restaurant. We were making so much noise that he instantly heard and saw us. He came over to the table.

WARNER: (*Ignoring Alice and Phil*) What the hell are you and Peter doing in Palm Springs?
    (*Peter and I look at each other.*)
PETER: Do you mean, as the titular head of Warner Brothers, that you don't know that the second lead is ill with pneumonia?
ME: I'm ashamed that you're apparently unaware that we are on lay-off until Mr Greenstreet returns to the studio. Right now, we are having a miserable time.
WARNER: (*Leaving*) I'm aware of that.
PHIL HARRIS: (*Lifting his glass in a toast*) Here's to a miserable time.

We all immediately burst into loud laughter, making more noise than before.

*

Peter and I apologized to Sidney for looking so fit and tanned.

SIDNEY: (*Looking pallid and wan*) It gives me great pleasure that while I was convalescing in bed, you two youngsters were recuperating in Palm Springs.
PETER: You must have lost at least a pound.
    (*Sidney pats his ample stomach.*)
SIDNEY: (*Chuckling*) Coulouris is getting too big, but not big enough to fill my breeches.
ME: With your permission, we'll use that line in the script. Let's do the scene where the professional thief explains to you how to open a locked and dead-bolted door from the outside.
SIDNEY: Who did I get out of prison to help me?
ME: Clyde Cook. A very funny man.

And that's where I made a serious mistake. The scene was well written, full of laughs: a small-time professional thief telling the former Inspector of Scotland Yard how to pick several locks from the outside. The unknown murderer would do his dastardly deed, then leave, locking the locks from outside the door. Unfortunately, I played it 'funny'. I let the actor do all sorts of eccentric movements. I should have made him play the scene straight, then it would have been funny. When I saw the dailies, my error was most apparent. It was a good lesson to learn: never play a funny scene 'funny'.

Ever since the picture started, I had been having trouble lining up my various set-ups. The staging should not have given me too many problems. Although *The Verdict* was my first feature, considering the shorts, second units and montages I had directed, it was ridiculous that I couldn't, without Ernest Haller's help, stage the scene properly. There was only one person to blame: me. Or was there?

Bette Davis was about to do a test. I was informed by Tenny Wright that Ernest Haller, Bette's regular cameraman, would do the test, starting tomorrow. Robert Burks would be his replacement. During the five days I worked with Burks, I not only had no trouble at all in lining up my shots and staging my scenes, but I had a great deal of fun. In addition, when I looked at the dailies, I thought they looked better than Haller's work. Plus another interesting fact: I made an average of fifteen set-ups a day. With Haller, I was lucky to get four.

Haller returned to *The Verdict* and Bob went back to Stage 5. I was ready. I started to lay out a shot. Peter entered the room and went over to Greenstreet's desk. But I didn't allow my actors to do anything. Instead, I asked Haller what took place in this scene.

HALLER: (*Smiling*) Well Don, you're the director. If you don't know, we're in trouble.
ME: I don't think I'm in trouble. You are if you don't answer my question.
HALLER: (*Uneasy*) What question?
ME: I asked you what takes place in this scene.
HALLER: Rehearse the scene with your actors and then I'll help you.
     (*I cross over to Haller, script in hand.*)
ME: Where's your script?
HALLER: I don't need my script.
     (*I grab Haller by his shirtfront and shove him hard into a nearby chair.*)
ME: (*Opening my script*) You dirty bastard, you haven't read page one. Here's the scene. Read it.

He looked at me and decided to read the scene. We rehearsed with the actors. After he lit it, we shot it. We made ten set-ups that day. The next day, he came on the set prepared. He knew the script. But that wasn't good enough to compensate for all my feelings of insecurity and misery.

ME: Each day we shoot, you'll first sit down and read the new scene. (*I hand him the scene in my script.*)
HALLER: But I know the scene. Peter goes over . . .
ME: (*Interrupting*) You'll read the scene each morning before we start, or two things are going to happen to you. I'll hit you flush in the nose. Then I'll drag you, bleeding, into Warner's office.

He sat down and read the scene. He believed me and so did I.

*

When I suggested to Jack Warner that Tommy Reilly should be my editor on *The Verdict*, he thought I was crazy. My first feature film and I use an assistant cutter as an editor. It turned out that Warner was right.

Each night, when shooting was finished, I would search for Tommy. I would wander around the whole of Warner Brothers to find Tommy, inevitably, huddled over a bar, drinking. I would grab him by his arm, pay his tab, which told me how much he was drinking, and we would go back to his cutting room to run the film he had edited on the movieola. We might work for two or three hours. This went on all throughout the picture. That was all I needed. A hopeless alcoholic for an editor.

*

Bill Jacobs, Tommy Reilly and I drove out to Warner's house to run the first cut of *The Verdict*. I knew I was dead when, in the car, my two companions praised the film and my work.

JACOBS: You've done a great job, Don.
ME: I wish I thought so.
REILLY: Warner will love it. Why do you pretend that he won't like it?
ME: My vibes are telling me how can Warner like it when so many pictures under the Warner Brothers insignia stink.
JACOBS AND REILLY: You're crazy.

Warner was gracious as we were taken to his private projection room. The picture had no surprises for me. I had seen it in various forms about 2,000 times. Frankly, although I was nervous, *The Verdict* bored me. I thought it would never end. When Greenstreet was revealed as the murderer, Warner let out a sigh of surprise. Jacobs nudged me with pleasure. Tommy leaned to my ear and whispered, 'What did I tell you? He loves it.' The picture ended. The lights went on as the screen was covered with a heavy curtain. Warner looked at us, puzzled.

WARNER: Greenstreet can't be a murderer.

JACOBS: But J.L., you bought the book, *The Big Bow Mystery* by Zangwill. In the book, the Inspector of Scotland Yard committed the murder.

ME: We didn't add Greenstreet murdering an innocent man – it's all in the original book.

WARNER: (*Getting up-tight*) I don't give a shit about the book. So I bought it. Now make the changes so that Greenstreet isn't the murderer.

ME: (*Tense*) If you do that, there's no picture. It won't make any sense. It will cost plenty of extra loot and still won't work.

WARNER: (*Taking his time*) What if, instead of finding out at the end of the film that Greenstreet killed somebody, we show the audience some clues that Greenstreet might be the guilty man. That way, it won't be such a shock to the audience.

JACOBS: That could be done. It won't cost much money and won't change the original story.

WARNER: Good, Bill.

ME: Yeah, good Bill. What clues are you talking about?

JACOBS: (*Winging it*) Well, when he takes off his coat, the black gloves fall out of his pocket.

WARNER: That's it, Bill.

ME: Yeah, we can have a 'stinger' music cue.

WARNER: How about Greenstreet going up the stairs wearing black gloves?

JACOBS: We can do those things easily and cheaply.

ME: Will it improve the picture? He's still the murderer.

WARNER: It will improve the picture. Do it as soon as you can.

JACOBS: We'll get right on it.

WARNER: (*Relaxed now*) The picture's not bad. Why, Don, did you have so much fog?

ME: You may recall that at the time there was a strike on. The only way I could keep on shooting was by hiding the modern buildings with heavy fog.

(*Warner gets up. Like robots, we get up too.*)

WARNER: (*To Jacobs*) Be sure to let me know when I can see the new version. Good night, boys.

(*He leaves us still in the projection room. We slowly amble to the front door, saying nothing. Outside, we get in the car and start off.*)

ME: (*To Reilly*) Still think I'm crazy, Tommy?

REILLY: I think Mr Warner's crazy.

JACOBS: Now fellows, let's keep our cool. Let's give J.L. what he
 wants. It won't hurt the picture all that much.
ME: Tonight, when I'm not sleeping, I'll be thinking about 'all that
 much'. And when I'm trying to figure out how much is 'all that
 much', I'll be thinking of you, Bill, and the man who, in my book,
 is 'crazy' Jack.

We rode the rest of the way in silence.

Although I felt strongly that the revelation of Greenstreet as the
murderer should come as late as possible, there was nothing I could do
about it. Of course it made no sense. Once one starts to suspect
Greenstreet, considerable suspense is lost. The fact that J.L. was genuinely
surprised to learn the truth about Greenstreet proves that we had been
successful in the execution of the film.

We made a shot of Greenstreet entering his room, taking off his
overcoat. A black glove falls to the floor. I could hear the music stinger:
'Dum de dum dum'. Pretty dumb of J.L. We made a shot of Greenstreet
climbing the stairs to the second floor wearing *black gloves*: 'Dum de dum
dum'. Maybe we should call the film *Dum De Dum Dum*.

The end result: Warner saw the changes and liked them. The final cut
was seen and okayed. Warner felt he had 'saved' the film. He was happy.
The critics, not so happy. The returns, just fair. At least my first feature
was behind me. A milestone had been reached.

Vendetta

One Friday I was leaving the lot at about 5 in the afternoon. The cop at the
gate stopped me. Trilling wanted me to call him. I got out of my car and
called him from the booth. I was put through at once to him.

TRILLING: I'm sure glad J.L. liked the picture. His changes worked
 fine.
ME: (*Somewhat abrupt*) Is this what you wanted to talk to me about?
TRILLING: Not exactly. J.L. would like you to play tennis with him at
 his house on Saturday afternoon.
ME: I'm sorry, Steve, but I'm booked up solid on Saturday.
STEVE: Well how about Sunday afternoon?
ME: Steve, I might as well tell you the truth. Unless it's business, I never
 go to anyone's house if I would not invite him to mine. I'm sure
 J.L. will understand.

I hung up. I knew it was stupid of me. On the other hand, I didn't trust myself to play against J.L. I'd never be able to resist smashing a ball directly at him. My lay-off would run concurrently with his stay in hospital.

*

I got a call to see J.L. in his office. On my way up, I speculated on what this was all about. Of course, he could be angry at my refusing to play tennis with him, but it was unlikely that he would let me know how he felt about it. What I thought most likely was some sort of discussion about my next assignment. Warner completely surprised me.

WARNER: How did you get to know Howard Hughes?

ME: I've never met Mr Hughes, or even spoken to him by phone.

WARNER: (*Disbelievingly*) He made a strange request.

ME: I've also never written to him, or received a letter from him. My hands are clean.

WARNER: Mr Hughes is a very important man. He wants you to see his movie, *Vendetta*. It needs fixing. He wants your help.

ME: (*Completely confused*) Why me?

WARNER: I don't know. I want you to co-operate fully with Mr Hughes and do whatever you can to help him.

ME: Did Mr Hughes see *The Verdict*?

WARNER: Hey, that must be it. We let the more important executives in the industry see our product before releasing them to the theatres.

ME: (*Tongue in cheek*) Do you think he's going to make further changes in *The Verdict*?

WARNER: (*Getting impatient*) I told you what he wants. Go do it.

ME: One last question. Why, when you see and work on hundreds of pictures, didn't he ask for *your* help in fixing his picture?

WARNER: (*Irritated*) Stop asking questions. Do your job and report back to me when you've finished.

ME: Yes, sir!

I got out of there without further ado. I was more than a mite curious about Mr Hughes.

*

I arrived at Goldwyn Studios in my brand new convertible, tan De Soto. I wore a tie, button-down shirt and a suit, my best, store-bought. I was about five minutes early. Right on the dot, a 1937 dilapidated, dirty Chevy truck wheeled up in front of me and stopped. Out stepped a tall, slender man, wearing an open-necked soiled white shirt with a World War I leather jacket slung over his shoulder. The rest of his attire matched: wrinkled dungarees, sneakers with no socks. I recognized Howard

105

Hughes, but was too startled by his appearance to introduce myself. He came over to me and asked, politely, if I were Mr Siegel.

ME: Yes, Mr Hughes.
(*We shake hands.*)
HUGHES: Thanks for seeing me. Let's go over to the projection room. I'll explain what this is all about.

But he didn't explain anything. He asked me to run his film *Vendetta*, asked if my chair was comfortable. He showed me the button to push to alert the projectionist to start and left me all by my lonesome. I pushed the button and settled back to see the film, which I hoped wouldn't start a vendetta between Hughes, Warner and Siegel.

The picture made little sense. The continuity was confusing, the acting stiff and unbelievable. The only thing I knew about the picture (I may have fallen asleep) was that I didn't know what it was about. The lights went on and Hughes appeared. He sat down next to me.

HUGHES: What do you think?
ME: Not much, I'm afraid.
HUGHES: I was hoping you could take it over, completely.
(*I think this man must be crazy.*)
HUGHES: I don't have time to work on it.
ME: Mr Hughes, who directed this picture?
HUGHES: Preston Sturges and Max Ophuls.
ME: I can't believe it. They're two of the best. Please don't be offended by what I'm about to say. It's impossible that you didn't influence their work.
HUGHES: I gave them complete freedom. They let me down, badly.
ME: Well, I'm not going to do that under any circumstances. I honestly regret that I don't have the ability to help you.
(*He gets to his feet, as do I.*)
HUGHES: (*Shaking my hand*) Thank you for your time. I appreciate your honesty.

He went to his truck. I went to my convertible. As he drove off, I slowly followed. My thoughts were muddled. I had great respect for Hughes. If, by some miracle, I could at least make *The Vendetta* presentable, my future would be assured. But I didn't want to join Preston Sturges and Max Ophuls in letting him down. As I drove back to Warner Brothers, I decided not to report to J.L. Maybe the whole thing would wither away without further discussion.

Three days later, the note of 'doom' sounded. Even Warner's male secretary seemed strained.

SECRETARY: Mr Warner wants to see you *right now*.
  (*Warner literally snarls at me.*)
WARNER: Mr Hughes called to tell me you didn't even try to help him.
ME: That's not true. I ran the picture. I told Mr Hughes I didn't have the ability to help him.
WARNER: Why didn't you report back to me?
ME: Because I didn't want to quarrel with you.
  (*His voice surprisingly softens.*)
WARNER: You'll be doing me a personal favour if you'll look at the film again. Perhaps make some notes – you know what I mean.
ME: I certainly will do the favour you ask. What I can't understand is why you don't run the picture with me. You'll do Mr Hughes and myself a huge favour.
WARNER: I'm leaving tomorrow for Europe. Sales meetings every·day. I simply don't have the time to run the picture.
ME: (*Getting up*) O K, I'll do the best I can. By the way, I liked Mr Hughes. I also want to thank you for not losing your temper.

Warner gave me a friendly smile. I still saw no purpose in re-seeing *Vendetta*. However, I liked J.L. asking me for a favour instead of issuing an angry order.

*

One of Hughes's staff notified me that I was to run *Vendetta* the following night at 8 p.m. in the same projection room. A secretary would be provided. However, I declined that offer. I didn't want a secretary for the simple reason that I knew I was going to talk back to the screen when viewing the picture and I didn't want Hughes to read what I might say.

Just as I was about to start running the film, Hughes stuck his head in.

HUGHES: Everything all right?
ME: Fine. I'm about to start running.
  (*Hughes looks about the room.*)
HUGHES: Where's the secretary?

He immediately crossed over to the phone. I spoke up quickly to tell him that I had told whomever had called me that I *didn't* want one. Hughes totally ignored me, bawling out to someone that he wanted a secretary for Mr Siegel at once. I felt, being over twenty-one and an American, that I had the right not to have a secretary. As he left, he said over my objections that a secretary was on her way. I pushed the button to start the film.

I was about a reel into the picture when an out-of-breath, big-bosomed young secretary rushed into the projection room. She sat down in front of me, her hands clutching a pad and a bunch of sharpened pencils.

ME: If you as much as touch the pad with a pencil, I'll stop the picture and leave the lot.
SECRETARY: (*Still breathing heavily*) I know, I know, Mr Siegel. I promise I won't put pencil to pad.
ME: Thank you.
(*The picture continues. Occasionally, in a soft voice, I direct the actors to stop talking gibberish, to get the hell out of the scene, etc. Vendetta finally creaks to a halt. The lights go on. Hughes enters the room.*)
ME: (*To secretary*) Thank you, young lady, for your help.
(*She leaves quickly, still carrying her pad and pencils.*)

Hughes suggested we go to his office. In his somewhat modest room he poured me a scotch and soda. He drank nothing. I made my criticisms as brief as possible. They were more or less the things I had told him before.

HUGHES: Evidently, it doesn't improve on seeing it a second time.
ME: Nor I'm sure will it improve on the third, fourth or fifth time.
HUGHES: I thought up a new ending which I'd like to tell you.
ME: Fire away.

Well, he didn't exactly 'fire away'. He rambled on slowly, somewhat incoherently. He was dead serious, totally wrapped up in his creative thoughts. The phone rang and continued ringing. He paid no attention, continuing his soliloquy without pause. The phone stopped ringing. My thoughts raced. Mr Hughes is a very important man. Maybe the President wants to talk to him. Maybe the studio is on fire. Maybe Mr Hughes is deaf. The phone started to ring again. He was right at the climax of his story when I rudely interrupted.

ME: (*Loudly*) The phone is ringing. (*Louder.*) Someone is calling you.
(*Startled, he turns to the door and yells.*)
HUGHES: Come in. Come in!
(*I point to the phone, still ringing.*)
ME: The phone!
(*Hughes glances at the phone, shrugs impatiently and goes on with the new ending. The phone again mercifully stops. Ultimately, Hughes winds down. There is a brief silence.*)
HUGHES: Don't you think it would make an exciting ending?

ME: Indubitably.

HUGHES: Would you direct it for me?

ME: (*Loudly and determinedly*) Mr Hughes, I have a problem. I am
preparing a picture that I want to do. I just simply do not have the
time. However, I will write you comprehensive notes which I hope
will prove helpful.
(*We shake hands.*)

HUGHES: Again, I wish to thank you for your kindness. I shall not
forget it.

I left feeling sorry for the guy and angry at my guilt.

The next morning, I wrote him a three-page memo of what I hoped
would be construed as constructive comments. At the end of the letter, I
couldn't stop myself from adding: 'Whether, Mr Hughes, you have read
this far in this letter is unimportant. Nothing can save *Vendetta*.' I sent the
letter off to Hughes with a copy to Jack Warner.

Night Unto Night

My next assignment was based on a book by Philip Wylie. The script,
written by Kathryn Scola, was given to me by the producer, Owen Crump.
I read it immediately. Unfortunately, I didn't like it or understand it.
Certainly it wasn't a project for me. But I had no choice, no court to
appeal to. I was bound to a long-term contract, which spelled out in no
uncertain terms that I directed what was given to me, or immediate
suspension.

So I met with Owen Crump, script in hand. I knew him slightly. He
appeared friendly, well educated, with a track record of making pictures
that I knew nothing about. On the other hand, he certainly knew my case
history: one feature. Owen, good looking, in his early forties, was smooth.
When I raised objections about the script being obtuse, weighed down
with lengthy dialogue of little meaning, etc., he flattened my objections
with flattery; a facile tongue which expressed great enthusiasm for the
project. I brought up the name of the scriptwriter. He shook his head
helplessly.

OWEN: Kathryn Scola is a very difficult lady to work with. Frankly, I
found her to be hopeless. Very opinionated. (*Warmly.*) Why don't
we keep our changes in the family — just the two of us.
(*Naively, I think it a good idea.*)

ME: Do you have a copy of the book I could read?

OWEN: (*Smiling*) You'll probably find it tough going. (*Handing me a copy of the book.*) Don't misunderstand me. Philip Wylie is a great writer. Take your time reading it. When you've had time to digest it, let's have another chat about the book and the script too.

I left with the book and script. I hoped I would find the book palatable when I had 'digested' it. Philip Wylie may have been a good writer, but to me he was a dull one. I found it tough going – Owen was right. I began to feel uneasy about the project. I didn't understand the book at all. The leading character, a microbiologist, suffers from epilepsy. The leading lady, a widow, believes her house is haunted by her dead husband, an artist who gives them both endless, boring, philosophic, incomprehensible advice. I badly needed a 'chat' with Mr Crump.

Owen was patient and calm; his responses were polite but, to me, meaningless. I was unhappy, puzzled, not liking or understanding the project at all. I came up with an idea.

ME: Owen, I like you. You see and feel things in *Night Unto Night* that I can't digest. In point of fact, I threw up.
(*Owen frowns at my crudity.*)
ME: I have an idea – a viable one. I'm not the proper choice for the director on your project. Get someone who will share your enthusiasm, someone who will give you the picture you want. A director like George Cukor. I think he'd be perfect. Or there are many others for you to choose from.
(*Owen doesn't bat an eye. He engulfs me in meaningless rebuttal, with pleasantries, with encouragement.*)
OWEN: Both Mr Warner and Mr Trilling agreed with me that you would be the perfect choice for *Night Unto Night*. We discussed many directors, including Mr Cukor. I want you to be happy and will do everything I can to help you make a picture you'll be proud of.
(*There is no way I can stop his avalanche of words. I give up.*)
ME: Although the scriptwriter is difficult, I would like to meet with her.
OWEN: (*Unruffled*) Of course. I'm not sure, but she might be out of the country. But I'll get right on it.
ME: Thank you.
OWEN: By the way, tomorrow, in my office at ten, we're having a casting meeting with Biano and Kumen.
ME: I'll be there. (*Leaving.*) Thanks for your patience.

*

The two casting members and Owen were in perfect accord. It was brought out at the beginning of the meeting that Warner and Trilling had given their full approval of the casting suggestions. Obviously, I was just a mere formality to hurdle or cast aside. The unbelievable list included:

1 *Ronald Reagan* as the microbiologist who suffers from epilepsy.

ME: Reagan is too healthy. No one will believe him as an epileptic, nor as a microbiologist, whatever the hell that is.

2 *Viveca Lindfors* as the grieving widow who feels that her dead husband haunts her house.

ME: Miss Lindfors may be a fine actress, but she does have an accent, a strong Swedish accent. How do we account for the accent?

Silence was their way of accounting for it.

3 *Brod Crawford* as the philosophical artist who gives endless free advice to Reagan and Lindfors.

ME: Brod Crawford is a ridiculous choice for the verbose, philosophical artist. Brod is so well known in films as a tough, menacing villain that the audience, if there happens to be one, will laugh when he's giving gibberish advice to Reagan and Lindfors.

OWEN: (*To Kumen and Biano*) Report back to Trilling that we've had our first casting meeting (*looks at me*) and are considering the casting suggestions – and others.
(*Kumen and Biano leave.*)

*

Night Unto Night started in the middle of another strike; it was the only picture shooting at Warner Brothers. I began to suspect that I was the only director who would work during a strike. Again, the Screen Directors' Guild and my agent and lawyer insisted I had to report to work. I had picked locations with Pev Marley, an experienced, excellent cameraman; Hugh Retiker, an art director I didn't know; and Owen Crump. When we left the lot in a large bus, passing the jeering strikers, I insisted on sitting next to the window, Viveca sitting beside me. She thought it was very gallant of me to shield her from possible shattered glass if the strikers starting throwing things at the bus. I liked the idea of Viveca thinking me gallant, but I felt like a damn fool because again, as in *The Verdict*, I didn't know what the strike was about.

When we arrived at the beach where we were to shoot, Pev and I were very disappointed with the weather conditions. It was an overcast day; the sand, sea and sky were all the same colour. I suggested that we use this as a rehearsal day.

OWEN: (*Nervously*) We have to shoot.

ME: Of course. We will prove our point on film.

So we set up dolly tracks and dollied with Reagan and Lindfors, a four-page scene. I thought our actors were good, and they became better as the day went on. The three of us got along fine. I suggested to Owen that we rush the film through the lab and see it early in the morning there. If we got a good weather report, we would return to the beach and re-shoot the sequence in the sun.

OWEN: Shouldn't we let Warner and Trilling see it before we make up our minds to re-shoot it?

ME: Pev and I know how it's going to look. (*Challenging him.*) What are you afraid of?
(*Owen colours in anger, but he says nothing. The next morning at 6, we see the film at the lab.*)

PEV: It looks like shit. Someone tell me where the sand enters the water, and the water disappears into the sky.

8 *Night Unto Night*: Don Siegel with Ronald Reagan and Viveca Lindfors shooting at the beach

ME: (*To Owen*) What's the weather report?

OWEN: The forecast is sunny with spotty clouds.

ME: What are we sitting around for? Let's move it.

OWEN: You don't think. . . ?

ME: (*Interrupting*) No, I don't think. Blame it all on me.

So we re-shot the entire sequence. The actors were even better. The sand, sea and sky looked beautiful, as did Viveca. Viveca's husband, Mr Rogard, a huge, 6-foot 4 Swedish lawyer, suggested that I ride back to the studio with them in his limo. I gladly accepted.

On the way back, Viveca and I discussed the difficulties involved with making it believable that her dead husband haunts the house, that she talks to him.

ROGARD: (*Breaking in*) Do you play chess, Mr Siegel?

ME: The best I can say about my chess is that I know how to move the pieces. I don't know the literature of chess at all. (*Smiling.*) However, I used to play a fair game of checkers.

ROGARD: That sounds promising. Unfortunately, I don't have a chess set with me.

ME: I have several sets. (*Turning to Viveca.*) Is it all right with you if I show up after dinner, shaved and showered?

VIVECA: That will be fine. I'll haunt the apartment while the two of you play.

Unlike most games, there's no cheating in chess. Rogard moved his chess pieces quickly. I moved mine slow, dead slow and stop. In four moves, I should have given up. I lasted seven. I sensed sympathy from Viveca. We twisted the board around, both of us still silent. This time, I showed great improvement, I was checkmated in ten moves. We began another game. I continued to play slowly. I could do nothing against Rogard. I resigned the game and match and apologized for my poor play.

ROGARD: I am President of the International Chess Federation and a chess master.

Now he tells me. Of course, I could challenge him to a game of table tennis. But I knew one thing. One day I would get even; and not by playing chess.

*

The special effects turned out well. Actually, everything worked: the sets, the photography, even the actors, though woefully miscast. What didn't work at all was the script. The picture crawled along with pretentious dialogue. I must fault Crump. He liked the script. Also, for reasons I don't understand, he saw to it that I had no opportunity to work with the writer. On the other hand, I was stupid enough to let him get away with this charade.

It's always best not to let your cast see the dailies. Viveca looked particularly beautiful in a scene where she 'talked' to her dead husband. Her sensitivity and sincerity were excellent. So I ran the dailies for her. When the lights came up, she turned to me. I expected to be complimented.

VIVECA: Did you notice when I turned my head there were wrinkles in my neck?

ME: No, I didn't notice any wrinkles. I thought you looked lovely and that your portrayal was poignant and touching.

That taught me a lesson I never forgot. Unless a star insists, never run anything for them.

Ronald Reagan had definite opinions on politics and didn't hesitate to express them. At this time in his life he was left wing in speech and action. Maybe extreme left wing. One night, riding in the back of Ronald's car on our way to dinner, he spouted off endlessly to his wife, Jane Wyman, and to Viveca and myself. Wyman could take no more of it.

WYMAN: (*To Reagan*) Hey 'diarrhoea-of-the-mouth', shut up! Maybe we can get in a word edgewise.

But Ron continued soliloquizing.

*

During the strike, a few members of the cast ate in Warner's private dining room. Warner sat at one end of the table, surrounded by executives. Viveca and I sat at the far end, surrounded by writers, producers, heads of various departments. There were no other directors, as *Night Unto Night* was the only picture shooting. There was the usual din of conversation. Viveca looked at me strangely as I passed the ketchup across the table to Jerry Wald.

VIVECA: (*Softly*) I love you.

ME: (*Startled*) What did you say?

MACDOUGALL: Don, can you pass me the salt and pepper?

ME: (*To MacDougall*) What'd you say?

MACDOUGALL: The salt and pepper.

ME: Oh, sorry.

(*I pass the salt and pepper and turned to Viveca. She squeezes my hand beneath the table.*)

VIVECA: I love you, Don.

I couldn't believe it. This ravishing, adorable creature in love with *me*.

VIVECA: Don't you love me?
> (*I answer somebody across the table. I focus on Viveca, very much aware of our holding hands.*)

ME: To tell the truth, I fell in love the moment I first saw you. I didn't think I had a chance.

It was the damndest love scene ever played. She lifted my hand and pressed her lips to it. I wanted to grab her and kiss her and say sweet things. I pinched myself to find out if I was dreaming. Our immediate companions were a group of men busily eating and talking, occasionally addressing us. We finally got out of there, neither of us interested in food or conversation. I grabbed her and kissed her deeply. She responded with tears. From that moment, that was the end of my directing *Night Unto Night*. I was hopelessly, helplessly in love. Love may make the world go round, but it doesn't help directors directing.

After completing all my directing chores, including post-production, I decided to send a sarcastic letter of 'thanks' to Steve Trilling as a follow-up to a letter he sent to Tenny Wright criticizing my use of the boom in the film. Instead of reaching out to help me, his only contribution seemed to be 'the defender of the boom'. I'm afraid he took my sarcastic letter appreciatively, as he later thanked me for it. I used the boom because it made good shots and saved time.

End of an Era

Although I was preparing a picture, *Act of Violence* with Jerry Wald, Trilling called me to his office to tell me he was laying me off. The reason: they had other directors who had utilized their lay-off periods. One of them would direct *Act of Violence*. Then Trilling kindly suggested that if I could obtain employment elsewhere, Warner Brothers would not exercise their option on my contract. They publicly released to the trade papers that I had terminated my contract and had left the lot, which of course was a lie. This was a common occurrence with Trilling.

I notified my attorney, Loyd Wright, of what had taken place. He wrote a letter, an explicit one, to Jack Warner. Various memos followed each other rapidly, culminating in my parting company with the studio in exchange for a cheque of $1,750. Fourteen years of hard work at Warners were finally over. They were a strange lot. I learned the value of their vicious attitude. I was indeed happy to leave. I didn't expect the other side of the fence to be greener, but I knew it couldn't be worse.

9 *Night Unto Night*: Don Siegel (with pipe) with the camera on the boom

After fourteen years of being under exclusive contract to Warners, I gave little thought, certainly no worry, to whether or not my path would be under contract to a studio. What I didn't realize was that, outside Warners, I knew relatively few people.

I certainly didn't think being under exclusive contract was important in the making of pictures. All studios had stages and similar equipment. What difference did it make where I worked? Certainly the buildings had little meaning. It's the people who count.

I spent nine months writing a script in collaboration with a good friend of mine, Ted Pezman, who was a probation officer. It was about John Augustus, who in the middle of the nineteenth century in Boston, was the first probation officer. I'm afraid it didn't turn out very well, though years later we sold it for a pittance.

4

All the King's Men

Allied Artists 1949

About nine months after leaving Warner Brothers, I was offered a job on *All the King's Men*. Larry Butler, head of special effects, head of his own optical printers, etc., at Columbia Studios, insisted that I meet with Jack Fier, head of production. When I found out from Larry that it was mainly second-unit work, I was not interested. I felt that it was a step backwards. But reason prevailed. I found myself walking down the corridor with Larry to meet Jack Fier.

ME: I understand that Fier has the foulest tongue in the industry.

LARRY: (*Dismissing the idea*) His bark is worse than his bite.
   (*By this time, we are in Fier's office. Larry introduces us to each other. I stick my hand out to shake Fier's hand. Fier ignores it, but asks me a simple question.*)

FIER: Who in this fucking, crazy world ever told you that you could direct?
   (*As it is evident that Fier has no intention of ever shaking my hand, plus the air becoming blue with an endless stream of swear words, I turn to Larry and speak over Fier's foul tongue.*)

ME: Larry, I thought you told me that Jack Fier was one tough hombre. Hell, compared to Tenny Wright, Jack Fier is a flaming faggot.
   (*Fier looks at me astonished, his tongue stilled. Suddenly, he breaks into raucous laughter. I ask him a question.*)

ME: Would you be kind enough to explain to me what Orson Welles meant when he said, 'The only thing to fear is Fier himself'?

FIER: (*A warm smile*) Orson had a sense of humour; something like yours. (*His face hardens.*) Do you want the job?

ME: On one condition – I get *no* screen credit.

FIER: You think you're too good for the job?

ME: Of course.

FIER: Well, that settles it. You've got the job, starting right now. Larry, take this polite young man and introduce him to our director, Mr Robert Rossen.

ME: Oh, I did forget one thing.
> (*I reach across the desk and grab his hand in the style of Lee Anthony.*)

ME: A pleasure meeting you, sir.

FIER: (*Wincing from my handshake*) Larry, get his ass out of here before I . . .

*

I had become friendly with Bob Rossen during his writing days, which was sometime in the late thirties. He was a pugnacious man in his forties with a keen desire for two things: politics (certainly left wing) and getting a picture to direct. In 1947 he first directed *Johnny O'Clock*, then *Body and Soul*.

ROSSEN: (*Pacing up and down while I sit*) Don – I'm damn glad to get you to do the second unit.
> (*I keep my mouth shut, uncharacteristically. Bob appears somewhat ill at ease.*)

ROSSEN: The second-unit work is difficult and most important to the picture.
> (*He suddenly goes behind his desk, sits down and leans towards me.*)

ROSSEN: (*Dead serious*) I want your best work.

ME: I don't remember you ever giving less than your best, and that goes double for me.

ROSSEN: I'm going to level with you. You make me a bit nervous because I want you to direct exactly what I want.

ME: That sounds reasonable to me. I wish I had your record. *Body and Soul* is the best fight picture I've ever seen.

ROSSEN: (*A smile creasing his face*) Thanks.

ME: Could you let me have a copy of the book and your script?

ROSSEN: I'll give you the book, but I haven't finished the script.

ME: Aren't you supposed to start shooting in a couple of weeks?

ROSSEN: (*Somewhat strangely*) Just between you and me, I'd rather not start shooting until the script is perfect.

ME: (*Taking the book from Rossen*) A Pulitzer Prize-winning novel by Robert Penn Warren which you're writing, directing and producing. I'd say you know what you're doing.
> (*Bob shakes my hand and sees me to the door, his face beaming with confidence.*)

ROSSEN: Maybe I don't know what I'm doing, but I'm sure as hell going to make the picture – my way.

I left, still thinking it strange not to get some script.

*

The Fairmont stands high on Nob Hill overlooking the incredible city of San Francisco, my favourite city in the world. We stayed at this large, first-class hotel during the entire time we shot San Francisco and its environs. Only the crew stayed elsewhere. A big publicity party was held for the press to sing the praises of *All the King's Men* and its writer/producer/director, Robert Rossen. Shooting was to begin the next day. Although I had a list of shots and sequences to make, still I had not received a page of script. I decided to work directly from the book, which, by the way, was very well written. I could only presume that Rossen's script followed the book closely. How else could my second-unit work be used?

Shortly before lunch I got into the elevator to go to my room and Brod Crawford and his son in the picture, John Derek, followed me in. I pushed the fourth-floor button.

CRAWFORD: Man I'm starved. Hope the party's got plenty of booze. (*Noticing I've pushed the fourth-floor button.*) Why the hell you pushing four? (*Pushes the fifth-floor button.*) The party's in Rossen's big suite.
(*The elevator comes to a stop on the fourth floor and the doors start to open.*)
CRAWFORD: You're not thinking of leaving your buddies?
ME: I wasn't invited.
CRAWFORD: (*Laying a heavy hand on my shoulder*) Bullshit. You're coming with us.

I twisted myself clear and dashed off to my right. The corridors were wide. In a large rectangle that led back to the elevators, Brod lumbered to his right after me. I easily outdistanced him, but I didn't have a ghost of a chance when John sprinted to the left, caught and tackled me. I hit the carpeted floor hard. An out-of-breath Brod grabbed me under my armpits as John lifted my legs clear of the floor. They carried me back towards the elevator.

CRAWFORD: (*Still huffing and puffing*) Nice going, Johnny Boy. Like all directors, he's a dirty little sneak.
ME: (*Struggling in vain to get free*) Can't you get it through your thick heads that Rossen will never forgive me for crashing his party?

119

DEREK: If he protests, we'll throw him out of his party.

The doors to the sumptuous Rossen suite were wide open. I stretched my neck to see inside. The large drawing room was filled with press and cast. Rossen was addressing the milling groups, explaining that the book *All the King's Men* was in truth the story of the former Governor of Louisiana, Huey Long. There were *hors d'oeuvres* piled on *hors d'oeuvres*. The bar was manned by busy bartenders. Waiters wandered through the room serving endless imbibers and the air was fouled by cigarette smoke. I pleaded once more, but to no avail. Brod and Derek, gripping me firmly, started swinging me through the air, their loud voices attracting immediate attention: 'A-one – a-two – a-three!' I flew through the room, landing on a small table full of delicatessen goodies. The table flattened and there were screams from those who were splattered. Several of the media picked themselves up from the floor, but the din was topped and stopped by the angry, outraged voice of Rossen.

ROSSEN: (*Addressing me*) You son-of-a-bitch! What the hell are you trying to do?
(*By now the media has completely surrounded us, asking questions about who I am and scribbling madly.*)
ME: The law of gravity is entirely responsible for the mess I made.
(*Rossen is totally ignored as John and Brod are questioned by the media as to why they threw me into the room.*)
CRAWFORD: Don Siegel is a splendid director.
MEDIA: Who is directing the picture?
(*A groan of frustration from Rossen.*)
CRAWFORD: (*Helping himself to a double martini*) We should know that in a few days.
MEDIA: But why hurl Mr Siegel into the room?
DEREK: Siegel didn't want to go to the party. Rossen insisted he come. We are under contract to Mr Rossen. So, we had no choice but to do what we did.

By this time, everyone was drinking, including Rossen. This picture was rapidly turning into a drunken nightmare. John Ireland and Mercedes McCambridge, who in the film managed Crawford's campaign to become Governor, plied me with drinks. I went over to Rossen, who was drinking alone, to wish him luck. He looked up at me, his manner ugly. He spoke with passion and simplicity.

ROSSEN: Go fuck yourself!

I must have hurt his feelings, because I didn't even try.

The three musketeers, Brod, John and Don, 'did the town'. Brod, just sniffing his first martini, was as drunk as after he had downed his twentieth. A huge man with unlimited desire for trouble, he would often get into fights. The reason we didn't get hurt I can only attribute to the fact that Brod fought as a pro. Yet he could talk on most subjects as an erudite man.

I pointed out to him that I had to get up at 5 a.m. to start shooting as soon as the light chased the darkness away. Coincidentally, I was shooting Brod. Did he have any idea what we were filming?

CRAWFORD: Just give me the pages and I'll spew them out.
ME: (*Alert*) By the way, do you have a script?
CRAWFORD: I read a few pages with Ireland, Derek and
    McCambridge. Rossen took the pages away from us – apparently
    disgusted.

When Brod got up to 'wash his hands', I made a very quick exit to my room to get a few hours' slumber. The phone rang, awakening me from a deep sleep. I managed to knock the phone off the bedside table. I could hear Brod cursing.

ME: (*Talking into the phone lying on the floor*) Goddamn it Brod, I
    told you I was getting up at dawn. I don't think you're a bit funny.
    (*I hang up and crawl back to bed. The phone starts to ring again. I
    give up, stretching beside the phone on the floor.*)
ME: I've a brand new bottle of Dewar's White Label. It's yours. I hope
    it kills you.

In a few minutes, there was a pounding on the door. I picked up the fresh, unopened bottle of scotch and hurried to open the door before Brod broke through it. Brod, closely followed by his 'son', grabbed the bottle and opened it by knocking the top off against the edge of a corridor wall leading to my bedroom. A large hunk of plaster hit the carpet. I tried to pick pieces of glass from his bleeding hand.

CRAWFORD: Don't ever interfere with my drinking!
    (*He pushes me roughly against the wall. I sink to the floor.*)
DEREK: (*Stripping the bed*) Drip, drip, drip the blue blood on the sheet.
    There are no virgins anywhere.

Brod squeezed his bleeding fingers on the sheet. Then he took a careful sip of scotch. By now I was hoping he would eat the bottle too. Derek and Crawford picked me up from the floor and dumped me on the bloodied sheet.

CRAWFORD: Can you imagine the *nerve* of that McCambridge whore offering us *milk*?

I was wrapped in the sheet as they carried me out of my room, winding up at McCambridge's room. I closed my eyes and dropped off to sleep. The morning's work was just around the bend.

Somehow, I found myself at the location – an old grocery store in the middle of nowhere. When I picked this location, I emphatically told the owner *not* to clean it up. It was spotless. We got special effects to spread spider webs throughout the store.

Brod showed up with the make-up man, wardrobe man and hairdresser, a startlingly beautiful girl. He had bags under his eyes that dropped to his knees. I told the 'miracle workers' to get Brod ready sooner than possible. I said nothing to Brod. He was too hung over to do anything but breathe. But that was not good. I told the startlingly beautiful to pour a large bottle of Listerine down the bibber's throat.

By the time special effects had made the store look like a spider's nest, Brod appeared. I leafed through the book and found a suitable passage for him to use as one of his political speeches.

I explained to all the people in the store, most of whom were sitting round a wood-burning stove, that we would pay them $5 to listen to Mr Crawford when he gave them his political speech. I told the cameraman to start lighting, the assistant to see that none of our 'cast' wandered off. I then went directly to Brod.

ME: (*Handing him the book opened at the political passage*) Here's your dialogue.
(*Brod, still bleary-eyed but unbelievably improved, haltingly starts reading the passage. Before he has time to finish, I take the book away from him.*)
ME: That's all the rehearsal time. Remember who you are and, in the best tradition of Stanislavski, you'll have no trouble convincing the people you are talking to. In case you've forgotten, you're running for Governor of this glorious state.
(*A gleam appears in one of Brod's eyes. He puts on his dark glasses as he struggles to his feet.*)
CRAWFORD: (*Loudly*) I'm your next Governor!

A miracle happened. By the time we were set up, ready to shoot, he was ready to talk. Just as, when directing a Western, the moment I yelled 'Action!' the horses all bolted away, when Brod heard 'Action!' he took off, speaking quickly, with vigour and meaning. He was excellent.

I spent the rest of the day shooting Brod outside a barn, leaning on a fence, standing on a bridge, holding on to a horse that was pulling a buggy filled with elderly people and children. He never stopped giving speeches, talking at full speed. There was nothing for the director to do but gape and admire. I was truly thrilled with his performance.

*

The next day, Rossen was shooting a large square filled with people. I picked out a set-up at the end of the square on top of a three-storey building. To get there, one had to climb out of a second-storey window and up iron rings embedded in brick. The grips carried all their equipment, as did the camera crew, by using the iron rings. When we had the camera on a tripod, which looked good to me using a 35mm lens, I noticed Rossen on the street below and yelled down to him.

ME: Hey, Bob – wanna check the set-up?
ROSSEN: (*Looking up truculently*) Of course I do.
ME: (*Smiling*) You get to the roof from the second floor.

The reason I smiled was that I had a hunch that he'd never reach the roof and that he'd okay the set-up from the second-floor window. Sure enough, in about five minutes, I heard Rossen yelling, 'Don, Don!'

ME: (*Looking down from the roof*) How we doing, Chief?
ROSSEN: Does the set-up look good to you?
ME: I'm sure you'll like it. The thirty-five covers the entire square.
ROSSEN: Sounds good to me. Just be sure you've got film in the camera.

He disappeared. I felt good the rest of the day.

*

Some days later we had to shoot a scene at a football game and chose Hardin-Simmons versus the College of the Pacific. During the half-time I had dressed Crawford's double in a suit, covered by a full-length camel-hair overcoat. The double walked down the centre of the gridiron, doffing his hat to the spectators on both sides of the field. The spectators yelled and whistled. Obviously, they had no idea who this large, imposing figure was. We covered the sequence with shots of the double and many shots of the cheering fans. Our work finished, there was one flaw to our leaving: the game was tremendously exciting and none of the crew, including the director, wanted to leave. The game finally ended in a tie.

When we got back to the production office, a major change had taken place: the second unit was disbanded, because we had completed our scheduled work. We were told to leave for Los Angeles that night. I had no regrets. Some of the work I had found to be quite interesting.

The picture turned out great. Rossen, Crawford and Mercedes McCambridge all won Oscars. It was Mercedes's first picture and I shot her first scene.

Although Jack Fier, production manager of Columbia Studios had hired me, I discovered in looking up the credits that Allied Artists took credit for making *All the King's Men*. I really didn't know or care who the executives were. I was never given a script; I said goodbye to no one; I thought the football game made the second unit worthwhile. However, I reached a positive decision. No more second-unit work for me – unless I was directing the first unit as well.

5

The Big Steal

RKO 1949

Howard Hughes never forgot that I had turned down directing and producing *Vendetta*. To everyone's amazement, including mine, I became the first director he hired after buying RKO.

Robert Mitchum was serving time at an honour camp on a marijuana charge. Hughes found an impossibly dull script entitled *The Big Steal*, which he submitted to the court. He pleaded that the picture was ready to be shot. Many people would lose their jobs if it was not made because of Mitchum's incarceration. The court ruled that Mitchum would be given a second chance. He would be allowed to make the picture, providing that a probation officer was with him in Mexico. His sentence was reduced to three months. I knew then that, although Hughes had successfully got his huge aeroplane, the *Spruce Goose*, off the ground for a few seconds, he would never get RKO off the ground.

I immediately hired Robert Pirosh, a top writer with a wonderful sense of humour. Recently he had won an Academy Award for writing the screenplay *Battleground*. In case he had to leave RKO before we had finished the film, as he had other commitments, I hired another excellent writer, Danny Mainwaring. The script, thanks to the skill of these two, moved with pace and was filled with humour.

It was decided to start shooting without waiting for Mitchum. The plot was very, very thin. The story, what there was of it, was one continuous chase across Mexico. Patric Knowles drove a wild car escaping from Mitchum and Jane Greer, who drove a wilder car. They were closely pursued by Bill Bendix, who drove a faster car. He, in turn, was chased by a Mexican police captain, Ramon Navarro. And that was the story I was instructed to do.

Before I left to go to Mexico, I visited Mitchum at the camp to give him some revisions of the script. I put the new pages in a large manilla envelope. Two special RKO chocolate bars were placed between the script pages. While sitting in the visiting room, I noticed the mailman, briskly delivering the mail. I recognized him immediately as an old friend of mine,

10 *The Big Steal*: Robert Mitchum and Jane Greer

Bill Tilden, considered by many to be the greatest tennis player of all time. I turned to face the wall. I didn't want to embarrass him, or myself.

Mitchum never looked better in his life: deeply tanned with clear eyes. His waist couldn't have been more than thirty-two inches. He sat down opposite me, a healthy grin on his face.

ME: What the hell are you so happy about?
MITCHUM: Never felt better in my life – at peace with the world.
ME: (*Handing him the envelope*) I brought you some new pages.
    (*Mitchum is totally uninterested.*)
ME: I also brought you some RKO chocolate bars.
    (*Mitchum instantly becomes a con.*)
MITCHUM: (*Whispering out the side of his mouth*) Watch out for screws. How'd you get the goodies past the guard?
ME: He was as uninterested as you were with the new pages.

Mitchum slowly unbuttoned his blue work shirt. He took out the pages of script and apparently started reading them. In a flash, he had both bars of

126

chocolate in his shirt. Slowly, he re-buttoned his shirt, still pretending to be reading the pages. All I could think about was what happens if the screws take the chocolate away from Mitch, and supposing Hughes finds out? It may be the end of Mitch, to say nothing of me.

MITCHUM: You know, you're my favourite director.
ME: Oh, it's really nothing. Calm nerves, courage and hatred for authority.
MITCHUM: (*Beaming*) We share many, many things.

*

When Mitchum showed up on location at Tehuacán in Mexico with his probation officer, he had finished a bottle of tequila in the car from Mexico City. The probation officer was drunker than Mitchum. He passed out in his room. Pat Knowles and I made our first major mistake: we tried to sober up Mitchum. We got him in a steam room, where he proceeded cruelly to beat the tar out of Knowles. When I tried to grab him, he would spin his shoulder, which sent me spinning around the wet walls. We tried our best, but it was no contest. Mitch was in the best shape of his life. At the honour camp he had built endless brick walls. He was one tough hombre with a mean streak that we couldn't handle.

Mitchum, looking none the worse for wear, though Knowles and I had a few facial abrasions, appeared on the set ready for work. The cinematographer, Harry Wild, lined up on a scene with Greer, favouring Mitch. Suddenly there was no Mitchum. We lined up on Greer. When we were ready to shoot, Greer had disappeared. Wild and I figured out a shot, shooting up at Knowles looking out of Greer's window. When we were ready to make this historic and most unimportant shot, our work came to a shuddering halt. No cameraman.

The shooting proceeded like this all day. Everyone had Montezuma's Revenge with a vengeance, with one notable exception. I showed no sign of diarrhoea until early in the afternoon. Then Montezuma struck. We were working on a small stone bridge over a stream. Two strong grips grabbed me by my ankles and held me upside down while I threw up for what seemed to be hours. When their hands and arms gave out, they lifted me up from the stream and carefully laid me outstretched on the bridge. That night, Ramon Navarro got me a Mexican doctor, who gave me some unpronounceable Indian pills. Ramon explained to me that one should always use local knowledge. Gringo pills might be all right in South Dakota, but were practically useless in Mexico. He was right. The next day, half our cast never got out of bed. Apart from feeling weak, I was O K and put in a full day's work.

Mitchum took pride in the fact that he never studied his lines. After several rehearsals, he would be letter perfect. No matter who he was working with, he would play the scene without much vitality and generally in a low voice. This made the actor he was playing opposite appear to be overacting. Whenever I arrived in the morning with rewritten pages, Mitch would have a certain amount of trouble in memorizing the new lines. The more I got to know him, the more certain I was that his claim never to have studied his lines was an affectation. His attitude of not caring was a pretence. I was also aware that he was a talented actor with a most original style. Nevertheless, I felt he was quirky.

I encountered a complicated problem. By the time Mitchum got out of jail, I had already shot the chase material with Pat Knowles, Bill Bendix and Ramon Navarro. At that time, the trees were bare. When Mitchum joined us and drove madly with Jane Greer after Knowles, the trees and flowers were in full bloom. No one at RKO ever noticed anything amiss. In fairness to the critics, there wasn't enough time to notice anything. Also, Jane Greer was four months pregnant. With a little care in how I shot her, no one was aware; but I must confess that at times I worried about a miscarriage.

*

At lunch in the large dining room, over 100 Gold Star Mothers, who had lost their sons in World War II, trooped in. Their eyes bulged when they noticed the movie stars: Robert Mitchum, Jane Greer, William Bendix, Patric Knowles and Ramon Navarro eating their lunch. Patric nudged me. I followed him into a large bar adjacent to the dining room.

KNOWLES: Do you think Bendix would be thrilled to buy drinks for a hundred Gold Star Mothers?
ME: He'd have a heart attack and his wife would join him.
KNOWLES: You may be right, but duty calls . . . it has to be done.

He called over the head bartender and explained his plan, slowly and carefully. The bartender was to take the drink orders from the Gold Star Mothers and explain to them that this was a gift from Mr William Bendix. When all the ladies had received their drinks, they were to stand up and raise their glasses, toasting Mr Bendix. After they were seated and their toasts acknowledged by Mr Bendix, the bartender was to hand Mr Bendix the bill for all the drinks and immediately go back to the bar.

KNOWLES: Comprende?
BARTENDER: (*Beaming*) Sí, sí Señor Knowles.

Patric and I returned to our table to await developments. We were aware of the ladies giving their orders for drinks. They feasted their eyes and interest on Bendix, paying no attention to anyone else. The 'ham' in Bendix rose to the occasion. He smiled graciously back with warmth and pride, obviously pleased that he was the only actor given this attention. The ladies received their drinks. They all raised their glasses in a toast to Mr Bendix. Bendix stood up, a glass of water in his hand as he acknowledged their attention with pleasure.

The bill arrived, delivered to Bendix by the bartender. Before Bendix had a chance to examine it, the bartender disappeared. Bendix studied the bill closely. His face turned red, his breathing became short and heavy. God forbid. Maybe he was about to have a heart attack.

BENDIX: (*Voice cracking in anger*) Where the hell is that waiter who gave me this lying, fucking bill?

ME: (*Interrupting strongly*) Are you crazy? Do you realize that what you did was the cleverest publicity stunt I've ever seen?

BENDIX: (*Bewildered*) But why should I be stuck? (*Picking up bill.*) Why don't I share it with Mitchum?

ME: It's incredible how stupid you are. Mitchum is a big star. You're as good an actor, but your career needs work. Those hundred ladies will spread your name around wherever they go. They'll never stop singing your praises. Throughout Mexico, the States, indeed throughout the world, your name will become better known than Mitchum's.
(*While Bendix is digesting my soliloquy, Patric nudges me. We go back to the bar. The bartender asks us what our pleasure might be.*)

KNOWLES: I would like that big malt-shaker. Also, I need your largest glass. (*A look of the devil creases his face.*) I shall make the drink for Mr Bendix, full of the nectar of every bottle you have in your magnificent bar.

ME: Please don't kill him. But it's a hell of an idea.

Knowles placed the malt-shaker on the bar. From every bottle in view, and there were close to 100, he poured a few drops. Never in the history of drinking was a drink made with more different kinds of liquor, ranging from sweet liqueurs, whiskeys, tequila (about ten brands), dark and light beers, white and red wines, port, gin, vodka, etc. When the malt-shaker was full, Knowles turned on the shaker to mix up this hideous concoction. Finally, he called for me to see his masterpiece. It bubbled in the largest glass extant. The colours were rainbow: mainly purple, lavender, violet, blue, plum, lilac and puce. Knowles tipped handsomely, giving instructions that this strange smelling drink was a gift to Bendix from the Gold Star Mothers.

When Bendix received this large glass of 'witches' brew', he looked and sniffed it suspiciously. However, when told that it was a gift from the ladies, he rose to his feet. All the Gold Star Mothers stood up too, glasses upraised. Bendix gallantly lifted his glass in both hands and took a healthy sip. He looked puzzled. However, he took two more sips, each one larger than the one before. I couldn't take my eyes off him. Beads of moisture appeared on his brow. He swallowed once more, then offered it to his wife. She quaffed a greedy swallow, turned to Bendix and said, in a voice filled with enthusiasm, 'It's one of them foreign drinks. It's delicious.'

In order to get them out of the dining room while they were still able to make it, I suggested that we go bowling. Bill and his wife, still grasping the glass firmly, thought it was a 'fun' idea. They waved goodbyes to the ladies and then started off towards the bowling alleys, closely followed by Patric and myself. Every once in a while they would stop to share another gulp. When we arrived at the bowling alleys, they were feeling no pain. In actual fact, they were growing affectionate. I caught Knowles's eye. He shook his head solemnly, putting his finger to his lips, warning me not to say anything. The pins were set up.

MRS BENDIX: (*Handing the glass carefully to her husband*) I'll be first.
BENDIX: (*In love*) You'll always be first, my love.

Mrs Bendix carefully put her fingers into the three holes on the bowling ball and let fly. Unfortunately, she couldn't release her fingers. Mrs Bendix and the ball swept down the entire length of the alley, knocking all the pins asunder. She lay still – very still. Bendix, followed by the rest of us, rushed down the alley to help his wife. Unfortunately, he fell on top of her. They both lay still. In Spanish, Knowles ordered the Mexicans to get a doctor and two stretchers, *muy pronto*. Saying we had to continue shooting, we escaped, *muy, muy pronto*! I might add that for two days the Bendixes were neither seen nor heard from. They were suffering from a bad case of '*turista*'.

*

Being under exclusive contract to RKO was entirely different from Warner Brothers. For one thing Hughes had nothing to do with the making of *The Big Steal* – except which lady was playing the lead role. All the other executives were in fear of my connection with Hughes. They had absolutely no contact of any sort with him, so I was completely left alone, exclusive contract, no bother at all.

After finishing the picture, I saw Hughes and asked that my exclusive contract be broken, as I didn't like the pictures he was thinking of making. He was sorry I wanted to leave and thought I was making a mistake. But he graciously let me go.

6

No Time for Flowers

RKO 1952

In 1952, behind the Iron Curtain, Viveca Lindfors, Paul Christian, Ludwig Stossel and a host of foreign actors worked on a US–Austrian co-production titled *No Time for Flowers*, filmed in its entirety in Vienna. The producer, Mort Briskin, a burly man in his forties who wore a conspicuous hearing aid, had strong likes and dislikes, mainly concerning the acquisition of money. His taste was questionable. For example, to try to win favour with the American Vice-Consul, he gave him a gold champagne swizzle-stick made in the shape of a penis. Exit Vice-Consul, embarrassed. He made a strong point never to see or hear from Mr Briskin. There were times when we could have used his help.

A well-known, experienced American director, Frank Tuttle, was hired. He was fired by Briskin when it was discovered that he was a diabetic. Briskin was afraid that the rigours of directing would be too much for Tuttle. This made no sense, as the rigours, at least physical, were minimal. Or maybe Briskin thought that diabetes was contagious. Wrong again. Now comes his classic mistake. He hires me to replace the diabetic director. Apparently he had never found out that I have been a diabetic since I was twenty-seven years old. I might also add that I have never missed a day's work due to being diabetic. I didn't know a thing about Frank Tuttle until I was shooting the film. Briskin filled me in on stories depicting the hopeless horrors of being cursed with that illness. Inasmuch as diabetes is *not* contagious and you are at least 90 per cent your own doctor, Briskin must, in his confused state of mind, have been thinking of gonorrhoea, or some other venereal disease. Or, of course, leprosy. Given that I've never had any of these despicable diseases, I learned a great deal about them from Briskin. Perhaps he spoke from experience.

*

Some months earlier, I had married Viveca Lindfors in Paris, in the sixteenth *arrondissement*. The jolly little man who married us, the Maire, wished us happiness, health and lots of 'little Oscars'. I was now on my way to the British Airport, near Vienna, totally surrounded by Russian territory, to pick her up. We were travelling in a big Buick, driven by the head of publicity, Shapiro. He hated Communists to the point of insanity. Accompanying us in the back seat was my Hungarian assistant director, Ladislaus Ronay. In order to enter the Russian environs of the British Airport, it was absolutely mandatory to have a properly stamped 'grey card'. I had one for myself and one for Viveca Lindfors Siegel. As we approached the divided road, one going to Prague, the other to the airport, a Russian soldier carrying an automatic, similar to the Sten automatic, appeared. He slowly crossed the road, presumably to examine our papers. The idiot Shapiro suddenly stepped hard on the gas pedal and we careened out of sight. I slid down the passenger seat, expecting a hail of bullets to come slamming into us. I cursed Shapiro as he slowed down and stopped his Buick in front of the airport. A Swedish plane was about to make a landing. I rushed off to see and embrace Viveca.

Ronay piled Viveca's suitcases on the back seat and in the trunk. There was barely room for him to squeeze in. Viveca, looking happy and in love, sat between Shapiro and me. She looked puzzled when I warned Shapiro that if he didn't stop for the armed Russian guard on our way back to Vienna, I would throttle him and throw him out of the car. Sure enough, the soldier was standing in the middle of the road facing us; his automatic rifle, cocked, was ready to fire. Shapiro lurched to a reluctant stop. Viveca threw me a worried look. Handing her her grey card and holding mine, we waited for the soldier to approach the car. Shapiro, now totally crazed, swore at the soldier in German and let out his clutch. Before the car could have moved more than a foot, the soldier raised his automatic to shoot. I heard a thud in the back seat. Ronay had hit the floor of the car. Shapiro let out a harsh torrent of German.

I screamed to the idiot to shut up! I held Viveca's and my grey cards above our heads towards the soldier. Behind us, a Scandinavian bus pulled to a screeching halt. The officers of the plane rushed to the soldier. Some spoke Russian. They explained who Viveca was and that she carried a Swedish passport. Viveca handed the soldier her passport and grey card. After a surprisingly brief exchange of words, Viveca and I, along with all her luggage, were allowed to enter the bus. Shapiro and Ronay were ordered out of the car. The soldier's gun was trained on them at all times, still cocked. Standing in the crowded bus, we thanked our Swedish friends. As we pulled away, we saw the small figures of Shapiro and Ronay being pushed and shoved. They finally reappeared in Vienna to work on the picture three weeks later.

We decided to celebrate our still being alive and unscathed by wandering through the streets of the Russian sector of Vienna. We found the best Russian restaurant with the best caviar. The sturgeon was indescribable! Placed on our table was a very large, ornate sterling-silver tureen, set on a silver tray. It was filled to the brim with grey caviar. A large serving spoon was placed at each end of the tureen. Plates, depicting snow scenes, were set in front of us. Smaller spoons were placed beside each plate. No attempt was made to serve us. Viveca ordered an ice cold, small bottle of their finest Vodka. We attacked the tureen. We ordered another small bottle of Vodka. Neither we, nor the waiters, suggested any other food or beverage. I had no idea of the amount of caviar we consumed, or what the price was. I just knew it was the greatest. After a while, we ate slower and slower. We didn't finish the second bottle of Vodka. We held hands, looked deeply into each other's eyes, silently showing our love.

VIVECA: Do you think we can make it back to the hotel?
ME: I don't want to go back to the hotel. Let's sleep here.
VIVECA: Just so we hold each other in our arms and keep ourselves
    from falling down, we'll find our way back.
ME: Do you have any idea what the name of the hotel is?
VIVECA: (*A pause*) It'll come to me. That's where we'll make love –
    and sleep, and sleep, and sleep.

I ordered the bill by scribbling in the air. The tureen, now about two-thirds full, was removed from the table. Unbeknownst to me, it was weighed. When full, it had been weighed too. They knew exactly how much caviar we had eaten. When I was handed the bill, I gasped. I emptied my wallet. I couldn't pay the bill, even if I left no tip. I leaned towards Viveca and whispered.

ME: Do you have any money?
VIVECA: How romantic. (*Going through her purse.*) Do you think I
    could sell my body?

She gave me all her money, mostly Swedish. I thanked her for the lovely dinner and handed everything I had to the waiter. We got up, somewhat unsteady, and left what had been the most expensive dinner and most enjoyable experience in my life. We had no idea what it cost and couldn't have cared less. I thought only of love and sleep. Somehow, in a circular route, we made it back to the hotel. The first thing I did was to leave implacable instructions that under no circumstances were we to be disturbed. And that included fire, earthquake and war. I smiled at my lovely bride.

*

Vienna – a beautiful city. It used to be capital of the Hapsburg Empire. Consequently, there are many old state buildings – perhaps more state buildings, opera houses and churches than in any other city of its size. When I started to line up my shots, I was immediately told I couldn't show St Stephen's Cathedral, or any other recognizably Viennese building because *No Time for Flowers* was supposed to be set in Prague. Why shoot in Vienna when it's supposed to be Prague? There were times when I pointed my camera north. I was told 'no dice'. I pointed it south. I was shooting at a Russian military building. A nervous 'no' was quickly uttered. East and west were impossible because the Hapsburg Empire buildings didn't exist in Prague. I cornered Briskin, who saw no problems. I just couldn't shoot in any direction that might be recognizable as Vienna.

ME: (*To Briskin*) You must be crazy, or a fool. Probably both.
(*Briskin just smiles.*)
ME: Why not shoot on Universal's or MGM's backlot? At least I could find something that apparently looks like Prague and, with luck, fits the picture.
BRISKIN: (*Putting his arm around me*) We have no choice. The money to make the picture comes from Vienna. (*Voice hardens.*) And that's their orders.
ME: I've got a great idea. You know this city and the script much better than I do. You give me your okayed set-ups.
BRISKIN: I'm not a director.
ME: You're telling me . . .

At best, *No Time for Flowers* was a poor man's *Ninotchka*. It was bad enough that the storyline was dull. Viveca, living in Prague, is working for the government. Her boss, a spy, is Paul Christian, who has just returned from the States. He's obviously on the make and gives her American stockings, dresses, etc. Instead of talking about love, he seems only interested in the wonders of capitalism. Instead of reporting to the authorities about this, they fall in love and ultimately escape from the communist city of Prague and live happily together in a capitalistic world, which is more than most Americans can boast about.

We missed three important bits of casting. First and foremost, Don Siegel was a poor substitute for the brilliant Ernst Lubitsch. Paul Christian was much too stiff and without the charm and fun of Melvyn Douglas. Viveca Lindfors was not only Swedish, but a distinguished actress in her own right. If she had worked for Lubitsch, she would have given Greta Garbo a run for her money. To make matters worse, Briskin was really only concerned with making his money before we made the picture.

We shot a post office scene in which the Russians opened all the packages that were mailed from America, hoping to steal the contents. Briskin promised me fur coats, cameras, dresses, shoes, in the various packages: the money for the contents was already in the budget. When we opened the packages, they were all empty. It made for another stupid sequence. After all, Briskin could have rented the clothes and practically got his money back.

ME: (*To Briskin, angry*) If you cared about the picture, who knows – you might have made a successful film. But you're too greedy and stupid.

There was another sequence where pictures of Churchill, Roosevelt and Stalin were hanging in a booth. If you could knock the pictures down with a ball, you received a prize. This set was to be located in the Prado Park, a *Russian* Park. I suggested that this shot might have dire consequences. In fact, it was a dangerous sequence to shoot. Imagine some Russian army officer seeing Stalin knocked off his perch. Briskin pooh-poohed the chance of any danger.

ME: I'll tell you what we'll do. You stand next to me in the park and I'll shoot the scene.

Briskin paled and built a set on a stage where we were relatively safe. I told him he finally made sense. Because if anything happened to me, I'd point my finger at him and yell: 'That's the producer who told me to throw hardballs at Stalin.' He walked away, a little shaken.

Notwithstanding the hopelessness of the project, both *Newsweek* and *The Commonweal* had nice things to say about *No Time for Flowers*. Needless to say, it failed to make money. I wasn't surprised.

7

Duel at Silver Creek

Universal 1952

I received a call from a well-known agent, Phil Gersh. He wanted to know if I would sign up with him if he got me an immediate picture to direct at Universal.

ME: Why not? It sounds good to me.
GERSH: You'll hear from me within the hour.
ME: Don't bother calling if you fail.

Phil took me to meet the producer, Leonard Goldstein, who seemed surprised to see Phil. I soon found out that early that morning Phil had tried to sell another director to Goldstein. But Leonard said he wasn't interested in Phil's client; he wanted me. Before Leonard could get hold of me, I was already a client of Phil's. There was no embarrassment on Phil's face. Just pleasure at his gaining a quick 10 per cent. It calls for a certain kind of a critter to be an agent. Always think of your 10 per cent. If you can get a client a job, great. If you can't, don't waste time. Get rid of him.

When I received the script from Goldstein, entitled *Duel at Silver Creek*, I told him I'd read it and immediately get back to him. We shook hands. He didn't get up.

GOLDSTEIN: Bad ticker. (*Looking at notation on notepad.*) Go to
    Room Twenty-three in Building B. Next door to your office is your
    writer, Joseph Hoffman. Don't talk to him before reporting back
    to me. Be seeing you.

I left, script in hand.

Duel at Silver Creek was interesting. There was no duel and no creek. Also, the names of the characters in the picture were unbelievably amusing.

Audie Murphy: The Silver Kid
Stephen McNally: Lightning Tyrone
Faith Domergue: Opal Lacy

Susan Cabot: Dusty Fargo
Gerald Mohr: Rod Lacy
Eugene Iglesias: Johnny Sombrero
Walter Sande: Pete Fargo
Lee Marvin: Tinhorn Burgess
James Anderson: Ratface

I wanted to rush next door and compliment Hoffman on his imagination, creativity and originality. There was no doubt in my mind that those names were tongue-in-cheek. I hoped the whole script would be written in the same style.

Outside the names of the characters, however, the story was well trodden. The Silver Kid rides into town for some excitement and winds up as deputy to Sheriff Lightning Tyrone. He gets the job because the former deputy, Dan Music, has been murdered. The deputy and sheriff together defeat an ill-assorted group of villains, including Tinhorn, Opal Lacy, Ratface and Johnny Sombrero. The story was quite routine and needed work. I hoped Goldstein had a sense of humour. At least he appeared to like the names of the main characters, which, considering the script, showed hope.

I saw Goldstein as soon as I had finished reading the script. I levelled with him. At this stage, I didn't even know who got the girl – the Silver Kid or Lightning Tyrone. But I did like their ridiculous names. Obviously, I needed more time to work with Hoffman, whom I still hadn't met.

GOLDSTEIN: I don't give a shit who gets the girl. I've done nineteen pictures already this year and I haven't done them by pushing them back. Get moving on it.
ME: May I call you Leonard?
GOLDSTEIN: I don't give a shit what you call me. Get with Hoffman and fix the script as soon as possible.
ME: I'm leaving right now to have a story conference with Hoffman. Do you think he'll mind if I call him Joe? (*Before he has a chance for his traditional answer.*) I know – you don't give a shit.

I left immediately for a story discussion with Joe.

I liked Joe immediately. His eyes twinkled and his face had a friendly grin. He listened to my criticisms politely. He appeared champing at the bit to start working.

HOFFMAN: Mr Siegel, there are many things wrong with the script.
ME: The name's Don. I assume yours is Joe.
HOFFMAN: That's what I like to be called.

ME: Good. Don't you think Faith Domergue's dialogue needs not only fixing, but editing?
   (*Joe takes out a lined pad and pencil and starts scribbling.*)
ME: Who gets the girl?
JOE: (*Graciously*) Anyone you say.
ME: Stephen McNally will never be a star. Audie Murphy may not be able to act, but a lot of stars fall into that category.
JOE: Anything you say, star-maker.

We churned out the pages for several days as fast as we could. I thought Joe was doing as good a job as possible, considering the material. I told him so and he seemed very pleased.

   I took a break to get some coffee. As I strolled slowly back to Joe's office, sipping black coffee from a styrofoam cup, I realized that Joe and I had been putting in a lot of hours on the rewrite. Maybe Joe didn't feel it, but I was bone tired. A voice hailed me. It was Ross Hunter, an actor with whom I had never worked, but had met at several parties.

HUNTER: Sorry Don, I haven't seen you at Mr Goldstein's office. I'm the associate producer.
ME: Have you given up acting?
HUNTER: Yes and I'm very happy about it. By the way, I've read all the revised pages you've sent on to Mr Goldstein. They are a great improvement. Keep up the good work.
ME: Well, thank you Ross. Frankly, I've been so bushed that I haven't had a chance to sit down and read them from page one.
HUNTER: So far, the pages look very good indeed. I'm off to see Mr Goldstein right now.
ME: Thanks for the kind words. We should be finished within the week. I hope the fifty cups of coffee keep me awake.
   (*I tell Joe the good news from Ross. He is very pleased.*)
ME: When do you figure you'll finish?
JOE: Less than a week. You realize we're very short.
ME: There's a simple, easy solution. When you get to the final shoot-out, make it a series of staccato cuts. Drop two spaces to 'cut to' and two spaces to each 'shot description'. If it's still short, make it three spaces instead of two.
JOE: You're a genius.
ME: Another thing. From this point on, make the scenes and the dialogue longer.
JOE: There will be a day of reckoning.
ME: There always is.

A week or two later, I received a telephone call from Goldstein's office.

GOLDSTEIN'S SECRETARY: (*Nervously*) Mr Siegel, Mr Goldstein wants to see you as soon as possible.
ME: Tell him I'll be there in ten minutes.
(*I stick my head into Joe's office.*)
ME: Hear anything from the moguls?
JOE: Not a whisper. Anything wrong?
ME: Don't know yet. Mr Goldstein wants to see me right away. I'm sure it's not to compliment us. Maybe they found out the script's short.

I closed the door and sped on my way.

When I was admitted to Leonard's office, the atmosphere was heavy with gloom. Ross was standing next to a seated Leonard. At least I knew I had a friend in court: Ross loved the new pages.

ME: Please tell me the good news. The picture's been cancelled.
(*Leonard lifts his head. Ross looks surprisingly blank.*)
GOLDSTEIN: It's not funny, kid. Miss Domergue doesn't like the new script.
ME: (*Getting angry*) That's ridiculous. I'm not defending Joe's script; but compared to the earlier script, the rewrite will win an Oscar.
GOLDSTEIN: (*Funeral note*) Don, it's no joke. Her agent says she won't do it. She greatly prefers the first script.
(*Suddenly, I remember Ross.*)
ME: Ross, what do you think about the two scripts?
(*Ross fidgets and then smiles placatingly.*)
HUNTER: You know how it is, Don. Some like one script; some prefer the other.
(*I explode, grabbing Ross by the throat. A squall of protest is heard from Leonard. I remember his bad heart. I let go of a frightened Ross, who collapses over the desk.*)
ME: (*To Leonard*) That miserable excuse for an associate producer told me about a week ago that he thought the new script was a great improvement over the original. If he so much as appears on my set, or locations, I'll wring his neck like the chicken he is.
GOLDSTEIN: Please, Don, I don't feel well.
ME: (*A course of action occurring*) Leonard, I know exactly what to do. Call Faith or Faithless Domergue to meet me in my office at once. I'll clear up this mess. If it doesn't work, I'm off the picture.

GOLDSTEIN: (*Weakly*) You want to see her alone, without her agent or anyone else?

ME: I won't see her if I can't talk to her alone.

GOLDSTEIN: I'll get her in as soon as possible.

ME: The sooner the better. (*To Ross.*) Don't ever cross my path again. I mean it! (*To Leonard.*) I'll be in my office expecting our 'star'. I won't leave until I hear from you. I'm positive we won't lose Faith. Just quit worrying and keep the faith.

I stormed out of the office. I might wring Ross's neck anyway.

Back in my office, I told Joe everything. It was the first and last time I ever saw him angry. He wouldn't talk about Ross, but he had plenty to say about Faith. I told him my plan. I was going to be seated next to Faith. The first script would be in front of her. Joe's script would be in front of me. We would go through both scripts, page by page. The phone rang.

GOLDSTEIN'S SECRETARY: Mr Goldstein is not feeling well. He's going home. You can reach him there. Miss Domergue will be in your office in twenty minutes.
(*She hangs up.*)

ME: (*To Joe*) She'll be here in twenty minutes. So vamoose. If you hear a woman's scream, ignore it. If you hear me yell, save me.
(*Faith, looking beautiful, knows the house rules: we will discuss both scripts. I want to know why she prefers the original by Gerald Drayson Adams.*)

FAITH: I never said I preferred the Adams script.

ME: Mr Goldstein called me in his office and said you wouldn't do Hoffman's script but would do Adams's script.

Before she had time to deny further what she, or her agents had told Leonard, I started with her, closely examining both scripts, page by page. I explained why Joe and I had made changes, mostly small ones. In every instance, when I asked her which page she liked the most, she picked Joe's script. Finally, after going through about twenty-five pages with her still choosing the second script, I figured out the solution to this annoying charade.

ME: (*Smiling at Faith*) I think I've figured out why in each case you've picked the page in the second script. I want to thank you for your honesty and politeness. The reason Mr Goldstein was told by your agent that Adams's script was the one you wanted to do (*looking her straight in the eye*) was that you had more words to speak in that script.

FAITH: That's certainly true.

ME: Yes it is, but the dialogue is not as good as Hoffman's. Supposing I promised you that you would have as much to say in the second script as in the first. Which script would you prefer?

FAITH: The second one, of course.

(*I close both scripts.*)

ME: You made the correct choice. Mr Goldstein will be very happy; as will Hoffman and yours truly.

(*I kiss her on the cheek and see her to her car. I rush back to my office, yelling through Joe's door.*)

ME: You've won one hundred per cent!

(*I then call Leonard's home and ask for Mr Goldstein, if he is well enough to talk.*)

GOLDSTEIN: (*After a pause*) What happened?

ME: I know it's going to make you immediately well. Faith Domergue pefers every page in Hoffman's script.

GOLDSTEIN: Gee, that's great Don.

ME: The only thing she wants is to have as many lines as she had in the first script. It's a cinch to fix. I promised her she would have what she wanted. Is that OK with you, Leonard?

GOLDSTEIN: Are you kidding? I feel like a million bucks. Let's have lunch tomorrow. I'll buy the food and drinks.

ME: Thank you, sir.

*

On the set it felt as if we were getting it; and, more importantly, the dailies looked good. The few reels of edited film, which no one other than Russell Schoengarth, the editor, and yours truly were allowed to see, made us enthusiastic.

I like to see my dailies during my lunch break; it saves me a lot of time. I hate to hang around until after 6, when I'm tired, before I can view them. Also, I don't like the executives, heads of departments and production people seeing my dailies, for the simple reason that if they report back to me what they didn't like, I have no realistic answers, not having seen what they have criticized.

One day, when I went to a small theatre to run the dailies, I was told by the projectionist that the head of the studio, Mr William Goetz, was running my dailies in his private projection room, thereby making the film unavailable to me. I decided to telephone him during the afternoon to complain. I finally got hold of him on my third try.

GOETZ: Hi, Don. I saw your dailies and liked them very much.

ME: Always like to hear nice things. Thank you. On the other hand may I make a small complaint?

GOETZ: Fire away.

ME: I always make it a point to see my dailies at lunch. I bring a couple of sandwiches and a piece of fruit. This saves me valuable time, as I don't have to see them after I'm finished shooting when I'm tired.

GOETZ: I understand completely and please accept my apologies. The reason I ran them is because I'm off to New York for at least a week. I thought I might get the feel of how your film is going to do by at least seeing the dailies.

ME: You're quite the most decent head of a studio I've ever talked to. May I ask a further question?

GOETZ: How can I turn you down when you say such pleasant things?

ME: I'm particularly worried about the length of the film. My gut reaction, at this early stage, is that it is going to be too short.

GOETZ: When your film looks great, full of action and constant pace, don't change a thing. Continue to keep the picture moving.

ME: (*Relieved*) It shall be done, sir.

The picture, when we had finished editing, turned out to be fifty-four minutes long – if I may use the word 'long'. When Goldstein rightly complained, I, of course, had the perfect answer. Mr Goetz, to whom I had spoken about my fears of running short, had told me definitely to keep shooting at the same pace and not to change a thing.

We settled on a new prologue and epilogue. I had the brass tell Joe, 'No double spaces, please.' He wrote a surprisingly good prologue and epilogue. We fattened the picture from fifty-four minutes to seventy-seven minutes. We weren't a second too short. I became known at Universal as the fifty-four-minute director.

Years later, Ed Muhl, who was then head of Universal, stopped me one day. I had no idea who he was.

MUHL: You're Don Siegel, aren't you?

ME: It's an ugly rumour, but I'm afraid it's true.

MUHL: I'm head of this studio and what I remember about you is *not* an ugly rumour. You're known as the idiot who brought a picture in that ran fifty-four minutes.

ME: Were any of the fifty-four minutes usable?

MUHL: Let me put it this way. You watch your step, or you won't be working for me.

When *Duel at Silver Creek* was released, the reviews were surprisingly good – 'A cracking good western with pace, characterization, a suspenseful plot and reels of arresting camera angles in vivid Technicolor,' according to *Newsweek*. When reviews are good, I believe in them. If I know they are bad, I don't bother to read them. Most critics don't like their work. They would much rather write movie scripts, be a director or producer, but, mostly, be a mogul. I'm surprised that more critics don't become moguls. They are well qualified for the job. Both have very little of the technical and artistic knowledge necessary to make pictures about anything.

8

Count the Hours

RKO 1953

Ben Bogeaus ran and possibly owned a piece of the studios where he made pictures. His career became suspect when he started to make cheap, uninteresting pictures. He called me in to discuss the possibility of directing a film and gave me an outline that, ultimately, after ninety changes of title, became *Count the Hours*. It was written by Karen de Wolfe. I read the outline and decided to invite Karen for lunch at Lucy's, opposite Paramount. I was working on a possible project at Paramount and was about five minutes late for our lunch date.

Karen, in her fifties, attractive both in looks and attire, was sipping a double martini. She had ordered one for me. I told her that we had a story conference with Bogeaus right after our lunch. I would probably fall asleep, though I wouldn't blame her work, just the double martini. After we ordered our food, I started asking her some questions.

ME: Would you mind filling me in on what your skimpy pages are about? (*She orders two more martinis, one for herself and one for me. I push my glass back to her.*)

ME: (*Sweetly*) With six martinis, this should be one hell of a story. The kind I like – sexy.

KAREN: You're sweet. Well, here it goes. I'll try to tell the story in shorthand. (*Drains her second martini.*) I like starting my stories with action, with fear. A middle-aged couple are murdered at their farmhouse. (*Gulps her drink.*) From this moment on, the terror mounts. The hired hand is arrested and, in protecting him, his wife throws his revolver into a nearby lake. A public defender is assigned to represent the hired hand and, in the process, alienates the town and almost loses his fiancée. The real killer is tracked down by the police, but they let him go free when they can't prove his guilt. The killer is finally caught when new evidence is revealed. End of shorthand. (*Sipping on her sixth martini.*) You may be relieved that the picture has now come to an end.

ME: That's the best and most exciting part of the picture.

KAREN: (*Finishing her drink*) That's the sweetest thing you could have said.

ME: Not at all. By the way, aren't you going to eat your lunch?

KAREN: When I work on stories like *Count the Hours*, I count my calories and drink, not eat.

ME: Do you feel up to telling Bogeaus your yarn?

KAREN: Pay the bill, and thanks for the lunch.

Although I kept dozing off, Karen, full of spirit and wide awake, told her story now in longhand. Bogeaus seemed to like it. He thanked her and saw her to the door. He crossed over to me and gave me a mogul stare.

BOGEAUS: Thank God we won't have story problems. She'll write a great script. But I have other problems. You must promise not to shoot over twelve days. I just don't have the money to shoot a longer picture.

ME: If you get me a good crew and don't hold me up waiting for sets to be completed, etc., I'll bring it in, come hell or high water, in twelve days.

BOGEAUS: You'll get everything you need.

ME: How about money?

BOGEAUS: (*Face tightening*) You'll get seventy-five hundred.

ME: Make it ten thousand, or no deal.
     (*I stand up to go.*)

BOGEAUS: You drive a hard bargain, but OK. If you go over twelve days, *no* ten thousand.

ME: When do we start shooting and with what cast and crew?

BOGEAUS: I'll see you tomorrow morning at nine and we'll settle everything.

I got up slowly, realizing something was wrong. I soon found out. Bogeaus didn't have enough money to shoot more than an hour. I was heading for happy days with the worst faker I had ever run into.

*

In the next two days, we settled all our cast and crew.

John Craven: Hired Hand
Teresa Wright: Hired Hand's Wife
MacDonald Carey: Public Defender
Dolores Moran: Carey's Fiancée
Adele Mara: Killer's Wife
Jack Elam: Killer

We were scheduled to shoot at the beginning of the following week. The script, which miraculously appeared, made sense; possibly because through the haze of endless martinis, Karen de Wolfe wrote with abandon.

The actors were all good. Jack Elam used to be an accountant for Hopalong Cassidy; he had thousands of metal coins showing Hopalong on his horse. He had also worked as an accountant for Bogeaus. When I read with Jack, I thought he was very good and, as Bogeaus didn't need an accountant and he wanted an actor, I insisted that Elam get the job. Bogeaus finally gave in because he wanted to start shooting and realized that he was wasting time arguing with me.

Teresa Wright and MacDonald Carey were fine actors. Dolores Moran, who was married to Bogeaus, had no problem with me. She was also a beautiful girl. Adele Mara pleasantly surprised me with her talent. The only person I had trouble with was Teresa Wright. It should have been obvious that, with the speed at which we were forced to shoot, everyone had to be ready to do their scenes at the drop of a hat. Not Miss Wright. She insisted on being treated as a star. I simply didn't have time to 'baby' her. I admired her acting ability, but thought she was plain stupid to try to play games with me. If you accept the assignment, don't bitch because it has to shoot at top speed.

We were working at Nasser Brothers Studio where Bogeaus had a beautiful office. I was called in to see him.

BOGEAUS: I had a house for you to shoot in, but lost it. Are you familiar with the new Joan Crawford set on Stage Three?
ME: Not really. I saw it when Revue was building it.
BOGEAUS: Get down there as fast as you can and figure out how to shoot the opening of the picture.
ME: But the Crawford set is new and chic. The sequence I'm shooting takes place in an old house in poor condition. It won't work.
BOGEAUS: Make it work. But remember, you can't remodel or redress the set.
ME: Any other stupid instructions?
BOGEAUS: Get your ass down there and start shooting.

I was sitting alone on the set trying to figure out how to shoot it so that it might make some sense. I didn't have a clue, as electricians and grips started to appear. A voice hailed me. It was Jennings Lang, a top executive in the industry.

LANG: What are you doing here, Don?

147

ME: I'm trying to figure out the impossible. This set doesn't make any sense with what I have to shoot.

LANG: You're not thinking of shooting our brand new set for Joan Crawford, are you?

ME: My instructions from Ben Bogeaus are to shoot it whether it works or not.

LANG: (Angrily) This set belongs to Revue and you can't use it.

ME: Don't cry on my shoulders. See Bogeaus, or the Nasser Brothers. Get me kicked off this beautiful set and you'll be my friend for ever.

Jennings, eyes glaring, spun round and hastened off the stage. We were kicked off the set. Bogeaus found another house, which he 'borrowed'. We somehow managed to finish the sequence. We were now on our ninth day of shooting. It was unbelievable, but we were also on our last day of shooting. John Alton, who had written a book entitled *Painting with Light*, literally did just that. He shot without any overhead rigging. He talked Bogeaus out of half the money he saved. When we entered our last location, the house that Bogeaus talked a friend into 'loaning' him, I laid out a shot with Alton. All the action stayed away from any windows with the sun shining through.

ALTON: Don, why are you shooting against walls so that we never see windows?

ME: And why are you 'pulling my leg'? You know better than I that if we photograph the windows with the sunlight streaming through, the background will look like a white sheet. (Sarcastically.) We don't have any jellies to put on the glass to kill the glare. Or do we, Mr 'Paint with Light'?

ALTON: (Smiling) No, we don't have any jellies and we can get by without them.

ME: Miracle man, be my guest . . . Shoot through the windows.

I left him to talk to Archie Dalzell, Alton's excellent camera operator, who also was the first operator I had ever worked with. I trusted his opinion, so I explained what Alton was doing and asked if it were possible.

DALZELL: As the camera operator, I can only answer that I don't know how it's possible to balance the shot. But remember the night shot, Don? He insisted that using flashlights crossing the lens with moving beams of light would work. Every other cameraman, including yours truly, *never* pointed a flashlight at the camera. We were afraid of flares.

ME: You're right. It looked great with flares, reflections, broken beams gleaming in the darkness.
DALZELL: He's a strange one. No rigging to enable him to shoot his lights down on whatever he wants to see. Everything shot from the floor. Take a chance with him. I'm still learning.

*

Up to now, the crew had been in excellent spirits and most co-operative. But a change had taken place. They never stopped talking and moved at three speeds: slow, dead slow and full stop. I swore at the crew and bitterly complained to my assistant director. He was very embarrassed.

ASSISTANT DIRECTOR: Mr Siegel, there's nothing I can do. Nobody's been paid a cent. That includes electricians, grips, camera crew, labourers and me.
ME: (*Yelling*) Kill the lights. Shut up everyone. Let's have an immediate meeting.
(*Cast and crew gather round me in an ugly mood.*)
ME: We can't just *not* shoot.
(*There are audible signs of dissension.*)
ME: Under no conditions will Mr Bogeaus ever get the last day's dailies, or even see them, until we get paid in full.
(*Everyone quietens down.*)
ME: Herb Aller, the Cinematographers' Union business manager, will safely put away our last day's dailies. Let me remind you again. Until all of us get our full salaries, no one but Aller will know where the film is.

Before anyone had a chance to argue, I yelled 'Hit the lights.' We finished all our shooting and met outside Aller's office at Consolidated Film Lab. I explained everything to Aller and handed him the reels of exposed negative. He told us he would talk to Bogeaus, who would see us within the hour on Stage 2 at Nasser Brothers Studio. He disappeared with the film.

Bogeaus looked as if he was wearing a death mask. We all settled on Stage 2. Bogeaus spoke from a small platform, shared by Aller. Bogeaus appeared nervous, but he pulled himself together.

BOGEAUS: I apologize to all of you for not getting paid. There is a simple, painful reason. The 'money people' lied to me, broke their promises and caused this dreadful trouble with you. Everything is now with a new group. I give you and Mr Aller my solemn word of honour that all of you will get paid, in full, tomorrow at four p.m. in my office. I'm sincerely sorry and want to thank all of you for working so hard and so well.

Everyone got paid, including me. I cut the film with James Leicester, my former montage editor. He is a whiz with the scissors. We ran our first cut for the RKO brass. They loved it. They paid Bogeaus many hundreds of thousands of dollars as immediate profit. There's a lesson there somewhere. Maybe it pays to be dishonest.

My only comment on the picture: years later, I saw *Count the Hours* on television – the nine days showed. I don't know why I expected to see a better film. Naiveté, I suppose.

In *Rediscovering the American Cinema*, William Routt and James Leahy wrote of *Count the Hours*: 'Made in nine days by one of the strongest directors of the underground, this film cannot be called a masterpiece by any stretch of the imagination. Yet, it is one of the most amazing examples of economy, of overcoming seemingly insurmountable obstacles, that the American Cinema can show.'

9

China Venture

Columbia 1953

Ben Kahane, second only to Harry Cohen at Columbia, discussed the possibility of my directing *China Venture*. The story took place in China during World War II. Tentative deals were made with Edmond O'Brien, Barry Sullivan and Jocelyn Brando. He asked if I liked the cast. I told him that O'Brien and Sullivan were excellent, but I wasn't familiar with Jocelyn Brando. If she was anything like her brother, she was tops in my book.

KAHANE: (*Handing me a script*) Read the script. Let me know what you
    think of it. If we agree, we'll set up a meeting with you and the
    producer, Anson Bond.
ME: Thanks, Mr Kahane, for the opportunity. I'm looking forward to
    working under the Kahane banner.

He smiled and graciously said he too looked forward to working with me.

As I took the script with me, I thought it rather strange that the producer, who had credit on the title page, hadn't been at the meeting with Mr Kahane. But I forgot all that nonsense when I read the script. It moved. That was a pleasant surprise.

In the story, an American patrol has orders to find a Japanese officer in the Chinese jungles. He is dying from a strange malady. It is absolutely critical to the success of the mission that the officer be found before the Japanese get their hands on him. Apparently, the officer has top-secret information on how to defeat the Americans and win the war.

The patrol is headed by Captain Matt Reardon (Edmond O'Brien). Commander Bert Thompson (Barry Sullivan), who speaks Japanese, has one mission: get the vital information from the Japanese officer and under no circumstances let him fall into the hands of the Japanese, even if it means killing him. Lieutenant Ellen Wilkins (Jocelyn Brando) is the nurse who helps Dr Masterson (Dayton Lummis) take care of the dying officer. The entire patrol consists of about ten more men.

The patrol fights its way through a raging storm, overcoming two Chinese patrols before meeting and dining with a crazed Chinese War Lord

(Leon Askin). The ending comes somewhat abruptly. Sullivan gets the essential information from the Japanese officer before he dies. He gives the top-secret information to O'Brien, who takes off immediately with the remnants of his small patrol. Sullivan covers for them and is killed. The picture actually ends on an atom-bomb explosion, leading us to believe that the dying Japanese officer knew about the atom bomb, though it is never spelled out.

I thought the ingredients for an exciting picture were there. Kahane was pleased with my reaction. When I want a job, I don't go into the script or story too deeply. I give the impression that I'm going to xerox it directly on to the screen. They always like that. Kahane got Anson Bond on the phone and told him that I was coming right over to meet him to discuss the story.

KAHANE: (*To Bond*) I don't want any delays on the picture. I considered your ideas and turned them down. Work everything out with Siegel.

His remarks puzzled me.

I met Anson in his office. He was wearing an expensive-looking suit, complete with vest. It was a hot day. I was dressed in lightweight trousers and a short-sleeved sports shirt. As usual, I was smoking my pipe. Anson had beads of sweat on his forehead and looked uncomfortable.

ME: I'm glad we finally met. I couldn't understand why you were not at the first and second meetings with Mr Kahane. Is there anything wrong?
BOND: Frankly, yes.
ME: Anything I can do about it?
BOND: (*Dead serious*) I had several other choices for a director. It looks like I lost.
ME: If I do a good job, won't that satisfy you?
BOND: Frankly, no.
ME: Have you seen any of my pictures?
BOND: No. I have no desire to see any of them.
       (*He is beginning to get under my skin.*)
ME: Well, for that matter, I have not the slightest idea what you've produced, if anything.
BOND: I haven't done much, but at least I liked the people I was associated with.
ME: The fact that we've never seen each other before doesn't mean that we can't work well together.
BOND: I think it does.

(*I get up and start pacing about his office. Anson must be crazy or sick.*)

ME: Obviously, if Mr Kahane wants me to direct, I don't see how you're going to stop it. In fact, you can't.

BOND: I'll check it out with my attorney. My contract is pretty tight.

By now, I didn't care what I said to Anson. The name Anson Bond sounded like a wholesale clothier. He was in his late thirties, looked soft and definitely carried around too much weight.

ME: Just out of vulgar curiosity, what in the hell have I done to you?

BOND: Nothing.

(*I lean over his desk.*)

ME: Well then, tell me what you don't like about me.

BOND: It's not you, it's your pipe.

(*I fall into the nearest chair.*)

ME: You mean that the only reason you don't want me to direct your picture is because I smoke a pipe?

BOND: I find it noisome and sickening.

ME: I'll make a deal with you. I'll never smoke in your office, or wherever we eat.

BOND: (*Beaming*) That's very decent of you, Don.

ME: However, I do reserve the right to smoke in my office, or on the set, or location.

BOND: (*Shaking my hand*) It's a deal.

ME: Great.

(*I knock out the ashes from my pipe in an empty waste basket and stick the pipe in my shirt pocket.*)

ME: I think the script needs a polish. I'd like to suggest an excellent constructionist – Richard Collins. He doesn't cost an arm and a leg; plus the fact that he's fast, pleasant and doesn't smoke anything.

BOND: I'll try to get him to pick up a script today.

ME: While you're doing that, I hope I have your permission to visit the john. See you later, with or without your OK.

I hustled out of his office on a mission that was of extreme importance to me. Anson seemed amused as he picked up the phone.

*

Anson hired Richard Collins. The three of us worked hard on the script. In the meantime, the art director, Edward Llou, agreed with me that we should build the damndest, impenetrable jungle on the largest stage we could find. The stage we ultimately picked, on the Columbia lot in the San

Fernando Valley, was a bit rickety. I intended to use torrential downpours, which might float the stage away. We decided to tell no one how I meant to shoot the jungle. I knew I'd get along all right with Special Effects: they were as nutty as I.

The studio didn't mind if I had a reading of the script at my house, just as long as nobody went on salary. This meant I had to call all the main protagonists on the phone and explain that I wanted a reading at my house, not a rehearsal. This way, we would get to know each other and bring up anything in the script that they didn't understand or like. Ideas for changes were most welcome. I didn't promise I'd make the changes unless I thought it improved the scene. It might spark me into new channels of thought. Of course, they'd have to join our reading group without pay. That was the mandatory studio policy. Everyone always agreed to do it, realizing that it was primarily for their own good and the picture benefited greatly. I had never been turned down, until I ran into an actor I greatly admired – Edmond O'Brien. He astounded me because I knew he took his work seriously.

ME: Eddie, why can't you show up?

O'BRIEN: I'm tired, Don. I just finished a tough picture.

ME: The cast will certainly appreciate your co-operation.

O'BRIEN: My throat's been bothering me.

ME: May I send a doctor to treat you?

O'BRIEN: My brother's a doctor. He's taking care of me.

ME: I know you and Viveca don't like each other ever since you didn't get along with her in the play *I've Got Sixpence*. I've managed to steer clear of the squabbling.

O'BRIEN: What the hell's the matter with you? What's *I've Got Sixpence* got to do with *China Venture*?

ME: Can you get it through your dumb *mick* head that if you don't come to the reading, I'll have to read your part? There's no one even close to my inadequacy. The cast and I will love you.

O'BRIEN: I'm sorry, Don. I can't make it.

He hung up. I was surprised and felt let down. I decided O'Brien was full of guile, perfidy and sham. I lost the respect I had for him. Oh well, the sun's shining and who knows – maybe I'll read O'Brien's part so well that I'll replace him with me.

When we started the picture on our jungle set, I noticed that O'Brien seemed clumsy. He'd make his way climbing over fallen trees, or hacking through deep vines and foliage with undue caution. By good fortune, I gave him certain directions, which he appeared to appreciate. The tension between us eased off. On another day, a huge tree which had fallen to the ground blocked our group. Everyone but Eddie climbed and scrambled on to the tree. On the other side, I had the grips build a small ladder, which was nailed to the lower side of the tree trunk. This enabled Eddie to grab the ladder and pull himself on top. Once on top of the trunk, they were fired on by Chinese snipers. They were supposed to 'hit the deck' and fire up at the snipers on all sides, high in the trees. Some of our patrol threw themselves to the ground and some got hit. Ultimately, the snipers were hit and killed by their falls. I couldn't believe that a tough street-fighter and athlete like Eddie was so inept. After lengthy rehearsals, we finally got a master shot. Later, I used five cameras to cover the complete action.

In order to continue shooting with Eddie, I decided to take away some of the difficult physical things that he would be called upon to do. I rewrote several sequences, with Sullivan and others in the patrol doing them. The next day, I went over the new pages with Eddie. He immediately yelled in desperation for 'Charley'. When Charley came on the run, Eddie broke down.

O'BRIEN: Don, I can't see. That's why I have Charley read the lines to me each day, and I memorize them. The reason I didn't go to your reading was because the cataracts in both eyes make it impossible for me to see. I knew if you told the studio about my condition, I was dead. I'm sorry, Don.
(*I put my arm around him.*)
ME: Everything will work out fine. These new pages have taken out the difficult physical actions that you previously were called upon to do.
(*Tears appear in his eyes.*)
ME: You get with Charley and work with him.

He thanked me and walked off with Charley. I felt terrible about the whole situation. I realized how gutsy Eddie was. From that moment on, we became the best of friends. I hope I learned the important lesson not to leap to false conclusions.

*

The meeting with the War Lord presented certain difficulties. The patrol sits down inside an elaborate tent, and unless one arranged the actors in a U-shape with the War Lord centred and the others seated so as *not* to surround him, one was going to have trouble. If you have no open U-space, the left to right, right to left gets all screwed up. Imagine a table with four people seated, two at opposite ends of the table and two sitting opposite each other in the middle of the table, so there is no empty space. You may have to shoot certain exchanges of dialogue and looks between the actors two ways: left to right, and right to left. This is a waste of time and film, which costs money.

However, I did run into trouble. The Chinese food was excellent. Everyone, including the War Lord, but especially O'Brien, started to eat during rehearsals. I warned them all *not* to eat until we were making a take. My words of caution fell on the deaf ears of O'Brien. We had a number of rehearsals where he over-indulged himself. As the day wore on, he ate less and less during the actual takes. Remember, he had to match the amount of food he had established in the first printed take. He also had to match the manner in which he ate. He started to look green, got up quickly and ran to his trailer, which served as his dressing room, and threw up all over the place. He cleaned himself up and was forced to eat again. I was reminded of Bavarians in Munich drinking too much beer. They would go out in the street, put their fingers in their mouth and vomit. Then they would return to the bar and start drinking again. Disgusting? Yes. But in O'Brien's case it was necessary, or we wouldn't get the shot. He told me years later that he still had trouble eating Chinese food.

*

Production people, headed by Jack Fier, rushed over to the set when they heard of the amount of water I was using for the torrential downpours. I thought it looked good and said so.

FIER: I don't give a shit how it looks to you; the stage will start floating and collapse.
ME: It's too late now. We have to match it. Anyway, we're almost finished.
FIER: I'll tell you this, wise guy: if the stage floats away, you'll float out of this studio with it.
ME: (*Addressing all production executives*) Get off the set immediately! If the stage crashes down, I don't want to kill you. Let's roll 'em!

The complainers hastily left the stage, screaming dire threats. We continued with the wild rain the rest of the day. The film looked great when I saw the dailies. I thanked the special-effects men, but warned them no more heavy rain.

The picture, which I thought was pretty good, attracted no attention whatsoever. It was a typical Siegel picture of the time. You had to catch it the first day at your neighbourhood theatre, or it would be gone, only to arise years later in a mutilated form, squashed in a television box.

10

Riot in Cell Block 11

Allied Artists 1954

Walter Wanger was dedicated to the making of a prison picture. He knew about the inequities of prison life, the unfairness, the cruelties. He had been incarcerated at an honour camp for shooting at the genitals of an agent who represented his wife, the actress Joan Bennett. He suspected them of having a continuing affair, and when he realized that they were indeed seeing each other, he put an immediate stop to it. Walter insisted on paying the penalty by admitting his guilt.

Wanger met me in his office at Allied Artists. We discussed my directing a prison picture entitled 'Riot'. I was confused, as I expected it would be something concerning honour camps, which I always thought didn't have riots. He handed me a first-draft script, written by Richard Collins.

WANGER: Can you read the script right now if I put you in the next office?

ME: I like to read a script the first time to enjoy it. From then on, I read it critically and hopefully constructively – not destructively. So, unless you mind, I'd rather see you tomorrow, at your convenience.

WANGER: (*Thinking a moment*) I would prefer seeing you today because the moguls here at Allied Artists want to start shooting yesterday.

ME: That's a common disease at all studios. The important thing is *not* how I read the script, but if you're pleased with what I have to say. I'll see you as soon as I finish reading it. It gives me a good alibi. Obviously, I won't have enough time to read the script properly.

Wanger laughed as he pointed to a door on his left. I felt good, leaving him with a smile. I returned in a couple of hours. I had time at least to think about the project. I'm sure he understood that. Wanger sounded well-educated, with a sense of humour.

WANGER: (*Touch of sarcasm*) Did you make all your notes?

ME: I didn't write anything. It's all in my head ready to spill out.

WANGER: Tell me what you liked and what you didn't like.

ME: Well, I don't like the moguls wanting it yesterday. Seriously, the Collins script is very good. He obviously knows a great deal about penology. It's really a semi-documentary. No women at all, no crooked district attorneys. The prisoners stand for better conditions. Their demands make sense. The Warden is honest. Believe me, that's unusual. He listens to the prisoners' demands. He's trying to settle this dangerous dispute as fairly as possible. He's a man I'm rooting for.

WANGER: What do you think of the various prisoners?

ME: Dunn, the leader of the riot, is fantastic. He's tough, relentless and in complete control of the riot.

WANGER: We'll have to find a terrific actor to play the role.

ME: You make it sound like I'm going to do the picture.

WANGER: I'll let you in on a little secret. You're going to do the picture.

ME: I never argue with the producer.

WANGER: I've been told you're feisty. I expect trouble because you don't like producers.

ME: Depends on the producer. You look and sound pretty good to me.

WANGER: Do you mind coming in tomorrow to have a chat with the writer? I've an appointment I can't break.

ME: I've worked with Dick before. He's perfect casting for this picture. Will you be kind enough to have your secretary set it up?
(*Wanger stands up offering his hand.*)

WANGER: Welcome aboard. Everything will be taken care of. By the way, who is your agent?
(*We shake hands.*)

ME: Ingo Preminger. I'm not doing this picture for the money. Nor am I doing it for the executives. I should say I'm doing it for you. That's partially true. But the complete story is I'm doing it for myself.

WANGER: Drive safely home and re-read the script. When you start working with Dick, I want the best damn script possible, so you can make the best prison picture ever. I don't like being second best in anything.

I agreed and left.

Next day I met Richard Collins in his office.

ME: There's no question about the high quality of your writing. But Wanger talked to me yesterday about doing the best prison picture ever. Your attack on the main protagonists is too set and ordinary.

DICK: The prisoners are full of terror and represent violence and death to the guards, the Warden and any prisoner who doesn't join in on the riot.

ME: All true and well executed. But take the character of Carnie, who is a psycho who runs amuck. On the other hand, he may think in conventional terms. Indeed, he may be a conformist – an ordinary person. He may have a sense of humour. When he looks into a mirror, he, just like us, rarely sees the truth. He and you and I see a misunderstood man. To wrap it up, I think crazed prisoners like to eat, go to the toilet, snore when they sleep, etc. That's why I want the audience to see these rough toughs occasionally as gentle souls.

DICK: I don't want to fool the audience.

ME: Just surprise them. Spark them into thinking.

DICK: I'm beginning to understand Mr Wanger. He wants to turn the world upside down.

ME: Hasn't he?

DICK: Touché. I'll take a cock-eyed approach to what I thought was a semi-documentary.

ME: Look in the mirror. Write the truth as you see it, which reminds me, I'd like to see the pages before Wanger.

DICK: What if he demands to read them first?

ME: Dicky Bird, I'll tell him you've decided that you want me to see them first.

DICK: *(Drily)* Thank you, sir.

I made a quick exit before he had a chance to change his mind.

*

My desk was so full of books, pamphlets, periodicals that Wanger gave me, that if I had read them all I would *still* be reading about the ramifications of penology. Fortunately, Walter liked what Dick was writing. He read the pages of the revised script after I had worked on it with Dick, which proved that Walter knew what he was doing. He decided on a welcome change of pace: he wanted to take me to Alcatraz, San Quentin and Folsom prisons. Poor Dick was left behind to continue writing.

We arrived at Alcatraz on a small boat that carried the prisoners to the island, but only rarely back to the docks of San Francisco. I was excited at the opportunity to see everything at Alcatraz. The California State Board of Corrections had given orders that we were to see anything we desired. Before we were taken up the steep grades to have lunch with the Warden, we had to pass through an outside metal-detector. Two prison guards watched as Walter breezed through. As I strode through, a loud bell started to ring. Not until my heart had skipped two beats did it stop, as my body cleared it.

WANGER: (*To guards*) He's undoubtedly a felon, heavily armed.
FIRST GUARD: Empty your pockets of change, nail-clippers, or
    anything else you might be carrying. Now, try it again.
    (*The instant I enter, the bell rings. As I step through, it stops. I am
    embarrassed and puzzled. Walter starts to laugh.*)
WANGER: I'll eat with Warden Swope. You can stay here, if the guards
    let you.
SECOND GUARD: May I see your glasses?
    (*I hand him my sunglasses, which I hadn't realized I am wearing.
    He examines them closely.*)
SECOND GUARD: Try it once more.
    (*Again, I go through the detector: only this time, thank God, the
    bell doesn't ring.*)
ME: (*Smiling weakly at Walter*) You've had more experience.

Warden Swope treated us as honoured guests in his large private dining room. The view of San Francisco made that extraordinary city even more beautiful. The Warden carefully pointed out that the prisoners who served us were all murderers. When Walter asked, 'Why?' the Warden calmly declared that these men were the best-behaved prisoners at Alcatraz – perhaps because they knew they were there for life, whereas prisoners with lesser sentences were more alert to trying to figure out how to escape. We thanked him and his 'staff' for the excellent food and the superb view. We saw everything at Alcatraz, most of it depressing. I felt that it would be extremely difficult to stage a riot there. I doubted that we'd ever get permission to stage one. I suggested we see San Quentin.

San Quentin was much better for shooting than Alcatraz. There were, however, the usual negatives. The prison was terribly overcrowded. How the guards would protect us during the riot was beyond me. Wanger was all for pushing on to Folsom, to which I heartily agreed.

A miracle happened at Folsom. Deputy Warden Ryan showed us a complete, huge two-tier cell block. So what? It was completely empty with solid iron doors. They had no intention of ever using it. It was absolutely perfect for our picture. No one could get in or out to bother us.

We purposely made no attempt to see Warden Heinze, who ran Folsom with a very firm hand. We didn't want to chance a turn-down. Wanger would have further talks with the California State Board of Corrections. He would let the studio production people make all the deals.

ME: I congratulate you, sir. In my wildest imagination, I never dreamed I'd have a huge set perfect for the picture.
WANGER: Don, we'll get out of here as fast as we can. Back at Allied Artists, we can start immediate casting. Get your crew set and complete the script with Dick. Let's get on the plane and drink a toast to the best prison picture ever made.
ME: God bless Folsom. I must be going crazy. I believe every word you say.

*

The casting started immediately. We agreed we didn't need a star for the main role of Dunn. We saw at least 100 candidates, each one meaner than the next. Most of the actors could do it, looked and talked like the leader of a riot, but Walter and I felt no great excitement.

Then a man entered our casting session. His gaunt face showed poignancy. He was lean and tough. His voice, as he expressed deep feelings about the script and prisons in general, sounded guttural and gravelly. We discovered that he was the fourth most decorated soldier in US history. He had killed hundreds of men during World War II. But most importantly, when I read with him I was thrilled and excited. He had a passionate belief in the rights of the prisoners.

WANGER: You're the director. You have to work with Neville Brand. If you want him, you've got him.
ME: I'm not saying he's the only pebble on the beach. I thank you for trusting me and believing in Brand. Excuse me, but I've got to tell him the good news.

Neville was pacing up and down when I entered the office. I didn't beat around the bush.

ME: Congratulations. (*We shake hands.*) I've never had more belief in anyone's talent. You are, to put it mildly, sensational. Mr Wanger feels exactly like I do.
(*Neville's eyes glisten with relief and appreciation.*)
BRAND: There's only one way to thank you. I'm going to play the part of Dunn . . .

(*His voice breaks.*) Shit – I am Dunn.

ME: If you need anything, Dunn, sing out. I feel so damn lucky to have
  gotten you.

(*He embraces me, lifting me off my feet.*)

BRAND: This is the happiest moment of my life.

The next bit of casting was the part of the psycho killer Carnie. He was
Dunn's second-in-command. When we finally saw Leo Gordon, a frightening man both physically and mentally, Walter flipped out, as did I. After
listening to him read, we instantly gave him the part. That afternoon, Leo
came to see me in my office. He looked haggard and worried.

GORDON: I don't want to let you guys down. I can't accept the part.

ME: (*Angrily*) I know you're paranoid, nuts and stupid. What pit have
  you buried yourself in?

GORDON: I'm an ex-con. Served five years in San Quentin for first-
  degree robbery. I was shot in my guts by the arresting officers. I
  had pulled my gun, but didn't fire it.

ME: Let us worry about getting the officials to let you work. Mr
  Wanger, who's also a con, will get the California State Board of
  Corrections to help us. Learn your part. You're going to get it.

I had a long talk with Walter. He was furious. Walter had quite a temper,
but I kind of cooled him off.

ME: If you can't give a man a second chance, we shouldn't make the
  picture. If we can get Leo to remain on the picture, it makes
  shooting 'Riot' worthwhile and meaningful.

WANGER: (*Irritated*) All right, all right. Let's get on with the casting.
  What about the Warden?

ME: Emile Meyer looks the part and fits the character.

WANGER: I know Emile. A good choice. Have him see me. I'll hire him.
  I saw Frank Faylen for the State Mediator. Remember, he rejects
  the demands of the prisoners.

ME: He's a fine actor. Hire him. The rest of the cast presents no
  problems. I suggest that I annoy Dick and get more pages.

WANGER: Do that. Remember, we were supposed to get everything
  done yesterday.

I saw Dick and read all the pages he had written. I had told him about our
fabulous, massive 'set'; he couldn't believe our incredible luck.

ME: What I want to do, script in hand, is lay out how I'm going to
  shoot.

COLLINS: Good idea, but I'm changing the title. When the prisoners, headed by Dunn, call the Security Central Control, they can't simply yell 'Riot.' The guards won't know where the riot is. It's necessary to identify the cell block where the riot is taking place. I'm identifying the place as 'Riot in Cell Block 11'. Do you like it?

ME: On a scale of one to ten, you're batting eleven. The way you're doing it now, the security people, guards if you prefer, know exactly where the riot is taking place. *Riot in Cell Block 11* has a nice ring to it. Do you suppose Mr Wanger will approve?

COLLINS: He may change the number of the cell block, but he can't simply use the one word title 'Riot'.

ME: When I finish 'walking' the script at Folsom, get out a revised script proudly titled *Riot in Cell Block 11*.

The phone rang. Walter wanted to see me. I waved 'so long' and was off.

*

On the wall behind Walter was a large poster naming all the films he had produced. I studied them while he was writing. Walter, a sturdy, white-haired man, had a great deal of experience. He held many executive posts with various studios, as well as making his own films. He produced such films as *Queen Christina*, *You Only Live Once*, *Algiers*, *Stagecoach*, *Foreign Correspondent*, *The Trail of the Lonesome Pine*, *The Long Voyage Home*, *Salome Where She Danced*, *Scarlet Street*, *Joan of Arc* and *Tulsa*. No wonder I had great respect for him. He looked up and stopped writing.

WANGER: Sorry to keep you waiting. I need a favour. I'd like you to use as an assistant a young man, Sam Peckinpah. His family has a great deal of influence with Pat Brown, the Attorney General of California.

ME: Does he belong to any guild or unions? Has he had any experience?

WANGER: (*Sighing*) No and no, and it's not necessary. Use him as your personal assistant. I'll get him to your office after two. OK?

ME: I'm fully cognizant of the importance of getting as much help as we can, but I simply do not have the time to conduct a seminar in how to direct pictures. For one thing, I'm not sure I know how. But before you blow your stack, I'll see him and try to figure some way to make it work.

Sam Peckinpah, a bright young whippersnapper, thin as a rail, was waiting for me in my outer office. He lept to his feet as I told him to follow me into my office. He stood at attention, so I suggested he relax in one of the chairs beside my desk.

ME: I know you don't have any experience. What do you expect to do?
PECKINPAH: I want to work for you.
ME: Doing what, Sam?
PECKINPAH: Anything.

I found out that he had studied film-making at the University of Southern California. I liked his wit, charm and ambition. I told him I had never had a 'gopher' before.

PECKINPAH: What's a 'gopher', sir?
ME: Oh, someone who 'goes for' anything and everything: coffee, paperclips, girls . . . you name it.
    (*Sam grins his crooked little smile.*)
PECKINPAH: Girls! That's the job for me, sir.

*

The entire crew met at Folsom. We all squeezed into Warden Heinze's office. The Warden, a perpetual frown on his face, was scribbling on a pad. I was introduced as the director. He didn't look up.

WARDEN HEINZE: (*Rough voice*) How long you gonna be at Folsom?
ME: Sixteen shooting days, sir.
    (*For the first time, he looks up at me.*)
HEINZE: You're full of shit.
ME: (*Replying quickly*) You may have a point there; but if we get your co-operation, we'll finish the picture in sixteen days.

The Warden went through the rest of the crew like a dose of salts. Obviously he didn't like any of us. Standing in front of the Warden's desk was the lowest man on the totem pole: Sam Peckinpah. When Sam was introduced, the Warden looked up quickly.

HEINZE: Are you related to the Peckinpahs in Fresno?
PECKINPAH: (*Drawing himself up proudly*) Yes, sir. They're my family.
HEINZE: Are they judges and lawyers?
PECKINPAH: Yes, sir.
HEINZE: You ever been on the Peckinpah range of mountains?
PECKINPAH: I've hunted there since I was a kid.
    (*The Warden does an extraordinary thing: he stands up, sticks his hand out and smiles.*)
HEINZE: It's a pleasure meeting you, Mr Peckinpah.
    (*Inasmuch as he has met all of us, he now walks around the*

table, puts his hand on Sam's shoulder and walks with him to the door.)

HEINZE: If you run into any trouble, or have need of any information, be sure to see me, personally.

He left the room without so much as a glance at the rest of us. We were stunned and surprised. It was our first exposure to the 'Peckinpah mystique'. I decided to put it to immediate test.

ME: Sam, I need twenty-five, hard-bitten, ugly, tough men to be the core of the prisoners we'll use every day. They must look like real prisoners. 'Gopher' them.
SAM: (*Instantly*) I'll have them here the first thing in the morning.

The next morning, early, there they were. A more dissolute group I had never seen. They made the regular Folsom prisoners look like sissies.

By now, Dick was finishing his third revised final, tailored to the actual locations at Folsom. The script was officially titled *Riot in Cell Block 11*, which Walter approved. The picture was entirely cast. No stars – just damn good actors who fit their parts.

When Warden Heinze heard about the ex-con, Leo Gordon, he turned him down flatly. But Wanger put up strong resistance. He pointed out that the California State Board of Corrections unanimously agreed that Gordon should be given a second chance and that since getting out of San Quentin he had worked industriously as an actor and as a writer.

HEINZE: (*Making up his mind*) OK, Mr Wanger. As you know, at a maximum-security prison we can't afford to take chances. Each day Gordon reports to work, he'll be admitted through a side gate. Guards will strip and search him, both on entering and leaving.
WANGER: I shall report back to the Board of Corrections to thank you for your kind co-operation. I greatly appreciate it.

*

As we shot our cast with other prisoners and guards walking back from the yard to Cell Block 11, the prisoners in other blocks greeted us with boos, hisses, foul language and yells of derision. Some of the regular guards tried to stop them. I told them it was exactly what I wanted to happen. They looked at me as though I were crazy. They ignored the prisoners, although they didn't like, or approve the din.

Once we got inside our 'home', Cell Block 11, we started shooting the actual riot. It was scary, but exciting. Neville Brand acted like a man possessed, a man born to lead the riot. Several actor guards were beaten up and thrown in cells. Leo Gordon was truly a madman. Each cell was stripped; mattresses, beds were thrown from the second tier to the floor below. I had difficulty in making myself heard and obeyed. Finally, Brand gets security headquarters on the phone.

BRAND: (*Yelling into phone*) Riot in Cell Block 11!

It was chilling. Later, when Brand screamed the prisoners' demands to the Warden and to the State Mediator, Frank Faylen, all hell broke loose when Faylen rejected their demands. In the mêlée that followed, Faylen got hurt.

The next day, units of the State Militia tried to subdue the prisoners. By now, I didn't know our hired prisoners from the real prisoners. I was standing on a high parallel when a large group of prisoners burst into the yard and tried to overturn the parallel. With all our cameras rolling, we got realistic, violent, documentary material. The riot ultimately subsides. The Warden agrees, when the hostages (guards and a few prisoners) are released, to the terms demanded, such as better food, the end of the guards

11 *Riot in Cell Block 11*: Leo Gordon and Neville Brand

166

mistreating them, and no more being thrown naked into the hole for weeks at a time.

Brand was magnificent in his fervour. Every prisoner wildly celebrates. They have won! But, unfortunately, Brand is double-crossed. The Warden is helpless. Officialdom rules the day. Brand has an extra thirty years added to his sentence. Gordon is sent to a prison for the criminally insane.

*

When we ran the film for the top executives, Walter was seated in the last row between Dick Collins and myself, on the aisle. When the picture was over and the lights came on, the theatre was absolutely silent. As they walked past us, someone sympathetically pressed my shoulder.

ME: (*To Walter and Dick*) I guess we're dead.
WANGER: There won't be one change. When *Riot in Cell Block 11* is released, they'll fall all over themselves taking credit.

I think it is one of my best pictures. A lot of credit must go to Walter Wanger, Richard Collins, the crew and an amazing cast, especially Neville Brand.

12   *Riot in Cell Block 11*: Walter Wanger and Don Siegel at Folsom prison

II

Private Hell 36

Filmakers 1954

I was vacationing in Phoenix, Arizona, enjoying the fruits of success. *Riot in Cell Block 11* was well received by the critics, moguls and the public at large. My fanmail increased enormously, from zero to hundreds of letters. One letter particularly interested me. It was from Ida Lupino. She wanted to see me at my earliest convenience. Would I telephone her if her coming to Phoenix would upset my 'social' life. The friends with whom I was staying had no extra room. I would get Ida a suite at the Biltmore Hotel, which was near where I was staying.

She arrived the next day. I was flattered that, after seeing *Riot in Cell Block 11*, she wanted me to direct her next picture, *Private Hell 36*, for her company Filmakers. I teased her that just because I had used the number eleven in my title, she was using thirty-six in hers. I respected her work as a director, especially *The Bigamist* and *The Hitchhiker*. I knew I was a goner, as I can never say 'no' to anyone who likes me and my work.

LUPINO: (*Fixing two vodka and sodas*) Just think, Don, we'll be the only two directors who can openly love each other.
(*We click our glasses and drink.*)
ME: That suits me fine, but will I be able to direct while you act and produce?
LUPINO: How can we fail with a cast that includes me, Howard Duff, Steve Cochran, Dorothy Malone and Dean Jagger? In addition, Collier Young and I are doing the screenplay. Collier is the producer.

I couldn't help laughing. When she asked what I was giggling about, I told her the odds were against me.

LUPINO: What in the world are you mumbling about?
ME: *Private Hell 36* is a family picture.
LUPINO: I don't follow you. There's a great deal of violence and sex in the picture.

ME: I like that, but it's not what I was referring to. Before I explain myself, would you be kind enough to give me a capsule idea of what the picture's about?

Picking up her cue like the pro she was, Ida told me a brief outline. There was violence and sex galore. It was certainly not a family picture, but my rebuttal would come later.

In the story, Duff and Cochran, following a lead on some stolen money, break up a burglary. They meet a nightclub hostess, Ida Lupino, who on being questioned by the two detectives finally admits she can identify the man who has the money. When she does, there is a car chase and the man is killed. In the car, a suitcase filled with money is found. Cochran grabs a number of money packets and hurries off to call for help, despite Duff's protests. Jagger, the Police Captain, remains silent on his suspicions. A penitent Duff watches Cochran hide the money in a trailer, number 36. Lupino learns from Cochran that she'll get the money she wants and Cochran too. Guilt-ridden Duff scares his wife, Dorothy Malone, by getting drunk. Duff threatens Cochran to return the money or he'll do it. Cochran tries to kill Duff, who is saved by Jagger killing Cochran.

LUPINO: Well, what do you think?

ME: It's impossible to tell until one reads the script. What does bother me (*taking a long swig*) is that it's a family picture.

LUPINO: (*A bit annoyed*) You're crazy.

ME: Indisputable proof. You and Duff, the romantic leads, are Mr and Mrs in private life; yet, in the picture, you both make love to different people. A beautiful family set-up. To further my case, a strange sort of consanguinity takes place. The script is to be written by you and Collier Young; the picture to be produced by Young; you are still partners in Filmakers; Young is your next-to-last husband. Now, what happens when, in the picture, you make love to Cochran? And pray tell, what part of the family does the poor tired director play?

LUPINO: Play your cards right. There's no telling what may happen to the 'family'.

I agreed to make the picture. I never got a straight answer about when the script would be completed, or, for that matter, how far along with it Ida and Collier were. I was to report as soon as possible, so I could start preparing the picture. Ida kissed me goodbye. She assured me that making the picture would be a 'ball'.

*

When I showed up and read about forty pages, I began to feel uncomfortable. They wanted me to start shooting as soon as possible. I wanted to start not only when they were finished with the script, but after I had had a chance to add my input. Ida and Collier were great con artists. They struck me as pretentious in thinking they were artists. They felt they could wing their way through a picture without rehearsals and shoot with great speed.

When we started the actual shooting, the fact that the cast was knowledgeable and talented helped me a great deal. Then, lo and behold, the producer would appear sipping a glass of vodka over ice. He drank vodka under the mistaken idea that one's breath did not smell of liquor. This opened the gates to the rest of the cast to start drinking vodka and ice, with the exception of Dean Jagger, who not only disapproved of drinking on the set, but didn't get along with the rest of the cast. Dean and I became the best of friends.

Ida started drinking the non-halitosis vodka, closely followed by Duff and Cochran. The 'family' turned against me and the liquor helped their cause. I lost my vantage ground. On one occasion, I planned a way to shoot a sequence in which Cochran opened his hotel door to reveal the closest two-shot possible of Ida and Cochran. I set this shot first. Then, when Ida walked down the corridor and knocked on Cochran's door, I panned Ida to the exact spot where Cochran opens the door. They were already in the closest two-shot possible. It was not necessary to dolly, only to pan with Ida. By shooting this way, I was able to make the sequence in one take. Or so I mistakenly thought.

LUPINO: (*Acidly*) Aren't you going to break up the shot?

ME: No, Ida, the two-shot couldn't be closer.

LUPINO: If you make two over-the-shoulder shots, you'd at least see my two eyes and Steve's two eyes.

ME: Shooting it the way I did, I was able to finish the entire sequence in one shot.

LUPINO: (*Tension mounting*) I don't give a damn about your one shot. I want my two eyes seen.

ME: And I don't give a damn about your two eyes.

I left the set to line up a new sequence. I realized that I was being stupid, but the die was cast. Ida had every right to ask for the extra over-the-shoulder shots; not necessarily because she was right, nor because she was the star, or the writer, or the owner of the company making the picture; but because she was a fine actress and director. Out of consideration and courtesy, I should have graciously made the shots she wanted. But I was stupid and angry, not capable of thinking straight.

*

Out of continuity, I was making the last shot of the picture. The cameraman, Burnett Guffey, and I were riding a huge boom high in the sky. We had been shooting throughout the night and had just pulled away from a close shot of Cochran's dead body, with Duff and Jagger standing looking down at him. A row erupted over the *raison d'être* of the shot I was lining up: Ida and Collier insisted on intellectual explanations of what I was doing. The air, heavy with accusations and overladen with a sickening odour of vodka, was my excuse to leap aboard the boom and escape by swooping up high in the air. I refused to discuss anything until they explained, in simple language, what they were trying to say in their inexplicable script. Jagger broke in with a loud, angry voice.

JAGGER: The script is meaningless. Why don't you get off Don's back and let him work?

Cochran, presumed dead, had passed out, for which I thanked him. Up in the sky, alone with Guffey, it was peaceful.

GUFFEY: Why argue with them? They make no sense. The picture is a mess. Why not do it their way, if you can figure it out?
ME: You mean you wouldn't fight them even though you know they're dead wrong?
GUFFEY: Hell no!
ME: Drop me to the ground.

Guffey had the grips lower the boom to the ground. I waited patiently to climb off until my weight was balanced with lead weights; if I had got off any sooner the boom would have shot up in the air. Without disturbing Cochran, I addressed the rest of them.

ME: (*Calmly and lucidly*) It's apparent that you don't like what I've been doing. So, Miss Lupino, Mr Young, Mr Duff, lay out the shot for me. I'll do exactly what you want.

A shocked stillness resulted. Finally, Ida and Young begged me to continue shooting. I couldn't believe my ears. I whirled around and got back on the boom.

ME: We will be ready to shoot in five minutes. Assume your positions and, please, don't disturb Mr Cochran. (*Whispering to Guffey.*) Are you pleased?

GUFFEY: Very, very pleased.

Finally, I apologized to Ida for my rudeness in not shooting a couple of over-the-shoulder shots in the earlier scene: 'It's not a question of who was right. Common courtesy demanded that I pleasantly acquiesce to your request. I'd like to make the shots before some idiot tears down the set.' She thanked me.

That afternoon, a large movieola was wheeled on to the stage. Ida and Steve watched the shot I had made. It was simple to make the additions Ida wanted. Steve made no comment. Suddenly, Ida noticed something in the tight two-shot.

IDA: I must show this to Guffey. I think it could be better lit.
    (*She fetches Guffey and has him look at the film.*)
GUFFEY: There's no problem with the over-the-shoulder shot.
IDA: I wonder if you would mind re-shooting the tight two-shot.
GUFFEY: Whatever for?
IDA: I believe I could look better.
GUFFEY: (*His face reddening with anger*) As far as I'm concerned, you
    couldn't look any better. I'm certainly not re-shooting it.
    (*He exits quickly, but I am hard on his heels and catch up with
    him. I grab him and spin him around to face me.*)
ME: Do you remember on the boom your saying, 'Why argue with
    them?' 'Why not do it their way?'
GUFFEY: (*Icy cold*) Let go of me.
ME: And when you said, 'Very, very pleased.'
    (*He tears himself from my grasp and rushes around a corner.*)
ME: (*Laughing*) It all depends on who it's happening to, Guffey boy!

I enjoyed shooting the added scenes. Guffey spoke to no one. I guess that Walter Wanger spoiled me. I had complete control on *Riot in Cell Block 11*; I was encouraged to shoot freely and with confidence. On *Private Hell 36*, every move was decision time. They'd argue, vindicate, sound unreasonable and be illogical. I must be to blame. I should have joined the 'family'. Instead, I fought them. What I most regret is that the picture did not come off. The director must be chastised. I liked Ida personally and admired her talent. We just couldn't communicate.

12

An Annapolis Story

Allied Artists 1955

Apparently, anything can be done if the studio wishes to do it. When I came to direct *An Annapolis Story* for Allied Artists, I must confess to being startled to learn that we were not shooting a foot of film in Annapolis. The plan, if it can be called that, was to beg, borrow, steal and occasionally buy any kind of colour stock footage dealing with Annapolis. This included shooting Technicolor photographs.

The picture was to be shot on Allied Artists' backlot. The backlot was minuscule; it was also run down and ill equipped. In the history of motion pictures, no colour film could compare to the mishmash of pieces of colour film we ended up using – all sizes and shapes, including 16mm and 8mm. We used an old Technicolor camera in a huge casing. The oddity was that, despite the clumsy, hot, uncomfortable casing, it was manned by a most brilliant cameraman, Sam Leavitt. His knowledge pulled us through many an awkward problem.

The story was simple and familiar. Two brothers, midshipmen John Derek and Kevin McCarthy, experience a series of disasters (a sea rescue; a boxing match), hopefully to gain the favours of Diana Lynn. This rivalry, fortunately, is never settled.

Derek wanted to play McCarthy's part. I pointed out to Derek that his was the better role, but he obviously didn't believe me. So they changed parts. It actually made not the slightest difference.

The producer, Walter Mirisch, called me from an ocean liner to finish the picture as quickly as possible. I told him that, although I was enjoying it, I would continue to shoot as fast as I could. I also asked him if he had ever seen an old Technicolor camera in a huge casing? The camera had one speed: slow. Mirisch unabashedly said, 'You can do it, Don.' That gave me great confidence.

The picture *was* fun to do. I liked my cast; I liked my crew. Unfortunately, the one thing I didn't understand was the picture. I should have understood it. I had seen other versions many, many times. I'm afraid the supposed audience agreed with me.

*

It's better to be a large frog in a small pond than to be a small frog in a large pond. Certainly, Allied Artists was a small studio.

I first became aware that I was the 'big frog' director at Allied Artists when a scurrilous character handed me a script like a dirty French postcard. He told me that Mr Broidy said that if I would direct the picture, Mr Broidy would make it. The script was not only full of filth, it was dull. I saw Broidy in his office.

ME: I can't believe you would make this dreadful script.
BROIDY: Hold on there, Don. I said if *you* wanted to direct it, the
    project is OK with me.

Two more depraved characters sidled up to me, with different scripts, and told me the same story about Steve Broidy. I went to see him on two separate occasions. He stuck to the same story. All I had to do was to approve the script and our distinguished president would OK it. Otherwise, the projects would never be made at Allied Artists.

The day after my third visit to Steve, a phenomenon occurred. My brain started ticking. Broidy had paid me a great compliment. Three times he had told me that he would make the pictures if I directed them. An idea began to develop. Why not come up with a good property – hopefully, an excellent one? Obviously, if I gave Steve the property to read, told him I was enthusiastic about it, he would let me make it.

I ran into incredible luck. A friend of mine, Don McGuire, a former actor who was now a producer/writer, suggested that I read his latest script. I thanked him and read it that afternoon. I couldn't wait to speak to him. I got him on the phone and told him, sincerely, that it was the best script I had ever read. We made a date to meet in my office to discuss all possibilities.

Naturally, McGuire was walking on air. I had explained my situation with Steve Broidy, which sounded impressive. McGuire asked me to join him for a late lunch at the Brown Derby in Beverly Hills to meet with Joel McCrea, who was as excited about the script as I was.

ME: McCrea is the top star at Allied Artists.
MCGUIRE: And you're their top director. An unbeatable combination.
ME: The most important element is the script.
MCGUIRE: (*A wide smile*) I agree with you. (*Getting up.*) See you at
    three on the dot.

We shook hands, very pleased the way things were progressing and equally pleased with ourselves.

Joel McCrea was most pleasant and most enthusiastic.

MCCREA: I had no idea that I'd be entertaining the idea of going back to work. But my God! What a script.

MCGUIRE: Well, at least the millions of people who want to see you again owe me a debt of gratitude. What's the next step, Don?

ME: Get back to the studio and lay the script on Broidy's desk. It's been a thrill to have met you, Joel. (*To McGuire.*) I'll call you the second I know anything.
(*The moment I get back to my office, I call Broidy.*)

ME: Can I see you for a moment?

BROIDY: I'm leaving in ten minutes.

ME: I'll see you in one.
(*I rush to his office and hand him the script.*)

ME: I know you're in a hurry, so I'll make it brief. The script that you're putting in your briefcase is the best screenplay I've ever read. Don McGuire wrote it and owns it. I met Joel McCrea this afternoon. He feels about the project exactly the way I do. We're itching to get going as soon as you give us your blessing.

BROIDY: I've never seen you so excited.

ME: I've never read a script like this before.

BROIDY: (*Getting up to leave*) I'll read it tonight. Be in my office at eleven a.m. sharp. (*Walking out the door.*) I'm kind of excited myself.

At 11 o'clock on the dot, I bounded into Broidy's office. His face looked grave, his attitude seemed uncomfortable.

BROIDY: Sit down, Don

I sat down realizing that something smelled rotten in the state of Denmark. What had happened to his congratulatory handshake, his warm smile, his words of praise, the magic words, 'We'll make it'?

BROIDY: Making pictures is like horse racing. There would be no horse racing if everyone agreed.

ME: Mr Broidy, I agree with your feelings on horse racing. But I'm not here to talk about Hollywood Park or Santa Anita.

BROIDY: I believe in making up one's mind by instinct. My mind is made up. The answer is no.
(*I try to speak calmly, but my voice trembles.*)

ME: When you told me that you would make three poor scripts, providing I directed them, were you motivated by instinct?

176

BROIDY: I'm not saying I'm right. It's my decision and I'm sticking to it.

ME: (*Trying not to lose my cool*) That, of course, is your right; but I'd appreciate your answering a few questions. What don't you like about the story?

BROIDY: (*Getting fed up*) I don't believe I'm on trial.

ME: Do you want more sex in the picture, like a girl taking a bath in the middle of nowhere, yet visible to voyeurs?
(*Broidy's face is set, his mouth shut.*)

ME: Or would you prefer more violence or less?

BROIDY: Once my mind is made up, that's it.

ME: I feel badly about your reaction. I felt certain that once you had read it, plus knowing about McCrea's and my reactions, you would be one hundred per cent for making the picture.
(*I head slowly for the door.*)

ME: (*Deflated*) Anyway, thanks for reading it and thanks for seeing me. I honestly feel you are making a mistake.

I closed the door silently. When I told McGuire, he said he was on his way to MGM. He sold the script immediately. The picture was made in a couple of months on a distant location. A town was built next to railroad tracks on which a steam engine pulled a passenger train. It stopped at the railroad station. John Sturges directed an excellent cast that included Spencer Tracy, Robert Ryan, Walter Brennan, Lee Marvin and Ernest Borgnine. The title of the picture: *Bad Day at Black Rock*.

13

Invasion of the Body Snatchers

Allied Artists 1956

Walter Wanger, the superb producer of *Invasion of the Body Snatchers*, discovered the story in *Colliers Magazine*. It was written by Jack Finney. Wanger gave me a copy of the story after he got Allied Artists interested in making the film. I suggested Danny Mainwaring to write the screenplay. Walter agreed and his enthusiasm was matched by my excitement. Despite the absurd title, which cheapened the content of the story (Kevin McCarthy suggested a Shakespearean title, 'Sleep No More', which naturally the executives didn't like), we recognized that a most original film could be made – not only entertaining, but frightening as well.

With Wanger's full blessing, Danny and I proceeded at once on the actual screenplay. Danny likes to work closely with the director, talking out a sequence, writing it, then showing it to me. Once we agreed on the pages, I would hand them over to Wanger. He usually liked our ideas and would make a few suggestions, which Danny would rewrite. Then we would plunge ahead to the next sequence.

The story concerns alien beings taking over the bodies of humans. The aliens assume the exact likeness of real people while gestating in pods. But these 'pods' possess no soul, emotion or culture. They exist like cows munching grass, without a care plaguing them. They are incapable of love; passion is unknown. They simply live – breathing, eating, sleeping. Danny and I knew that many of our associates, acquaintances and family were already pods. How many of them woke up in the morning, ate breakfast (but never read the newspaper), went to work, returned home to eat again and went to sleep?

*

The picture begins with Dr Miles Bennell (Kevin McCarthy) arriving in the small town of Santa Mira, a suburb of Los Angeles, by train. The name of the town we used is Sierra Madre, which we picked because it fit the story and worked out very well. We shot in the city and its environs for about a week. We also used Bronson Canyon, with its tunnels, in the Hollywood Hills.

Miles's secretary, Sally (Jean Willes), meets him at the station. As they drive off, Sally tells him that his calendar is full. Most of the patients are making the strange claim that their relatives are not their relatives, although they look exactly like them. Suddenly, a small boy, crying, darts across the country road, hotly pursued by his grandmother. Miles spins his wheels, braking sharply, narrowly avoiding hitting the boy. Miles questions the grandmother. She tells him she doesn't know what's wrong with the boy. He insists that his mother isn't his mother. Miles frowns and tells her to bring the boy to his office.

His office is full of helpless people, fearful that their close relatives are strangers to them. He gives each patient a sedative, including the small boy dragged by his grandmother into the office. There is no doubt that the doctor is puzzled and disturbed. He sends all his patients to Dr Danny Kaufman (Larry Gates), the town's psychiatrist. Dr Kaufman admits to Miles that he has treated other patients whom he diagnosed as suffering 'mass hysteria'. He pooh-poohs the idea that it could possibly be anything more serious.

Miles meets his former sweetheart, Becky Driscoll (Dana Wynter), who is now divorced. They appear to have taken up where they left off. Miles gets a strange call from Jack Belicec (King Donovan) and his wife Theodora (Carolyn Jones), and goes to their house with Becky. They discover a blank pseudo-human, lying on a billiard table. His size is exactly that of Jack. They rush off to see Dr Kaufman.

To prove to them that they are all suffering from mass hysteria, Dr Kaufman returns with them to the house. There is not a trace of the body. The police obviously feel that the whole story of a disappearing body is ridiculous. Dr Kaufman pokes fun at them, but Miles becomes convinced that what is wrong is the *theory* of mass hysteria.

Miles discovers that the pod can't change into the likeness of a person as long as that person remains awake. The next morning, Miles finds huge seed pods in Belicec's garden hothouse, which open up and release the likenesses of himself and Becky. Next to them are the opening pods of Theodora and Jack. Sending Jack and Theodora to get help, Miles tries to kill the pods with a pitchfork. He discovers it is impossible to kill them.

My brilliant art director, Ted Haworth, figured out a way of creating the pods that was simple and relatively inexpensive (around $30,000). The most difficult part was when the pods burst open, revealing exact likenesses of our leading actors. Naturally, they had to have naked impressions of their bodies made out of thin, skin-tight lastex. Foaming soap bubbles would gradually disappear, revealing, yet still concealing, their entire bodies. Ted was worried about the executives' reactions to nudity.

ME: You forget, Ted, that the top executives at Allied Artists are all pods. They couldn't care less about nudity, sex or dirty words. They have no real feeling about anything.

HAWORTH: I hope the pods react as you say they will.

To my astonishment, one of the executives hadn't changed into a pod yet. He called me into his office and flatly ordered that there were to be no naked people in an Allied Artists picture. I noticed he looked sleepy. After playing innocent, pretending I didn't know what he was talking about, I rushed over to Haworth and told him to make the impressions secretly. I was sure that before the impressions were made, this executive would have become a pod too.

*

At the climax of the film, Miles and Becky, the only two people in town who have not been turned into pods, are trying to escape into the hills, pursued by a large number of townspeople pods.

Hidden in Bronson Canyon is a steep cement stairway, with iron rails to help pull yourself up the steps. The head grip suggested building a small camera dolly, with wheels, riding the top of the rails. I'd never seen one before, or since. It enabled me to dolly with Miles and Becky, and later, their pursuers, led by a policeman, Janzek (Guy Way). A siren suddenly starts to blare.

I made a close dolly shot of Miles and Becky climbing the steps as quickly as they can. They are forced to stop and catch their breath, as the siren continues to wail. Miles helps Becky to start climbing again. Then a long down-angle shot shows them toiling up the stairs. As they near the top, Becky stops, unable to continue, gasping for breath. Miles, breathing hard, turns back to help her. Far in the background below them, Miles sees Janzek's police car appear, followed by the vanguard of the running crowd. In a reverse two-shot we see Miles taking Becky's hand and practically pulling her up the stairs. Reaching the top, they disappear over the brow of the hill.

Janzek stops his police car and gets out. The growing crowd follows him as he makes his way to the stairs. As he reaches the bottom of the stairs, the camera dollies up with him, and the crowd follows. Miles and Becky plunge down a steep slope into a ravine, the camera panning them along the ravine. A long up-angle shot follows, showing the moving line of men and women extending behind Janzek, now almost at the top of the steps.

Miles pulls an exhausted Becky up the brush-covered slope, while Janzek studies the terrain from the top of the stairway. In the far distance, the tiny figures of Miles and Becky are seen as they cross open country. As

13 *Invasion of the Body Snatchers*: preparing the stairway shot

Janzek points them out, the townspeople swarm down the slope. Out of a
draw in close foreground, Miles appears, pulling Becky after him. They
are exhausted. As they stumble past, the camera holds on the crowd
following across the rolling hills. Miles catches Becky as she nearly falls.
He scoops her up in his arms, staggers around the corner of a cliff and into
a large tunnel, which looms directly in front of them. Faintly, they hear
distant voices. They lean against the wall of the tunnel, Miles unable to
take another step. He sets Becky on her feet. They gasp for cold air as they
struggle to move further into the tunnel, hearing people approaching from
the distance. The silhouette of a man (Sam Peckinpah) approaches the
tunnel's entrance. He shouts back to the crowd that they could be inside,
and his cry echoes and re-echoes throughout the tunnel.

In a shored-up section of the tunnel, water drips from the ceiling, which is supported by heavy timbers. Boards cover an excavation in the ground. Miles and Becky are pulling up boards with all their strength, discovering a narrow aperture under one. They manage to pull another board off. The babble of voices grows louder. Miles desperately lifts Becky inside, climbs in beside her and replaces the boards with a last stupendous, incredible effort.

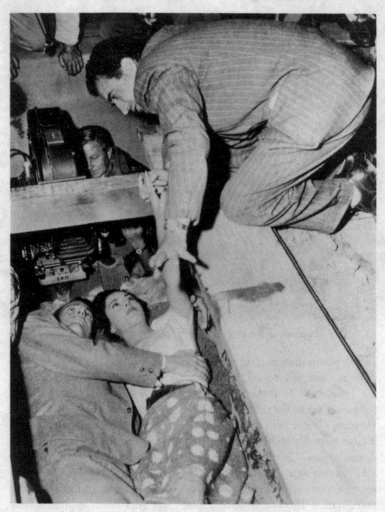

14   *Invasion of the Body Snatchers*: Don Siegel with Kevin McCarthy and Dana Wynter in the tunnel

There is a close shot of Becky and Miles, arms around each other, as they lie on the wet earth. The voices grow louder. Then light from several flashlights pierces the darkness. We shot at an angle up past Miles and Becky, through the cracks in the boards. Rushing feet and flashes of flashlights are seen directly overhead. The babble of voices is deafening. Miles and Becky draw even closer together.

Later that night, there are no sounds of the pod people. Becky and Miles wash their faces in a small pool of water to keep awake. They hear faint music off scene. Miles kisses Becky. He says that pods wouldn't be playing music, and leaves the tunnel to find the source of the music. He discovers that from a very large greenhouse people are packing pods into trunks. The music is coming from a radio in one of the trucks. Miles quickly returns to the tunnel.

When he arrives, he discovers that Becky has fallen asleep. Alarmed, he picks her up and carries her in his arms to another exit from the tunnel. He slips on the wet ground and falls, still holding Becky in his arms. She opens her eyes and sees his exhausted face. Miles tenderly lifts her to him and kisses her. He realizes that she has become a pod.

15   *Invasion of the Body Snatchers*: The 'pods' being disseminated

In the last sequence of the film Miles has reached the freeway and tries desperately to warn the oncoming drivers of the dangers they face from the pods. All of the shots, supposedly on the Hollywood Freeway, of Kevin trying to communicate with the drivers, stopping traffic, etc., were shot on a crossbridge scarcely used. The police allowed only our cars and trucks, about fifty, driven only by stunt drivers. No second unit was used here, or anywhere else in the picture. There was no process in the picture: every shot was authentic. The shots of Kevin's final scene were filmed just before dawn, and Kevin was in real danger, considering that he was at the breaking point of complete exhaustion. The stuntmen knew this and were alert to the fact that he might fall down, but happily there were no accidents.

Miles tries to stop several cars. He is almost run over, as the drivers swear at him. A large truck brushes slowly past him. He spins against it. On its side are the names of the cities the truck is going to. Miles pulls himself up into the back of the truck: it is full of pods! In a state of shock, Miles falls off the back. Cars screech to a halt. He staggers to his feet, as cars drive on past him, avoiding him.

MILES: (*Tortured, yelling at the top of his lungs*) You're next! You're next!

When the lights came on in the theatre, people glanced worriedly at those seated on either side of them. Were they pods too?

*

Several notable things happened during the making of the picture, which took nineteen days to shoot and cost under $300,000.

One night, I broke into Dana Wynter's house and slipped a pod under her bed. By this time, the pods had become a scary, realistic, believable possibility to cast and crew. The next morning, when Dana found the pod, she was in a state of near hysteria.

*

My idea, which Wanger seconded strongly, was to confront the idea of pods taking over the world as normally and naturally as possible. Obviously, in real life if one were to say, 'Look out! Pods are about to take over!' no one would take this preposterous notion seriously, and rightfully so. We therefore had the various characters in the picture, when first learning about the pods, pay little or no attention to this silly rumour. But when they were suddenly face to face with the monstrous horror, their reaction was startlingly frightening, as it would be in real life.

Allied Artists, bursting at the seams with pods, took Wanger's and my final cut and edited out all the humour. In their hallowed words, 'Horror films are horror films and there's no room for humour.' I translated it to mean that in their pod brains there was no room for humour. The studio also insisted on a prologue and an epilogue. Wanger was very much against this, as was I. However, he begged me to shoot it to protect the film, and I reluctantly consented. The epilogue started with Miles being taken back to the town's hospital, trying to convince the incredulous psychiatrist (Whit Bissel) and the hospital doctor (Richard Deacon) of the pods taking over the world. An emergency case is brought in whom the ambulance driver says was injured when a truck full of pods turned over. The psychiatrist looks at Miles, picks up the phone and asks for the FBI.

Oddly enough, in Europe and in the 'underground' in America, *Invasion of the Body Snatchers* was shown with the prologue and epilogue edited out. Like this, it was known as 'the Siegel version'.

14

Crime in the Streets

Allied Artists 1956

Crime in the Streets began as a television series, written by Reginald Rose
and directed by Sidney Lumet; both are extremely talented. I was asked to
direct the feature version for Allied Artists.

There are important differences between the small screen and the large.
In television, one doesn't have the time on film to develop characters
properly. The length of the show, twenty-four minutes, forty-eight
minutes, defeats any chance to make sense of the continuity and meaning
of the story. One is being constantly interrupted by advertisements, and it
is often difficult to get back to the mood of the show, particularly as the
photography of the ads is much better than the show. There is no art form
I know that gives a rigid amount of time to tell a story. It might be terrible
at forty-eight minutes and wonderful at fifty-seven minutes, but come hell
or high water, it must come in at exactly forty-eight minutes. Who are
these TV moguls who know what's good, bad or indifferent? Do the
letters ABC, CBS, NBC stand for quality or quantity?

It became absolutely essential that I make cinematic changes for the
feature. Although I never met Reginald Rose, I heard from my producer,
Vincent Fennelly, that Reginald was not happy with some of my changes.
I wish I had had the opportunity to meet with him and discuss our
differences. One thing was certain: I wasn't going to xerox his teleplay on
to the theatrical screen and make believe that I had made a feature. He
and Sidney Lumet wouldn't have liked it. Nor would John Cassavetes
and Mark Rydell, the two excellent actors who were in the original
version.

*

Vincent Fennelly came up with a single set idea, which would include both
indoors and outdoors. Everything in the picture was shot on this one huge
set, with the exception of the opening rumble, and that was shot outside
the single stage we used on the Goldwyn backlot. Fortunately, we had two
talented people who made it all work: creative sets from our art director,
Serge Krizman, and inspired originality from Sam Leavitt, our camera-

186

man. The complicated set cost about $35,000, but, more importantly, it enabled me to save a considerable amount of time in shooting.

Crime in the Streets takes place in the New York City tenement section: old, filthy and crime-ridden. Frankie Dean (Cassavetes) lives in a cold-water flat. Ourside his window is a fire escape. Most of his meetings with his gang, Baby Giola (Sal Mineo) and Lou Macklin (Rydell), take place on the fire escape and in a dingy, dirty, narrow dark alley nearby. Mineo lives with his parents over their small grocery store; he worships Cassavetes. Across the street in a shabby brownstone apartment house, directly opposite the alley, lives Rydell. We never see, or know with whom he lives. When he sings a strange tune, without lyrics, but with a chilling beat, one realizes he is dangerous – capable of anything.

Cassavetes is slapped around by an older man who lives on the block. The trio meet in 'their' alley and come up with a plan to kill the man. A social worker, Ben Wagner (James Whitmore), tries to influence them, but fails. Mineo is scared of what they are plotting, but goes along with them because he's more frightened of Cassavetes and Rydell. The film ends in catastrophe for the gang when the ordinary citizens of the street, outraged, decide to take action.

When I was shooting the gang meeting in the alley, Cassavetes sat at the end of the alley facing the street. Mineo joined him, sitting beside him. When Rydell joined them, he faced them with his back to the street. Across the street was the brownstone apartment house. I tried to continue shooting in one direction so that the cameraman could also light in the same direction. Naturally, the back of Rydell's head and the faces of Cassavetes and Mineo were visible to the cameraman. After breaking up the sequence by making close-ups of Cassavetes and Mineo, I fully intended to shoot at Rydell when the time came to light in the opposite direction. In the meantime, I continued shooting other sequences before lighting the other way.

Rydell, a typical New Yorker, suspicious of the jerks from Hollywood, challenged me as to when I was going to shoot at him.

ME: (*Mock sincerity*) Mind if I ask you a simple question?
RYDELL: I'd sure like some answers.
ME: Have I seen your face in the picture?
RYDELL: No, you haven't; and I want to know why.
ME: Not having seen your face at all, how do you think the audience will react when they suddenly see your face? It will upset the smooth continuity and flow of the picture. They'll want to know, 'Where'd that guy come from?'

187

RYDELL: (*Near tears of anger*) Do you mean I ain't gonna be seen leaving my house, ever?

ME: I don't see how. I trapped myself. I don't know how to get out of it. (*I turn and wink at Cassavetes.*)

ME: John, I don't have time to argue with your New York friend. Maybe you can explain it to him.
(*John puts his arm around Mark and leads him out of the alley. His explanation sounds like gibberish. Mark blows up.*)

RYDELL: I tell you he's crazy!

*

On the night of the contemplated murder, John was photographed first. He was in bed. I showed his face with the alarm clock on a bed stand. When the clock went off, he quickly turned it off and leapt out of bed. Sal was sound asleep. When the alarm clock went off, he jumped out of bed, turning off the alarm and quickly started to dress. When I was laying out the bed shot for Mark, for variety, I decided to shoot it differently from the others. I shot Mark through the bars at the head of the bed. It was an interesting shot as I could only see the back of his head. The clock was on a chair near the foot of the bed. Mark complained bitterly. I explained that the situation was still the same. Mark had tears of frustration when he saw the camera being wheeled in behind the bed.

A young lady, Maria Giola (Denise Alexander), had a difficult scene to play with Cassavetes. She was relatively inexperienced, so I asked John privately if he would do me a favour. His scene with Denise was to be shot in about two weeks. I would appreciate it if he would get to know her by occasionally rehearsing with her. I was so busy that I simply didn't have the time to rehearse with her so far ahead.

CASSAVETES: It will be my pleasure. By the way, if you don't shoot Mark's face soon, he'll crack up.

ME: I'm shooting him sometime tomorrow. He's a hell of an actor.

CASSAVETES: (*Grinning*) I'd hate to tell you what he thinks you are.

ME: Keep it a dark secret.

*

The work with Mark went smoothly and well, though he didn't trust me for a second. His brooding eyes studied me. I tried to explain to him why I shot so peculiarly.

Whenever I ran into John, I asked how Denise was doing in rehearsals. He was certain I would be very pleased and surprised with her performance. I thanked him. On the day I was scheduled to shoot her scenes with John, I began to rehearse. My worst fears were confirmed.

ME: (*Sternly*) How many times did you rehearse with Denise?

CASSAVETES: (*Somewhat embarrassed*) I couldn't help her, so I left her alone.

ME: Ever think of reporting that interesting fact to me?

CASSAVETES: (*Smirking*) I didn't want you to get mad at me.

ME: Reginald Rose wrote a great line for your mother when she's angry with you. She said, 'You're garbage.' I'd like to repeat it, John. You're garbage!

Denise got better and better. When I shot it, I liked her performance much better than John's. Of course, that was the only road I could travel.

15

Spanish Affair

Paramount 1957

Bruce Odlum, a producer in his early thirties, invited me to visit him on his father's Coachella Ranch at Indio. I arrived late in the evening and apologized. All I knew about Indio was that it was past Palm Springs. I got lost in the wonderful aroma of the area.

The next morning, Bruce asked if I'd like breakfast. When I nodded 'thank you', he went to the refrigerator. All that was revealed was a slice of stale cake with white icing and several cans of grapefruit juice. He opened up a can and gave it to me.

ME: How many acres is this Coachella Ranch?
ODLUM: Two thousand.
ME: Would you mind terribly if I walked six feet from the house and picked a succulent grapefruit?

He didn't seem to mind, but looked at me peculiarly. I returned the look, wandered outside and picked two of the best-looking grapefruit. When I returned, Bruce was finishing my can of juice. I sat down and ate both Coachellas, the best I had ever eaten.

ODLUM: Dick Collins recommended that you direct this picture, which takes place entirely in Spain.
ME: That's very decent of him. I'd appreciate reading the script.
ODLUM: First, I want you to meet my father, Floyd. If he okays you, you'll get the script. Let's get going.

We came upon a huge swimming pool. Although the atmosphere temperature was in the high 90s, steam filled the air. Bruce explained that his father suffered from severe arthritis. He was in a floating, inflated chair, talking into a phone which was set up to float beside him. Sunning on a patio lounge was an attractive woman in her fifties. Bruce introduced his stepmother, Jackie Cochran, the famed aviatrix. She nodded a cold hello, then turned in a fury on Bruce.

COCHRAN: How dare you let your damn dogs run loose on the golf course?

ODLUM: The dogs got away from me.

COCHRAN: (*Angrily*) Four of my shots disappeared in fresh turds.

ODLUM: I'm sorry.

COCHRAN: Sorry? Next time, the dogs, the turds and you will not be welcome at the ranch.

(*She shifts her body away from us.*)

ODLUM: (*Surprisingly unembarrassed*) Father's finished on the phone. I'll introduce you.

(*We go over to his father, still floating on the steaming water. I am sweating profusely.*)

ODLUM: Father, I'd like you to meet Don Siegel, the man I would like to direct *Spanish Affair*. My father, Floyd Odlum.

ME: A pleasure, sir.

FLOYD ODLUM: (*All business*) What do you think of the script?

ME: I haven't been given an opportunity to read any material on the project.

BRUCE ODLUM: I thought it better to get your approval before he reads anything.

FLOYD ODLUM: Do you know Spain?

ME: When I was fifteen years old I was to go to Spain to study guitar under Segovia. My father was a mandolin virtuoso and played the guitar quite well.

FLOYD ODLUM: So, you didn't go to Spain?

ME: I did considerable reading on the history and customs of the people.

(*The phone starts to ring.*)

FLOYD ODLUM: After Mr Siegel reads the script make up your own mind if you want him.

(*He starts a long business conversation.*)

BRUCE ODLUM: Would you care for a swim? There are plenty of trunks in the pool house that will fit you.

ME: Lead the way, leader.

It was impossibly hot. Bruce and I, wearing our trunks, dived into the water. I barely made it across the pool, as the water was extremely hot. I was too exhausted to pull myself out. Maybe this was a series of tests I had to pass to qualify as director.

*

I finally read the script, and immediately rushed over to Dick Collins's

191

office at Paramount. I didn't want to talk to Bruce before speaking to Dick. First, I thanked him for recommending me. I realized that it meant a lot of money for me – much more than I had ever earned before. But I was puzzled about a number of things.

COLLINS: (*Smiling pleasantly*) I'm glad you're not mad at me because you're making six figures for the first time in your hectic life.

ME: That part I like. But let's get down to the nitty-gritty. What do you think of your script?

COLLINS: There are many incredible locations: Segovia, Madrid, Toledo, Barcelona, etc. With that background for the story, I feel it has a chance.

ME: The Odlum family are somewhat peculiar. Bruce apparently is going to run the show. Can't we dream up something – anything – and rewrite the picture?

COLLINS: Bruce won't let me make a change. He loves it.

ME: Can you tell me the basic outline in précis form? There's no point at this time in going over the script page by page.

COLLINS: It's not only simple – it's simply not any good. (*Draws a deep breath.*) An American architect, Richard Kiley, designs a hotel for a Spanish three-man board. The architect goes to Madrid to see the first member of the board. He is turned down because his design is too modern. However, if Kiley can get an approval from either of the two other members, the first member will accept the plans. A translator, Carmen Sevilla, accompanies Kiley to Seville and Toledo, where Kiley is turned down by the two other board members. Carmen's jealous gypsy boyfriend picks a fight with Kiley. The gypsy is defeated. Kiley falls in love with Carmen and gives up on his design for the hotel.
(*Dick rests his head on the desk, spent.*)

ME: If we fail in getting Bruce to let us make changes, we are doomed.

COLLINS: Excepting one thing. We still get paid.

ME: I'm going to have a chat with Bruce before I join the world's oldest profession.

In my talk with Bruce, two things were very apparent. His father didn't want any changes. Bruce, in addition to obeying his father's word to the letter, honestly was proud of *Spanish Affair*. Very businesslike, he passed on the interesting news that Dick and I would pick locations with him within the week.

ME: I understand the casting is set.

BRUCE: The two main characters are set. Richard Kiley and Spain's number one actress, Carmen Sevilla. The rest of the parts will be cast in Spain.

ME: Kiley is a splendid actor and singer.

BRUCE: So is Carmen Sevilla.

(*I return to Dick's office. He looks tired and discouraged.*)

ME: I've joined the club. We're leaving for Spain within the week. With sensational locations, maybe we'll make the documentary of the year. I'm showing my faith. I'm taking the script with me.

(*Dick begins to perk up.*)

DICK: You'll love the dry sherry and olives.

ME: You'll love the food, period.

DICK: I think we're going to have fun. You're always so damn negative about your work.

ME: To tell you the truth, I don't know the tricks of the trade. I've never been a whore before.

*

The days passed swiftly. I stayed in Madrid at the Palace Hotel. Bruce and Dick were at the Plaza Hotel. I was very pleased with my accommodation. The food and wine were excellent and the service was superb. Dick was furious staying at the Plaza. The food, everything – including being in the same hotel as Bruce – was bad. As for Bruce, he showed no feeling about anything, which was par for the course.

We were to shoot most of our interiors at CEA Studios, the largest studio in Madrid. I noticed that the overhead rigging for different sets had no railings or rope. I questioned this. The Spanish production manager simply shrugged his shoulders uninterestedly.

ME: Do you have many accidents with electricians falling off?

PRODUCTION MANAGER: (*Coldly*) Maybe three or four.

Life in Spain was obviously cheap. The electricians had a remarkable way of getting around to set the various lamps. They straddled ladders of different sizes. They walked from one lamp to another as though they were on stilts. It looked precarious, but they were fearless and adept at walking ladders. While I was there and for the rest of the picture, I saw no accidents. Viva España!

Spanish Affair was a very poor affair. The picture was mainly a travelogue in a Pegaso, a wonderful Spanish racing two-seater. Dick Kiley drove and Carmen Sevilla was his companion and translator. One of the most interesting and exciting happenings was the 'poling' of the young bulls. A young bull would be chased by two cowboys, holding long poles, one on each side of the bull. When near enough, the bull would be knocked off his feet by pushing the pole into his haunches. If the bull ran away, he never entered a bull ring – just the butcher's shop. However, if he regained his footing and charged back at the horses, he was called a '*bravo bull*'; he would ultimately fight the matadors in the bull ring.

The poling of the bulls was the only exciting happening in the whole picture.

*

There's an old adage that makes sense: always shoot your exteriors before you shoot your interior sets. The weather was perfect, sunny every day. The production staff, who were idiots, believed that it would never rain, and for months they were right. All the cover sets at the studio were finished before we started shooting our exteriors, mostly on location.

In Barcelona, we shot outside at night a lovely *Sardana*, a Catalan dance. Suddenly, the clouds opened. All the dancers in their colourful costumes were soaking wet; they were a large, angry and unhappy group. When the rains stopped, we had to use our special effects for more water so that the sequence would match. They obviously didn't understand the necessity of wetting them further with hoses and sprinkers. Protesting, they moved on the small group of Americans huddled around the cameras. We tried to explain to them the reason why we were, in their eyes, rudely continuing to drench them. A riot broke out. Our group battled back, but we were overwhelmed by sheer numbers – there were over 100 of them. Fortunately for us, some of Franco's Guardia Civil appeared from nowhere to rescue us debilitated Americans, who were nearly at surrender point. By some miracle, we managed to complete the sequence – I suppose because the Guardia Civil looked like they all played tackle for Alabama.

*

Although I thought Richard Kiley an excellent actor and singer (I didn't know anything about Carmen Sevilla), he was not the star of the picture. The star was the Pegaso. It was similar to a Ferrari. The picture, which had the car in practically every scene, gave the film a documentary look. It had a companion, a mechanic, day and night, to tend to all its needs. One day, I decided to drive the Pegaso to the location. The mechanic was not happy. Jealous, I suppose. I screeched out of the Palace Hotel and sped down the road out of Madrid. I was aware that the 'star' was a fantastic piece of machinery. I had never driven anything like it before. It was too much car for my amateur talents. I was doing well over 200 kilometres when, off in the distance, I saw a large herd of goats blocking the road. I took my foot off the accelerator, which slowed the car down. I applied the foot brake slowly. I smelled rubber burning. The speed was still high as I neared the goats. I pressed further down on the brake pedal. The 'star' went into a long spin. I sounded the horn, which was a stupid thing to do as the goats scattered every way. I left the road, heading directly for a tree in my path – the only tree in sight. The 'star' co-operated. It stopped 4 inches from wrapping itself around the tree. I closed my eyes to the sound of frightened goats squealing and goatherds yelling. I opened my eyes. While they continued to curse me, I opened my wallet and gave them several hundred pesetas. They took their straw hats off. I took a silent oath never to drive the car again, if I ever reached the location. I started the engine. They swiftly cleared a path through the goats. I slowly, ever so slowly, pulled past the tree. When I arrived at the location, I turned the ignition off and got out of the car. I was asked how I liked the car. '*Viva España!*'

*

I do believe that Bruce tried to get me permission to shoot a sequence in the Prado Museum. Presumably his father, despite all his millions, couldn't swing it. Our Ambassador was helpless. Of course, the Spaniards were absolutely in the right. It was too dangerous. The paintings were priceless. Nevertheless, I was disappointed. I wanted to shoot exquisite photographs in colour of various paintings by El Greco, Velasquez, Goya, and others, which would be used for the main titles. Then, I would pull back on movie colour film from another priceless painting to reveal the interior of the Prado for the first sequence in the picture. The Prado had never before been shot by a motion-picture company.

At CEA Studios, they assigned a young lad in his teens to act as my assistant. The reason: he spoke excellent English. We were walking from my hotel to the Prado. Whenever I had some spare time, I would try to see as much of the museum as possible. I explained to my companion, who I referred to as 'Kid', my keen disappointment at not being allowed to shoot inside the Prado.

KID: (*Brash, confident*) I don't understand the difficulty.
ME: CEA said it couldn't be done. Our American producer, Bruce Odlum, failed.
KID: Do you know how the CEA refers to Mr Odlum?
ME: Haven't the slightest idea, Kid.
KID: (*Giggling*) The 'Smasher'. He screws up everything. The fact that he couldn't get permission from the Prado Museum means nothing.
ME: Well, how about his father, Floyd Odlum, many times a multi-millionaire? He made direct contact with the government.

KID: The American dollar means nothing in these kinds of negotiations.

ME: (*Somewhat nettled*) The American State Department failed, as did the American Ambassador.

(*By this time, I am paying our way into the Prado. The peace and quiet as we look at the many treasures calm my ire.*)

KID: May I break in on your thoughts for a brief moment, Mr Siegel? (*I don't disturb my reverie. I simply nod my head.*)

KID: (*Speaking quickly*) I know the Curator of the museum slightly. With your permission, I would like to talk to him about your problems.

ME: (*Practically ignoring him*) Kid, be my guest.

(*He disappears immediately. I am sitting on a bench in another room enjoying a collection of the immortal paintings of Velasquez when the Kid, out of breath, sits down beside me.*)

KID: (*Quietly, sincerely*) There are no major problems in your shooting in the Prado Museum.

ME: (*My full attention on him*) That sounds impossible. I take it that the Curator is the magician who will make all this happen. What is his actual job?

KID: (*Excitedly*) He is the person who is in actual charge of the museum. What he says, goes. He wants to meet you tomorrow at ten thirty a.m. in his office. Then, he wants you to show him exactly what you will be shooting. God willing, nothing should go wrong.

ME: I'd better have my cameraman, Sam Leavitt, with me so he'll understand the problems and difficulties.

KID: The fewer people, the better. Under no circumstances, please do not have the Smasher with you.

ME: You be sure to be beside me. Does the Curator speak English?

KID: Perfectly. (*Smiles.*) Just like me.

Everything worked out smoothly and easily. Sam was thrilled at the chance of shooting the masterpieces. He swore he would guard them with his life. The Curator couldn't have been more pleasant and helpful. I told him that tomorrow we would settle the day we would start shooting. Sam agreed with me that he thought we could complete all our shooting in one day. The only thing that worried me was the Smasher.

We started shooting the photographs of the various paintings early on Tuesday morning. It was a religious holiday. The Prado was officially closed. The Smasher refused to pay the Spaniards double time. The CEA people were shocked. I threatened to quit the picture, plus calling

Paramount and his father, Floyd Odlum. Bruce ultimately gave in. That was lucky for us, and for Bruce's physical well-being. There was one awful moment while we were shooting. We lined up to dolly back from a large Goya painting. My heart stopped beating as a careless labourer, carrying a plank, nearly scraped the magnificent painting. Both Spaniards and Americans nearly killed him right there and then. However, the opening scene, between Carmen and Richard, finally went perfectly, with no bloodletting. I thanked the Curator for making it all possible. Bruce amazed me. He asked the Curator what his favourite charity was: he wanted to make a donation.

I asked the Kid to have lunch with me. As we passed a jeweller, which was closed, I asked him what time it was.

KID: I don't own a wristwatch.
ME: For services above and beyond the call of duty, tomorrow I shall present you with the wristwatch of your choosing.
KID: I just did my job.
ME: That's more than ninety-nine per cent of us can say.

*

I wish I could say that the picture turned out well, or that it made a good documentary. Certainly Sam Leavitt could have won an Oscar for his brilliant camera work. I'm certain that Floyd Odlum made money by some intricate tax write-off, which he really didn't need. I'm sure we could have made a much better picture – but the Smasher did us in.

16

Baby Face Nelson

United Artists 1957

The producer Al Zimbalist gave me an uninteresting script by Irving Shulman on the life of Baby Face Nelson. Very little research had been done. Most of it was about John Dillinger. I went to see Danny Mainwaring and pointed out to him that I didn't feel I would be of much help to him in rewriting the script. I knew nothing about Baby Face Nelson. I had more good news for him. He had two weeks to write a new script.

Danny was an ex-newspaper writer. He suggested that the two of us go to the morgue of every newspaper in town: he felt certain we'd come up with plenty of material. First, he would read the script – fast – then we'd find out about 'Mr Baby Face'.

After our search, we met in Zimbalist's office. I told Al that time was of the essence: Danny would tell him the sparse outline as quickly as possible.

MAINWARING: Nice to meet you. Don and I visited all the newspaper morgues in town. The trouble with the script I read was that apparently very little research was done. It was not authentically the story of Baby Face Nelson. The script that I will write will be about Baby Face Nelson.

ME: (*Interrupting*) We've been so busy researching, coming up with ideas, that I forgot to tell you, Danny, that Mickey Rooney is playing Baby Face Nelson.

MAINWARING: My God – that's too good to be true. Magnificent casting, Mr Zimbalist.

ZIMBALIST: (*Pleased*) The moment I thought of Mickey, I knew it would be perfect casting.

MAINWARING: He's practically a midget with a chip on his shoulder, which drives him to be a tough guy. Outside of his size, he reminds me of you, Don.
(*Zimbalist laughs in agreement.*)

ME: I'm just feisty. The fact that I'm a lover is more important.
MAINWARING: As usual, you're wasting my time. Well, here it goes.
We pick up Baby Face Nelson coming out of prison, a hardened
criminal with such charming traits as being hopelessly psychotic
with an irrational, uncontrolled temper – all adding up to his
being a killer, which he enjoys.
(*Zimbalist is hooked. I keep my fingers crossed, hoping Danny will
continue in the same vein.*)
MAINWARING: The main components in this narrative development are
action sequences (fights, chases, murders, robberies). Dialogue
sequences are held to a minimum. (*To Zimbalist.*) Could I have a
cup of coffee, or a glass of water?
ZIMBALIST: Keep talking. I'll pour the coffee for you. Sugar, cream?
MAINWARING: The works. Nelson is approached to kill a union man.
He refuses, is framed, sent to jail, escapes, kills the men who
framed him. A pattern is set up throughout the picture. Violence,
flight, eat, drink, sleep, followed by more violence. (*Drinks coffee.*)
If your picture is as good as your coffee, we're in. A girlfriend, Sue,
is with Nelson when he robs a drugstore and Nelson is shot. Sue
takes him to a country hospital run by a sleazy underworld doctor.
The doc pays more attention to Sue than to Nelson, which enrages
him. Doc removes the bullet. He also attempts to remove Nelson's
fingerprints, but fails. For revenge, Nelson gets the doctor drunk,
which is not difficult to do. He gets him in a rowboat and
ultimately drowns him. At the hospital, Nelson meets a member of
Dillinger's gang, who gets him into Dillinger's mob. Dillinger gets
his robbery plans from an effeminate character, Fatso. During the
robbery, Nelson machine guns the guards while Dillinger is
wounded. Dillinger and the 'Lady in Red' go to a theatre in
Chicago. Dillinger is killed.
(*Mainwaring stops talking to catch his breath. Zimbalist
impatiently tells Mainwaring to continue. I nod my head,
indicating all is going well.*)
MAINWARING: Nelson takes over the gang. They commit a series of
bank robberies and murders. Nelson is totally out of control. He
evades an FBI trap and betrays the gang. The FBI traces him to a
forest cabin. Nelson and Sue attempt to escape. Nelson is shot and
crawls to a nearby country graveyard. Dying, Nelson learns
against a gravestone and asks Sue to finish him off. The picture
ends with a close shot of the gravestone. The camera moves in
close to the epitaph, 'The End'.

(*Zimbalist bounds to his feet.*)

ZIMBALIST: Absolutely great. Now get lost and write it. Remember, you've got two weeks to write the script.

ME: (*To Mainwaring*) It's really remarkable and I thank you for all your hard work. If you need me, call me – but I've got a strong feeling you can do better without me.

MAINWARING: I want to see you every day so you can go over the pages.

ME: So be it. (*To Zimbalist.*) I'm going back with Danny so he doesn't forget his story. I'll see you tomorrow morning.

We left a puzzled but happy Zimbalist.

*

Zimbalist was pacing up and down in his office when I arrived the next morning. I told him I had just left Danny, who was writing furiously. Come hell or high water, he would finish it in two weeks.

ZIMBALIST: I got lucky. I found a bunch of old cars.

ME: How old?

ZIMBALIST: Early forties.

ME: (*Disgustedly*) Brilliant start, Al. The cars can't be newer than early 1930s.

ZIMBALIST: (*Getting angry*) So what? They're all old cars.

ME: (*Implacable*) The picture is shot in 1930 to 1933. I'm not doing the picture with 1940s cars. That anachronism will ruin the believability of the film.

ZIMBALIST: Ackronish, smackronish. Do you know what 1930s cars cost?

ME: If you can't afford to make the picture properly, don't make it. I suppose you'll dress the cast in 1940s clothes. I've looked up your record, Mr Al Zimbalist. You've never made a successful picture. (*Getting to my feet.*) I'm quitting and taking Danny with me.

ZIMBALIST: (*Quick-change artist*) Let's talk casting. Rooney wants a beautiful young chick to play Sue.

ME: Naturally. He needs a gal to tire him out. What *we* need is an actress who can stand up to Mickey and hold her own. I've worked with a young, attractive actress, Carolyn Jones, who is sensational and I think she's brilliant in *Invasion of the Body Snatchers*. Why don't you meet her and work out a deal you can afford? At that end of the business, you're the champ. (*At least he writes her name down.*)

ZIMBALIST: What about the phoney doc?

ME: I'm not sure I can deliver this man, who is a good friend of mine, but he would give the picture a great deal of class.

ZIMBALIST: Don't tell me – Laurence Olivier.

ME: Close. Sir Cedric Hardwicke.

ZIMBALIST: You're crazy. For one thing, he wouldn't do it. And for certain, I couldn't afford to pay him.

ME: I'd offer him three days' salary. It's a good part.

ZIMBALIST: Give it a shot. I can always say no. What about Dillinger?

ME: Leo Gordon.

ZIMBALIST: Now you're making sense. I thought of him when I saw . . .

ME: *Riot in Cell Block 11.* He'd be perfect.

ZIMBALIST: How about Fatso?

ME: Jack Elam.

ZIMBALIST: Now I know you're crazy. Elam is as skinny as a scarecrow.

ME: My God, don't you know why Dillinger calls him 'Fatso?' He likes to insult people. If he gets tired of that, he kills them.

ZIMBALIST: I gotta admit I never thought of that. Now, get on your horse and bring me back Sir Cedric.

ME: He'll probably kick me out of his kingdom. Particularly when you offer him a nickel a day.
  (*I leave to call Sir Cedric.*)

Sir Cedric Hardwicke greeted me warmly in his small but lovely house. There were no horse guards, or servants, for that matter.

HARDWICKE: Still scotch and soda and no ice?

ME: Your memory astounds me. Thank you.
  (*We sit on the terrace enjoying our drinks.*)

HARDWICKE: To what evil end have you honoured me with thine presence? I memorized that line once, but the source escapes me.

ME: I shall be blunt. My eyes, ears, nose and throat warn me that what I'm about to tell you will kill our respect for each other. I'm not referring to your abominable left-handed tennis.

HARDWICKE: You know by now that I like my lovely ladies succulent.

ME: (*Suddenly to the point*) I'm directing a gangster movie starring Mickey Rooney.

HARDWICKE: I've heard of that name.

ME: In the picture, *Baby Face Nelson*, is the part of a doctor who is licentious, dissolute, debauched and a crook.

HARDWICKE: Sounds absolutely heavenly.

ME: I'm offering you three days' pay, which is the run of the part. It's not badly written. You get murdered. The salary is $3,000, which will probably ruin your career.

(*Cedric gets up, his face wrinkled in thought.*)

HARDWICKE: There are two parts I've always hungered to play. A clown and a bloody gangster. I accept your generous offer.

I fainted dead away.

*

Mickey Rooney and I were about to have dinner at his house off Laurel Canyon in the San Fernando Valley. As usual, Mickey was sipping a beer. The house was quite nice, but the grounds were literally swarming with snails. While telling Mickey about the script and the proposed cast, I was busy killing snails. Mickey – tough Mickey – jumped up with horror and demanded that I stop killing them. He couldn't stand anything helpless being killed. I refused to stop until we sat down to dinner. He screamed for his wife (no. 6) to get dinner ready. A beautiful redhead opened the front door and screamed back that dinner had been ready for over an hour. That was the end of my killing snails.

Mickey is one of the most talented actors I've ever worked with. However, the combination of Mickey and a six-pack was usually a disaster. He'd become vicious, morose and very stubborn. I liked him. He was a superb athlete. But with a beer can in his hand and twelve swirling around in his stomach, he became a perfect parody of Baby Face Nelson. To get a good performance from this great actor was not always easy. If one could hold down that wonderful energy that he would burst out with, he had no peer. But if twelve cans of beer took charge – look out. To give the devil (and he was one) his due, I admired his skill and loathed his personality. Somehow, we staggered through the picture as good friends. He wasn't too smart. He could have had 45 per cent of Zimbalist's end. That represented a lot of money. But Zimbalist settled for cash. That was about enough to keep Mickey in beer.

*

Early in the morning of the seventeenth day of shooting, Zimbalist informed me that I had to finish the picture that day.

ME: I can't do it. There are at least three more days of difficult shooting.

ZIMBALIST: You've no choice. I've run out of money.

ME: Do you remember when I sneaked you, the cast and crew on the studio lot of Twentieth Century Fox? We shot every sequence possible: bank robberies, the train hold-up, the lake, the hospital, etc. We shot for two whole days. If we hadn't shot at Twentieth, God knows how long it would have taken. Come to think of it, you never thanked me.

ZIMBALIST: I thank you now. Nevertheless, I'm out of money. I'm pulling the cameras tonight.

When he left, I rushed over to Mickey's trailer. I explained what was happening and that I was worried about his death scene, car chases and gun fights. Rooney appeared concerned. He said he would make a hell of an effort to straighten things out with Zimbalist. He left to see him while I went to prepare my first set-up.

Sometime later, Scott Hale, my dialogue director, rushed over to me. He whispered that he had overheard a conversation between Zimbalist and Mickey. Rooney said that if Siegel wouldn't shoot the scenes to finish them today, he would be happy to take over and direct the rest of the picture. The kind snail-saver was an evil man. To prevent the betrayal, I decided to lay out every shot. I shot only the amount of film that I would use in actual editing. There would be no extra footage. Each set-up was different from any of the others. Every foot of film I shot, I used. There's no trick in shooting a lot of set-ups, but to make difficult and important shots, shooting at top speed, is demanding and challenging. The sequences ranged from shooting at the FBI when Rooney and Carolyn are forced to flee from the cabin in the woods; a breakneck attempt to escape by car; Rooney wounded, but managing with Carolyn to crawl to the cemetery; Rooney dying and begging Carolyn to finish him off, which she does; Rooney, dead, sliding down the gravestone. It took me fifty-five tough set-ups to finish my last day's work. Carolyn and Mickey were magnificent. I never mentioned at any time that I was aware of Rooney's dastardly attempt to victimize me.

*

Some time later, I was shooting *The Lineup* in San Francisco when I received an urgent telephone call from Danny. He sounded terribly upset.

ME: Take it easy, sonny, before you have a heart attack.

MAINWARING: Do you remember ever reading a script *Baby Face Nelson* written by Irving Shulman on yellow pages?

ME: I only remember reading a script written by Shulman on white pages. That was given to me by Zimbalist. I have no recollection of reading any script written on yellow pages. What does Zimbalist have to say?

MAINWARING: He doesn't remember.

ME: Figures.

MAINWARING: To make matters worse, Shulman has pre-dated his
yellow pages so that it appears that he wrote it before I wrote my
script.

ME: Are the yellow pages an exact copy of your white script?

MAINWARING: The SOB made some minor changes of no importance.

ME: I hate to say this, but it appears that he has executed a perfect
crime.

MAINWARING: What the hell can I do to disprove this scurrilous
plagiarist?

ME: What's the Writers' Guild's position?

MAINWARING: There's no way they can prove that Shulman didn't
write the yellow pages before I wrote my script. As soon as you've
finished your present film, you'll be asked to testify in front of an
Arbitration Board. So will I, Shulman and Zimbalist.

ME: I'm being bugged to get back on the set. Send me a copy of the
yellow script and your script immediately, so I can compare the
two. Frankly, it appears that you've been reamed. A perfect crime
is an extremely difficult operation. I'm sorry about all of this. I'd
like nothing better than to nail Shulman to the cross. But
remember, Danny, it's not the end of the world. Good luck and
God bless.

There were about six members of the Writers' Guild Arbitration Board,
with a court typist, who miraculously got down everything that everyone
said. Danny, pale and angry, was present, as were Zimbalist, Shulman and
myself. *Baby Face Nelson* was shot in 1957, *The Lineup* in 1958. I am
writing this in 1988. I have no records of the arbitration. The best I can do
is paraphrase the hearing and edit it.

HEAD ARBITRATOR: Mr Siegel, why would Mr Shulman copy Mr
Mainwaring's script and pre-date it?

ME: I suppose there's a certain fascination in committing a so-called
perfect crime. However, this is a very strange perfect crime, as the
only payment is a writing credit. I'm trying to point out that there
was no financial gain, nor, for that matter, artistic recognition.
After all, *Baby Face Nelson* took seventeen days to shoot. It is
obviously considered a small picture.

HEAD ARBITRATOR: Did you read Irving Shulman's script written on
yellow paper?

ME: Yes I did. However, it was not written. It was typed. I also read
his first script, which was typed on white paper.

HEAD ARBITRATOR: Was there any major difference between the white and yellow scripts?

ME: They were entirely different scripts. Other than the title and the date on the yellow script when presumably written, there were no similarities.

HEAD ARBITRATOR: Was Shulman's yellow script similar to Mainwaring's script?

ME: They were identical, except for an occasional word change. But, more importantly, the yellow script pre-dated Mainwaring's. Shulman wanted to give the false impression that Mainwaring copied his script. The reverse was true.

HEAD ARBITRATOR: We hope you appreciate that we must come to a conclusion based on the written scripts.

ME: That would be true if Mr Shulman had been successful in committing the perfect crime.
(*A stillness suddenly prevails. Shulman and Zimbalist stare at each other. The Arbitration Board is alert.*)

HEAD ARBITRATOR: Do you have information that we don't possess?

ME: You possess it, but are unaware of it. Take the Shulman yellow script and the Mainwaring script and turn to the passage where Dillinger is betrayed by the 'Woman in Red'. Now, you will read that the woman's name is Ann Saper. The correct name is Anna Sage. She was under FBI pressure because of her involvement in criminal activities.

SHULMAN: (*Loudly*) So what?

HEAD ARBITRATOR: Mr Shulman, be quiet. Mr Siegel, we are confused about the importance of Ann Saper.

ME: Danny wrote the script in two weeks. When we got to the Woman in Red, we didn't have time to check out whether she was alive, or whether there was another woman named Anna Sage, who might sue. I said, let's not waste time. Let's use another name. Danny agreed: 'Give me a name.' 'How about using Ann Saper, my mother's maiden name?'
(*Confusion erupts.*)

ME: I thought it might be fun to have my mother linked up with the top gangster Dillinger.
(*Danny has a huge smile on his face. Shulman is in shock.*)

HEAD ARBITRATOR: (*After conferring with other members of the board*) Mr Siegel, is your mother alive?

ME: Very much so.

HEAD ARBITRATOR: Are there people who can substantiate your
statement concerning your mother's maiden name?
ME: Yes. My uncle is Jack Saper. He is my mother's youngest brother.
Mr Saper works at Paramount Studios. He is head of production
for Hal Wallis Productions. They are boyhood friends.
HEAD ARBITRATOR: Thank you, Mr Siegel, for your astounding
information.

A perfect crime calls for intelligence and luck. Shulman's luck ran out.
One day I'll direct a film about a perfect crime . . . and it won't be
plagiarism.

17

The Gun Runners

United Artists 1958

There's an old adage: never make a sea picture with a C budget. Clarence Green, a small, pleasant man, and surprisingly good as an amateur boxer, was producing *The Gun Runners*. The star, Audie Murphy, asked for me to direct the picture. United Artists, who were happy with *Baby Face Nelson*, gave their OK.

When I read the script, written by Paul Monash, I was astounded to learn that it was based on Hemingway's *To Have and Have Not*, which had been filmed in 1944, starring Humphrey Bogart and directed by Howard Hawks. Then Michael Curtiz remade it in 1949 as *The Breaking Point*, starring John Garfield. I decided to find out why Green wanted to remake it again.

We met in his office. Apparently, he was a successful producer in partnership with a director, Russell Rouse.

ME: Now I understand why Russell showed good common sense in not directing the third version.
GREEN: Don't you like the script?
ME: Not particularly. But that's not what irks me.
GREEN: Everyone here, including me, thought you'd be the perfect choice to direct the film.
ME: Thanks. Nevertheless, *To Have and Have Not* is the best version and cost the most, notwithstanding that it was physically the easiest to shoot. *The Breaking Point* is not as good, but cost almost as much. Your version, which is much more difficult to shoot than the first two, will have to be made quicker and cost less. It's a stupid trick at best, if you can pull it off.
GREEN: We'll pull it off.
ME: How can you compare a Bogart picture, or a Garfield picture, with an Audie Murphy picture?
GREEN: You'll make it work.
ME: Thanks again. By the way, are you satisfied with the script?

GREEN: I'm never satisfied.

ME: Great. I'd like you to hire Danny Mainwaring for the rewrite. He's gotten me out of similar messes.

GREEN: I'll set up an appointment to see him.

ME: Why not send him a script immediately? I'm sure he's seen the two better versions, as have most movie-goers. Before I leave, I want to level with you. I'm amazed that you want to do a remake of a remake. Why not do an original story?

GREEN: (*A bit miffed*) My instincts tell me to do the third version.

ME: Your instincts will win because you're the producer. I hope I'm wrong, but in the end, you'll lose.
(*As I start to leave, I turn back.*)

ME: Who do I have to fuck to get off this picture?

GREEN: (*Ignoring my crude remark*) Tomorrow we'll talk casting and story. I think you'll be happy with my choices.

The next day Green and I were huddled over his desk going over a cast list, which he had already prepared.

GREEN: Audie Murphy, the owner of a fishing boat, has . . .

ME: Excuse my interrupting, but do you consider Murphy as good an actor as Bogart or Garfield?

GREEN: Of course not; but he's considered a box-office name.

ME: Not by me.

GREEN: There is a lovely girl, Pat Owens.

ME: Do you think she has the box-office name of Lauren Bacall?

GREEN: (*A little angry*) When Bacall made her first film, she had no box office.

ME: True. And equally true of Pat Owens. When she finishes *The Gun Runners*, she will also have no box office.

GREEN: To continue. Murphy's drunken assistant is Everett Sloane.

ME: I'd prefer Walter Brennan, who is in a class by himself.

GREEN: The gangster who blackmails Murphy to deliver guns to the revolutionaries in Cuba is Eddie Albert.

ME: An excellent choice.

GREEN: Hooray! There's a mechanic who chases Murphy to get money owed to him for repairs, played by Jack Elam.

ME: Another hooray.

GREEN: The rest of the cast are Cubans and stuntmen.

ME: I was waiting in vain for one laugh. Remember how funny *To Have and Have Not* was? Your story has pace, danger and action. Your cast, on the whole, is workable. I do not think the picture, which you are blindly stubborn about, is going to make a dime. Plus, it's going to be physically extremely difficult to do. Have you picked your crew?

GREEN: No one is signed, sealed and delivered.

ME: (*Getting up to leave*) I suggest you hire Hal Mohr as the cameraman. He's had enormous experience. Also, Scott Hale as my dialogue director. I'm off to see Mainwaring. He doesn't like the script. If you don't mind, I'm going to try to get some humour into it.

GREEN: Let *me* level with you. I just want you to be happy. That way, I know we'll get a good picture.

ME: (*Leaving*) I sure hope you know what you're doing.

*

I got Audie and Pat Owens together to rehearse. Audie is a very shy person. Maybe it sounds strange that the number one hero of World War II is shy, but here's how the rehearsal went.

Audie, who was supposed to be in love with Pat, refused to look at her. He would turn his body away from her. I caught a pleading look for help from Pat. I had her follow Audie so he had to look at her. We ran the lines and I told both of them to change any that they felt were awkward, and, considering they were married in the script, they could be much more relaxed. Pat was dead game. She'd caress Audie's face, sit on his lap and attempt to kiss him. It's hard to believe, but I couldn't get any response from Audie. By twisting and turning, he managed not to look at her once. Oh Bogey and Johnny, where were you when I needed you?

One night, Audie was driving. We were going out to have dinner alone. When he parked his car, he opened the glove compartment and took out a large 45 Western revolver and stuck it in his belt. As we entered the restaurant, the revolver was not visible, hidden under his sports jacket. We sat at the bar waiting for our table. I ordered a scotch and soda, Audie a draught beer. I studied him. He was always polite and quiet with me, never any trouble. We liked each other.

ME: Why the arsenal?

AUDIE: You never know when you might need it.

ME: You're not expecting trouble?

AUDIE: No. (*Taking a long sip from his beer.*) But if it's coming, I'll blow it away.

I believed him. I realized that Audie, not all that big and strong, was one of the mighty reasons that the Western Allies won World War II.

18

The Lineup

Columbia 1958

Frank Cooper and Jaime Del Valle were the producers and owners of the television series *The Lineup*. I was hired to direct the pilot, which was sold immediately. The series ran successfully for many years. When Columbia decided to make a feature based on the series, it was also entitled *The Lineup*, and I was asked to direct it.

Frank Cooper was an agent who also put together deals – a deal-maker, not a picture-maker. Jaime Del Valle was strictly a television producer. *Lineup* was his first feature. I got him to hire Stirling Silliphant to write the screenplay. Stirling was enormously talented, with many years of experience. He not only wrote fast, he frequently wrote two scripts, for different producers, at the same time. Like Danny Mainwaring, he liked to work with the director.

We both felt strongly that it was a fatal mistake to use the title *The Lineup*. Most people would confuse it with the series, which they were seeing each week on TV. We felt a title like 'The Chase' would fit the picture and entice people into the theatre.

An extraordinary thing was taking place. Stirling was writing a superb, exciting, chilling movie about two killers, Eli Wallach and his mentor Robert Keith. They arrive on a plane in San Francisco. Their mission is to recover narcotics that have been hidden in the belongings of three passengers coming off a boat from Hong Kong. The dialogue between the older man, Julian (Keith) and Dancer (Wallach) is unique and strangely effective.

While approaching San Francisco in the plane, Julian is teaching Dancer grammar. Dancer is frustrated by the subjunctive tense.

JULIAN: (*Concerning 'if'*) How many characters on a street corner can say, 'If I were you'?
DANCER: (*Puzzled*) It's gonna be a tight day.
JULIAN: (*Calmly*) No, Dancer. It's going to be a good one.

I told Stirling that my vibes felt good about what he was writing. I didn't like any of *The Lineup* stuff. Should I see our producers and tell them how we felt? He agreed with me one hundred per cent, but gave a wry smile as he wished me luck. He didn't think they would have the foggiest idea why *The Lineup* was an impossible title for the picture.

Stirling, as usual, was right. Cooper and Del Valle felt that the title *The Lineup* could only help the picture. The success of the series practically guaranteed that the feature would have equal success.

ME: How about the failure of *Dragnet*? When I shot the pilot *Lineup*, neither of you had any idea of what to do to make it acceptable to the networks. Now, both of you know even less what is essential to make a money-making motion picture. You're making a serious mistake. Stirling agrees with me.

COOPER: Even Columbia approved it.

ME: That proves my point. I guess Stirling and I will have to live with it. It's going to be a chiller despite your lame contribution. Be seeing you – hopefully not soon.

I left before they had a chance to reply.

*

The killers wear conservative clothes. They pick up a driver, Sandy McLain (Richard Jaeckel). He is a hell of a driver with one bad habit: he is a closet drinker. Dancer carries a briefcase, inside which is a gun with a silencer, which he uses to get the narcotics by killing two of the carriers. He picks up the third carrier, a mother (Mary La Roche) and her little girl, holding a doll. Dancer, lithe and graceful, grabs the doll, violating it as he searches it for heroin. He discovers that the little girl has powdered the doll's face with it. He takes them to 'The Man', as proof that he hasn't stolen the heroin. 'The Man', in a wheelchair, arrives for the pick-up. Dancer moves quickly to him to report what has happened. 'The Man' replies simply, 'You're dead.' Dancer goes berserk, shoving the wheelchair backwards on to an ice-skating rink 100 feet below. Led by Dancer, they all rush to the car.

An impossibly scary chase begins with the police pursuing them. I try to make escapes and chases as hairy as I can. A near-miss is more exciting than one that's too far. That chase was difficult and dangerous to do. Years later, when I returned to San Francisco to shoot *Dirty Harry*, a police sergeant came up to me and pointed at his grey hair.

POLICE SERGEANT: You did that to me when we worked with you on *The Lineup*. I'll never get over that chase. How we didn't kill anybody, I'll never know.

And I didn't know myself. The shot in which the car comes to a sudden stop at the edge of the unfinished freeway was no trick shot. There was a five-storey sheer drop. We were photographing the action from the fifth-storey window of the city's YMCA. The stuntman who drove the car, Guy Way, had to be part insane. His girlfriend, doubling the mother, was in the car with him. She was hysterical for days after the shot. Dick Jaeckel was doubled by Way; the rest were doubled by other professional stuntpeople. There was no way we could protect them. We went over the scene many times before we shot it. Way knew what he was doing, but I was as nervous as the San Francisco police. If a tyre blew, or he slid too fast, they were all dead.

I cut the chase together without any dialogue or sound effects of tyres screeching and motors roaring, then ran it alone for Jaime Del Valle. When it was over, the projection room lights came on.

DEL VALLE: Not very exciting, is it?
ME: (*Stunned*) It's just the best car chase ever made.

Del Valle shrugged his shoulders and left the projection room. I pulled myself together and realized I had made a stupid mistake. There was nothing wrong with the film. What was wrong was running it without any sound. I had the editor carefully cut in sound effects and occasionally dialogue, consisting of the mother and daughter screaming, Julian yelling and Dancer enjoying it, laughing maniacally. I ran it again for Del Valle. This time, when the lights came on, he shook my hand in congratulations. His palm was wet with sweat. I learned an important lesson: the importance of sound effects. Frame for frame, exactly the same film. First running, without sound: a disaster. Second running, with sound: greatest chase ever.

19

Edge of Eternity

Columbia 1959

The setting of *Edge of Eternity* is one of the wonders of the world – the Grand Canyon in Arizona. The producer of the picture was Ken Sweet. All I knew about him was that he was a sound editor.

I read the script at Jack Elam's house. I liked the idea of doing a picture that took place in the Grand Canyon, but soon found out that the various studios were not interested in making a picture with Ken Sweet at the helm – a man who had absolutely no experience in producing pictures. Ken wanted Jack to play the lead. Jack was an excellent actor, but certainly no star and all the studios turned down the suggestion. Columbia had a commitment with Cornel Wilde and were interested in Cornel playing the lead, even though he was recuperating from a detached retina. They wanted me to direct the film, which was full of excitement, action and which would play well against the fantastic beauty of the Grand Canyon. As a further incentive, I was given the title 'associate producer'. I accepted, before I found out that I was being paid zilch for being an associate producer.

After scouting locations with Ken Sweet, we hastily (Columbia's way of working) cast the picture and picked our crew.

Cornel Wilde (detached retina still evident): Deputy Sheriff
Victoria Shaw (under contract to Columbia): Janice Kendon
Mickey Shaughnessy (comic relief turned villain): Scotty O'Brien
Edgar Buchanan (a former dentist, but sensational actor): Sheriff Edwards
Jack Elam (excellent actor, both comic and villain): Bill Ward
Ted Jacques (weightlifter): Suds Reese
Tom Fadden (elderly man): Eli
Screenplay: Knut Swenson and Richard Collins.
Cinematographer: Burnett Guffey
Editor: Jerome Thoms
Art Director: Robert Peterson

Music: Daniele Amfitheatrof

Our base was a motel in Kingman, Arizona. We decided to start shooting the second unit first. Each day, in a DC3, Ken Sweet, Burnett Guffey, electricians, grips, special effects and the production staff would fly from Kingman to land on a small plateau 1,500 feet above the floor of the canyon. I flew in a Cessna 180 with a bush pilot. (I learned to fly the plane. Actually, it was much safer than the DC3, a much larger plane.) On the plateau, a 50-foot ladder led to a small building which housed a bucket (cable car), which would swing and sway to the other side of the canyon, where there was an enormous bat guano cave. A scary experience – not only the ride; inside the cave were literally thousands of bats. With their mysterious radar, they would swoop down and just miss us. There was a danger of their biting or scratching. Rumour had it that they might have rabies. We beat a hasty retreat.

At first, on the plateau, when we were near the edge, we would lean backwards. The thought of slipping off to certain death was too frightening. But after a week, amazingly enough, we grew accustomed to the drop on all sides and didn't give it a thought. When the first unit arrived, I started to shoot a scene between Wilde and Elam where I tried to get them to stand near the edge of the plateau. When I got them somewhat in position, they were leaning backwards at a 45° angle. Disgusted and without thinking, I positioned myself between them and the edge. They screamed in terror.

ME: How in the hell can you play the scene bending backwards?
WILDE: If you don't get off that edge, we're quitting.
ELAM: I'm leaving now.

I pushed my way through them, explaining how ridiculous they looked. I told them I wasn't showing off and explained how I had felt exactly as they did when I first arrived. Finally, after lots of coaxing, they played the scene in an almost upright position. But they sure hated me and swore revenge.

*

The picture opens with two men fighting near the edge of the plateau. One of them falls to his death, while the other escapes. Deputy Sheriff Wilde is in his car waiting for any speeding vehicles. An elderly man (Tom Fadden), out of breath, staggers to Wilde and gasps out an incoherent story about a man who was attacked and almost killed. A car roars by. Wilde immediately sets chase, ignoring Fadden. Victoria Shaw is given a ticket by the Deputy Sheriff. We learn that her father owns a silver mine in the vicinity. When Wilde returns, he goes with Fadden to his cabin, where a murdered man is discovered. Sheriff Buchanan assigns Wilde to the case.

Fadden is murdered. Wilde tracks down a clue which leads to a friendly bartender, Shaughnessy, who turns out to be the murderer. Wilde finds evidence that Victoria Shaw's brother was in league with Shaughnessy in stealing silver from their father's mine. Shaughnessy murders the brother. He tries to flee across the canyon, but Wilde manages to jump on the swinging bucket, where he battles with Shaughnessy. After a desperate fight, Wilde manages to punch out Shaughnessy, who falls out of the bucket to certain death.

Cornel Wilde, for whom I have a great deal of respect as an actor and director, suffered throughout the picture from the detached retina, a very serious and painful handicap. When he had to climb the 50-foot ladder to reach the cable car, he hesitated. Without thinking, I scrambled up and down the ladder to show Wilde there was nothing to it. I wasn't showing off. Actually, I was scared to death. Wilde let us shoot him climbing the ladder – a brave but foolish thing for a man with a detached retina. If he appeared somewhat stiff in the picture, he had good cause. Wilde was a great athlete, a world-class sabre champion.

Poor Victoria Shaw was terrified of heights. She literally had to be carried up the steps with her eyes closed. Fortunately, she was supposed to look frightened. She gave a great performance.

Some of the things we did on the picture were the most dangerous stunts ever. Guy Way, who doubled Mickey Shaughnessy, actually dangled from that bucket, 1,500 feet in the air. A steel chain, wrapped around Guy and fastened securely to the bucket, rasping as it rubbed against the bucket, was the most terrifying noise I'd ever heard. Two professional high-wire stuntmen quit the picture. Guffey, the cameraman, and I had to take a helicopter to the bottom of the Grand Canyon, where not only had there never been any two-legged animals like us, but there had never been any four-legged ones either. The only signs of life were gnats. The helicopter swooped away to pick up equipment and an assistant cameraman. We wondered what would happen to us if the helicopter crashed and couldn't come back to pick us up. We planned an escape route. When the helicopter did come back and we completed our shooting (I started on a close shot of a wildflower, tilted up to the dancing bucket swaying out of control from the fighting of the stuntmen in the bucket), I asked the pilot to follow the route we had planned. We discovered, to our chagrin, that it led to a sudden straight drop of over 1,000 feet.

*

We worked with the enthusiastic help of the Arizona Sheriff's Department. One of the deputies had presumably worked in Hollywood. He put on airs that he knew the movie business from A to Z. The other deputies didn't like him and encouraged me to 'show him up'. I had no business in showing up this deputy. It was stupid of me to get involved. However, one of my many weaknesses is teasing. I couldn't resist the temptation, particularly when everyone on the set was in on the gag.

Early one morning, after giving Guffey the line-up, I went over to the 'Hollywood' deputy.

ME: Have you had any experience with acting – movie acting?
HOLLYWOOD DEPUTY: (*Eager*) Sure. I used to hang around Gower Street with the cowboys.
ME: (*Full of guile and other things*) I've got a difficult part of a heavy-set man in his thirties who has been attacked by a crazed man.
HOLLYWOOD DEPUTY: Hey – that's right up my alley.
(*I call the make-up man over.*)
ME: I want you to make up this deputy sheriff as though he ran into a buzz saw. Take your time. When you've finished, show him to me.

I started shooting a sequence with Cornel Wilde and Mickey Shaughnessy. Throughout the day, the make-up man would bring me the Hollywood deputy. Blood was coming out of his mouth and nostrils. I suggested blood running down from both eyes and ears. Later, when I saw that apparition, I suggested deep, bloody scars across his forehead. The next time, I suggested that the poor man have his throat slit. The sun would start setting within the hour. It was now or never with the most hideous man extant. I explained what I wanted.

ME: You look great. You know what it means when I yell 'Action'?
HOLLYWOOD DEPUTY: Yeah. I take off.
ME: (*Demonstrating*) Perfect. Now, when I yell 'Action', you take off as fast as you can. When I yell 'Stop' – and this is very important – you must stop on a dime.

I began to worry about the crew, actors and the rest of the deputies. I warned them not to give me away by laughing. There was no film in the camera. The make-up man freshened the Hollywood deputy's make-up.

ME: All right, roll'em!
SOUND MAN: Speed!
ME: Action!

The Hollywood deputy charged across the terrain, the empty camera panning with him.

ME: (*Without warning*) Stop!

He didn't stop on a dime – maybe a silver dollar. I walked over to him, my face showing my disappointment.

ME: You didn't stop on a dime. The camera stopped on 'Stop'. You didn't. Think you can do it? Soon there won't be any light.
HOLLYWOOD DEPUTY: Give me another chance.
  (*I hear someone giggling.*)
ME: (*Angry*) Damn it! Keep quiet! (*To Hollywood.*) Remember, run as fast as you can and be sure to freeze the instant I yell 'Stop!'

He did the best he could, which was miraculous. He stopped on a half-dollar. I went over to him and thanked him for his efforts. We had to stop shooting as we had run out of light.

ME: (*Hesitating*) I hate to ask you this, but your make-up took all day. Would you mind, terribly, if you kept your make-up on tonight? That way, we could start with you first.
HOLLYWOOD DEPUTY: Shucks, no.
ME: Are you married?
HOLLYWOOD DEPUTY: Sure am. Sarah'd never believe me if she didn't see me with her own eyes.

We packed up and left. My conscience bothered me.
  That night, the Mayor of Kingman gave a dinner in our honour. I sat next to him. Behind my back was a large plate-glass window through which could be seen and heard the main traffic of Kingman, mainly cars and trucks. I was called to the phone in the lobby of the motel.

ME: (*Picking up the receiver*) Hello, this is Don Siegel.
HOLLYWOOD DEPUTY: (*Voice cracked with tears and anger*) You dirty SOB. You think you're a wise guy . . .
  (*My heart skips three beats. Not only is he a big guy, but he wears a big revolver and is a deputy sheriff. I assume my best, icy-cool English manner.*)
ME: Now, old boy, there's absolutely no cause for anger . . .
HOLLYWOOD DEPUTY: (*Openly crying in rage*) You made fun of me! I'm leaving for the motel. I'm going to shove my gun up your ass and keep pulling the trigger!
  (*I am really scared. I try to pull myself together.*)
ME: I'm sitting next to the Mayor at a dinner in our honour. Sheriff Edwards is at the other end of the table. (*Swallowing.*) You'll be most welcome.

217

HOLLYWOOD DEPUTY: (*Still in a crazed rage*) Fuck the Mayor. Fuck
   Sheriff Edwards. But mostly, you bastard, *Fuck you!*

He slammed the receiver down. My heart beating furiously, I seated
myself next to the Mayor. People were talking to me on my right and left. I
turned around and stared at the street. My God! Hollywood could skid to
a stop directly opposite the back of my neck and fire away through the
plate-glass window. I turned back to practise sliding underneath the table,
as Cornell and his wife seated themselves opposite me.

WILDE: What are you looking for, Don?
   (*I pull myself up to a sitting position.*)
ME: Oh, nothing. I dropped my napkin.
   (*Cornel leans forwards and studies me. Each time I hear a car, I
   flinch.*)
WILDE: You look pale as a ghost. Are you feeling faint?
   (*I shake my head.*)
WILDE: Can I get you medical attention?

Something clicked. Why was Cornel so concerned about my well-being?
When I was on the phone, he wasn't at the table. Most people didn't know
it, but Cornel was a great mimic. I almost fainted with relief.

ME: (*Gaining strength*) I enjoyed our telephone conversation. You have
   a dreadful Arizona accent.

Silently, I swore revenge.
   On one of my many flights to the Grand Canyon with the bush pilot, I
innocently asked Cornel if he'd like to join us. It was the only way to fly.
Happily, he agreed. When we took off, Cornell sitting behind me, I waited
until we gained altitude before taking over the controls. I immediately
pulled back on the stick, gaining altitude rapidly.

WILDE: (*Uneasily*) I didn't know you flew.
   (*The pilot is in on my plot and plays his part well.*)
PILOT: He doesn't. I just wish he'd remember that this is an old plane.
   I wish he'd quit trying to reach the sun.
ME: (*Laughing manically*) One day, I'll reach the heavens.
CORNEL: You know I have a detached retina. This is not good for me.
ME: Really? Well, how about this?
   (*I push the stick forwards and the plane plunges straight down. It
   feels like the speed is Mach 1.*)
CORNEL: (*Screaming*) You're crazy!
ME: (*To the pilot*) Ain't that fun? I can't pull the stick back.

PILOT: I've got it. We'll pull out now.

The ground was rushing up to meet us at terrific speed. I was feeling queasy. I heard a moan from Cornel. I smiled. As the plane pulled out of the dive, I turned to him.

ME: You look pale as a ghost. Are you feeling faint?

I must confess that no matter what happened from there on, nobody would feel as scared as I did from Cornel's mimicry of the Hollywood deputy.

*

Edge of Eternity is the first picture I did in Cinemascope. I don't like the proportions at all. Look at the great paintings in museums: they are not in the shape of Band-aids. I prefer the older, rectangular aperture.

20

Hound Dog Man

Twentieth Century Fox 1959

Hound Dog is a delightful, funny book set in the South. I must confess that I loved its simplicity. But complications immediately set in. Jerry Wald, the executive producer, wanted to star a neophyte actor, Fabian. He also wanted him to sing at least twelve songs in the picture. Fabian, though one of the nicest kids I ever met, couldn't sing and knew it. The title *Hound Dog Man* reminded me of Elvis Presley's great hit song. I pointed out to Wald that Presley fans wouldn't go to the movie because he wasn't in it. I wanted to make Fred Gipson's excellent novel into a film which didn't feature any songs. Wald turned me down flat. My reply fell on deaf ears.

ME: Sam Peckinpah wanted to do a picture based strictly on the book. I'm sorry he didn't do it. He would have done it the way it should have been made – small.

I lost, but decided to have as much fun with the picture as possible. All but one of Fabian's songs were interrupted abruptly – as when the villain, Claude Akins, rides into the middle of a Fabian song yelling for Fabian and Stuart Whitman to quit bothering his hogs; or a girl loses control of her buckboard before Fabian can sing more than a phrase. Wald seemed puzzled at how easily the picture went together.

I had never done a picture in this genre. It was a welcome change of pace to direct a film that children could go to see. I wish I could do more. My reputation may be as a director of violence – stemming from my second-unit days – but that doesn't mean I can't, or don't want to do comedy, or love stories. My favourite picture is *Brief Encounter*, a simple, small movie.

It's difficult to get over in a précis the fun, the beauty, the splendid acting, the wondrous feeling of robust freedom in *Hound Dog Man*. Stuart Whitman wrapped up his carefree part with the ease of a brilliant actor. The woods and countryside are his domain. He takes Fabian and his kid brother on a hunting trip with Stuart's closest friends – his hounds.

Carol Lynley, who wants to marry Whitman, waylays the group. Whitman still prefers the hounds, though Carol is beautiful and wholesome. Claude Akins, known as Hog, suddenly looms on the idyllic scene threatening one and all if they tarry on his property. L. Q. Jones joins his good friends and promptly, in his ebullient manner, breaks his leg. They rush to get the doctor, Edgar Buchanan, who quickly sets L. Q.'s leg. Any happening is a good excuse to have a party. The celebration of the setting of L. Q.'s leg is rudely interrupted by Hog Akins, who, pulling a gun, tries to shoot Whitman for fooling around with his wife. Arthur O'Connell, Fabian's father, a quiet, subdued man, steps into the imbroglio and faces Hog, never uttering a word. Carol Lynley stands beside Whitman. Hog disappears into the night, searching for his wife. Fabian, proud of his father, tells him so. O'Connell simply says, 'All I done was what had to be done.' All ends in happiness when Betty Field, O'Connell's wife, tells her younger son that he can keep the hound dog he was given by Whitman.

Stanley Kauffman, writing in the *New Republic*, said, 'The picture creates an easy, bucolic Huck Finn feeling.' Philip T. Hartung, in *The Commonweal*, wrote, 'Their adventures in this lovely Southern country are full of nature lore, excitement and humor.'

21

Flaming Star

Twentieth Century Fox 1960

Nunnally Johnson, one of Hollywood's most respected writers (*The Grapes Of Wrath, The Gunfighter, The Three Faces of Eve* and a number of other distinguished films), wrote a screenplay about the trials and tribulations of a half-breed specifically for Marlon Brando. Incredibly, it became a vehicle for Elvis Presley.

The producer, David Weisbart, an old friend from Warner Brothers days, gave me the script to read. It was based on a story by Clair Huffaker, a well-known Western writer who always dressed in complete Western attire. I felt the need for a straightforward chat with David.

WEISBART: What do you think of the project?

ME: The script shows great promise. I must admit I'm confused. Why Presley?

WEISBART: (*Smiling*) He's a big box-office star.

ME: You ought to know. You gave him his first break in *Love Me Tender*.

WEISBART: Don't you think he can do it?
(*I fall back on my old usage of the word 'refocusing'.*)

ME: Surely you are aware of the need to refocus on the script?

WEISBART: Certainly he's no Brando. On the other hand, Brando's no Presley. What I'd like you to do is get with Clair Huffaker. Clair told me that a rewrite would work.

ME: What about Nunnally?

WEISBART: He won't talk with me, or the studio.

ME: In a way, I'm glad to hear that. I was beginning to think I was crazy. Realistically, you realize that we've got, without looking for trouble, a *considerable* rewrite.

WEISBART: Make yourself and Clair heroes. Let me see the pages on the rewrite as soon as you're satisfied with them. (*He stands up, shaking my hand.*) Good luck.

ME: I'll need it, and your prayers. God bless.

I left worried, but happy to be working for one of the industry's gentlemen.

The problem facing my Western writer, his boots up on the table, was simply this. Would the public accept a serious story with Elvis playing a half-breed – not accepted by the white neighbours for having an Indian mother (Dolores Del Rio), a white father (John McIntire), a white brother (Steve Forrest) born of an earlier marriage of his father to a white woman? To compound the problem, in the story the Kiowa tribe, headed by their Chief Buffalo Horn (Rudolfo Acosta) insist that Elvis and his mother return to their people. There were other problems. The studio wanted Elvis to sing at least ten songs throughout the picture. I told Clair, whom I liked and trusted, what I had done with Fabian in *Hound Dog Man*.

HUFFAKER: (*Laughing*) I saw the picture. Every time Fabian started to sing, someone, or something, interrupted him. (*He grows serious.*) But there's more than a bit of difference. Most folk think Elvis is the best singer in all America. Fabian doesn't sing a lick.

16 *Flaming Star*: Elvis Presley protects Dolores Del Rio

ME: Unfortunately true. But supposing we had Elvis sing over the main titles and sing one simple song at the party, less than a minute into the picture?

HUFFAKER: You'll never get away with it.

ME: How can Elvis sing 'rock songs', or any kind of songs after the traumatic experiences that constantly plague him? A white family leaving the party, massacred by the Kiowa tribe; the townspeople hating Elvis and his family; the Indians not accepting McIntire's offer to live together in peace; Elvis's mother shot by a deranged white man; Elvis becoming an Indian; the Indians killing McIntire; Forrest, in revenge, killing the Chief, but getting severely wounded; Elvis attempting to save his brother by tying him to his horse, hoping the horse will return to town; Elvis fighting the pursuing Kiowas; Forrest's girlfriend, who loves him and in a dramatic scene at McIntire's cabin learns that Elvis is in love with her, accompanying Forrest to meet Elvis, approaching the town slowly on horseback, mortally wounded; Elvis telling his brother that he has seen the Flaming Star; Elvis wheeling his horse about to go and die like an Indian. . . . (*Pause.*) Now that I've told you the story, more or less, do you feel that Elvis can sing his way through it?

HUFFAKER: Frankly, I reckon you're right. And you can quote me. But Don, in all honesty, the deck is stacked against you. There's not a smidgen of a chance.

ME: I'll see David. I'll use your quote. Be seeing you, cowpoke.

I saw David, always charming, a good listener and always fair. I told him that Elvis couldn't sing ten songs in his picture and that Clair agreed with me.

WEISBART: (*Stalling*) At least the rough outline sounded promising. There's no question that Elvis can play the part well. I don't know if the front office will accept Elvis only singing over the main titles and at the party. But I agree with you and I'll do my best to convince them. What if I get turned down? Will you accept their decision?

ME: I'll accept your decision.

WEISBART: I appreciate that. I've some strange casting news. We're pretty well set on the picture, except for the part of Forrest's girlfriend.

ME: Doesn't appear to be a major problem. There are about two hundred actresses who'd give more than uttering their lines to play opposite Elvis.

WEISBART: The studio wants a tall, black-haired English actress to play the part. Barbara Steele. She's had very little experience and is not a good actress. I don't like the leading lady towering over Elvis.

ME: Let me have a go-around with the head of casting. I promise, I won't quit.

WEISBART: Just don't punch him out

Owen McLean, head of casting, whom I knew and liked at other studios, had become a pompous ass. He said the reason I didn't like Barbara Steele was because she had black hair. I told him flatly that the only reason I didn't want her in the picture was to protect Presley. She couldn't act. In addition, I feared Elvis's reaction when he was asked to stand on an apple box to be eye-level with her. Owen had a brilliant idea. He would shoot a test of Miss Steele in a golden wig. He was adamant that we would flip out when we saw her.

ME: What about her height and her English accent?

MCLEAN: I'll shoot her in a scene from the script with an actor the size of Elvis.

ME: Why the big fuss about her?

MCLEAN: Because I think she's perfect for the part.

ME: What about the studio?

MCLEAN: They love her.

ME: (*Slyly*) Literally?
    (*He gets to his feet, angry.*)

MCLEAN: I'll see you and David when I've shot the test.
    (*As it is a 'no-no' to punch the idiot out, I decide to indulge in my favourite pastime, teasing.*)

ME: I'll report our conversation to my karate partner, Elvis.
    (*He appears terror-stricken.*)

MCLEAN: Under no circumstances mention a word of our meeting to Elvis. Is that clearly understood?

ME: (*Getting up to leave*) I think I got the message.

A week later, Weisbart and I saw the test with Owen. Miss Steele had blonde hair, a slight stoop and a Western accent straight from Birmingham. When we demurred, we were told that the studio had already made an irrevocable decision: Miss Steele was playing opposite Presley. We thanked Owen for his efforts on our behalf and left. Weisbart was upset.

WEISBART: I've never run into a situation like this.

ME: Something smells rotten in Greece. In the social world that I travel in, I heard a faint, very faint rumour that Chairman of the Board, Mr Skouras, is interested.

WEISBART: My God! We're dead.

ME: Not at all. Let's start the picture, do our best and see what happens.

On that happy note, we left for our respective offices.

*

We started the picture at the Twentieth Century Fox Ranch, near Malibu. Miss Steele, in her blonde wig and slippers, was very pleasant. I liked her personally, but her woeful lack of experience and strange Western accent, plus her height, proved her undoing. I tried to help her, despite some strange looks from Presley. Weisbart looked on glumly. Late in the afternoon, I took him aside.

ME: All you have to do is run the dailies with the executives. If necessary, put the blame on my shoulders. It probably won't be necessary, as the film speaks for itself.

WEISBART: I'm leaving right now to set up the running.

ME: I'll shoot around her so that she won't be embarrassed.

The next day, at about 11.30 a.m., I received a telephone call from David.

WEISBART: We've won: but I don't know who we've won. The moguls are busy casting an experienced actress.

ME: Congratulations.

WEISBART: I'll accept that when I know who we are getting. Please do me a favour. Have a talk with Miss Steele. I know you feel sorry for her. She's a pleasant girl and doesn't deserve this kind of treatment.

ME: Shall do, and I shall send her back to the studio. Maybe you can get some flowers and a note expressing your thoughts.

WEISBART: Good idea . . . and thanks.

I had lunch with Miss Steele in my trailer. I tried to be as gentle as I could. I explained that she was miscast. It wasn't fair to her. To my astonishment, she seemed relieved.

STEELE: I told Mr McLean and other executives that I was uncomfortable in the role. I'm happy I'm off the picture. I want to thank you and Mr Weisbart for being so kind.

Two days later, Miss Barbara Eden, an experienced, beautiful blonde actress, appeared on the location. There was no question that she would give an excellent performance. One thing did bother me, though. In the picture, she lived in a small, isolated Western town. I felt that her hair should at least be unkempt, but it was coiffured with great care and style. Her clothes, which should have been homespun and plain, were expensively tailored. She looked much, much too well dressed for this frontier town of about twenty people. I decided, after checking with David, to leave well enough alone. At least she was considerably smaller than Elvis.

*

Presley surprised me with his sensitivity as an actor. Colonel Parker, his mentor and personal manager, thought there should definitely be more songs. He was wrong on two counts: Elvis could have become an acting star, not just a singing star; also, he would have been happier. Colonel Parker was strictly interested in the buck. He had a strong Machiavellian influence on Elvis.

When it came to karate, Elvis had few peers. I hired a black-belt stuntman, who was an instructor for the Marines, but when they had their scene, a rough, tough fight, Elvis proved embarrassing: he was twice as fast and twice as good as the Marine instructor.

There was a difficult scene in the cabin in which Elvis is supposed to try to kill a white doctor who arrives too late to attend to his mother's wounds. Elvis is pulled off the doctor by his brother Forrest in front of a horrified Barbara Eden. The moment of truth hits Elvis as he declares his unrequited love for Barbara. Elvis felt he couldn't do the scene: he felt that his acting talent wasn't equal to the sequence. When I pointed out to him that we would rehearse until he was satisfied with his performance, he begged for more time to prepare. Almost childlike, he offered me the use of his brand-new black Rolls-Royce until we had to do the scene. He was so upset that I decided to push the shooting date back as far as possible. I took him up on his offer to use his Rolls-Royce, and for two weeks I felt like a millionaire, driving his superb car. When the inevitable time came to do the scene, I returned his Rolls-Royce. To Presley's amazement and mine, Elvis gave his finest performance ever.

Flaming Star proved challenging. The burial of Dolores Del Rio, I felt, was one of the key scenes in the picture, certainly the most poignant. I tried to do it with as much meaning as possible, yet with simplicity. I made it with the five people (Elvis Presley, Steve Forrest, Barbara Eden, Ford Rainey and John McIntire) at the grave on different levels, with each turning to walk away towards the house in descending order of their closeness to the dead woman. The scene closes with her husband, McIntire, standing there alone and the others fading in the distance.

22

Hell Is for Heroes

Paramount Pictures 1962

On a Sunday evening, after dinner at my house, six couples started to get
ready to leave to view a current film at MGM. The phone rang, and I took
the call in my office. It was Marty Rackin, recently named head of
production at Paramount, speaking authoritatively.

RACKIN: Do you remember where I live?
ME: Where else but Beverly Hills? I was at your house a week ago with
Eddie O'Brien.
RACKIN: I want you to meet me here as soon as possible. Then we'll
drive to Paramount.
ME: What for?
RACKIN: I have a script I want you to read.
ME: There are six couples at my house, ready to leave for MGM to see
a movie. Can't I see you Monday morning?
RACKIN: No. I'm offering you a directorial assignment, providing you
like the script.
(*The full import of Marty being the boss suddenly hits me.*)
ME: (*Weakly*) I'll be right over.

When I announced to the group that I couldn't go with them, as I had to
pick up a script at Paramount, all the wives threw sharp, questioning
glances at their spouses. Everyone knows that you don't pick up a script
on a Sunday night. For one thing, the studio is locked, closed until
Monday morning. I apologized and saw them all to the door.

When I arrived at Marty's house, to my surprise he was waiting in his
car. The moment I sat beside him, he tore off for Paramount. He uttered
no greeting, no clue about the script, nothing.

ME: How do you like being a mogul?
RACKIN: It's a hell of a lot of work and no fun.
ME: Why are you doing it?
RACKIN: (*Looking at me queerly*) Money.

(He stops at the main gate at Paramount and speaks to the cop in the cubicle.)

RACKIN: I'm Marty Rackin and I have to get into my office.

COP: You could be Houdini and not be able to get in.

(Marty loses his temper and is somewhat embarrassed in front of me. He gets out of his car and rifles through his wallet.)

RACKIN: I'm head of production. Call Mr Balaban and tell him I want in.

(The cop stares stupidly at Marty.)

RACKIN: *(Handing over Balaban's card)* And don't take all night about it.

The cop called. Immediately, the gates opened. When we were inside Marty's office, he found a script and threw it petulantly on to his desk. I opened the first page and paled. The script, *Hell Is for Heroes*, was written, produced and directed by Robert Pirosh.

ME: Marty, there's some mistake. Bob Pirosh is one of the most respected talents in Hollywood and one of my best friends.

RACKIN: Well for crying out loud, who do you think gave him the assignment? If you don't want to even read it, there're fifty directors waiting in the wings.

ME: I'm sorry, but I couldn't replace him.

RACKIN: *(Exploding)* You schmuck head, he's walking off the show. He doesn't want to do it. He and Steve McQueen don't agree on anything.

ME: I'm sorry about that.

RACKIN: Here's the final word – and I mean final. You read the script tonight; call me at nine tomorrow morning if you want to do it. Under *no* circumstances call Bob. The deal with him is not set.

ME: Well, let's get back to your house where I can pick up my car – that is if the cop will let us out.

I drove away from Marty's house hating myself for taking the script from him. As soon as I got home I called Bob and told him that Marty had given me the script to direct.

ME: What the hell's the matter with you?

PIROSH: One word: McQueen. Second word: Rackin.

ME: You're getting a royal screwing, but at the same time, you're stupid. So you don't direct the picture – but at least produce it and write it. I can take some of the pressure off as the director. How about it?

PIROSH: I'll admit we had fun doing *The Big Steal*, but I don't want anything to do with *Hell Is for Heroes*.
ME: Bob, have you anything against my directing your picture?
PIROSH: On the contrary, good luck – you'll need it.

*

I met Steve McQueen in Marty Rackin's office. Others were there: Dick Carr (writer), Al Manuel (Rackin's associate), Hilly Elkins (McQueen's personal manager). With the exception of a very tight McQueen, everyone else was positively beaming.

MCQUEEN: I don't understand all the happiness. My name goes on the picture and I still don't like the project.

Protestations came from all of us, but Steve was more than equal to holding his own. First, he took on Marty. He blamed him for letting Pirosh get away with an inferior concept. He then whirled on Carr and accused him of being a company writer – a hack. Before Carr could defend himself, he bawled out Hilly, who didn't look after his interest, always taking the easy way. Al Manuel was a joke hiding behind Rackin. Then he turned to me. He explained how he worked with a director. He hoped I didn't mind if he looked through the camera on every shot.

ME: I don't mind. The cameraman might though.
MCQUEEN: (*With modesty*) Now, I throw ideas at the director all the time. Maybe four or five hundred. I don't say they're all good. Maybe only one hundred and fifty are usable.
ME: (*Breaking in*) I don't care who I get the ideas from – the grip, the electrician. My name goes on the screen as the director. But there's one thing you better be damn sure you understand (*hitting the desk hard so everything bounces about*): I'm the director! Come hell or high water.

I thought at first that Steve was suffering an epileptic attack. His face contorted and he appeared to have difficulty breathing. He attempted to exorcise the evil that was torturing him. He struggled to attack me – and no one grabbed to stop him. I heard a loud laugh down the hall, which I recognized as my agent, Marty Baum. I leapt for the door and rushed down the corridor to Baum.

ME: (*Quickly*) Make the deal – any deal. I think I've blown it.
(*I run back to the office. Everyone is standing outside in the quadrangle. I go straight up to Steve.*)
ME: Are we going to have lunch?

STEVE: (*Having difficulty speaking*) Don't ever do that again.

RACKIN: Got to get back to my office.

    (*No one pays any attention to him except Al Manuel, who follows close behind. I decide to have it out with Steve.*)

ME: I'm bored with people who think they are the only ones who care whether a picture is good, bad or indifferent. I want this picture to be better than you do. And one last thing: I'm *not* a company man.

ELKINS: Let's cut the chit-chat and go to lunch.

To my astonishment, Steve led the way to the commissary. At lunch, he told me all the troubles he was having with Rackin. I was properly sympathetic. Right on cue, Marty loomed over the table. Things were going well until that moment.

RACKIN: (*To Steve*) I want you to start getting your wardrobe in shape. Don, you go with him. Then I want you, Steve, to go to the gallery and get some photos taken.

    (*Without warning, Steve shoves the table hard against Marty, who looks surprised and frightened.*)

MCQUEEN: (*Hissing*) Don't push me, Marty.

I was drinking a bottle of beer. The thought flashed through my head: what if I crash the bottle on Steve's head? Would that mean that Marty would figure I had saved his life, that my job would become a sinecure? Marty spun away and left the commissary. I finished the beer.

*

In *Hell Is for Heroes*, McQueen's hair is butch cut, his face bearded as he arrives to join an army squad as a demoted sergeant, now wearing no stripes at all. His only concern: his weapons. He carries a chip on his shoulder and appears crazed by the scars of war. The squad is taken to the front, led by the company sergeant, Fess Parker. We learn that Fess and Steve have known each other at the beginning of the war. Fess tells the squad he is fearful the Germans might break through. At this point, Steve, suspicious of anyone, looks disbelievingly at Fess. Harry Guardino is left in charge of the squad. Before Fess leaves to scout the area, he instructs Harry to have the squad make sufficient noise to give the impression that a full company of men, not just a squad, is encamped on the hill. James Coburn skilfully attaches all sorts of contraptions to make a jeep sound like a tank. Bob Newhart discovers a German bugged phone and uses it to give the impression that the hill is crowded with a full company of soldiers. Bobby Darin and Mike Kellin march furiously about. Nick

Adams, a Polish refugee, goes to Steve saying he wants to kill Germans. Steve says nothing while ominously sharpening his knife and bayonet. A few Germans attack their position and are shot down. Harry is found and killed, leaving James in charge. He asks Steve for help. Steve replies truculently that they have only one chance: to attempt to blow up the German pillbox across the open mine-field that controls the section opposite them. The whole squad is very brave, crawling through several mine-fields on their perilous way to the pillbox. James, following Steve, is shattered by a mine. The pillbox opens fire and mortally wounds Mike. Fess suddenly appears. He questions the remaining men to find out who was responsible for leading the attack. Steve, on the brink of a nervous breakdown, admits that he was. Several companies attack the pillbox. Steve immolates himself by rolling into it with a package of dynamite. The pillbox is destroyed as soldiers run by, dying.

*

The censor notes made little sense. Those responsible eliminated such naughty expressions as 'they're gonna be damn sure . . .'; 'Where the hell . . .'; 'we'll be damned near pinned . . .'; 'I don't give a damn what you think . . .'; 'gonna be damn sure . . .'; 'What the hell?'

I don't feel that the words 'damn' and 'hell' are *bad* words – and these men were, after all, supposed to be in the army and under fire. The result of all this stupidity – we used them anyway.

*

The temperature in the shade, and there wasn't any, was 117°. A retired colonel in charge of our welfare refused to be responsible for our health if we worked in this impossible heat. Need I add: we worked. In other group endeavours, people are trained to climb mountains, ford rough waters, work in freezing temperatures, etc. But the studios take untrained people and *tell* them to do their job, no matter how dangerous it might be. And in the land of the free, we do it.

Special effects spent a whole day getting over 100 big charges ready to explode. The terrain was rocky and dangerous, not only to the actors and stuntmen but to the whole crew, all of whom had to wear hard hats. Every explosion was numbered on a big board. The gravest danger was the possibility of blowing up running soldiers, more than 100 men, if they were too near the heavy, spectacular explosions. Possibly because I had spent seven years in special effects, the board was handed to me. That meant if something went wrong, it would be my fault.

I went through my usual spiel about making it as good as possible without anyone getting hurt, then, board in hand, I talked to the actors, stuntmen and extras. I explained in detail where the explosions would go

17 *Hell Is for Heroes*: Steve McQueen – 'the strongest eyes in the world'

off. There would be lots of smoke and fire. Rocks would be flying through the air. If they felt they were too near the explosions, they must hit the deck, then start up again, always with their backs to the seven cameras I was using. If the going got too tough, they were to pretend they were hit, take a fall to the ground and lie still as though killed. I asked if there were any questions. There were none. They were ready to charge.

On 'Action', I set off two huge explosions. The captain led his company as they ran, stumbled and fell on the terrain. I concentrated on where the men were when I let the charges go. Bobby Darin stumbled to the ground. Without warning, he got up, turned to the cameras, stretched his arms out helplessly and slowly started back up the hill. I yelled in my hand mike, 'Cut! Cut! Cut!' That was the end of shooting for the day.

The next morning, everything worked. Bobby fell down again, but Fess Parker grabbed him by the scruff of the neck and rushed him out of sight. Nobody got hurt and the action looked sensational.

After we had made the big shots of the battle, Marty Rackin insisted that we return to the studio to finish the picture. I used an entire stage full of rocks and trees. For one scene I wanted a close-up of Steve crying. I had a long talk with him about his motivations for breaking down. We both had worked with the Stanislavski method, and I felt confident that Steve, face set, eyes straight ahead, military bearing, when he walked from an extreme long shot into a huge close-up, would start crying. We shot it. Nothing, absolutely nothing in those bitter blue eyes. Not a glimmer of a tear. We didn't give up. When Steve walked into his close-up, we blew chopped onion shreds directly below his eyes. It might as well have been chopped liver.

Steve probably had the strongest eyes in the world. I decided on desperate measures. This time when I yelled 'Action', as steely-eyed Steve started walking I slapped him sharply across his face – then dived over an embankment, expecting him to tackle me. Instead, he walked on and, as usual, nothing happened.

My eventual solution wasn't what I wanted, but it worked. We put drops into Steve's eyes to make him look as if he was crying. I made a one-foot dissolve from the huge close-up to an insert of his eyes crying. It worked for me – I felt great empathy for him.

*

I would never make a war picture unless it was strongly anti-war. No side wins a war. How hypocritical warring nations are. Both sides have their priests and ministers pray to the same God for victory. War is senseless and futile. It is true that hell is for heroes. It is equally true that for heroes there is only hell.

23

The Killers

Universal 1964

Back in 1946, the producer Mark Hellinger was preparing a picture at Universal based on Ernest Hemingway's short story 'The Killers'. He asked Jack Warner to negotiate for my services as director of the film. Warner, who hated Hellinger and loathed me, said an immediate, 'No', and hung up. This was stupid of him, as I had just started to direct my first feature. It would have made me an important property for Warner Brothers to have under contract. Robert Siodmak directed the picture starring Burt Lancaster, Ava Gardner, Edmond O'Brien and others.

Seventeen years later, in 1963, I was in Lew Wasserman's office at Universal. He was President of the company and wanted me to direct a new version of 'The Killers'. It was going to be the first two-hour movie made for television. I told him I didn't want to make a xerox of the Mark Hellinger picture. He said he certainly didn't want that either, that's why he was prepared to hire me to produce and direct the remake.

I told him that the story was one of my favourites. Inasmuch as it was used in its entirety for the beginning of the original movie, I would have to come up with a different opening. The only idea from the picture I wished to use was the catalyst of a man knowing he's going to be killed and making no attempt to escape sure death. Not one word of Hemingway's dialogue would be used, nor would there be any scenes similar to those in the movie. Wasserman and I enthusiastically agreed on telling the story from the killers' point of view.

ME: Mr Wasserman, I'm really excited about the project. We seem to agree on our attack on the story. Who do you think should write the screenplay?

WASSERMAN: Gene Coon. He's written many scripts for me. He's intelligent (*smiling*) and fast.

ME: When do I start?

WASSERMAN: (*Getting up and shaking my hand*) You're on salary. (*Looking at his watch.*) You're also behind schedule. (*Looking at his desk pad.*) It's urgent that you prepare to shoot pre-production of the Sixth Annual Riverside Grand Prix on October thirteenth, two weeks from this coming Sunday. I suggest you meet with Paul Donnelly to work out the details.

ME: Paul's an excellent man. I'll need all the help I can beg, borrow or steal.

Paul, head of the production department, was Irish, black-haired and handy with his fists. He and I were good friends. I trusted his expert opinion. The only rub was that he was a loyal 'company' man. I was primarily interested in doing the work as well as possible, period.

DONNELLY: It's a tough job. We've got to make the race date. There will be over a hundred thousand spectators, plus at least thirty racing cars. We sure as hell can't stage the Riverside Grand Prix.

ME: I must meet with Gene Coon as soon as possible. I not only have to figure out what I need, but how to do it.

DONNELLY: Remember, you only get one crack at that race.

ME: I'll get back to you when I've finished with Gene. I hope by then I'll have it figured out.

DONNELLY: Whatever I can do to help, you can count on it.

ME: (*At door*) I wish I could count on your getting me a second unit to do the work.

DONNELLY: Wasserman would throw me off the lot.

ME: (*Going out*) We'll go down the drain together.

Gene Coon, a thin man in his late forties, had the tired expression of *déjà vu*. He had written so many scripts, he was not only tired but also bored. When I told him of my conversation with Wasserman, his only reaction was, 'Let's call the film "Johnny North".' I told him that was fine with me, particularly as it certainly wasn't Hemingway's 'The Killers'.

COON: I've been told to get right on the screenplay. They want to make it as soon as possible. I hear you're shooting the Riverside Grand Prix on October thirteenth.

ME: Have you any ideas on how to shoot it?

COON: Not a clue. You're the director. Shoot it.

ME: I think we should work together. Certainly I should see the pages as soon as possible.

COON: Just as long as you don't slow me up.

ME: My job is *not* to slow you up. My job is to help you write a better script. After all, I'm producing and directing this show. (*My face*

236

tightens.) So let's be sure that I get your pages without delay. If you want to talk about anything, I'm available.

COON: I think I can handle it.

I left aware that I'd better start figuring out how to shoot the race sequence.

*

Bill Brademan and Jere Henshaw, casting executives, finally read the script and we held a meeting with what I thought were excellent suggestions from them. We decided to submit only the best actor available for each part. On one part no one was suggested, as none of us felt we had come up with the right actor. I was impressed. Previously, I generally had about ten actors for consideration. In a number of pictures, many of the ten selected for each part were not good. Here is the cast we were going to try for:

Lee Marvin: Lee Strom (the older, experienced killer. All business.)
Clu Gulager: Charlie (the younger killer. He kills because he likes it. Psychotic sense of humour. No dissipations. An exercise nut.)
John Cassavetes: Johnny North (expert racing-car driver. Fearless. An eye for the wild ladies.)
Angie Dickinson: Sheila Farr (a racing-car buff. The attractive gal friend of many men. The mistress of the boss gangster.)
Jack Browning (boss gangster. No realistic suggestions for actor.)
Claude Akins: Earl Sylvester (close friend and partner in racing of Johnny North.)
Norman Fell: Shorty (a gangster. Owner of gym.)
Virginia Christine: Miss Watson (in charge of High Sage Home for the Blind.)
Kathleen O'Malley: Receptionist (for Jack Browning.)

I went to see Lee Marvin, whom I liked and admired. He moved like a cat, a ballet dancer, but there was nothing homosexual about him. On the contrary, he was mucho macho with an eye for the ladies. He could be dangerous when drunk. He liked to fight and was very knowledgeable about street-fighting and karate. We talked about the part of the older killer. His curiosity was relentless over why Johnny North, knowing he is about to be killed, doesn't make any effort to escape. He liked that. On the other hand, he didn't like the fact that there were two killers. Why split the part? He'd rather satisfy his curiosity about Johnny on his own.

MARVIN: Perhaps I should play the part of Johnny, who doesn't run away. He's a hell of a racing driver. Plus the fact that he's playing the title role, 'Johnny North'. (*Grins.*) Of course, you're only the producer/director and I suspect strongly also the co-writer, so you wouldn't be aware that the part of Johnny North is larger than both killers together.

ME: Everything you've said is true and spoken like the cunning actor you are. You can play any part in the picture you want. But I'll tell you this – the best, most interesting, most exciting, most dangerous, most original part in the picture is the older killer. (*Lee studies me for a long moment.*)

MARVIN: Who is playing the younger killer?

ME: Don't know yet. I wanted to talk to you first. I'll tell you who I'd like to get. Clu Gulager.

MARVIN: Damn good actor. I'll have to watch myself or he'll steal the show.

ME: Are you going to play the older killer?

MARVIN: Always was from day one.

ME: Figured.

*

Clu Gulager, dressed as a cowboy, sauntered into my office, sat down on a chair and put his boots up on my desk. He was a good-looking, 6-foot, well-built man of about thirty. He had a chip on his shoulder and a silly, challenging grin on his face.

ME: I hear you're temperamental, difficult to get along with.

GULAGER: That about sums me up.

ME: If you weren't temperamental and difficult to get along with, I wouldn't be interested in working with you. (*Clu looks puzzled. It is a common rumour that he spent most of his time quitting the TV series* The Virginian.)

ME: I'd like you to play the younger killer in 'Johnny North'. The older killer, Lee Marvin, has just accepted the part of your mentor. (*Clu takes his boots off the desk. He learns forward like I have hooked him.*)

GULAGER: Lee's a hell of an actor.

ME: That's what he said about you. (*Clu looks pleased.*)

ME: Including that you'd try to steal the show.

GULAGER: Fat chance stealing anything from Lee.

ME: Well, I'll tell you something that I hope doesn't scare you. That's exactly what I want you to do. I don't want two killers that are two peas in a pod. I want you to be exactly what *The Virginian* doesn't want you to be. In the picture, Lee is methodical, all business, which he knows better than anyone. He's ruthless, but calm. No wasted motions. You, on the other hand, are crazy, capable of anything. You take good care of yourself. Lee drinks scotch and smokes. You drink milk, or orange juice, and you don't smoke. You're an exercise nut. Lee has no sense of humour. You're always doing screwy things, the unexpected. You like scaring people, including snuffing people out. Lee kills for solid reasons. The two of you get along, but your approach to killing is poles apart. You have fun; Lee has success.

GULAGER: Sounds great. In reading the script, I had no conception of the part; or the script, for that matter.

ME: I have a conception, but it's not in the script . . . yet. Do you want the part?

GULAGER: Mr Siegel, I. . . .

ME: (*Interrupting*) The name's Don, Clu.

GULAGER: Don, I'll do the picture for nothing.

ME: There's nothing in this picture you'll do for nothing. Now get lost and start thinking. Come up with insane ideas.

*

Script in hand, I went to see John Cassavetes at his house. I offered him the role of Johnny North and handed him the script. He didn't take it. I thought that a bit peculiar. John was one of my best friends – a quadruple-talented man, an actor, director, producer and writer. Also, sometimes, a huge pain in the neck.

ME: (*Sitting down*) You afraid you might strain your hand if you took the script?

CASSAVETES: I don't have to read the script. If you want me, I'll do it.

ME: You don't read the script, I don't want you.

CASSAVETES: I need the money, so it doesn't matter what I think of the script.

ME: I not only insist on your reading the script immediately, but I need your input.

CASSAVETES: Whatever for? You're making it. I'll memorize the lines and be a good boy.

ME: Something's bugging you and I don't like it.
(*I get up, script still in hand, and start for the door.*)

CASSAVETES: What happened to your sense of humour?

ME: Gone, totally. Kiss Gena for me. Why that lovely gal ever married you is the Greek mystery of the week.

CASSAVETES: (*Joining me*) She's Welsh – I'm Greek. Give me the script. Well, what do you know. Am I playing the title role?

ME: (*Still trying to figure him out*) You're Johnny North, under certain rigid rules.

CASSAVETES: I'll sit right down and read it before your very eyes.

ME: When you've digested it, call me and let me in on the big secret. What do you really think about the script? I'll be waiting for your call.

I was still bugged at John as I left.

*

Wasserman's secretary told me to come to his office at 11.30. I was shown in immediately.

WASSERMAN: I've seen the cast list and I'm impressed.

ME: Thank God you like it.

WASSERMAN: All the major roles are cast except for the part of Browning. It's an important role that we must cast as soon as possible, as we're going to try to start this film on November twenty-first.

ME: What about the script?

WASSERMAN: It's almost completed.

ME: Have you read any of it?

WASSERMAN: No, but Coon knows what he's doing.
(*He gets up and gazes out of his window, then turns back to me.*)

WASSERMAN: I have a good idea for the part of Browning. Ronald Reagan.

ME: I don't remember his ever playing a villain.

WASSERMAN: True – and that's where you come in. I want you to talk him into playing that role.

ME: Has anyone tried to get him to play this part?

WASSERMAN: Yes. They all failed. That's how I found out that you've been doing most of the casting.
(*I get up and join Wasserman by the window.*)

ME: If I fail, we're no worse off than we are now. I'll give it a whirl. Ronnie and I are good friends and the part's interesting. Outside of no mention of money, I'll make it awkward for him to turn me down.

WASSERMAN: Let me know how you make out. (*Shaking my hand.*) Good luck.

Ronald Reagan met me for lunch in the Universal commissary. He looked tan and fit. He had matured since we had last worked together. I had grown older.

REAGAN: (*Pleasant as usual*) Good to see you, Don.

ME: You still trying to break your neck jumping horses?

REAGAN: Horses are like people. Treat them with respect and love, and they'll do their best to give you what you want.

ME: In *Night Unto Night* you won your argument with Owen Crump that a horse wouldn't step on a body lying in the sand. I agreed with you and the reason I agreed was apparent – you know horses.

REAGAN: Thanks for recognizing that fact. Owen, to this day, is miffed at me.

ME: He didn't like that I sided with you. Also, that the picture might have benefited by our having a writer at our beck and call, other than our 'would-be writer/producer', Owen Crump.

REAGAN: You're right, of course. It seems to me it is very beneficial to surround yourself with people of talent.

ME: How about a Cobb salad? You can eat while I talk.

We ordered our salads. Many of his friends dropped by our table. Ron was well liked. I felt sure that he knew why we were having lunch. I started our conversation by attacking.

ME: You puzzle me. I can't understand for the life of me not playing a part, if it's well written . . . maybe something different.

REAGAN: (*His face set*) I've never played a villain and probably never will.

ME: Why?

REAGAN: The salad's good, but I'll never get a chance to finish it.

ME: I'm sorry. You eat, which eliminates rebuttals. I'll talk. Many of your best friends in the industry have played, or are playing villains. That certainly doesn't make them a bad person in your eyes. Take Jim Cagney, Clark Gable, Edward G. Robinson, and, of course, Humphrey Bogart. Do you remember *Treasure of the Sierra Madre*? Did playing 'bad men' hurt their careers? Did you dislike them because they made successful pictures? Many of them had a wide range of parts, like Sidney Greenstreet and Peter Lorre, who also played comedy roles. These actors were not only good friends of yours, but were loved by millions of people throughout the world. Now that you've finished your salad and I haven't started mine, you do the talking – I'll do the eating.

241

He watched me eat and actually finish my salad. I knew Ron to be stubborn and fearless. But I also knew he was fair.

REAGAN: What kind of a part is 'Browning'?

ME: He's the boss. He's well educated and charming, yet rugged when necessary. He is in direct conflict with the killers, Lee Marvin and Clu Gulager.

REAGAN: Who else is in the picture?

ME: John Cassavetes, Angie Dickinson, Claude Akins, Normal Fell and many more. In my opinion, it's an excellent cast.

REAGAN: What kind of money are they talking about?

ME: I have nothing to do with money negotiations. That's up to you, your agent and Lew Wasserman. But I know they want you badly. I'm certain the deal can be worked out to your satisfaction.

REAGAN: The trouble with you is that you make sense. I'll get in touch with my people and find out if a deal can be made. You still crossing your fingers when you make a take?

ME: It works for me. I'm afraid not to. I want and need you in my picture – for your talent, for not being a 'dese, dose and dem' kind of guy.

(*The waitress comes by with the bill. I grab it out of Ron's hand.*)

ME: Surely you have no objection to Universal paying for our lunch.

REAGAN: (*Smiling*) Frankly, no.

*

Paul Donnelly and I met with Wasserman in his office. I went right for the jugular.

ME: I want to know two things. One, if you, Mr Wasserman, feel I'm on the right track. And two, if Paul feels I can deliver the race on schedule and on budget. Incidentally, I haven't told Paul what I intend to do. I might as well strike out twice.

WASSERMAN: Three strikes and you're off the team.

ME: There are over thirty cars lined up at the start. How can I possibly tell which car is going to win the race? Paul, there are nine Ford Cobras in the race. They look exactly alike, except for different numbers. If you can get more Cobras, the odds will favour me. If you can get better drivers, again, the odds will favour me.

DONNELLY: I don't exactly dig why the chances of your being successful depends on the number of Cobras.

ME: Because I'll have seven cameras, including the Titan crane, to cover the race. I'll concentrate on the Cobras. But I'm not interested in who wins the race. If any one of the Cobras has an accident and I get it on film, the quicker it happens, the better for the picture. I'll pick up Cassavetes, see him stagger out of his car matching the film of the actual race. I'll cover what's called for in the script and I'm on my way back to Universal.

(*Both Paul and I look at Wasserman.*)

WASSERMAN: What do you think, Paul?

DONNELLY: It has dangers, but the conception is terrific. I think Don can do it both on schedule and budget.

WASSERMAN: Would more cameras help you?

ME: There are four different units shooting the race. I might get kicked out of the racetrack if I get in anyone's way. We are definitely the fifth unit. The boom should ensure victory.

WASSERMAN: I agree with Paul. Your concept is good providing something happens to one of the Cobras. Did Coon help?

ME: I asked him if he had any ideas on how to shoot it. He replied, 'Not a clue. You're the director. Shoot it.'

WASSERMAN: If you have any time before shooting the pre-production on the race, continue working with Coon. I've told you he knows what he's doing, but he needs your help. The casting is complete. I thank you for your co-operation. Good luck on the race.

(*Paul and I thank Wasserman and leave.*)

DONNELLY: Wasserman really liked your ideas.

ME: I'll tell you what I liked. You told him what you thought of what I intended to do *before* knowing whether he liked it or not. The Irish in you came to the rescue. Now, all I've got to do is shoot it.

*

The crew and equipment arrived at the track shortly after dawn. I hoped to be able to place the various cameras in the best possible positions. Also, I wanted to get the 'feel' of the track. It was essential that the men knew the numbers on all the Ford Cobras in the race. They had to be loose and confident. Seven grips, one gaffer and two electricians showed up, along with my first cameraman, seven camera operators and seven assistant cameramen to load and focus the cameras. But the man who had the admission tickets and permits to all the places I wanted to go didn't show. He was Eddie Dodds, the unit manager. I sent out scouting parties to try to locate him. No luck. I tried to get our 'army' through the gates. No tickets, no permits: no admission. I asked if I could buy the necessary tickets for admission, parking and for placing our cameras where they would do the most good. The answer a flat 'No!'

The race started at 1 p.m. It was now past 10 a.m. and no unit manager. The best-laid plans of men sometimes go astray, but I must admit I had never figured on this. I could visualize Wasserman facing me on Monday morning after learning that I hadn't made a single shot. Looming behind him would be an angry Irishman, Paul, with a look of disgust and disappointment.

Finally, Eddie showed up, his face drawn and worried. It was obvious that he was suffering from a massive hangover. I didn't bawl him out or report his late arrival to the studio because I knew he'd be instantly fired. I'll say one thing for him, however. He didn't talk – he *moved*. We all got through the gates and rushed for the best vantage points. The other four units couldn't help but be impressed with our men and equipment.

The starter's flag whipped down as thirty cars roared off the starting line. My Cobras were competing with Ferraris, Maseratis and also a Lotus, a car I had never seen before. Numerous cars spun out at the twisting turns around the course. My forefinger and middle finger were numb from keeping them constantly crossed. One hundred thousand spectators, screaming at the top of their lungs, were drowned out by the tyres screeching, engines howling and brakes locking, when suddenly it happened. Number 98, a Ford Cobra, was inching past Number 41, a red Ferrari. The Cobra's right rear tyre suddenly blew. Hopefully, we had it covered as Johnny North's car. The Cobra broke loose and flew off the track. It rolled and rolled, bursting into flames. I immediately checked with our camera operators. Three of them, in different angles and sizes, had it. No question about that.

We picked up various shots. The boom shot straight down from the bridge crossing our track. The cars were travelling about 140 m.p.h. on the straight. The colours were blurred and stretched out – a remarkable effect. While we had time, we made closer shots of feet pressing down hard on throttles, tachometers bouncing crazily from 'o' to '2000'; exhaust pipes belching smoke; tyres burning rubber. We also made shots of the thousands and thousands of spectators yelling, drinking, screaming and kissing.

If the film was any good, after cutting it together I'd come back to the track with members of the cast and finish everything I needed. I would try to talk Paul into 100 extras, but would settle for fifty. In addition, I'd need at least fifteen cars, as I had to shoot the pit area where they repaired and tuned up their engines.

The dailies were a huge success. We were lucky and knew it. We could finish the pre-production with the necessary cast at any time. In addition, the driver of Cobra 98 had miraculously escaped with only bruises and scratches.

Within two weeks, Angie, John and I drove to Riverside to rehearse at the track. I discovered, to my horror, that John barely knew how to drive. I got one of our best drivers to teach him how to drive a Ford Cobra.

The pre-production schedule seemed to make sense. Later in the week, Ronald Reagan, Claude Akins and Norman Fell showed up. The first thing I shot were plates, or keys for process. I shot straight back, straight forward, 45° left to right and right to left. With plates going in all directions, my neophyte expert driver, John, would look like a pro, sitting in his Cobra with process plates making it appear that he was driving at high speed, fearlessly and recklessly. The pit area was shot with Angie, John, Claude, and later with Ronald, Norman and seventy-five extras – a compromise on which Paul gracefully gave in. I used the extras in the pit area and in the stands, pressed tightly next to Ronald and Norman, as spectators. I had to be damn careful not to show any blank areas where 100,000 spectators were supposed to be milling about, or the whole sequence would appear phoney.

18 *The Killers*: setting up a car shot with Angie Dickinson and John Cassavetes

245

The start date of 'Johnny North' was officially set for 21 November 1963. I felt we were ready, except for Coon's revised script, which had just arrived. I read it immediately and found many things I didn't like. I had been able to complete only about sixty pages of my own first draft. It would probably turn out to be the kiss of death, but I had to know: I set up an appointment with Lew Wasserman. Considering that he was one of the busiest executives in the world, I was always amazed when he gave me an early appointment. Three o'clock that very afternoon.

When I was admitted to his office, I was carrying two scripts: a thick one by Gene Coon and a thin one by me.

WASSERMAN: Any problems?
ME: Mr Wasserman, there are always problems. Mostly of our own doing.
WASSERMAN: What's wrong?
ME: Me, probably. I'd appreciate your advice.
WASSERMAN: That's why I'm here.
ME: (*Lifting my left hand*) In this hand, I have Gene Coon's revised script. (*Lifting my right hand.*) In this hand, I have about sixty pages of my first rough draft. Not only because I'm a slower writer than Gene, but he had a big head start on me.
(*I place Coon's script on Wasserman's desk, followed by my thin version.*)
ME: I would like to suggest that you read Coon's script first. It is complete. Then read mine, which is all the pages I have. I know I'm sticking my chin out, but I've boxed and have been knocked on my ass many times before. (*Starting for the door.*) Thanks for seeing me.

As I reached the door, I noticed that, contrary to my wishes, he had opened my script and seemed totally engrossed in it. I received it back within the hour, delivered by a messenger boy. On the cover was attached a small white memo headed 'Lew Wasserman'. The message read: 'Keep writing. I like it. L.W.' I felt good – real good. I decided not to get too fatheaded and called Gene to tell him I was dropping over to his office. He was lying on his couch, eyeing my thin script.

ME: No wonder you look tired. Have you heard from anyone concerning your script?
COON: How could I until you turned it in?
ME: You're right. At three o'clock this afternoon, I turned your

complete revised script over to Mr Wasserman, plus my revised
sixty pages.

(*Gene gets off his couch and sits down behind his desk.*)

COON: Did you discuss my script?

ME: All I said was that you had finished it, and laid it on his desk. I
also gave him this thin script, which was all I had been able to
write. Upon leaving, I suggested he read your script first and then
read mine, which obviously was unfinished. As I was closing the
door, he was already perusing mine.

COON: (*Looking a bit grey*) I'd like to read it.

ME: I had a feeling you would; that's why I brought it over. But there
are certain complications.

(*I handed Wasserman's note to Gene. He reads it slowly, fully
digesting it.*)

COON: Jesus, didn't he like mine at all?

ME: That's the only message I received. Give me the note back. I think
I'll have it framed.

(*Folding it carefully and sticking it in my wallet.*)

You're a stupid SOB; but if you meet my conditions, maybe we
can work things out. I'm not interesting in writing the script. What
I still want to do is to work *with* you, not *against* you. (*Handing
him my script.*) I want you to read my script carefully and slowly.
If you weren't so fast and scared, you could improve my script
enormously. From here on out, it's not *my* script, it's *yours.*

(*Gene breaks down, tears streaming down his face.*)

ME: I'm getting the hell out of here before I break down too. Let's turn
out the best script possible. Adios, amigo.

*

Apparently Universal's idea of proper scheduling was to shoot the end
(literally) of the picture on the very first day of shooting. Two people, Lee
Marvin and Don Siegel, never discussed this absurdity.

As Lee hadn't appeared, I began shooting Ron's arrival in his car, which
he parked in the driveway of a house in Toluca Lake. This house was
obviously picked because it was only minutes away from the studio. He
entered the house quickly, carrying his rifle with him. I next shot Angie as
she parked her car in the garage and entered the house. There were so
many things to work out that I was grateful Lee hadn't arrived. I wasn't
too concerned about the staging and shooting of the last sequence in the
picture, but the small details did bother me. How much blood would be
visible on the dying Lee and on his clothes? How should we use the

briefcase? Is it covered with blood? Does Lee make it back to his car? Is there a shoot-out between the police car (the first one we've seen in the entire picture) and Lee? What happens inside the house between Lee, Angie and Ron? Do we see Lee kill them?

No wonder Lee showed up late. He was carrying a bottle of 7-Up filled with straight vodka. How insulting and ignorant to expect an actor the stature of Lee Marvin to perform, faced with the same problems that had been worrying me. As I talked with him about the last scene in the picture, he had a silly grin on his face. It was strictly a one-way conversation. I put my arm around him. He smelled like a brewery.

ME: First, I want to apologize for attempting to shoot the last scene of the picture first. I'd like to waltz the scene with you.

Lee had a theory about drinking. If you didn't talk, no one could smell you. Also, if you didn't open your mouth, your speech wouldn't be muddled. So we continued our pleasant one-way conversation.

Executives wandered around observing everything, understanding nothing. The head of TV production, Allan 'Pinky' Miller, called out to me.

MILLER: Excuse me. I'd like a word with you, Don.
ME: Be right with you, Pinky. (*To Lee.*) Where's your briefcase?
    (*Lee shrugs and, as a further piece of information, shakes his head.*)
ME: (*Yelling*) Property! Get Mr Marvin's briefcase. (*To Pinky.*) Sorry to keep you waiting.
MILLER: Are you going to be able to film that drunken bum?
ME: I don't blame him for being what you so kindly refer to as 'drunken bum'. Was it your brilliant idea to start the picture with the ending? Lee, the actor, is as unprepared as I, the director.
MILLER: I didn't know a thing about it.
ME: Well, Pinky, stick around. Maybe you'll learn something.
    (*The propman appears with a scuffed-up, dirty old briefcase.*)
ME: Who picked that out of which pawn shop?
PROPMAN: Nobody told me nothing.
ME: Well, I'm telling you to go to my trailer and bring back my new Gucci briefcase. And see to it that it doesn't get damaged. If blood gets on it, carefully clean it off.
    (*The propman scuttles off. I call to my cinematographer, Richard Rawlings. He hustles over.*)
ME: I want a Titan crane and the largest zoom lens you can get, on the double.

RAWLINGS: I've got the zoom lens and I'll get a Titan crane, or the next largest one within thirty minutes.
(*He yells for his gaffer and head grip. I yell for my assistant director. I have never worked with him before and have already forgotten his name. The assistant moves slowly up to me.*)
ME: Hope I'm not disturbing your slumber, but I want to rehearse with Lee immediately. Have the wardrobe, make-up and property men stand by next to me; and that goes for you, too.
(*I notice Pinky staring and listening intently, his mouth agape. I cross over to Lee.*)
ME: Lee, you've just killed Ron and Angie in the house. You're dying, badly wounded from rifle bullets. When you become aware of a police car slowly approaching . . . (*To assistant.*) Get hold of the police-car driver to watch the action. (*To Lee.*) Sorry, Lee. Lift your empty gun hand in a reflex gesture with your pointed finger. Then, keel over on the grass, the empty briefcase in your hand. It's the last gesture you'll ever make. Now, let's rehearse with you coming out of the house. Leave the door open.
(*Lee staggers from the house, carefully closing the front door, and stumbles across the grass.*)
ME: (*Shouting*) Look to your left, see the police car approaching, raise the empty briefcase, point your right forefinger and keel over, dead.
(*Lee looks to his right, points his left forefinger and sprawls flat out on the grass, the briefcase falling on top of him.*)
ME: Excellent, Lee. Make-up and wardrobe, fix him up.
(*By this time, the Titan crane looms in front of the house.*)
ME: Dick, you've seen one very rough rehearsal. Strictly *entre nous*, I'm not going to make this shot today. However, we can practise now and shoot it later in the schedule.
RAWLINGS: (*Worried*) Does Lee know this?
ME: No, and he will never hear it from me. If the studio wants to play dirty pool, I'll be happy to oblige them.
RAWLINGS: It's a bitch of a shot. When the Titan pulls back and up, I have to time it perfectly with the zoom. It's almost impossible to tie the movement of the boom with that of the zoom without a bump.
ME: I don't know your crew. I believe if they are given plenty of time to practise, you'll make it. I've made a number of shots linking the boom with the zoom. We will practise today while Lee rehearses.

We laid tracks for the boom to pull back and raise to its full height, as Lee gracefully sank to the grass at least twenty times. As the boom eased into its fullest position, the zoom took over the final moments of the shot. Lee got better and better, never complaining once. Dick wasn't fooling: it was extremely difficult to work out the timing. But we took it slowly. No pressure. We were making progress on the technical aspects of the shot. Finally, I apologized to Lee for our not being able to make the shot. We had received word that we would stick to the original schedule tomorrow: shoot the gymnasium with Norman Fell, using a steam cabinet, Lee and Clu turning up the heat until Norman literally wilts and gives them the information they want.

LEE: (*Smiling*) I'll take a steam work-out tomorrow morning. Who knows, I might get sober.

It had turned out to be a fun day.

*

The main gym was full of apparatus that encouraged big muscles and heart attacks. A door led to the steam room. Sure enough, Lee was sopping wet in a hot steam cabinet, feeling no pain. Norman and Clu were standing on each side of him singing 'Jingle Bells'. I gave Dick the line-up and went off to go through wardrobe with Angie Dickinson.

A bunch of clothes was strewn about. Angie was excited and happy. The ladies' costumer rushed in with another dress. Several wardrobe girls were standing by, waiting to fit Angie. The morning started off as mornings should. Angie rushed over to me and planted a big, wet lipstick kiss on my dry, nervous lips.

ANGIE: We'll go over to the fitting room and as soon as I'm fitted, I'll come out and show them to you for your approval.
ME: After that kiss, there's nothing to okay.
ANGIE: (*Kissing me again*) That's for the seal of approval.

As I waited, I heard a radio playing country music. I smiled as I wiped off my lips. The music didn't fit the chic, smart clothes. Finally, the lovely vision in red made her appearance. She was beaming as she twirled about.

ME: One guess. When you're shot by Lee at the end of the picture, you'll steal the show wearing that exquisite red gown.
DICKINSON: Brilliant idea. I've ninety more dresses to show you.

As she gaily started off to the dressing room, the music abruptly stopped. An announcer's voice immediately came on the air.

RADIO ANNOUNCER'S VOICE: We shockingly regret to inform you

that President John Fitzgerald Kennedy has just been assassinated in Dallas, Texas. The whole country is in turmoil . . .

A loud, piercing scream from Angie cut through the announcer's voice. I rushed to her as she started to topple to the floor. I grabbed her in my arms and carried her into a small dressing room. I stretched her out on a couch and yelled to someone to get first aid. She was crying hysterically. I whispered to one of the wardrobe girls to turn off the radio. I tried to comfort Angie by pointing out that radio announcers would say anything for a story. Probably someone had pointed a revolver and was immediately wrestled to the ground. The first-aid man appeared. He gave her a shot to stop her hysterics. When she had calmed down, I told the head of wardrobe *not* to let her drive home but to order a car and driver to take her home. She appeared to be resting quietly. I sneaked off and rushed over to Paul Donnelly's office. There was complete confusion and grief at the studio.

After I had explained to Paul what had happened, I received my instructions.

DONNELLY: Mickey Rooney told me he couldn't work. I called Mr Wasserman. He said to send everyone home and to call all the studios and have them shut down. He also said to declare November twenty-fifth a day of mourning.
ME: (*Feeling queasy*) Do you expect any trouble?
DONNELLY: Of course; but they'll cave in when Mr Wasserman insists.
ME: I must confess I admire him. Two quick questions and I'll get out of your hair. Do I shoot Tuesday what I was scheduled to shoot today? Also, can I have a new shooting schedule?
DONNELLY: Yes to both.
ME: Thanks, Paul.

I went to the set and filled in the cast and crew with all I knew. One wise guy, a gaffer and a member of the John Birch Society, wanted to work out the day and come in on Monday, 25 November, the day of mourning.

ME: You'd better not, or there will be a new gaffer on Tuesday. (*To cast and crew.*) I'm in a state of shock, as all of you are. See you Tuesday. I know that most of us are members of the 'no bigot' society.

It was tragic, watching the funeral on television on the 25th. We returned to the studio the next day. Somehow, life goes on.

*

In the garage scene with Clu and Lee, Claude Akins was roughed up by them. Lee was quite drunk and let a few punches fly that he didn't mean to. Claude was a big man who could handle himself; he also happened to be a close friend of both Lee and myself. I spoke quietly to him: I was going to have an understanding with Lee. If he flattened me, I'd pick up every tool, bolt and nut and let fly.

AKINS: It's not a good idea. Lee's tough and has been drinking too
    much. You might get hurt.
ME: I know that ugly fact; but remember, I have an advantage. He likes
    me.
    (*I cross over to Lee.*)
ME: I'd like to talk to you about this scene. Let's go to my trailer.

There was no question. Lee was drunk. He pulled himself together and followed me into my trailer. I fixed up two drinks. We didn't toast each other; we just drank.

ME: You're trying too hard in the scene.
    (*Lee's expression doesn't change.*)
ME: The truth is, you can't work when you've had too much to drink. I
    could shoot it and possibly use it; but I wouldn't like it and you
    sure as hell wouldn't trust me. So, let's go through it one more
    time for show, call it a day and do it right tomorrow.

We made the shot, Lee doing his damnedest to do his best. It really wasn't any good and he knew it. I didn't print it. I called a 'wrap' and announced to one and all that we'd shoot the garage sequence the next morning. Lee casually crossed by me.

LEE: How about joining me for a drink across the street in the Chinese
    bar?
ME: Thanks. See you in fifteen minutes.
    (*When I arrive, Lee has ordered me a scotch and soda. He is
    finishing a margarita. He turns around and faces me.*)
LEE: I like the fact that you talked to me alone.

That was it. He didn't stop drinking, but he wasn't drunk again on the picture. Working with him was fun.

*

It had been bad working outside on the racetrack with John Cassavetes. He drove the car with nonchalance. His left elbow would be hanging outside the door and he looked like an eastside punk. He never could figure, in spite of lessons, why he had to shift down going through hairy

252

curves. But now that I was shooting him in the process, I felt confident he would do OK. He was worse.

There were two-by-fours on each side of the Ford Cobra that rocked the car in sharp jerks. In addition, wind machines blew John's curly locks in all directions. I hit the camera with staccato bumps, which caused him to lose his concentration.

CASSAVETES: Do you have to rock the car so much. I've got a splitting headache. (*Angrily.*) It's impossible and unnecessary to shift the gear handle down, then up. It must look like I'm going round in circles. (*Sarcastically.*) Did you invent process? Don't you think you're overshooting with all these stupid angles?

ME: Let's quit the process shots for now so you can get some rest. I've got one line-up where you're with the blind kids showing them how an engine works.

CASSAVETES: (*Getting out of car*) That should be fun.

I had had trouble getting the studio to allow me to use real blind people in the picture. Ultimately I won, but it was tough going: the studio didn't think it necessary. For this shot I had the assistant gather all the blind children around the engine, then put John where the camera could see him. I got on a 15-foot ladder and asked Rawlings for his finder. I peered through it, apparently having difficulty in lining up the shot. John was getting restless and moving about.

ME: Would you mind, John, holding your position?

CASSAVETES: I don't know what the hell my position is.

ME: (*Still peering through the finder*) Would you please move six inches to your left.

(*John moves 6 inches to his left.*)

ME: Please come forward two inches.

(*John moves 2 inches forward.*)

ME: I don't know why I can't place you in the right position. Everyone else is perfect.

CASSAVETES: (*Voice tense*) Are you sure you're looking through the right end?

ME: (*Sarcastic*) I'm not sure that I've got the right actor.

(*Mad, John leaves the group and starts to climb the ladder to push me off, to punch me out or to topple the ladder over.*)

CASSAVETES: Well, fuck you and your fucking line-up.

(*I burst into song, followed by everyone on the set.*)

ME: Happy birthday to you. Happy birthday to you. Happy birthday dear Johnny, Happy birthday to you.

The singing propman carried in a large cake depicting John driving a Ford Cobra 98, slouched behind the wheel. About thirty candles were lit. Instead of swearing at me or hitting me, John, in one big breath of air, blew out all the candles.

CASSAVETES: How'd you know it was my birthday?
ME: Because I'm your West Coast mother and you've been a naughty baby all day.

*

On Christmas Eve not much work is done and a great deal of celebrating throughout the studio is expected. Generally, the studio closes down right before lunch.

That day I was to shoot Lee and Clu on a train (process), sitting in a fawn-coloured compartment behind a blood-red door. The porter would bring Clu a large glass of fresh orange juice. In an equally large glass, Lee would be served a scotch and soda. Under normal conditions, Lee's glass would be filled with ginger ale. I decided to gamble. I called the propman over.

ME: If Lee is served ginger ale, he'll undoubtedly demand scotch. See that the porter gives him a full glass of straight scotch.
PROPMAN: My God, he'll drain the glass and that's the end of the day.
ME: Probably. Nevertheless, do what I say.
PROPMAN: OK, Governor. It'll be a short day for all of us.

We started rehearsing in the compartment car. Clu got his orange juice and, unbeknownst to Lee, he had his full glass of scotch. Clu kept sipping his juice. Lee took one sniff of his scotch and his eyes sparkled with astonishment; but he put the scotch back on the table and didn't touch it again throughout the scene. We had another rehearsal and the scene played better. This time Lee didn't even touch his glass. I suggested to Clu that he drink some of his orange juice, toasting their successful mission. Lee totally ignored him.

ME: I don't understand you, Lee. You order the scotch and then don't touch it.
LEE: (Miffed) There's no rule that spells out you must drink your scotch immediately.
ME: There's no rule that says you don't touch your scotch during the entire scene. It looks odd, particularly when Clu toasts you with his juice.

LEE: That was an addition to the scene I didn't like. Anyway, I frequently order a drink and don't drink it.

ME: I never saw you do that.

LEE: (*Getting angry*) Well, you're seeing it now. I think it's silly, Clu drinking orange juice and me drinking scotch.

ME: (*Playing it casual*) Let's not make a big thing out of it. You're probably right, or you wouldn't feel so strongly about it.

We shot the scene and printed it. In breaking it up, I couldn't finish before lunch and I knew Lee would have a couple of drinks then. After lunch, we made three more shots. Absolutely perfect.

ME: It's a wrap. Merry Christmas and please drive home safely.

(*The propman comes up to me.*)

PROPMAN: How did you figure that Lee wouldn't drink?

ME: I didn't. I knew he'd drink, so I made it easy on him.

PROPMAN: Mr Siegel, you're not only a lucky gambler, you're a genius.

*

For some time I had been suspicious that executives did not look at dailies. I decided to put it to the test.

I shot a scene in which Clu and Lee enter the large foyer of a hotel, with rounded sofas forming a circle in the centre of the room. They step on the sofas and over them in a straight line to the information desk. After announcing themselves at the desk and asking for Angie Dickinson, Clu leads the way to the waiting elevator. As he steps in, Lee notices a sign, 'Cocktails', pointing up to some nearby stairs. He immediately steps quickly up the stairs. Clu dashes after him and forces him back into the elevator. He presses a button. The elevator door closes and the elevator rises out of shot.

I printed that shot. Then I made a second shot which I didn't print, but held. This shot, when printed two days later, showed Clu and Lee walking around the sofas to the information desk. When Clu enters the elevator, Lee follows him in. Clu pushes the elevator button, the door closes and the elevator rises out of the shot.

As usual, no one mentioned the ridiculous shot I had printed for the dailies. I did several shenanigans like this during the picture. No one in authority ever noticed them. It's possible they may have been asleep.

*

Lee, followed by Clu, walked quickly through the outer office to Reagan's office. A young secretary tried to tell Lee he couldn't enter Mr Reagan's office without being announced. Lee brushed by her without a word. Clu picked up a bunch of paperclips and smiled.

Ron played his scene while Lee and Clu played theirs. I had never seen Ron angry before. His face flushed as he stood up and kicked his desk, muttering something about lack of manners. Lee and Clu asked questions about getting in touch with Angie, which Ron entirely ignored. To my amazement, he showed absolutely no fear of Lee, or Clu. An interesting scene was beginning to develop, which was quickly running out of control.

ME: Cut! (*To Lee and Clu.*) Take it easy. I want to talk to Ron.
(*I cross over to him.*)

ME: What's wrong, Ron?

REAGAN: (*Kicking his desk again, his voice trembling with anger*) They have no right in not allowing that young lady to speak her lines. I was President of the Screen Actors' Guild from 1947 to 1952. They're not going to get away with it.

ME: Ron, the first run-through of a scene is unimportant. I assure you that the young lady will say all her lines before Lee brushes past her.

REAGAN: (*Still angry*) And I assure you, Don, that I won't play the scene unless she does.

ME: I admire you for taking your strong position. But it really isn't necessary, as I hired Miss O'Malley, who is my girlfriend, to play the part. May we start rehearsals?

REAGAN: (*Calming down*) I can't stand a bully.
(*I cross over to Lee and Clu.*)

ME: Let's rehearse; only this time, listen to the receptionist before you ignore her by brushing past her.

Both Lee and Clu were totally unaware that Ron was angry about anything. We went into rehearsal with Miss O'Malley getting all her lines in and successfully holding up Lee and Clu before allowing them to enter the office. The rest of the scene played scary until Ron promises to find out where Angie Dickinson was staying. This scene was a key one.

*

Lee lies on the floor, his pistol, with silencer attached, held in both hands, pointing at Ron and Angie. The reverse shot from the floor, using an 18mm lens, distorts Lee's face and makes the pistol menacingly huge and inevitable. Mortally wounded, Lee asks for the money and is about to shoot. Angie pleads with him to listen to why he was double-crossed, in a voice that captures the frustration of a lifetime of lies.

MARVIN: Lady, I just haven't got the time.

We cut outside the house and hear two sickening shots made with a silencer. Lee staggers out of the house, the shot becoming the famed last strip of film – the marriage of the Titan crane and zoom.

*

The picture's title became: Ernest Hemingway's *The Killers*. That title made no sense. There was not a word in the motion picture written by Hemingway.

The picture was quickly edited and a temporary pre-dub was finished, with much help from my editor, Dick Belding. We were totally exhausted. We would work from early in the morning until 3 or 4 a.m. I had promised Lew Wasserman that we would run the completed version with him at 9 a.m. one Sunday. We checked out the print at 4 a.m. that Sunday. When

19   *The Killers*: Ronald Reagan slaps around Angie Dickinson

20   *The Killers*: Lee Marvin and the menacing pistol

21   *The Killers*: the death of Lee Marvin

we had finished, we looked questioningly at each other. We had lost our ability, through utter fatigue, to be able to judge whether the film was good, bad or indifferent. We broke down into hysterical laughter, tears running down our faces. We were left with one big problem: the running with Lew.

We met Lew and Jennings Lang (which surprised me) at Projection Room 1. We were unshaven, haggard and our clothes were wrinkled. Lew and Jennings looked immaculate, as usual. In the projection room they sat by the controls, we sat by ourselves.

ME: (*To Wasserman*) I didn't think there was a prayer we'd finish.

They said nothing. Lew pressed the start button. I crossed my fingers. We were off on the unknown journey. When the lights came on, Jennings's head was bent over. Lew turned to me, getting up from his seat, which was the cue for the rest of us to stand.

WASSERMAN: Excellent job, Don.

We followed him outside the projection room. Jennings said nothing.

ME: Mr Wasserman, my editor, Dick Belding, was of great help. Thank you for the kind words.
 (*We split, going opposite directions. Jennings yells to me.*)
LANG: (*Peculiarly*) I'll tell you one thing, Don. The picture was much better than the script.
ME: Isn't it supposed to be? I'd sure as hell be disappointed hearing you say 'The script's better than the picture.'

The Killers was supposed to be the first two-hour TV movie. However, it was much too violent for the time. Wasserman liked it, particularly when it was shown on 16mm. It sold more than any other 16mm picture of its time, and when it was released as a feature it did very well critically and at the box office. The reaction to the violence in *The Killers* was one of shock in 1964, although later the film was considered to be quite tame.

24

Crime Without Passion

1964

John Cassavetes had a brilliant idea. Why not let him rewrite Ben Hecht's classic 1934 film *Crime Without Passion*?

ME: What would you want me to do?

CASSAVETES: Produce and direct it for Universal, you idiot. I need you to cross all the Ts and dot all the Is. Seriously, Don, you're hot stuff with Wasserman after *The Killers*.

ME: I remember how magnificently Claude Rains played the villain; but my memory is somewhat faulty about the rest of the picture. It's been about thirty years since I saw the black-and-white print. Let's see it together. I'll call you when, or if, I can get a print.

By the time the lights went up in the projection room, I could see great possibilities in making another classic. It was remarkable how a thirty-year-old picture kept us in its grasp.

CASSAVETES: Do you believe I can bring it up to date and lose none of Hecht's talent?

ME: If I didn't, I wouldn't see Wasserman about your writing it. I'll call you the minute I get a 'No', 'Yes', or even a 'Maybe'.

*

Jennings Lang and I sat opposite Lew Wasserman. After my spiel about John rewriting *Crime Without Passion*, their faces seemed cold and passionless.

LANG: I can think of a lot of writers who could do the job; but John . . .

WASSERMAN: I agree. Has John any writing credits? I don't think he even belongs to the Writers' Guild.

ME: On reflection, John is very much like Mr Hecht. When Hecht wrote his classic script in 1934, he was young, energetic and full of talent. He was a rebel and full of brass. How better could I describe John than by repeating the same words? John is young, energetic and full of talent. He is a rebel and full of brass.

LANG: It's full of danger.

ME: Jennings, I don't follow your logic. Full of what danger? He will write the entire script for absolute minimum. And that goes for whatever changes we want.

WASSERMAN: Set up the deal, Jennings. Remember, we want to see the very first draft as soon as possible.

*

John had the office next to me. We shared a secretary. We were both pleased as punch that we had the opportunity to work together on a project that gave such promise. John was champing at the bit. After working on an outline that we both liked, he took off like Ben Hecht at his best. He promised to give me the pages as soon as he finished each sequence, and he lived up to his word.

I liked what I was reading. His style was terse and taut, which was not characteristic of John. In addition, the words were warm and full of fun. My criticisms were few and carefully chosen. I didn't want to get into an argument on whether a comma or a dash should be used. He could get stubborn and waste three hours on a needless discussion. Whatever suggestions I might have, I had our secretary immediately type them up and give them to John.

As the script neared its end, I noticed that John's style was undergoing a change. He wrote, particularly in prose, in florid, rococo, flowery words. It shocked me. Before going home, the secretary long gone for the weekend, I wandered into John's office, his script in my hand.

CASSAVETES: (*Busily writing; looking up*) Sneaking off as usual?
　　(*I sit down, wondering how to handle the situation.*)

ME: Not exactly. But I have noticed a change.

CASSAVETES: (*Icily*) Such as?

ME: Throughout the script, I've enjoyed your way with words. Your style is avant-garde. Now, in a number of scenes, you've suddenly become old-fashioned.

CASSAVETES: Where?
　　(*I open the script.*)

ME: Turn to page sixty-six, paragraph two.
　　(*John turns the pages of his script and stops to read. His face hardens.*)

CASSAVETES: I didn't write that shit!

ME: (*Relieved*) You didn't?

CASSAVETES: No. I thought you did.

ME: But John, I didn't write a word. Turn to page eighty-six, paragraph four.

CASSAVETES: (*Reading the page*) That stinks worse than the other! Who could have written it if you didn't?

ME: (*Thinking a moment*) Our dainty secretary, who obviously figured she was a better writer than you, John.
(*John paces his office, his face contorted in anger. He slams his desk.*)

CASSAVETES: If she shows up Monday morning, I'll punch her out.

ME: Pick all the scenes you thought I wrote and I'll pick all the scenes I thought you had written. I'll call the secretarial pool and get a new secretary. It's so insane, it's kind of funny.

There was no bloodshed on Monday. John rewrote all the necessary changes. The new secretary had strict instructions about not changing a word. On 14 May 1964, we had John's first draft screenplay xeroxed. I toasted John and he toasted me. We both toasted the script.

ME: I'm going to drop two copies off at Wasserman's office. Let's have lunch together.

CASSAVETES: Can't. Gotta earn a buck. I think I can get a quick job acting.

ME: You've been acting all your life. It's a waste of time, because you're a better writer than an actor.

CASSAVETES: Flattery will get you everywhere. Deliver those scripts to Lew and good luck to us.

Three days after delivering the two scripts, I received a call to see Wasserman as soon as possible. I grabbed a script and hastened over. I waited in the outer office at least 30 minutes. This made me somewhat uneasy, as Lew always saw me with a minimum of waiting. Also, his bright, efficient secretary never failed to greet me warmly. This time she didn't greet me or give me the slightest smile.

When finally I entered the president's office, Wasserman picked up Cassavetes's script and angrily slammed it on his desk. I was shocked into silence. I had never seen, or heard, Wasserman angry. To the best of my memory, he showed very little emotion. He was a distinguished-looking gentleman, dignified and polite.

WASSERMAN: (*Voice trembling*) How could you write a script like this? John I know only too well. He's capable of anything.

ME: I'm not defending John, although I have not the slightest idea why you are so displeased with us.

WASSERMAN: I hate the script.

ME: I changed the title to 'Champion of the Damned'. Maybe that will help. Everyone has the right to hate a property. But I'm not learning anything. May I ask, Lew, at the risk of rousing your ire, why you hate this script?

WASSERMAN: (*His voice rising*) How could you submit a script like this, knowing that NBC hates violence?

ME: (*Trying to placate him*) But Lew, on page two of the script, a man, Tasby, kills his girlfriend's lover, Prince, in the ocean. We don't actually see the crime committed.

WASSERMAN: Damn it, he did kill him.

ME: The only other violence in the entire script is at the end, page 117, where the girl, April, fires a gun, committing suicide, falsely implicating the lawyer, James Gentry, of killing her. And that, sir, is the total violence in the script.

WASSERMAN: Nevertheless, there are two killings. I don't want to go through another fiasco like *The Killers*.

ME: *The Killers* could never be made to pass the odious television censor code. I tried and you know it.

WASSERMAN: I want you to make *The Hanged Man*.

ME: (*Losing control*) You mean the remake of Robert Montgomery's *Ride a Pink Horse*? In changing it to *The Hanged Man* you've complicated the shooting enormously by adding in the New Orleans Mardi Gras. It also might interest you that instead of two acts of violence, there are at least eight. I'm not only puzzled by your attitude, I'm upset.

WASSERMAN: (*Loudly*) Get out of my office! Post-haste.

ME: (*Getting up and leaving*) It'll be a pleasure.

I went directly to John's house and told him everything that had happened with Wasserman. I emphasized how oddly Lew had behaved. For the first time, he had acted rudely and senselessly. John came up with a viable idea. He would see Lew with his business manager, Morgan Maree. Inasmuch as Lew didn't like the script at all and there was no money to speak of invested in the property, both he and his manager thought they could buy the script at a fair price.

CASSAVETES: What do you think?

ME: Until very recently, I thought Lew was the smartest, shrewdest, fairest man I had ever met. Now, I must confess, I think he's odd.

I'm afraid he falls in the category of not wanting to make it; on the other hand, he probably won't allow anyone else to make it, in case they make a successful picture, which would make Lew look bad.

CASSAVETES: I'm going to give it a whirl.

ME: Count me in. Good luck and God bless.

John came over to my office the following week. He and Morgan Maree had had a very pleasant chat with Wasserman, who had listened attentively and politely. When they offered $30,000 for the script, Lew smiled and said he would get back to them after discussing it with his associates.

Wasserman's counter-offer was short, sweet and to the point. John could buy it for $330,000. Lew smiled, but wouldn't budge a penny. John got angry. Lew's only reaction was a practised, warm smile.

JOHN: So, it was fun while it lasted.

ME: You wrote an excellent script, John. I think the only thing to do is to forget it. Lew's acting quirky.

25

The Hanged Man

Universal 1964

I was getting to be known as the 'remake' director. The director/actor of *Ride a Pink Horse* (1947), Robert Montgomery, did an excellent job on his picture, and *The Hanged Man* was poorly based on it. The advantage that Montgomery had over me, other than his talent, was that he had a simple story to tell. It was not cluttered with backlot Mardi Gras nonsense.

Right in the beginning of *The Hanged Man*, the audience sees that Harry Pace (Robert Culp) has a cancelled cheque made out by a Swiss bank for $50,000 and signed: 'Arnold Seeger' (Eddie O'Brien). We are immediately told that O'Brien, head of a crooked union, has killed Whitey (Gene Raymond) for the incriminating cheque, although, obviously, he has failed to get it. Raymond is Culp's best friend. Culp, as in many other pictures, sets off to find the killer, O'Brien. Unfortunately, Culp becomes involved with two gypsies – Uncle Picaud (J. Carrol Naish) and a young girl, Celine (Brenda Scott). They both believe in tarot cards and try to persuade Culp that his tarot card indicates death: the Hanged Man. Nevertheless, Culp keeps trying to find O'Brien.

The story then becomes hopelessly convoluted. When Culp finds O'Brien's wife Lois (Vera Miles), she claims she has found the cheque and has given it to Raymond. The cheque rapidly becomes the worst-kept secret in the annals of filmdom. Culp does not believe that Raymond was going to blackmail O'Brien. Miles claims her husband was going to ransom her (shades of the Southern States, 1750). Culp doesn't believe that Raymond would say, 'Here's your cheque back, now give me your wife.' (I think Culp has a viable point there. On the other hand, the audience might start laughing. In actual fact, only the producer, Ray Wagner, believed it.) Every character in the picture, including the little gypsy girl, knew about the cheque.

We learn, totally out of left field, that Raymond is not dead. He faked his death so that he and lovely Miles could take the blackmail money from Culp (we don't know how) and escape without being found by O'Brien.

(This isn't explained either.) Culp hides a letter (what were Miles and Raymond doing?) and is conveniently followed by an IRS man (Norman Fell), who is certain that Culp can help him get O'Brien for tax evasion. We don't know if Culp is convinced. O'Brien comes out of left field and agrees to pay Culp something for the letter. Culp naively goes to collect. Two of O'Brien's killers trap him in an alley. Culp kills one man and wounds the other, but is shot as he disappears in the Mardi Gras crowd. (Sorry, Mr Wasserman.) What makes it worse, if possible, is that Raymond appears and threatens to kill Brenda Scott and Naish, who are taking care of him. (They must have been lax in how they were taking care of him.) O'Brien, in the middle of the happy, gay Mardi Gras, gives the money to the badly wounded Culp. Just as Raymond is about to take it from Culp and shoot him, Fell kills Raymond. (Again, my apologies, Mr Wasserman.)

*

We made the picture in New Orleans at Mardi Gras time. I made use of the costumes to parallel the tarot cards and the superstitious ideas that they were meant to portray. Raymond appeared dressed as a clown, which in the tarot deck represents foolishness; Miles dressed in black tights (which I suppose is naughty); and Brenda Scott in virginal white (I would have preferred her as a clown repesenting foolishness). Culp, the hanged man, wore a cowboy suit, which had nothing to do with the tarot motif. It was his own idea. Apparently, he saw himself as a new Gary Cooper.

I like Culp. He's talented not only as an actor, but as a writer. As an actor, he occasionally works at a very slow pace. In our picture, he had to cross a street leaving a hotel. I didn't expect him to run across the street. He didn't. He approached the curb, looked one way for traffic, then the other way. He waited for traffic to appear, then crossed the street cautiously and very slowly. I realized that there was no danger of a short picture.

The producer, Ray Wagner, a pleasant, nervous man in his forties, did a rather strange thing. I needed a lapse of time from one street to another. I noticed, to my astonishment, that on the backlot where we were shooting was an enormous moon. We got out our biggest zoom and pulled back until we picked up Culp walking down the street. I thought the shot worked perfectly, as did the rest of the crew. It looked even better on film. Ray seemed equally enthusiastic. However, when I turned the completed film over to him, without saying a word to me, he cut the moon shot entirely out of the picture. I wondered why he made that cut, but I never asked him. I didn't think the picture was worth arguing about.

266

26

Stranger on the Run

Formerly 'Bad Day at Banner'
Universal 1967

Stranger on the Run is set in 1885, in the inhospitable south-west. Railroad tracks bisect the town of Banner, which shows the scars of raids and train robberies: they have left most of the desolate town in charred ruins. An ancient train belches to a jerky stop. A dirty, unshaven itinerant, Ben Chamberlain (Henry Fonda), is thrown by the brakeman from a freight car into a weed-choked yard. A single passenger, Mr Gorman (Lloyd Bochner), is met by Vince McKay (Michael Parks). He is assigned by Gorman as the railroad's chief deputy. The only deputies he can enlist are gunmen and roustabouts. McKay reluctantly hires O. E. Hotchkiss (Dan Duryea), Mercurio (Rudolpho Acosta), Blaylock (Sal Mineo) and Leo Weed (Tom Reese).

Ben, without a penny in his ragged pockets and with an insatiable craving for a drink, gets a job from the general-store owner, Abraham Berk (Walter Burke). At day's end, he tells Berk that he has a message for a local bar girl. Berk smiles, saying she lives in an old shack on the outskirts of town. When Ben goes to the shack, he finds her dead. He quickly takes off on foot away from town. When McKay learns about the woman's death, Berk remembers that Ben had enquired about her whereabouts. The search is on when it is discovered that Ben has disappeared.

Ben leaves an easy trail and is soon found by the posse. But McKay perversely decides to prolong the hunt. He gives Ben a horse, a canteen of water and an hour's head start. Ben is grateful for his reprieve and bolts off. Later that night, he wanders into the camp of two cowboys, Arlie Dockstatter (Rex Holman) and Dickory (Bernie Hamilton). Arlie's brother has been killed by a railroad posse. Ben is welcome to travel with them.

The next morning, the posse catches up with them and a gunfight ensues. Blaylock is critically wounded, forcing McKay to order his men back to town. Arlie is killed and Dickory is hit in the shoulder. He leaves Ben at Valverda Johnson's (Anne Baxter's) ranch and goes on alone. Valverda thinks Ben is going to rob her, but knows better after he helps her cow deliver a calf. When her son Matt (Michael Burns) comes home, the three of them return to Banner.

Blaylock is in the town's only hotel awaiting a doctor. Ben is detained there to await trial. Valverda has fallen in love with him and sneaks him a gun. When the deputies come for him, shooting begins. Blaylock is mistakenly fatally shot by one of the deputies. Ben runs out of bullets and surrenders, but McKay refuses to allow him to give himself up. McKay will kill him with his bare hands. Leo Weed is discovered by Hotchkiss to be the real murderer of the bar girl and is gunned down. McKay begins beating Ben mercilessly. Suddenly, he stops. He realizes that Ben is innocent; that he has discovered his manhood. McKay walks away from Ben, no longer interested in gaining power to kill.

As Matt and his mother are leaving to return to their ranch, Ben finally decides to join them. He, too, climbs aboard and the three turn the buckboard towards the ranch, leaving Banner to whomever will have it.

*

The studio was worried about the cost of shooting the film on location. George Santoro, an ex-assistant director and unit manager, who was working in some capacity for Jennings Lang, senior vice-president in charge of television at Universal, was instructed to show my producer, Richard Lyons, a cherubic, pleasant but nervous chap, and me how to shoot the picture on the backlot.

The successful TV series *The Virginian* had its own period train and town, Virginia City. There were possibilities in using that; but George was not properly prepared and I wasn't satisfied. The picture starts as the train stops in the town of Banner. George showed us that by moving the freight car not more than a foot or two, all we would see in the background would be the freight car and the ground.

ME: (*Sarcastically*) Brilliant. Exciting thinking, George. Unfortunately the train stops at the town and leaves. The town needs work to fit our story.
SANTORO: (*Shocked*) You can't touch Virginia City. Nor for that matter, can you see it in your picture.
ME: Dick, as my producer, do you have the foggiest notion what this idiot is talking about with reference to how to shoot the freight car and how *not* to shoot Banner?
LYONS: I think we had better talk to production about the Virginia City situation.

We explained the whole situation to Paul Donnelly. He looked at Santoro as though he were crazy.

DONNELLY: I don't give a damn what you or Jennings is up to.
Virginia City can't be touched, George. Have Jennings talk to Lew.
That'll be the end of both of you and the project. Try to find the
town in a nearby location. It would be great, Dick, if we could
travel to it each day. We'd save a fortune.

Dick, a location man and yours truly took a studio car and driver and
started looking. After seeing several locations which added up to nothing,
Dick remembered that Burt Kennedy, a director he knew, was shooting a
Western with Hank Fonda somewhere in Conejo. It was a miracle.
Kennedy was shooting Fonda in the main and only street of a badly
burned town. I was introduced to Kennedy and Fonda.

ME: (*To Kennedy*) Are you planning to continue burning your
interesting little town?
KENNEDY: (*Laughing*) Hell no. The last time we set fire to it, we damn
near burned it to the ground. You're looking at a reconstructed
town.
ME: I'm looking at the perfect town for our picture. About all we have
to add is a train and tracks that run through it.
LYONS: How much longer have you got to shoot?
FONDA: I was just asking that same question.
KENNEDY: Shouldn't be more than two, maybe three weeks, if Hank
remembers his lines and kills off everybody in the town.
ME: It's been a pleasure meeting you gentlemen; but we have to run
and nail the town down before some SOB beats us to it.

Paul Donnelly solved our problems. He and his staff took a look at the
town, which they all liked very much, and Conejo was immediately
rented. In about six weeks, when *The Virginian* company took a long lay-
off, Paul would get their train and engine loaded on flatbed trucks and
taken to Conejo. The complete train and tracks cost $8,000 to be
delivered to the location and returned to the Universal backlot. I had no
idea he could get it delivered so cheaply.

The art director used about a couple of hundred feet of iron track. The
rest of the tracks, going east and west out of Banner and disappearing in
the distance, were made of wood and looked as real as the iron tracks.

*

When we got Henry Fonda to play the lead, a weak man physically,
mentally and spiritually, I knew we were in. Hank is one of America's
greatest actors, plus being a wonderful, kind man. We got along great.
When I heard that the name of the picture had been changed from 'Bad

Day at Banner' to *Stranger on the Run*, I fainted dead away. Generally, my pictures have titles that do their best to discourage people from seeing them, such as *Invasion of the Body Snatchers* instead of 'Sleep No More'.

As we approached our start date, I was busy working on the script with Dean Riesner. He was writing his usual excellent script. When I wanted certain dialogue changes, he would smile and say, 'Why not? It's only words.' The only real problem I had was with Michael Parks. He was a young man for whom the studio had high hopes. There was no question about his talents, but he had a stubborn disposition and could be ornery. He insisted on a moustache that drooped down on each side of his face. I thought it was an absurdity: I didn't want him to wear the damn droopy moustache, but he flatly insisted. I got hold of Jennings Lang and explained my predicament. He wouldn't even come to the make-up department to look at it.

ME: How about if I take him up to your office?
LANG: I'm busy, Don. I'm sure it will look OK.
ME: Maybe you're not aware of it, but we're not purposely making a comedy.
LANG: I hear you've found a great town; you've got your train; you've got a great star, Fonda. You can't win them all, Don.
ME: I'm going to paste that moustache on your face and shoot you down in the middle of the commissary. Goodbye, Senior Vice-president.

The first two days of shooting went reasonably well. Fonda, of course, was incredibly good. He looked terrible. Unshaven, hair dishevelled, smudges of dirt on his face and wrinkled clothes.

The scene with Michael Parks and Lloyd Bochner presented difficulties. Not only did Michael mumble (possibly because of the moustache), but he played childish games with the camera. Bud Thackery, a seasoned cinematographer, put his camera on a high hat (on the ground) and shot up at Michael, hoping to get a glimpse of his face. After the second day, Dick and I went to the dailies, accompanied by Michael, who had asked for permission to come. Most actors say nothing, but not Michael Parks. Before I had a chance to get out of my seat to go to my office to discuss the dailies alone with Dick, Michael started talking, with no mumbling.

PARKS: I didn't like Bochner at all.
ME: Really? What did you think of yourself?
PARKS: I thought he hurt my performance.
ME: (*Getting angry*) What performance are you talking about? All I

saw was you staring at the ground, always away from Lloyd and the camera. All I heard was some indistinct mumbling. No wonder you thought little of Lloyd. He not only couldn't hear you, he never made eye contact.

(*I get out of my seat, as does Michael and a placating Dick.*)

LYONS: (*Quickly*) Now boys, let's relax and take it easy.

PARKS: He insulted me.

ME: Let me tell you something. Instead of worrying about the other actors, you'd better start worrying about yourself. (*Shouting.*) Because as an actor, you stink!

I left the projection room and hastened to my office. I could hear, very distinctly, Michael threatening to quit the picture. Dick was doing his best to calm him down. I was so mad that I went into the wrong office. When I found my own, I picked up my thickest pipe, filled it with an English tobacco 'Smooth as a Baby's Bottom', lit it and rushed out to continue the fray. Dick and Michael were standing outside the projection room arguing, with Dick doing most of the listening. I stood in a darkened area. I figured it was a good spot to hit Michael with my heavy pipe. If I landed it, he'd have a broken jaw.

ME: (*Yelling*) Dick! Let the bum go. He can keep his moustache as a memento.

Michael turned from Dick and I thought he started towards me. However, he totally ignored me and disappeared through the studio gates. I couldn't help but admire his complete indifference to me. When an agitated Dick Lyons appeared, I went back to my office and telephoned Paul Donnelly at his home. Dick just stared at me, stricken. I explained everything to Paul and suggested he get a new director.

DONNELLY: Listen carefully, Don. You be on the set early. If anyone quits, it'll be Parks. See you in the morning. These things have a way of blowing over. Eat your dinner and get some sleep. If you're late on the location and if Parks doesn't hit you, I will. Good night.

The next morning at 7 a.m. I arrived at the location. Bud Thackery was preparing a 'day for night' shot. In between munching on a doughnut and sipping a cup of hot coffee, he was explaining to me the beauty of the picture he was painting with lights and proper exposure. In the daylight, it looked ordinary. When I saw the long shot of the town in dailies, it was resplendent and picturesque. Magic. Michael showed up. I gave him the same treatment he had given me. I totally ignored him. My assistant director came over to tell me that they would be ready for a run-through.

ME: Great, Earl. One thing. I want you to give all the directions to Michael. Have him come out of the hotel, go down the street and enter the store.
BELLAMY: Yes, sir.

The next shot, on the boom, showed Michael walking towards the shack on the extreme outskirts of the town. There were no roads or trails leading to it. Just dirt and dust. Earl gave Michael his directions and we shot it. I just let him walk. It was about half a mile. As Michael strode towards the cabin, Bud thought I had forgotten to yell, 'Cut.'

ME: Turn your camera off whenever the mood hits you. But do it silently. I want Michael to walk up to the cabin. If I'm lucky, maybe he will sprain his ankle.

I watched Michael stride resolutely to the cabin. I turned away to give Bud a line-up on our next shot when I saw something interesting on the ground. It was a small piece of wood with one end pointing down and the other end pointing up. I became excited with a preposterous idea. I asked the nearest grip for a piece of adhesive tape the length of the stick. I folded the tape carefully so that the adhesive side would stick to my moustache and to the stick. It worked perfectly. I had a drooping moustache on the left side and an upturned moustache on my right side. I patiently waited for Michael. As he walked by me, of course never looking at me, I called out to him.

ME: Michael! I want to explain the next set-up to you.
(*He walks over to me slowly, his eyes examining the ground.*)
ME: The reason I didn't have you rush back to get your deputies and horses is because there's never a thought that Hank could possibly escape.
PARKS: That's true. Actually, I enjoy making a manhunt as difficult as possible.
(*He looks up at me casually, then suddenly bursts into laughter.*)
ME: (*Playing it straight*) What's bothering you?
PARKS: (*Tears in his eyes from laughter*) That's the damnedest moustache I've ever seen. Wish I'd seen it before you. That's the one I would have been wearing.
(*In the background, Paul steps up to us.*)

DONNELLY: You guys aren't supposed to be laughing. (*Starting to laugh.*) What the hell is that contraption on your face?

ME: I decided to make Michael jealous.

PARKS: Yeah, I'm gonna pout my way through the entire picture.

DONNELLY: Don, why don't you give Michael your moustache?

ME: Because he won't give it back to me. I'll tell you one thing Michael, it's fun laughing with you.

*

In the middle of nowhere, early in the morning, I was standing with Fonda. No belching tractors, no cars, no people, just an empty vista. We were planning the route Hank would take when he was captured by Michael and his deputies. Far in the distance, I saw some animals grazing.

ME: (*Pointing*) What kind of animals are those?

FONDA: Horses, you brilliant Western director.

ME: You're a big Western star. You know these things.

FONDA: It's going to be one hell of a Western with a director who doesn't know what horses look like.

ME: I don't even know how to ride.

FONDA: I hate horses.

ME: I'm going to tell them what you said.

FONDA: The only way you'll get me on the treacherous beasts is to pay me.

(*I light up my pipe, puffing up a storm. Hank starts to cough.*)

FONDA: What a stupid habit, despoiling the clean, clear air.

ME: I've been smoking a pipe since I was sixteen.

FONDA: Look at your clothes. There are burn holes everywhere. Why don't you quit smoking? Your throat would feel clean and the air about you wouldn't smell like horse turds. Over the long haul, you would be surprised how much money you would save. I gave up smoking eight years ago. I haven't regretted it, or missed it.

ME: I can't give up my pipes in the middle of a picture. But I'll tell you what. I'll try. The day after we finish the picture, I'll make the strongest effort to quit.

(*Hank fastens his clear blue eyes on me.*)

FONDA: You make the effort to quit smoking and I promise you that I'll never mention it again.

We shook hands. Hank was dead serious. I liked him so much that I hoped I wouldn't let him down.

*

In the final confrontation between Fonda and Parks outside the hotel,

273

Dean Riesner had written an excellent scene where Hank, regaining his manhood and courage after taking a terrible beating from Parks, wins the final encounter. Michael took the position, about a week before the fight took place, that it was ridiculous for a twenty-nine-year-old deputy chief, in excellent physical shape, to be beaten in a fight by a sixty-year-old former drunk. To my surprise, Hank agreed with Michael. I got hold of Dean and told him all the details. He took it in poor grace. He liked what he had written. Everyone on the show had approved it. In good conscience, Dean couldn't rewrite it. I was nominated and approved to do a rewrite – I might add, against my will. I took a simple approach, which I thought might work. It was true that in a hand-to-hand encounter Hank would have little chance. It was also, hopefully, true that Michael might recognize Hank's new-found courage. Every time Michael knocks Hank down, he staggers to his feet. Michael, in huge close-ups intercut with huge close-ups of Hank, ultimately realizes the futility and stupidity of the fight. He leaves the scene of battle with Fonda still on his feet. I don't believe that my version was as good as Dean's. Dean agreed, as he made clear later.

RIESNER: Don wrote a new ending and shot it. He did an outstanding job of taking the wrong ending and making it come off. I would have been more pleased if he had blown it and they had to do the thing my way.

27

Madigan

Universal 1968

After *Stranger on the Run*, I remembered my promise to Hank to try to give up smoking. I didn't light up a pipe. I knew that when I got my next assignment I would undoubtedly start smoking again, but at least Hank would know that I tried. He would have to live up to his promise of never mentioning anything about smoking. I found it difficult not to think of my next picture when I would surely start smoking. However, a miracle occurred. My next picture was *Madigan*, starring Hank Fonda – a thousand to one shot. My heart sank. Hank was extremely proud of me. He didn't give a tinker's damn about my directing – only that I no longer smoked. I couldn't let him down. As luck would have it, I never smoked again; but I sure missed it while working on the film, which was full of woe and problems.

*

Prior to *Madigan*, its producer, Frank Rosenberg, wanted me to work on the television series *Arrest and Trial*. When I told him I didn't want to direct any of the segments of the series, he refused to release me from my contract with Universal. I went to Allan 'Pinky' Miller, senior vice-president in charge of television, and explained my predicament. He got me away from Frank, for which I was most grateful. I wondered, now that Frank was to produce *Madigan*, if he held a grudge.

I met the writer, Abraham Polonsky, in Frank's office at what I thought was going to be a story conference. Polonsky was a blacklisted writer and for many years was unable to obtain work. Rosenberg gave him the job of rewriting Howard Rodman's script. This was very decent of Rosenberg, and also smart. Polonsky had a very good reputation as a screenwriter. He had a pleasant grin and the appearance of an erudite chap; but, to my astonishment, he never opened his mouth at the meeting.

Abraham and I watched Frank write. He wrote quickly with a small pencil and frequently sucked on its pointed lead. I assumed that when he was finished he would let us read it; or he would read it to us. Once, when he was sucking on his pencil, he looked up at us and smiled.

ROSENBERG: You know, I've written more material than both of you put together.

(*I think that a strange remark. I look over at Abraham, who smiles back at Frank. When Frank finally finishes writing, it is obvious he likes it.*)

ROSENBERG: I'll send you both typed copies.

ME: It will be more sanitary that way.

(*Abraham laughs, but Frank's face becomes set.*)

ME: Notwithstanding the enormous amount of scribbling you do, I would like to discuss the script with Abraham, alone.

ROSENBERG: It won't be necessary. Anything you have to say to Abe, you can say in front of me.

ME: But Frank, there are things I wish to say to Abraham, if indeed he is the writer, that at this time I don't wish to discuss with you.

ROSENBERG: Don, I'm afraid that won't be possible.

ME: It's still a free country, unless you've taken it over. I always work with the writer.

ROSENBERG: (*Getting angry*) When you work with me, I'm the boss.

ME: (*Getting up*) You're the producer – but not my boss. (*Turning to Abe.*) I'm sorry to embarrass you, but could you have lunch with me?

(*Abraham finally speaks.*)

POLONSKY: It's ridiculous not to allow us to have lunch together. Actually, it's un-American. (*He stands up.*) I'll let you know everything we've discussed.

Frank looked at both of us with real hatred. I smiled back at Frank, expressing my interest in what he had just written. We left.

Polonsky and I ate alone at the commissary. He explained that Rosenberg was kind enough to hire him when no one else would give him a job. He felt greatly beholden to Rosenberg and, consequently, his hands were tied. However, if he felt that I had come up with ideas that would help the picture, he would tell Rosenberg what my ideas were. Unfortunately, Rosenberg was a stubborn cuss, but Abe promised to do everything in his power to get him to agree to use my material. I thanked him.

*

After weeks of picking locations in the general area of Los Angeles, the Universal backlot and several interesting sets built by the art director, George C. Webb, we flew to New York City where we met the Mayor, Chief of Police and other officials. Our locations were good. Frank came up with several ideas. I discovered that he seemed confused about the theory of left to right/right to left. He acted somewhat embarrassed. From then on, he left us alone; he tagged along, but kept his mouth shut. Our cinematographer, Russell Metty, considered to be one of Universal's finest, simply stayed in the comfort of his studio car. Frankly, he was too fat to climb up six flights of tenement stairs. I felt more comfortable without his obese presence.

In the meantime, my producer/*auteur*, Rosenberg, picked wardrobe with Edith Head without discussing it with me. He also picked standing sets, such as a huge hotel suite that was unbelievable, both in taste and credibility. In the picture, at the Captain's party, Dick Widmark and his wife were to be given the use of what had to be the Royal Suite, which made the whole scene appear unrealistic. Of course, it was a standing set. No Captain could have had a suite as large. But I grew to accept these stupidities. In fact, the two executives who ran the studio at Universal, Ed Muhl and Mel Tucker, approved everything and anything that Mr Frank Rosenberg wanted. However, I must admit that our final cast list was impressive and Rosenberg deserved a great deal of credit for it.

Richard Widmark:	Dan Madigan
Henry Fonda:	Commissioner Anthony X. Russell
Inger Stevens:	Julia Madigan
Harry Guardino:	Rocco Bonaro
James Whitmore:	Chief Inspector Charles Kane
Susan Clark:	Tricia Bently
Michael Dunn:	Midget Castiglione
Steve Ihnat:	Barney Benesch
Don Stroud:	Hughie
Sheree North:	Jonesy
Warren Stevens:	Ben Williams
Raymond St Jacques:	Dr Taylor
Bert Freed:	Chief of Detectives
Harry Bellaver:	Mickey Dunn
Frank Marth:	Lieutenant James Price
Lloyd Gough:	Earl Griffen

*

Detectives Madigan and Rocco Bonaro track down and arrest Barney Benesch, an old criminal acquaintance, who is wanted for questioning by a neighbouring precinct. But Benesch distracts them, grabs their weapons and escapes. It turns out that Benesch is actually wanted for murder, and Madigan's interference has now made the situation worse since Benesch now has Madigan's gun. The Police Commissioner Russell, who, as a stickler for procedure, is diametrically opposed to Madigan's methods, gives Madigan three days to bring in Benesch.

Madigan's guilt is intensified when Benesch kills two policemen with Madigan's gun. However, his efforts finally pay off when he and Bonaro track down Benesch, who kills Madigan in a shoot-out before being killed himself by Bonaro.

Through his dealings with Madigan, the Police Commissioner finds a way of dealing with his own problems.

*

The first day's shooting was the last and most poignant scene for Miss Inger Stevens. Frank felt comfortable with this peculiar scheduling, as did his two superior executives, Muhl and Tucker. I didn't know Inger Stevens, other than having met her at some minor rehearsals and, of course, by her excellent reputation. She came up to me, close to tears.

STEVENS: It's not bad enough that I play this emotional and bitter
scene with Henry Fonda and James Whitmore; but to add the icing
of ignorance, I have to shoot wardrobe tests throughout the day.
Dick Widmark has just been killed in the line of duty. As his wife,
it's a tremendously poignant scene for me and changing clothes
does nothing for my concentration.
(*I felt enraged and helpless. The studio must be crazy.*)

ME: I am appalled about this. Please accept my sincerest apology. The
scene you're about to do is at best – even if shot at the end of the
schedule where it belongs – extremely difficult. I admire your
courage and talent in attempting to do it. I do have one suggestion
that may ease your task. When you're playing this acrid, painful
scene with Mr Fonda, think of the hate you feel for Frank
Rosenberg, who is responsible for this ridiculous schedule. Make
use of Rosenberg. Think of him with the loathing you feel when
faced with Fonda. As for the tests, think of nothing. Go blank.

Miss Stevens gave a startling portrayal: she was truly magnificent and brave.

*

One incident in the opening sequence astounded and disheartened me. In rehearsing this scene, where Steve Ihnat, in the dim, early-morning light, bolts up in bed when Dick and Harry break into the tenement apartment, I had Dick go to the window and release the window shade. Naturally, Steve's eyes blink as a shaft of light enters the room.

Russ Metty, our corpulent cinematographer, sat in a high director's chair at the back of the set; his radio, softly throughout the day, played

278

nothing but news. Rarely did he ever get out of his chair. When he heard the assistant director yell, 'Roll 'em!', he turned off his radio.

I shot the first take after numerous rehearsals. I noticed that there was no change of light when Dick pulled the window shade up.

ME: Why no change of light, Russ?
METTY: Whatever for?
ME: Didn't you notice Steve blink when Dick pulls the shade up?

Metty's face flushed in embarrassment. He turned his radio off, waddled over to his gaffer and had him set a couple of lights, which went on when the shade went up. He didn't apologize. I must give the devil his due: he was very fast. On the whole, the film looked good. You may wonder why I didn't have a serious quarrel with Metty. Frankly, I was outnumbered. I didn't get along with Rosenberg, nor his bosses Muhl and Tucker. What I did do was to treat Metty politely and make it very clear, as though letting him in on a secret, what I hoped for from his excellent lighting. He appeared to me to be bored by the picture. My ploy was to impress him that the only chance that *Madigan* had lay in his expertise in lighting. I always complimented his work at the dailies. He took it in his stride, never thanking me or saying anything about my work. Maybe that was just as well, as I'm sure he wasn't impressed.

*

Because I was working until at least 7 each night, Rosenberg started looking for locations in the slum area of Los Angeles for the final shoot-out. The reason that we had to shoot it in Los Angeles was that the company ran into trouble in Harlem, where Widmark and Guardino's car was dangerously rocked by a large group of young kids and our propman was mugged by some thugs. After that Rosenberg went everywhere with two husky detectives. Unfortunately, every location that I was shown after work by Frank was unimaginative. None of them looked like Harlem and I didn't have the foggiest idea of how to shoot what he showed me, which should be a most exciting sequence. Finally, he showed me a parking lot in downtown Los Angeles. In back of the lot was the side of a large, old tenement building. Behind the front area of the parking lot was a busy bus station. The street was full of traffic. I was terribly depressed. I walked away, accompanied by George Webb, the art director. We browsed by ourselves from street to street. Suddenly, we found a location that had great character: railroad tracks, curving alleys covered with walkways overhead from one dingy building to another and the back of a run-down hotel. There was only one angle which showed that we were not in New York: the Los Angeles Civic Center in the distance. This could be easily fixed with a 'glass shot': painting out the Civic Center and painting in a New York skyscraper. Universal had the best matte artist in the business, Al Whitlock.

ME: Make sure you cover this location thoroughly with Polaroids. Do the same with Frank's location.

WEBB: There's nothing to shoot there.

ME: Shoot it anyway. Let's find our prestigious producer and show him our masterpiece.

We showed it to Frank, who was totally unimpressed. He insisted his location was the one I would have to shoot. Webb, who was the gentlest and politest man on the whole crew, exploded and walked out.

The next morning, at about 9.30, Webb showed me the Polaroids. My location looked great; Frank's, just dull.

ME: I can't thank you enough.

WEBB: Good luck. You deserve it.

I called Lew Wasserman's office. I explained to his secretary that I had to talk to him as soon as possible. It was urgent.

SECRETARY: Hang on just a moment. Mr Siegel.
    (*Almost immediately, Lew is on the phone.*)

WASSERMAN: What's your problem, Don?

ME: I'm in serious trouble. I must see you at your earliest convenience.

WASSERMAN: Can you be in my office at noon without upsetting your schedule?

ME: I'll be there at twelve sharp.

I hung up feeling a ray of hope. I recognized that I couldn't branch off on various tangents of despair. I had to stick to one thing: do I shoot Rosenberg's location, or mine? As I rushed back to the set, I knew one thing. I would never shoot the Rosenberg location.

At noon I rushed to Wasserman's office and was immediately shown in. I was conscious of my heart pounding as I sat down without waiting for Lew's invitation to do so.

ME: I've never been in a position before where the producer picked the locations. I wouldn't mind if there was a possibility of my doing a good job. Here are pictures of Rosenberg's location for the last shoot-out. He insists I shoot it.
    (*Wasserman lays them out on his immaculate desk. He says nothing.*)

ME: And here's what I found.
  (*He examines them slowly.*)
ME: I need *one*, possibly two matte shots so I can shoot in any
  direction. At the other location, there can be no reverses because
  of the busy bus station and busy street. It will be necessary to
  shoot on the weekend.
  (*Wasserman makes a note on his white pad.*)
ME: I have a suggestion to solve this problem. Inasmuch as I truthfully
  have no idea how to shoot this exciting sequence at Rosenberg's
  location, I respectfully request that I be replaced.
WASSERMAN: Did you show Rosenberg these pictures?
ME: No. We had already walked thoroughly through both locations. As
  I mentioned before, he insisted, vehemently, that I must shoot
  what he picked.
WASSERMAN: (*Dismissing me*) I'll get back to you before the day is
  over.
ME: (*Getting up to leave*) Thanks for seeing me.
WASSERMAN: That's why I'm here. May I keep the Polaroids?
ME: (*Smiling*) They were shot specially for you.

Charley Greenlaw, production head for Wasserman, came down to the set
to see me. He told me that Mr Wasserman okayed my entire location for
the shoot-out. Naturally, I was very pleased. Then Charley spoiled my job
a little by giving me a most unnecessary admonition.

GREENLAW: Don't take advantage of Mr Rosenberg because you won.
ME: That's about as stupid a statement as I've ever heard. I'm only
  interested in doing my work as well and as quickly as I can. The
  last person I would talk to would be Frank. You must be
  becoming senile in your dotage. As I will stay out of Frank's way,
  you'd better stay out of my way.

*

I decided to concentrate on preparing my set-ups for the final shoot-out.
First, I would make an editing continuity on how I thought it would be put
together. This was all important. Then I would mark this continuity in the
order that I intended to shoot it. If I was successful in doing this, it would
make my shooting quicker without sacrificing quality.

  The master shot, embracing the entire area by panning and dollying,
was the first set-up shot. We started preparing as soon as we arrived at the
location. This shot took more time to prepare than any other shot in the
sequence.

Shooting continuity	*Editing continuity*

1st shot

1st shot (Master shot)
On boom – shooting down towards east alley. A police car with red lights flashing. Several policemen stand near it, alert. They look off, south.
Camera pans south to narrow curving alley leading south. At the far end of the alley is another police car with flashing lights.
Camera continues to alleyway west. At the far end of the alley, beyond the gates, is another police car with flashing lights. Against a near wall are several detective cars.
Camera zooms in to Lieutenant Marth and other detectives, huddled against a wall. Some have their badges on; others are affixing badges to their coats.

16th shot

2nd shot
Close angle on Lieutenant Marth and other detectives as they look up.

2nd shot

3rd shot
Up angle at last window on the top floor (fifth) with red and yellow curtains.

8th shot

4th shot
Up angle at policemen with rifles on the roof.

17th shot

5th shot
Close up of Lieutenant Marth looking up and across from window to his right to the roof across the street at policemen with rifles.

9th shot

6th shot
Up angle – policeman, mounting fire escape and taking his position with a rifle.

14th & 15th shots

7th shot
Angle on covered corridor from one factory building to another across the street. Windows open up and two rifles are pushed out, aimed at the killer's window, also firing.

10th shot	8th shot
	Up angle at policeman on fire escape near Ihnat's window.

19th shot	9th shot
	Angle shooting north toward north alley. At the end of the alley, train tracks disappearing past another police car with lights flashing. Whitmore's car appears coming towards camera, which pans it down the west alley past Lieutenant Marth and other detectives. At the same time, in the distance is seen Fonda's limousine approaching rapidly. Whitmore joins Marth and the other detectives, turning to wait for the Commissioner to arrive.

24th shot	10th shot
	Camera pans at far end of west alley with emergency truck as it proceeds east along the alley in the area where Whitmore and Lieutenant Marth are.

18th shot	11th shot
	Angle on limousine stopping. Fonda leaps from the passenger side, a policeman behind the wheel. Fonda affixes his badge to his lapel, joins Whitmore and Marth, camera panning with them.

MARTH: Lieutenant Marth, Commissioner. Twenty-third squad.

FONDA: Where is he?

MARTH: Last window, top floor, red and yellow curtains.

Camera pulls back with Marth, Whitmore, Fonda and detectives headed by O'Brien and Linc as they proceed to peer up past the corner.

3rd shot	12th shot
	Up angle at window. We see the still window on the fifth floor, the red and yellow curtains.

WHITMORE'S VOICE: (*Offstage*) Cover the front and evacuate the entire fifth floor.

20th shot	13th shot
	Wide angle on detectives, headed by O'Brien and Linc as

they run north in the alley. Shots ricochet near them as they continue to run north.

4th shot	14th shot Up angle at Ihnat's window. He is firing through it.
11th, 12th & 13th shots	15th shot Up angles on various police on roof tops, fire escapes, etc., which we have previously established. They commence firing.
5th shot Use 3 cameras from various angles	16th shot Up angles at Ihnat's window as the glass is shattered by shots.
25th shot	17th shot Reverse angle, Fonda, Whitmore and Lieutenant Marth pressed against a wall. FONDA: I understand he's got a girl in there with him. WHITMORE: That's right. Makes it all a little tougher. They look off to their right.
26th shot	17A Point of view: three men in protective gear get off the emergency truck carrying shotguns, tear-gas guns and two metal suitcases.
27th shot	17B Close shot – Fonda. FONDA: No tear gas, or smoke if we can avoid it.
22nd shot	18th shot Angle shooting toward east alley. (*Matte shot* to get rid of Los Angeles Civic Center.) Police are setting up barricades from a truck, as spectators are pressing against it and are forced to stay beyond the barriers.
22A	18A Closer angle – some of the spectators scatter and run, shouting and panicking.
21st shot	19th shot Shooting down south alley. At the far end of the alley is a police car, its red lights still flashing. Other police are

setting up a barrier as Guardino's car swerves past it, coming at high speed towards the camera, which pans it careening, skidding down the west alley. It stops near an emergency truck.

28th shot
20th shot
Closer angles – Guardino and Widmark – as they jump out of the car and rush over to Whitmore, Fonda and Lieutenant Marth at the wall along the west alley.

29th shot
20A
Angle featuring Widmark, who has the plan of Ihnat's apartment in his hands. He gives it to Whitmore. Fonda looks on, silent.

WHITMORE: (*Studying it*) Good.

Pan Whitmore, Widmark and Guardino to the edge of a building in the west alley. They peer around the corner.

6th shot
21st shot
Up angle at Ihnat's window.

WHITMORE'S VOICE: (*Offstage*) Is that the kitchen?

30th shot
22nd shot
Reverse back to group.

WIDMARK: Yes.
WHITMORE: Now, which of you guys goes first?
GUARDINO: I do.
WIDMARK: He covers, chief. I go for the kitchen.
GUARDINO: (*Protesting*) Wait a minute.

31st shot
22A–B–C
Camera dollies with group as they join Fonda.

WIDMARK: I'm the senior man, Chief
GUARDINO: By two days . . .
WHITMORE: (*Abruptly*) Dick goes. Harry covers.

He looks at Rubin with a shotgun as the emergency truck moves closer.

WHITMORE: (*To Rubin*) If you have to use the shotgun, use it. (*To Fonda.*) I guess that's it, Commissioner.

Fonda looks at Widmark and Guardino.

FONDA: I know the detectives assigned have a personal score to settle in this. (*Looks at Widmark.*) Good detectives are hard to find. Good luck and God keep both of you safe.

As Fonda, Widmark and Guardino look at each other, the driver of the emergency truck on foot comes right up to the group carrying two metal suitcases. Behind him is Rubin, carrying his ten-gauge shotgun. The driver opens up the suitcases and hands the armoured jackets to Widmark and Guardino. Widmark throws the weighty jacket to·the ground, followed by Guardino.

WIDMARK: To hell with these things. We've gotta move fast.

22nd shot	23rd shot Dolly with group – Widmark, Guardino and Rubin. They hug the wall of the west alley, then start running down the wall of the north alley and continue their race to the rear entrance of the East River Hotel. While running, bullets are just missing them.
7th shot	24th shot Up angle at Ihnat's window. Pistol fire is rapid.
14th shot	25–30 Up angles at various police in various vantage points. Police are firing.
No shooting continuity on interior shots	31st shot Interior, fifth floor, being evacuated by a group of detectives led by O'Brien and Linc. Mothers and their small children, an elderly man in a wheelchair and a man and wife are hustled into an elevator, which is now crammed full. The doors close. Three detectives run down the stairs as the elevator descends. Linc and O'Brien remain on the fifth floor.
	32nd shot Interior, fifth floor landing. Widmark, followed by Guardino and Rubin move down the bare corridor. Linc and O'Brien join the group.

WIDMARK: (*To Linc and O'Brien*) Get every light bulb out.

33rd shot
Angle on Linc and O'Brien, who run softly down the corridor. O'Brien makes a cradle with his hands for Linc, who steps up and unscrews the lightbulb, then jumps lightly down. They continue until all the corridor lights are out. The corridor is considerably darkened.

WIDMARK: (*Indicating apartments on both sides of corridor*) Empty?
LINC: The whole floor . . . excepting 502.

34th shot
Tight angle – Widmark and Guardino, as they check their pistols. They quickly and quietly move on either side of 502. Rubin, shotgun in hand, follows. Widmark gestures to Rubin, who positions himself to blow the lock off Apartment 502.

WIDMARK: Just the lock. There's a girl inside with him.

35th shot
Close shot – shotgun. It fires.

36th shot
Close shot – lock, as the door breaks free of its lock.

37th shot
Wider angle – Guardino and Widmark on either side of the door as it slowly swings wide open. Five fast shots slam out, ricocheting in the hall. Guardino and Widmark jump to opposite sides of the open door flat against the wall. Rubin hits the floor. The darkened kitchen is dead ahead, beyond a small foyer. A door leads to a bedroom. A girl's scream rips out as two shots come out from the kitchen area. Neither the girl nor Ihnat is visible.

38th shot
Reverse on Widmark and Guardino.

WIDMARK: Stevey! You haven't got a chance. Use your head and come out.

IHNAT: (*Offstage*) I still got one of your guns, Dicky boy. How about it? Do you want it with a police special?

GUARDINO: It's all over, Stevey! Come out, or we're coming in to get you!

IHNAT: (*Offstage*) What're you waiting for, Harry? You and Dick lost your nerve?

39th shot
Close dolly and pan with Widmark until he has a good view of the small foyer and the opening of the kitchen. He gestures to Guardino.

40th shot
Close reverse on Guardino.

GUARDINO: You should be giving me cover. Let me go in.

41st shot
Close reverse on Widmark.

WIDMARK: Knock it off. (*Whispering.*) Keep him talking, Harry.

42nd shot
Reverse on Widmark and Guardino.

GUARDINO: Stevey! Send the girl out. She won't help you any!

IHNAT: (*Offstage*) (*Laughing*) How do you know? I might get bored.

GUARDINO: Come on, Stevey. She's got nothing to do with all of this. Let's talk it over.

IHNAT: (*Offstage*) I'm all through talking with you bums. Send me somebody important. The Mayor here yet?

GUARDINO: He couldn't make it, Stevey. He's busy with the budget.

Three fast shots smash out into the wall.

IHNAT: (*Offstage*) (*Wild, shouting*) You're a funny man, Harry!

Widmark crouches low, ready to dash into the room.

IHNAT: (*Offstage*) You want her alive, come and get her before I put a bullet in her dumb head!

NOTE: during the shoot-out, the short staccato cuts will be shot and edited as a montage.
At this moment, Widmark makes his move. Guardino has drawn his second revolver and as Widmark, gun in hand, goes in low, Guardino opens fire with both hands over Widmark's head.

43rd shot
Low angle favouring Widmark. Widmark slams in low against the wall to the left side of the kitchen door, not firing.

44th shot
Shooting down on Guardino. He keeps firing high.

45th shot
Close angle – Ihnat. He appears from behind the stove in the kitchen. He has a .45 automatic in one hand and Guardino's .38 police special in the other. He crouches low and covers the open kitchen door.

46th shot
Ihnat's point of view – Widmark jumping out and firing.

47th shot
Shooting past Widmark as he fires at Ihnat.

48th shot
Shooting past Ihnat with both pistols aimed at Widmark. There is a violent interchange of shots.

49th and 50th shots
Inserts – Widmark's pistol firing and Ihnat's guns both blazing.

51st shot
Angle favouring Widmark, as he is hit by a bullet, whirling him around.

52nd shot
Close shot – Widmark, as he falls to the floor, shooting all the while.

22 *Madigan*: Madigan (Richard Widmark) hit by a bullet

53rd shot
Close shot – Ihnat. He is hit, dropping to his knees, still shooting at Widmark.

54th shot
Angle on Widmark, who tries to twist out of range.

55th shot
Close angle on Ihnat, firing.

56th shot
Raking shot of Widmark, as he is hit in the thigh and abdomen.

57th shot
Pan Guardino, who jumps over Widmark into the kitchen. Ihnat has disappeared.

58th shot
Low wide angle – Ihnat lying on the kitchen floor before
the open door of a large closet. He is desperately trying to
crawl into it, but is mortally wounded and can't make it.
Inside the closet, Doreen is crouching on the floor,
screaming hysterically.

59th shot
Closer angle – Ihnat. He tries to raise his gun to shoot
her.

60th shot
Up close angle – Guardino. He fires three times.

61st shot
Down angle over Guardino on to Ihnat, as three bullets
thud into him. Ihnat lies still.
NOTE: End of montage of shoot-out.

62nd shot
Camera pans with Guardino, as he leans over Ihnat, guns
ready and turns him around.

IHNAT: (*His last breath*) I killed him, didn't I, Harry?

Ihnat dies.

63rd shot
Reverse angle. The apartment fills with police. Harry
picks up the .38 special and runs to Widmark as two
policemen start to bring Doreen, crying hysterically, out.

64th shot
Tight two-shot, as Harry kneels over Dick.

WIDMARK: (*In great pain*) I'm hurt bad, Harry.
GUARDINO: (*Half sobbing*) No, you're not, Dick. No,
  you're not.

32nd shot   65th shot
Exterior, East River Hotel. A Flower Hospital Ambulance, siren wailing, lights flashing, pulls up to the rear
exit of the East River Hotel. The siren dies out as the
driver and his partner rush out of the ambulance, open
the rear door and quickly wheel a gurney, piled with
blankets and a medicine bag, into the rear of the hotel.

33rd shot	**66th shot** Full shot. The crowd is now silent. Police start to come down from various vantage posts. Other police keep spectators from passing through the barricades.
34th shot	**67th shot** Dolly shot. The Commissioner and Chief Inspector Whitmore make their way to the rear of the hotel, near the back of the ambulance. They are surrounded by police and detectives. They look off at the rear exit to the hotel.
36th shot	**68th shot** Angle on rear exit. Several policemen appear, leading the way for the gurney with Widmark on it, covered with blankets. Guardino, in semi-shock, walks beside Widmark.
35th shot	**69th shot** Pan shot of reporters and photographers scattering out of the way of the police and making a beeline for the stretcher. There is a great deal of shoving, flashbulbs popping, etc.; but the police waste no time clearing the area, as Fonda, Whitmore and Marth form around the moving gurney as it is wheeled to the rear of the ambulance.
37th shot	**70th shot** Closer angle – dolly shot – Widmark. His eyes are closed against the brightness of the cold sunlight. Fonda, walking beside him, puts a hand out and holds it over his face to shield it. Widmark opens his eyes. FONDA: You're going to be all right, Dick. WIDMARK: (*In a whisper*) Thanks. (*Then recognizing the voice.*) Thanks, Commissioner.
23rd shot	**71st shot** Hand-held camera in gurney – close-up – Fonda. FONDA: Save your strength. You'll be at the hospital in two minutes. The gurney is carefully lifted into the ambulance.

GUARDINO: Can I go down with him, Commissioner?
FONDA: Go ahead.

Guardino gets into the ambulance. The doors are slammed shut. The ambulance moves off, its siren beginning to blare as the ambulance makes it way down the street (matte shot). Whitmore turns to Marth.

WHITMORE: Get Widmark's wife . . . (*pause*) . . . and a priest.

38th shot	72nd shot
	Close-up down shot, Widmark in gurney.
39th shot	73rd shot
	Hand-held camera in gurney shooting up at Fonda for a close-up. This will be cut in immediately following the close-up of Widmark in the gurney, shot 71.

*

I discovered, to my dismay, that the censor board of NBC cut out the entire beginning of *Madigan*. The picture started lamely, with Henry Fonda standing on his apartment porch on 57th Street. The reason for this seven-minute cut was a few fleeting glimpses of the naked girl in bed with Steve Ihnat when Widmark and Guardino break into the tenement apartment. The censors had no quarrel with the violence or dialogue in this sequence, which was most exciting. Apparently Rosenberg was unable to save the film, or he felt it wasn't important.

I saw Lew Wasserman and explained to him that I felt I could save the opening sequence by taking out a few frames of film. He gave me his blessing to do what I could. I took out literally just a few frames, which still enabled the audience to think they saw the naked girl. NBC gave me no trouble at all. By starting the picture excitingly, *Madigan* became a big success.

Given that Widmark was killed in the film, I was astounded to learn that Universal was planning on making a TV series entitled *Madigan*, starring Richard Widmark. It was an incredibly stupid idea. Even though Widmark is one of filmdom's greatest actors, the series bombed out, a financial and artistic failure.

28

Coogan's Bluff

Universal 1969

There was a mix-up at Universal. Clint Eastwood, whom I not only did not know but had never seen in person or on film, was considering two directors for his first starring feature at Universal. Their names were Alex Segal and Don Taylor. They were both pleasant, talented directors. All Clint had to do was to make a simple choice. But alas, in the basement of the Black Tower (the executive building) there existed proudly a brand-new computer. Two names were fed to the ever-ready computer: Alex Segal and Don Taylor. The computer, like all executives, made a mistake. The name that appeared was Don Siegel. Clint was puzzled. He asked the executive producer, Dick Lyons, 'Who the hell is Don Siegel?'

LYONS: He just finished *Madigan*. Before that, he directed *Stranger on the Run* for me. He's done many pictures, like *The Killers* . . .
EASTWOOD: (*Interrupting*) I'd like to see those films.

When I found out that Clint had run three of my pictures and wanted to know if I was interested in directing *Coogan's Bluff*, I responded that I'd like to see the three Sergio Leone pictures he had starred in. I thought they were great fun, magnificently photographed, very well directed and no question that a new star was born – Clint Eastwood.

Eastwood wanted to meet me at his home in Carmel. Jennings Lang wasted no time. He got Pat Kelly, head of casting, to fly me up to Carmel immediately. Before I agreed to meet Clint, I wondered why it was necessary. What difference did it make if he didn't like my bovine eyes or my acerbic tongue? The only thing that counted was the fact that he liked my films – at least three of them. But Pat, the wily Irishman who was well known for the lousy deals he made for people coming into Universal Studios, overwhelmed me with a line of blarney that I couldn't resist.

We met Clint in his surprisingly modest cabin. He was charming and gracious, 6 foot 4 with steely eyes of blue. I was tempted to say that he'd never make it as an actor because of his prominent Adam's apple, his deeply lined face. I wanted to find out if he'd pull a gun on me, or just pick me up with one hand and dump me. But after two martinis, during which time we discussed dames, golf, dames, the glorious weather, etc., I brought up the subject of hitting a few golf balls. Unfortunately, the phone rang. It was Jennings Lang. Clint talked to him in his usual taciturn manner.

EASTWOOD: Everything's fine with me. (*Pause.*) Jennings wants to talk to you, Don.
(*I cross over and take the phone.*)
ME: The fog's setting in pretty heavy. I'll come back tomorrow, if it lifts.
(*Clint laughs but the company man, Pat, grabs the phone away from me.*)
PAT: The weather's perfect. We'll catch the next plane out. I agree with you, Jennings. Fuck the golf. We'll see you tomorrow morning.

The first thing I did upon returning to Universal the next morning was to start reading all the material on *Coogan's Bluff*. Jennings called to tell me I was assigned to the project. I told him that I was already reading hundreds of pages that writers Herman Miller, Roland Kibbee and Jack Laird had produced. It would take me all day to read and digest everything. There was no doubt that a good script could be written. But so far, I felt it needed mucho work. I was working on a project with Howard Rodman. How about my letting him read the material? This would save time, if Jennings agreed that he could write it. Jennings agreed. Rodman agreed. He showed up at my office at 5 o'clock.

RODMAN: I read it all. It needs a complete rewrite. We should go to New York and write it to actual locations, which you'll pick.
ME: Do you think you can whip it in shape in a couple of weeks?
RODMAN: Make it a month.
ME: Let me set up a meeting with the two of us and Jennings around ten in the morning. I'll call him now.
(*My secretary, Ceil Burrows, gets Jennings on the phone.*)
ME: Can Rodman and your favourite director see you tomorrow morning?
LANG: I'm tied up tomorrow. How about seeing me right now?
ME: OK. Chill the martinis.
(*Jennings agrees to everything.*)
LANG: Go to New York. Buy the camera you and Rodman want and charge it to Richard Lyons. You can talk script on the flight. When can you leave, Howard?

RODMAN: Yesterday.

ME: Day after tomorrow. I want a penthouse for Howard and a gold typewriter. I'll chain him to his desk. Thanks for the martini. Don't you drink, Howard?

RODMAN: (*Smiling evilly*) When I drink, I get mad; which means I'll throw you out of the penthouse window.

ME: (*To Jennings*) Maybe you should come along with us.

LANG: Get moving. My secretary will take care of all the reservations.

We left happy and innocent. Ignorance is bliss.

*

New York has large buildings and New Yorkers speak with many tongues. I found Howard an honest-to-God penthouse at the Drake Hotel. We bought a Nikon camera, extra lens and a case. We charged it to Richard Lyons: $657. The gold typewriter presented difficulties. However, in the window of a pawn shop on Lexington Avenue was an old typewriter, gold-plated and in mint condition. Naturally, Howard took a picture of it. Then we went in and bought it. The price: $125. I gave the owner $100. A bargain. Later, we found out that it was painted gold, *not* gold-plated.

By cunning persuasion and stern exhortations, I managed to get Howard started on the screenplay. We talked every day until the early hours of the morning on a step outline, which by some miracle we agreed on. I was staying at the Regency Hotel on Park Avenue. In less than a week, we had found all our exterior locations. Incidentally, I did not chain him to his typewriter chair. He wrote swiftly and well.

I had to leave Howard to pick locations in the Mohave Desert. I took several xeroxes of what he had written so far – about fifty pages. He swore he would complete the script within two weeks. When he finished a sequence, he could special deliver it to me. I thanked him for his excellent work and was off. The locations in the Mohave Desert were easy to find. More important, they would work well in the picture. I had a studio photographer shoot stills. The main difference between his photos and Howard's was that the photographer didn't waste a shot.

Finally, I had a complete script. I sent xeroxes to Lang, Lyons and Eastwood's agent, Lenny Hirshan of the William Morris Agency. Although I thought the suspense was there, I missed humour.

The studio liked the script, and the basic continuity. Rodman was exhausted and resting in New York, which meant that he was shooting hundreds of stills. I heard from Jennings.

LANG: Be in my office at eleven a.m. Clint has read the script and wants to discuss it with us.

ME: Did he give any indication of whether he liked it?

LANG: No, but he's showing up with his entourage – his agent, lawyer and business manager.

ME: It sounds ominous.

LANG: Entourages are born to dislike everything. See you in the morning.

No use worrying because I knew one thing: Rodman's script was better than Miller's, Kibbee's or Laird's. It's strange about agents, lawyers and business managers. What the hell do they know about making pictures? They're wheeler-dealers, not picture-makers.

The next morning, without Richard Lyons, Jennings and I waited for Clint and his advisers. He showed up wearing sneakers, Levis and an open sports shirt. Everyone else, including Jennings and me, wore ridiculous suits and ties. No one shook hands. Everyone waited for Clint to speak.

EASTWOOD: (*Simply*) I hate the script.

Now everyone looked at me. I had a strange ambivalence. Obviously I was insulted, but at the same time I thought, 'Thank God I'm off the picture.' When he saw my shocked expression, he took up the slack.

EASTWOOD: I feel that the writer has gone away from the original concept. I don't like it and don't want to work on it.

ME: (*Getting angry*) How many versions of *Coogan's Bluff* have you read?

EASTWOOD: One.

ME: Well, there are three writers: Miller, Kibbee and Laird, with a total of at least seven versions. Naturally, I figured you didn't like Miller's first draft, or why where they written?

EASTWOOD: Damned if I know.

ME: I figured you didn't like it, so I steered Rodman in a different direction thinking you wanted a change.
(*Jennings leaps to his feet. He is a master con artist.*)

LANG: (*To Clint and me*) Look, you two guys are going to make the picture. Do whatever you want, but let's get it going. It's your picture.

So I left with Mr Six-foot-four for my office. I immediately pulled out all the written material and handed it to him.

ME: If we're to make this picture, you must read all this material.

EASTWOOD: Shit.

ME: You have to know everything I know. When you've read everything, let's meet again. I'll do my damnedest to give you what you want. But it's only fair that you read the same material that I did. If we don't agree, we'll call it a day, wish each other luck, have a brew and be friends.

EASTWOOD: (*Smiling*) You just struck me a low blow. I'll see you tomorrow, if I don't call you to forget it.

ME: That's fair enough. Glad you didn't hit me a low blow. Hope I see you tomorrow.

*

The next morning in my office, two grown men, Clint and I, were lying on the floor surrounded with pages from the various drafts by the four writers. We were having fun putting together a script based on their work; yet we were dead serious in what we were doing.

EASTWOOD: (*Scissors in hand*) Do you prefer the Rodman opening, or Miller's?

ME: I'll take either. Just so you don't use Kibbee's or Laird's.

Without further ado, he picked up the opening page of Miller's and compared it with Rodman's. He cut the first paragraph of Miller's and pasted it on a clean piece of paper. He then cut the rest of the first page of Rodman's and pasted it beneath the Miller opening paragraph. I read it.

ME: It looks like we're playing scrabble. But I've got to admit that it's a good opening.

EASTWOOD: How about going back to Miller?

ME: How about continuing with Rodman?

EASTWOOD: It really needs editing.

ME: Agreed. Slice away.

We both scribbled in bridges between the different scenes, and by lunchtime we had twelve pages that read pretty well. By the end of the day we had twenty-seven pages. Clint was tied up the next day, but he promised to be in my office the following day.

ME: I've an idea. Don't misread me, but we need a writer who can correlate our work.

EASTWOOD: Now we'll have five writers. I thought you liked what we've done.

ME: You have things to do and so do I. I know a writer, Dean Riesner, who will save us a lot of time and give us what we want.

EASTWOOD: You really think we need him?

ME: Yes. I just hope we can get him. I'd like to have him read all the material tomorrow, including our twenty-seven pages. We really don't have much time before we're supposed to start shooting. In addition to the script, we have to cast, pick wardrobe, get the best crew possible, ad nauseam.

(*Clint gets up from the floor, hands me the paste and scissors. He looks like a hurt kid.*)

EASTWOOD: I guess you're right. But I want this writer to give us what we think we need. I don't want him turning out a new script with his ideas.

ME: He'll do what we tell him to do. He's the best writer on the lot. Believe me, we need him.

(*We walk carefully through the mess to the door.*)

EASTWOOD: I enjoyed today. Let's keep up the good work.

ME: There's only one way to shoot, Cowboy. Aim high.

(*Clint smiles and we shake hands.*)

The next morning, Jennings got me Dean Riesner. Before Dean arrived, Dick Lyons handed me copies of all the material to give to him. He looked wide-eyed at the mess of cut pages on the floor. I had put a large sign on the floor, '*DON'T* TOUCH', so the cleaning lady wouldn't throw them into her waste barrel.

LYONS: I guess *Coogan's Bluff* is turning into a dirty script.

ME: Do me a favour. Make me four copies of this 'patched' version. Keep one for yourself.

(*He leaves and shortly afterwards Dean arrives. When he sees the mess on the floor he grins widely.*)

RIESNER: That's a nice touch: *DON'T* TOUCH.

ME: We need you badly to —

RIESNER: I would think so.

ME: — to correlate the various scripts so that they make sense. (*Handing him the material.*) Read it today and meet Clint and me tomorrow morning at ten.

(*There is a knock on the door. Dick's secretary enters and hands me three copies of Clint's and my work. I give Dean his copy. His smile grows larger as he quickly scans it.*)

RIESNER: It reminds me of my childhood. I used to secretly cut out paper dolls.

ME: There's a problem that —

RIESNER: There always is, Don.

ME: — we have to face. Clint wants you to fix up the already written
    material. He doesn't want you to write a new fifth version.
    (*Dean gets up and pats me on the cheek.*)
RIESNER: It's only words, Don. I understand.

He picked up all the material and with one 'oy vey', left the room.

The next morning there were three of us on the floor busily cutting,
pasting and scribbling. Bits of priceless dialogue filled the air: 'I think this
sentence might fit'; 'Here's a paragraph that blends right in'; 'There are a
couple of pages I found that are well written'; 'Hurray'. We had only one
bad moment when Dean criticized Clint for banging Linny Raven, a
young girl, in the hope that she would take him to her boyfriend. He
thought it was stupid. Clint thought otherwise, losing his temper. I eased
the situation with guile. From that moment on, we all got along fine.

Clint told us at the end of the day that he had to leave town. He was
leaving the script in good hands, our hands, and he thanked us. I said we'd
get out a short synopsis, or treatment, or step outline, then a script in,
hopefully, two weeks. As soon as we had it, we wanted Clint to read it
before the Black Tower saw a word.

When he left, Dean felt a bit depressed. I told him to get going
immediately on a synopsis, or whatever. As soon as we okayed it, he
would be off and running on the script.

ME: Keep feeding me pages. I know it's a tough job and I realize that
    you're not a xerox machine. Keep loose, quit worrying. You're
    going to turn out a hell of a script.

*

Walt Coogan (Clint Eastwood) is a modern-day primitive. An instinctive
hunter, he rarely fails to track down his prey, animal or human. This
makes him invaluable as a deputy sheriff in the badlands of Arizona's
Piute county. Coogan is also a loner, a trait which often gets him in
trouble with his superior, Sheriff McCrea (Tom Tully).

Coogan, tall, trim, tanned by the desert sun, has no lack of female
admirers. One of them, Millie (Melodie Johnson), is helping him take a bath
when McCrea appears. The Sheriff gives his deputy a special assignment. He
is to go to New York (his first trip to the Big City) to extradite James
Ringerman (Don Stroud), escaped Arizona killer, now under custody.

Accustomed to direct action, always willing to make his own decisions,
Coogan finds the machinations of the law in New York quite unlike
Arizona procedures. To begin with, Detective Lieutenant McElroy (Lee J.
Cobb) informs him he will have to cool his heels. Ringerman is not ready
to be returned. He has taken an overdose of LSD and is under treatment

at Bellevue. Not until doctors release him can he be moved. Coogan's dismay is slightly overcome when, in McElroy's office, he meets lovely Julie Roth (Susan Clark), probation officer. Coogan goes on the make, and it is apparent that Julie is enormously attracted to him, but she resists the swiftness of his advances, never before having been confronted with such animal magnetism.

Restless over the unforeseen delay in extraditing Ringerman, Coogan decides to take matters in his own hands. He bluffs his way into Bellevue. He fast-talks attendants into releasing the prisoner into his custody. Before leaving with Coogan, Ringerman whispers a message to his visitor, a mini-skirted swinger, Linny Raven (Tisha Sterling). The nature of the message becomes apparent at the airport, where, awaiting departure, with Ringerman manacled to his wrist, Coogan is called to the phone, only to be blackjacked into unconsciousness by Ringerman's confederate, Pushie (David F. Doyle), who frees Ringerman from the handcuffs. Regaining consciousness, Coogan is severely reprimanded by McElroy, who advises the deputy to forget about Ringerman; the New York police force, 28,000 strong, will handle the matter. Chagrined over the unexpected turn of events, Coogan is now more determined than ever to get his man. From the escaped prisoner's mother (Betty Field) he gets a lead on Linny, but in so doing he blows a police stake-out, thereby getting himself in trouble, once again, with McElroy. At the same time he receives a telegram from McCrea informing him he has been taken off the case.

Julie, feeling sorry for Coogan, invites him to dinner at her apartment. While she is preoccupied in the kitchen the deputy discovers, in her filing cabinet, an address for Linny, one of her probationers. Coogan takes off. He finds Linny at a psychedelic night spot where he fights off two of her would-be protectors armed with knives. She takes Coogan to her apartment. He makes love to her and she promises to lead him to Ringerman. Instead she takes him to a pool hall where he recognizes Pushie, the man who blackjacked him. Linny yells to Pushie that the deputy is unarmed, whereupon Pushie and eight of his friends, each armed with a billiard cue, gang up on Coogan. The deputy turns the tables, first by hurling well-aimed pool balls and later by grabbing a cue that one of the men drops. Bloody and mauled, Coogan returns to his hotel to tend his wounds. Later he returns to Linny's apartment. She is now fearful that he will kill her unless she leads him to Ringerman, and she guides him to the Cloisters in Fort Tryon Park. Ringerman is armed with Coogan's stolen gun, which he empties, futilely, at the deputy. Then he tries to make a getaway on a motorcycle. Coogan takes after him on another motorcycle. The two vehicles collide. Ringerman runs but Coogan brings him down with a diving tackle.

When police arrive, headed by McElroy, Coogan grins that he has made a citizen's arrest. Soon after Coogan once again has Ringerman in tow as he prepares to board a helicopter on top of the Pan Am skyscraper to take them to Kennedy Airport to catch a plane for Arizona. At the heliport to see him off is Julie. Their words are lost in the deafening whine of the helicopter, but from the smile on Julie's face it is clear the two have by no means seen the last of each other. Coogan and Ringerman get into the helicopter and it takes off. From Coogan's point of view, Julie is seen looking up at the rising helicopter. Her figure becomes smaller and smaller until she is indistinguishable in the vast panorama of Manhattan.

*

Jennings's office was beautifully furnished. All the paintings were oils and modern. They were very valuable and belonged to him. He appeared not to have a worry in the world; but I knew differently. A number of years ago he had been my agent; now he was my boss. He was genial, friendly and full of fun, a most likeable chap. As I sat watching him talk on the phone, I reminisced.

Jennings was tricky. My ex-wife, Viveca Lindfors, was represented by the powerful agency MCA. At that time, Jennings worked for the Jaffee Agency. Viveca asked me what I thought of Jennings as an agent; MCA didn't seem to be doing anything for her.

ME: I never recommend doctors, lawyers, business managers and particularly agents. As far as I'm concerned, Jennings is good.
LINDFORS: He wants me to leave MCA. He says they have too many clients. If Jennings represents me, he will handle my career personally.
ME: You are the only one who can make that decision.

She made it. She fired MCA and signed with the Jaffee Agency. About two weeks later, Viveca complained to me.

LINDFORS: I don't understand Jennings. I call him repeatedly. He never returns my calls.
ME: I don't feel responsible, but I'll see him to find out what's wrong.

I didn't see Jennings, but I quickly discovered what had happened. As soon as he had wooed Viveca away from MCA, they offered him a job at MCA. He took it and left Viveca without his services at Jaffee.
My reverie was interrupted by Jennings speaking to me.

LANG: There's no way that we can postpone *Coogan's Bluff*, Don.
ME: God may do it for you. We are scheduled to shoot in New York

during the month of November. Has it ever *not* snowed when you've been there in November?

LANG: Definitely yes.

ME: What happens if it does snow?

LANG: There comes a time when one has to gamble. Certainly if it snows you won't be blamed. Figure out what you could do if it does snow. You're a tricky fellow.

ME: Funny – that's what I was just thinking about you.

LANG: (*Looking at his watch*) I'm late for a meeting with Lew. If we ever get the script and it turns out good, we will cast it as well as we can. (*Getting up and walking with me to his door.*) Clint really likes you. It's going to be a cup of tea.

I wandered into Paul Donnelly's office, the antithesis of Jennings's. There were only a calendar and two shooting schedules on the walls. He was dressed as usual in a dark suit and tie. He looked in an ugly mood.

DONNELLY: If I hear one more complaint, I'll commit suicide.

ME: That's kind of tempting. Seriously, Lang insists it won't snow in November in New York.

DONNELLY: (*Writing on his desk pad*) I'm going to get a rundown on that piece of information. It'll make nice reading for Lew. When do we get the script?

ME: Riesner is not only doing a great job; he's fast. You should have a complete draft in one week.

DONNELLY: Seems to me I've read quite a few first drafts.

ME: Have you ever made three different shooting schedules for each day's shooting?

DONNELLY: What the hell for?

ME: I think I may have an idea that might help us if we run into occasional foul weather. The first schedule is for fine weather. Like the love scene between Coogan and Julie at Fort Tryon Park. The second schedule is for shooting without sun, but definitely possible shooting weather. Like anything around the Twenty-third Precinct exterior. The third schedule is for shooting in impossible weather, like heavy rain, fog, but particularly snow blizzards. This would mean the interior of the Twenty-third Precinct, including whatever interiors we build in one of the studios in New York. Like the hotel room where Coogan meets the prostitute, etc.

DONNELLY: It could work; although I don't know what you'd do if it snows during a long scene and stops, then starts again . . .

ME: Let's give it a try. With Jennings's luck, the sun will shine throughout the shooting.

DONNELLY: It's OK with me – providing I get the promised script.

ME: Why don't you go and cry on Lew's shoulder? I just left Jennings on his way to a meeting with Lew.

DONNELLY: (*Getting up*) That's a hell of an idea. Maybe I can get Jennings fired. Be seeing you.

He scooted out of the office, ostensibly to see Lew. However, it's more likely he went to the bathroom.

*

Throughout the writing of Dean Riesner's script, I read, worked on and discussed each sequence with him to our mutual satisfaction. When he completed the script, which I thought was excellent, I rushed off to have two copies hand-delivered to Clint. I enclosed a note reminding him of the urgency of hearing from him – good, bad or indifferent. The studio knew that the script was completed. They (Wasserman, Lang, Donnelly, Adler) couldn't understand why I was holding up the immediate distribution. I told them I had a number of important changes that I had to make; I thought it better that I didn't bring Clint's name into this.

Later that night, Clint called me at home. He was very pleased and thanked me. I asked him to call Dean, who would greatly appreciate hearing from him. Clint mentioned that he had a few minor suggestions. I told him that's why we had blue pages: in fact, before we finished shooting, the script would look like a rainbow – blue, green, yellow, pink pages with a few white ones scattered in between. I ended our telephone conversation by telling him how happy I was. I felt secure that the picture would be much better than the script.

When the script went into general distribution, the reaction from the moguls, production, heads of departments and the cast was too good to be true. The criticisms were relatively easy to fix, but in most cases were ignored. After many meetings with Lang, casting and obtaining Clint's approval, we finally cast the picture. I thought we did very well.

*

Our start date drew closer. I left for New York with my cameraman, his gaffer and head grip, location manager, unit manager and assistant director. I was turned down on taking the executive producer. He was to handle things back at the studio. However, when my dialogue director was turned down, I balked. For one thing, he lived in New York. Also, I had casting to do in New York and I needed Scott Hale badly: he was very knowledgeable about New York actors. They gave in.

New York was overcast and cold. We picked a studio, a small one with 10-foot ceilings. We were building three sets: a hotel room with corridor, a hospital room where Coogan is sapped and a Bellevue Hospital room where Coogan finds Ringerman and Linny Raven. That gave us three good cover sets in case of bad weather.

Lee J. Cobb and I had a seemingly endless dispute over a wig that he wanted to wear. I thought his bald head was perfect for the part of McElroy. Lee was a superb actor. I didn't want to lose him or the argument. I phoned him and suggested we have lunch at the Plaza Hotel. He agreed to meet me at 1.30.

COBB: I hope you don't mind if I don't wear my wig today. I'm having it altered.

ME: I greatly prefer you without your wig, altered or not altered.

COBB: Let's not quarrel over the phone. I'm not playing the part if I can't wear the wig.

ME: Well, at least we can have a pleasant lunch. I think I have a solution.

COBB: Great. Just so I wear the wig. See you shortly. I'm not only stubborn, I'm hungry.

Lee showed up promptly at 1.30. He handed his hat and light topcoat to a lovely-looking girl attendant and joined me at the window table where I was sipping a martini. We smiled at each other as he sat opposite me.

COBB: Fancy a window table. Directors have such power.

ME: How about joining me with a Bombay martini?

COBB: I've never had a Bombay martini. I'll be delighted. However, I must warn you that drinking will get you nowhere.

ME: You look in great shape. From head to toe. (*The maître d' appears.*) A Bombay martini straight up for Mr Cobb, very dry and cold, with an olive. Do you have Scotch salmon?

MAÎTRE D': We have excellent Scotch salmon, Mr Siegel.

ME: (*To Lee*) How does that sound to you?

COBB: You're the best director I've ever had lunch with.

ME: That will be two orders of Scotch salmon and another martini for me.

MAÎTRE D': Thank you, Mr Siegel.
(*Lee looks at me quizzically. I return his stare.*)

COBB: Rather than talk over what promises to be an excellent lunch, why not discuss my (*smiles*) bald pate.

ME: There's no problem.

COBB: You mean you've given in to my intelligent request?

ME: The word 'intelligent' offends me. What I meant by 'no problem' is simply this: you will *not* reveal your slight loss of hair; nor will you ever wear your wig.

COBB: You sound like a close relative of King Solomon. How do you account for this phenomenon?

ME: Simple. In scouting the location, the Twenty-third Precinct, I met your prototype: a lieutenant detective in homicide. Throughout our conversation, he never took his hat off. I have no idea if he was bald. So, if you wear your hat at work – and most people do as the heating at the Precinct is faulty – no one will ever know if you have a full head of hair. There will be no need for you to put on your wig.

(*A waiter appears with the martinis.*)

COBB: (*Raising his glass in a toast*) Here's to the confidence I have in your solving all my acting problems.

ME: And here's to the actor who has no acting problems.

We sipped our martinis, liking them and liking each other.

*

The weather was good in November when we started shooting with Clint. As Coogan, he arrives by helicopter from Kennedy Airport dressed as a deputy sheriff from Arizona: every New Yorker who speaks to him addresses him as 'Tex', 'Cowboy', or 'You're from Texas', and whenever Coogan points out that he is from Arizona, it only registers to New Yorkers that he is from Texas: his cowboy hat, his pointed boots, his accent. In Arizona, when hunting his two-legged prey by means of scent, 10/10 vision – and that includes girls as well as malefactors – Coogan used Western lore and knowledge. But in New York City he can only see across the street, his vision blocked by huge skyscrapers. He is assailed by a thousand scents. He is indeed a fish out of water.

Our three-way schedule was working smoothly. We shot every day, be it good weather, poor weather or terrible weather. Consequently, we made good time, despite our fear of running out of cover sets and being left to cope with a continuing blizzard.

One problem suddenly arose that caught me unawares. Scott Hale had arranged a rehearsal session for himself and me to work with Tisha Sterling. Tisha, who had wanted badly to play Linny Raven when she was hired in Hollywood, had now changed her mind. She wanted out of the picture. I realized I was dealing with a ding-a-ling. She refused to rehearse.

ME: What displeases you about your part?

STERLING: Everything.

ME: But Tisha, the only way you can get out of *Coogan's Bluff* is for your agent to see Mr Wasserman. Maybe he will say 'Good riddance', but I doubt it, because you fit the part and you are a fine actress. I must warn you that Universal plays rough. Your agent, I'm sure, will tell you the same story.

STERLING: I'm quitting.

ME: If you do, you'll be put on suspension, off salary. You will not be allowed to work for anyone else.

STERLING: I don't like you.

ME: I'm not exactly crazy about you. What have I done?

STERLING: (*Eyes filling with tears*) I was robbed of my location expenses.

ME: Believe it or not, I didn't steal it. In fact, this is the first I've heard of it. Was it stolen from your hotel room?

STERLING: Yes. And the location manager refuses to give me any more.

ME: Supposing I talk to him and try to get him to give you back your stolen allowance. Will you feel better about the script?

STERLING: Of course.

ME: I'll do the best I can. I'll wind up our 'rehearsal' by telling you to your pretty face that I don't like being blackmailed into making you like the script. I still think you will have fun with your part.

And that was that. We had no further trouble with her. She was good in the part.

*

I wanted to shoot a scene between Julie and Coogan in a lovely setting: Fort Tryon Park, near the Cloisters, in beautiful sunshine. Twice I failed, shooting the interior of the heliport, which could be shot in any weather. On my third attempt, the sky was overcast, so I decided to wait an hour or two, hoping for a break through of the sun. I began rehearsing Clint and Susan Clark so that if the sun peeked through I could immediately start shooting.

As ill-luck would have it, Jennings Lang made his first appearance in New York to watch our shooting. The sequence I was rehearsing ran five pages, and he sat quietly watching, having no idea that I didn't intend shooting unless the sun came out. Finally, after two hours, the actors looked good. Jennings came over to me.

LANG: I thought that last rehearsal looked excellent.

ME: So did I.

LANG: Why not shoot it? Doesn't Clint like it?

ME: He told me the scene couldn't play any better.

LANG: What in the hell are you waiting for?

ME: I thought you might bring me luck. This is my third crack at trying to shoot this lovely location in the sun.

LANG: Did the thought ever occur to you, Don, that this overcast day might be the best weather you'll ever get?

ME: It does now – but when I saw you, I could only think of one thing: your luck would bring out the sun. Now I think of you as my Jonah. I'm going to shoot this scene with or without sun in one hour. You'll notice my fingers are crossed. I suggest you bring me luck by leaving the location. Thanks for your co-operation.

I left him to go to my trailer. It was reported to me that he departed in ten minutes, after saying goodbye to Clint. Five minutes later, the sun came out strong. Ten minutes after that, we had the master shot. I stopped crossing my fingers. I put on my gloves. It was getting colder. The wind came up and the American flag waved bravely. We completed the sequence, which looked beautiful. My stars were excellent and I felt great.

The sequence in the continuity that immediately followed Fort Tryon Park was Julie's apartment. The last shot at the park is Coogan kissing Julie, the camera moving in close until nothing is seen but their heads. From a slightly different angle in an extreme close-up of Julie and Coogan still kissing, we pull back to reveal that they are in Julie's apartment. They have apparently just come in. A bag of groceries is nearby on a table, a package of spaghetti sticking out of the top of the bag.

ME: Cut! You certainly don't need any rehearsals. Put some make up on and change into your wardrobe and away we go . . .

Surprises never end when you're making movies. When Susan came back on the set, she was wearing an entirely new and different dress. I explained to her that this sequence immediately followed the Tryon Park sequence. She had to wear what she had worn in the previous scene.

CLARK: Why did we pick this dress if I can't wear it?

ME: We picked the dress in a great hurry. I thought it better if we 'over-picked' in case we needed something for you in an added sequence.

CLARK: As far as I'm concerned, this is the added sequence.

(*This is an entirely new Susan. Determined and stupid.*)

ME: But surely you understand that your wardrobe must match.

(*Her eyes fill with tears. She takes a most revealing stand.*)

23 *Coogan's Bluff*: Don Siegel directs Susan Clark and Clint Eastwood

24 *Coogan's Bluff*: Coogan (Clint Eastwood) with Julie (Susan Clark) in her apartment

CLARK: I want that dress. Otherwise, I won't play the scene.

ME: I'm going to pretend that I didn't hear what you said. I'm asking you a simple question. Supposing I managed to get you your new dress, which I agree is most attractive on you. Would you then play the scene, in the correct clothes, with Clint?

CLARK: Absolutely.

ME: Fine. Then you have no problems. What if the studio refuses to give it to you without your paying for it?

CLARK: I'll tell wardrobe you gave it to me.

ME: Good thinking. Now get into your proper clothing for this sequence as quickly as possible. Clint's been ready an hour. (*She looks worried.*) I'm not going to mention the reason for the delay. (*She dashes off to her trailer.*)

Susan and Clint rehearsed smoothly, intelligently and with talent, until I stopped the rehearsal and suggested that as Susan crossed behind the couch where Clint was sitting, he should reach out and pull her down to him for a fervent kiss. When she breaks free, she says, 'Dinner', picks up the bag of groceries and enters the kitchen. Susan disliked my suggestion quite strongly. She felt that I was making Clint too macho and over-emphasizing the kissing, etc. Clint spoke up, somewhat annoyed.

EASTWOOD: I like Don's idea of my reaching behind me, pulling you down to kiss.

CLARK: It's too obvious.

EASTWOOD: It's obvious you don't know what you're talking about. Let's shoot it, Don.

We shot the sequence and broke it up without further ado.

*

The weather was becoming bitterly cold. Snow was around the corner. I figured I'd better get the big motorcycle chase, where Coogan pursues Ringerman, before a big blizzard wiped us thin-blooded Californians off the face of New York State.

There was already frost on the ground. What made the chase particularly hazardous were the leaves on the ground and pathways, which were extremely slippery. Luckily, Clint was an expert motorcyclist. But Don Stroud, a surfing champion from Hawaii playing Ringerman, had never ridden a motorcycle. We had two racing champions to train Stroud and to ride the motorcycles. They took great risks. Our camera operator, Bruce Surtees, wearing a World War I aviator's leather jacket and leather headgear, sat backwards on the motorbike holding a hand-held camera,

25 *Coogan's Bluff*: Coogan (Clint Eastwood) makes a citizen's arrest

an Arriflex 2C, on the pursuing Clint or the escaping Stroud. When we
followed at high speed, either Clint or Stroud, or the two of them together,
the stunt drivers would wear an Eymo, a very light camera, fitted tightly to
camera helmets on their heads, the lens pointed forward. With cold,
blustery winds sweeping in from the Hudson River, the miracle was that
no one got hurt. There were plenty of hairy skids and scary falls, but no
blood. I wore out my crossed fingers.

The following morning, the city was covered with snow. We decided to
get out of New York while the getting was good; prognostications were

for a big blizzard to hit the city in a day or two. We would shoot the Mojave Desert as soon as we returned to Universal. Whatever interiors and exteriors we had not finished shooting in New York, we would pick up at the studio. I didn't feel we were in trouble. On the contrary, I thought we were damn lucky.

Mojave, California, represented the northern Arizona desert: a classic Western setting – raw, rugged, breathtaking terrain. A desert means to me a sweltering, broiling sun, an empty vista of shimmering heat. What we worked in was a frigid, bone-chilling atmosphere – a benumbing, biting wind of over 30 miles per hour. The howling winds blasted everything in sight with swirling, choking sand.

We shot a sequence where Running Bear (Rudy Diaz) shoots at Coogan in his jeep. The rifle cracks. The jeep is seen through the wide-spreading sand. Coogan is not visible. A crash of glass as the windshield is hit. Quickly, a second shattering of glass. Then silence, as the winds lift the sand from the jeep. The jeep door is open. The jeep is empty.

I didn't like the effect of the grease gun, which supposedly makes the windshield appear shattered as though by a rifle bullet. I purposely staged the sequence so that when the real bullets hit the windshield, Coogan is not in the jeep. There's a strict rule that no live ammunition can be used on location. When special effects turned me down, I talked to several deputy sheriffs, explaining my predicament. They were eager to help me. The executive producer, the location manager, the unit manager and the assistant director refused to give their approval. Clint, the deputy sheriffs and the stuntman (Buddy Van Horn) all gave me their enthusiastic approval. There was no danger. On a cue from me, one of the deputies, the best shot, fired two shots. The results were perfect: two shattered holes in the windshield.

The next few days were spent shooting in the bitter cold wind. Shots of Coogan and Running Bear, manacled to a metal hand-hold on the dashboard, travelling in the jeep. Shots of a sheriff's department car trying to find Coogan, siren wailing. Shots of Coogan evading and losing the pursuing sheriff's car. Shots of Millie's typical run-down ranch house, exterior and interior. The following morning, before dawn, I was rudely awakened by a loud knock on my motel door. When I opened the door, a blizzard was in full progress. We were immediately high-tailing back to the studio. The irony didn't escape me. We managed to escape the snow in New York, but were caught, totally unawares, in the Mojave Desert.

When we returned to Mojave, all the snow on the ground had disappeared. Only the distant mountains were still covered. No one, to my knowledge, ever noticed that change of scenery in the picture.

*

Universal moved fast. To my eyes, the sets were beginning to look as good as what I had picked to shoot in New York. The art directors, John McCarthy and John Austin, were prepared to work around the clock. They were professionals; none better.

I was proud of my studio. I decided to see Paul Donnelly about using the largest set on the lot for the psychedelic discotheque sequence. Paul asked me how the sets were coming along.

ME: I can't believe my eyes, but we should be shooting tomorrow. My congratulations and thanks.

DONNELLY: When we were moving your company back to the studio, we started working.

ME: Well, it's fantastic. I came over to talk to you for two reasons – to leave the workmen alone so they could move faster and to discuss the discotheque 'The Pigeon-Toed Orange Peel'.

DONNELLY: How'd you ever come up with that name?

ME: My son, Kris Tabori.

DONNELLY: It figures. I like it.

ME: The discotheques in New York were impossible to shoot. Much too dark and expensive. Wall-to-wall wildly dancing bodies. Is the *Phantom of the Opera* set available? I need the largest set on the lot.

DONNELLY: It's empty.

ME: How many extras do you think we'll need?

DONNELLY: Around a hundred. How many do you figure?
(*If he is going to play the numbers game, I'll join him.*)

ME: I figured around a thousand.
(*Paul's face reddens in anger. He gets up from behind his desk.*)

DONNELLY: You're crazy. Let's walk down to the stage. I'll pick up anyone who's free.

I left word for Bud Thackery to join us with his finder. Paul became the Pied Piper. He would yell to everyone he knew if they could spare a few minutes to join him on the 'big' stage to line up a shot. By the time we arrived at our destination, he had over fifty people following him. I was up in the rafters with Bud and his finder. Paul was on the floor, pushing and shoving the people apart, trying the impossible – to make the huge, open spaces on the floor look crowded. It was impossible. Bud and I would share the finder and yell down that the only thing missing was added people. Finally, Paul gave up to go back to his office. I thanked him without response. The rest of the 'crowd' left with Paul.

313

I explained to Bud, who had been with me seeing discotheques in New York, what I wanted. Strobe lights all over the place. Process plates of nude girls flickering on the walls. A black nude girl emerging briefly, as she swings over the dancing crowd below. The dance floor, made of thick squares of various coloured lights of unbreakable glass, etc. Bud said he needed at least one full day of photographic testing. I agreed, but told him not to bring it up. I would do that. I reminded him of what we had seen in New York. It would be impossible to make the lighting too busy. Bud smiled.

BUD: *You're* telling *me*!

Our budget for extras was 250 people. The huge stage built for *Phantom of the Opera* swallowed up this number, making the set appear quite empty. However, if 125 extras were used, the Extras' Guild allowed us to hire as many real hippies as we needed at a fraction of the cost of the

26   *Coogan's Bluff*: Coogan (Clint Eastwood) at the 'Pigeon-Toed Orange Peel'

extras. We wound up with 125 extras and over 400 hippies. It made the famed New York discotheque Electric Circus look second-rate.

Coogan made his way through the throngs of wigged-out types in front of the discotheque – beads, bells, beards and sandals; each in his own private Nirvana. He goes up the steps and enters – the camera holding on twinkling orange lights of the sign, 'The Pigeon-Toed Orange Peel'. Inside, bedlam! Six hundred hippies dancing, swaying, singing to the big, throbbing electronic beat. Strobe lights flashing everywhere. Process colour plates of nude girls intercut with wild animals shown on the side walls. Groovy types, various freaks, boys with boys, girls with girls, men with women, dancing madly on thick glass squares of constantly changing coloured lights.

*

I ran the first cut of *Coogan's Bluff* in mid-January. Frankly I thought it poorly edited. Dick Lyons, who had seen all the dailies, thought the film very exciting and agreed that it needed careful editing. Fortunately we had enough footage for me to experiment and play around as I tried to do justice to the picture. Everyone had great faith in *Coogan's Bluff*, and it had been fun to make.

29

Death of a Gunfighter

Universal 1969

I was working on a couple of ideas to be made into features. Richard Lyons, who shared my bungalow (actually it was his before it became mine), offered me the directing chores on *Death of a Gunfighter*, before it had a star. Among other titles, it was at one point called 'Patch' – an idea that came from Jennings Lang. Jennings had the bizarre idea that because John Wayne had a son named Patrick, Wayne might accept the picture. Wayne not only turned the picture down, I did also.

The story wasn't bad: a sheriff, over the hill in age, proves that he is still a man who is unafraid to stand up for what he believes is right. Jennings had another unbelievable idea: offer it to Clint Eastwood by making the sheriff considerably younger. I told Lyons that the whole premise of the story would be lost. I thought it a stupid idea. Finally, Richard Widmark was given the script. That choice was an excellent one, but I still didn't want to do it. It was a small picture, which could be shot almost in its entirety on the backlot. In addition, I thought the script needed a lot of work. I flatly told Lyons again that I didn't want to get involved with the project.

When I was producing the television series *Legend of Jesse James*, I used a young, talented director, Robert Totten, who had done a good job for me. He also did a number of *Gunsmoke* episodes, which turned out well. I suggested to Lyons and Lang that it would be good casting to give the script to Totten. He was a 'Western' man. He rode horses well, owned horses and raced them. So they gave the script, still called 'Patch', to Totten and that was that. But I was wrong.

Dick Widmark came to my office to try to talk me into directing the film. He didn't like Bob Totten.

ME: What's wrong with Bob?
WIDMARK: I don't like his thinking. We just don't speak the same language.
ME: You must remember, Dick, that Bob is a young man, no doubt in awe of you. You know you can be pretty frightening at times.

WIDMARK: Did you feel that way about me?

ME: Frankly, Dick, I don't remember our ever having a quarrel; differences of opinion, yes, but never in anger.

WIDMARK: Well, I don't like Bob. I was hoping, Don, that you would direct the film.

ME: May I remind you that on *Madigan* you didn't want me to direct the picture. Hank Fonda talked you into accepting me.

WIDMARK: (*Finally smiling*) Touché. Thanks for listening to my bitching.

ME: Give the guy a chance. Show him that you trust and like him. (*Dick shakes my hand and leaves.*)

I called Bob Totten into my office to tell him about my conversation with Widmark. He thanked me and declared that he had no idea why Dick didn't like him.

ME: Forget all that nonsense. That's in the past. What I want to talk to you about is working for Universal.

TOTTEN: (*Smiling*) They are somewhat peculiar.

ME: Now cut that right out of your vocabulary. Did you know that Universal has a super-duper computer in the Black Tower?

TOTTEN: No, I didn't.

ME: Let's say that the shooting schedule has allowed you three days to complete the opening sequence. You take one day. The computer figures you are shooting two-thirds better than the schedule. So when you are on schedule to finish shooting the picture in thirty days, the computer figures you are shooting two-thirds better. The computer points out that if you continue at that speed, you'll finish in ten days.

TOTTEN: But I can't shoot the picture in ten days!

ME: Really? And no one expects you to; but they quit worrying about you. They know you're going to bring the picture in under schedule. On the other hand, if the schedule shows that you are to shoot the sequence in one day and you take three, the computer will point out that on a schedule of thirty days, you will take ninety days.

TOTTEN: (*Shook up*) That's kinda stupid.

ME: What's worse, the front office starts worrying about you. They watch you and your work very carefully. That's why I want you to prepare your work, particularily in the beginning, as thoroughly as possible. And most important – you must be under schedule right from the beginning, so they can forget you.

TOTTEN: But I must do good work.

ME: The studio takes it for granted that your work will be good. But for Christ's sake, bring the picture in under schedule. If you do that, and you bloody well must, you'll be in no trouble.

TOTTEN: I'll do it.

ME: I know you will.

(*We stand up and shake hands. Totten starts to thank me.*)

ME: (*Interrupting*) All the thanks I want is for you to bring the picture in under schedule. Good luck.

Bob left my office beaming.

*

I had completely forgotten 'Patch'. Several projects looked promising as the weeks flew by. One day, around 3 in the afternoon, my secretary buzzed me. I picked up the phone.

BURROWS: Mr Wasserman's secretary is on the phone. Mr Wasserman wants to talk to you immediately. Don't lose your temper. I'm putting his secretary on now.

SECRETARY: One moment please, Mr Siegel. I'm buzzing Mr Wasserman.

WASSERMAN: Don, I need a favour.

(*My heart sinks. When Lew needs a favour, trouble lies ahead.*)

ME: You've never asked me for a favour before. I owe you one.

WASSERMAN: I want you to take over 'Patch', starting tomorrow morning.

ME: What happened?

WASSERMAN: Widmark refuses to work with the director you suggested.

ME: I don't think it's fair, Lew, to blame me for the present situation.

WASSERMAN: I'm not blaming you. I'm asking for a favour.

ME: I don't understand why it takes about twenty-five days for the studio to make up its mind that Totten's no good.

WASSERMAN: I agree with you.

ME: I'll have to look at what he shot today first thing tomorrow morning. The dailies should be put on a rush immediately by the editor. Plus, I'd like to look at today's dailies, what he shot yesterday, at the same time. Can you have someone take care of this for me?

WASSERMAN: I'll see to that immediately. I'll also notify Widmark. Thanks for the favour, Don.

318

He hung up. There was nothing I could do about it. His putting it as a 'favour' could easily change to suspension if I refused. I was angry with myself, Dick, Bob and Lew. I decided to pick up a script and duck out for home. Tomorrow was going to be a tough day.

At 7 a.m. next day, a group consisting of the editor (whom I didn't know), the assistant editor (whom I didn't know), Dick Lyons and me were in Projection Room 1.

LYONS: (*To me*) It's not my fault. Widmark and Totten hated each other. There was nothing I —
ME: (*Interrupting*) Have we got the new dailies?
EDITOR: Yes, sir.
ME: Run yesterday's dailies first, then have the light come up.
(*He picks up the phone and relays the information to the projectionist.*)

After a few minutes, the lights dimmed and yesterday's dailies started. They showed a corral filled with milling steers. Carroll O'Connor (doubled by Bob Burrows) dodged through the corral trying to escape from the sheriff, Dick Widmark, on horseback. Dick rode the horse through the cattle, which was no cup of tea. Then we ran the new dailies. They included point-of-view shots, hand-held, that I thought were excellent. The dailies ran out; the lights came on.

ME: I think the dailies are damn good.
LYONS: Totten did all the hand-held camera work, sitting backwards on a horse going through the cattle.
ME: It's not only done well, it's damn dangerous.

The dailies showed me exactly where Totten stopped shooting. It so happened that Widmark came out of the sheriff's office and played a scene in the street. It would be relatively easy for me to continue Totten's work. Everything he had shot looked good to me. In the two days' dailies, I saw nothing to re-shoot.

I went on the set to see Widmark and get the feel of the exterior of the Western street. Widmark was being made up in his trailer; he looked up and grinned.

WIDMARK: I can't thank you enough. (*Turning to make-up man.*) Get yourself some coffee and bring Mr Siegel a cup, no sugar or cream. (*Smiling at me.*) I have to talk to my director.
(*The make-up man disappears.*)
ME: Well, I've learned my lesson. What you want, you get.

WIDMARK: I'm really sorry to do this to you, Don; but I was trapped in a corner and had to do something desperate.

ME: Thanks. I've got to tell you, Dick, that I ran the last two days' dailies and they look good. I'm going to have to lean on you a bit. I'm kind of working blind.

(*The make-up man hands me a cup of hot, black coffee. Widmark gets up and suggests that he show me exactly where Totten stopped shooting.*)

ME: (*Sipping coffee*) Lead the way, Madigan.

The set-up was easy to shoot so that Totten's shot would smoothly cut into mine. As we walked down the street, I came up with a few ideas that had occurred to me after reading the script the night before. Widmark was elated, which made me feel better.

The cast, which was excellent, included, besides Widmark, John Saxon, Kent Smith, Larry Gates, Lena Horne, Carroll O'Connor, Victor French and others. Totten picked most of them. I, of course, had nothing to do with the casting.

I shot a prologue of Lena Horne standing beside the coffin of her husband, Richard Widmark, at a railroad station. I included a shot of a young boy walking behind the train. It felt interesting, different to me, strange to some people. The opening and the ending were my main contributions; in Totten's words, 'You made the book ends of the picture.' I worked nine or ten days on the film. Totten was on it twenty-five days. In re-editing the picture, picking up a few shots, I *guess* we broke about even on footage in the film.

I was somewhat embarrassed that Totten was on the set, taking on the responsibility of his two small children, who had minor parts in the film. He didn't direct them. He stayed away from the actual shooting. He was there just to see that they didn't get into any trouble. I would have much preferred a welfare worker to be responsible for them. Finally, the title was changed to *Death of a Gunfighter*, from a book of the same title by Louis Patten. Until then I hadn't known that the screenplay was based on the book. If I had, I would have read it immediately: I always go back to the original source of the material.

When I refused to take directing credit for the film, as did Bob Totten, the Directors' Guild made up a pseudonym for Totten and myself: 'Allen Smithee'. As the picture was well received, I told all my young friends who wanted to become directors to change their name to Smithee and take credit for the direction of the picture. I don't know if anyone did this. I still think under certain circumstances, they might have cracked the 'magic barrier' and become a director.

I'm sorry I got involved in the making of the picture. I thought Totten made a mistake in taking his name off the credits when I did, as he was truly the director of *Death of a Gunfighter*.

30

Two Mules for Sister Sara

Universal 1970

Clint Eastwood was co-starring with Richard Burton in *Where Eagles Dare*. When I went to London to loop Clint's lines in *Coogan's Bluff*, he handed me a script to read, *Two Mules for Sister Sara*. It was given to him by Elizabeth Taylor, who wanted Clint to co-star with her. He asked me to read it, as the producer, Marty Rackin, was preparing to make it at Universal.

I read the script, which was written by Albert Maltz, based on an original story by Budd Boetticher. I told Clint that I thought the story was great fun, perfect for Clint and Liz. It takes place in Mexico. Clint rescues a woman from being raped by three bad hombres by killing all three. He discovers, when she puts her clothes back on, that she is a nun. Reluctantly, he takes Sister Sara with him and they run into adventure after adventure.

Clint was delighted with my reaction. He reported to the powers that be at Universal that the three of us, Clint, Liz and I, were very keen to do the property and were eager to work with each other. Both the stars fitted the parts they were to play: Clint the Western adventurer, Liz the dark-haired, dark-skinned Mexican nun. The studio and Marty Rackin started negotiations. All went well until the fateful day when longitude and latitude killed the deal.

Richard Burton was set to do a picture entirely in Spain. Liz insisted that *Two Mules for Sister Sara* be shot there too. Her reason was unshakeable. She wanted, at all times, to be near her husband, whom she loved dearly. She felt that Richard needed her presence. If the picture could be made in Spain, all would be well. The studio balked and finally said firmly, 'No deal.' Both Clint and I felt terribly let down.

The studio came up with another female star: Shirley MacLaine. There was no question that Shirley was a fine actress with a great sense of humour. But her skin was fair, her face – the map of Ireland. She most likely would look ridiculous if she played a Mexican nun. Nevertheless, Shirley was assigned to the picture. She had just finished starring in *Sweet*

Charity and the studio felt they now had a big, successful flick. They were wrong. Naturally, the script had to be rewritten to fit her appearance.

Shirley was a 'night bird'. Although she tried, she couldn't withstand the hours outside in the broiling sun. Getting up early to start shooting at 8 in the morning was impossible. We hired a Mexican *peón* who held an open umbrella shielding Shirley from the rays of the sun from the moment she appeared on location until she left.

After working with Marty and Clint on the script, I made a startling discovery. Budd Boetticher, in addition to writing the story, had also written a script. He was a well-known director and a good friend of mine. When I read his script, which I thought had strong possibilities, I asked him why he wasn't considered to be the director. He claimed that Marty never gave him a straight answer. As he needed money, he sold his story and script to Marty, who took the property to Universal, got their OK and hired Albert Maltz to write another script. I felt funny about being the director. Budd laughed and told me that everything was settled with Marty long before I appeared on the scene. We remained good friends.

*

The trick in picking locations is to find the most difficult one first. For this picture, that was the period train that crossed a trestle over a large ravine. From that location, I found everything we had to shoot, including ideal living quarters within a radius of 50 miles. Many of our locations were 5–10 minutes from the magnificent hotel we lived in at Cocoyoc, a tiny city.

There were constant disagreements between Marty and me. He tried to save money in all the wrong spots, which, in the long run, cost us more dineros and hurt the picture. I wanted to use American motion-picture horses; Marty insisted on using good-looking but untrained Mexican horses. Marty won that one. I wanted an experienced American art director; Marty insisted on hiring an inexperienced Mexican, José Granada. Marty won that one too and the sets were unimaginable and unworkable. Also, I wanted in the beginning of the picture to use three American Western character actors as the men who were about to rape Shirley. I particularly wanted these villains to be Americans, not the usual heavies played by Mexicans. I strongly pointed out that if we started out poorly in the picture, we might never recover. My pleas fell on deaf ears. These parts would run only one week. Nothing mattered other than saving money. To give the devil his due, Marty did like the locations. But his attitude alarmed me.

When we returned to Universal, I worked very hard on making the script fit the various locations. There were still sequences that needed work. Albert Maltz was a pleasure to work with. Clint liked the script, but

323

was still worried about Shirley playing the part. We turned the script in to Marty for his input. He made a number of minor changes – mostly gag dialogue. He had multiple copies of the script made. When I received mine, I sat down to read it carefully. I never got beyond page 1.

My secretary got Mr Rackin on the phone. I told him I had just received the new script and would appreciate it if he could drop by my bungalow to discuss it. He graciously agreed to come right over. Marty looked great. The tan we had picked up in Mexico suited him.

RACKIN: I heard from the Black Tower. They like the script.
ME: Delighted. (*Turning to the first page.*) It says here: 'There are to be no changes in the script, without exception, unless you obtain the oral, or written approval of the Producer, Martin Rackin.'
RACKIN: (*Smoothly*) Oh, that's nothing. You must remember that you have a dialogue coach, Leon Charles. It's so that he can't make any changes.
ME: Leon Charles is your choice. Not mine. I don't know him. Why didn't you say that he can't make any changes without *my* approval?
(*The intercom buzzes. I pick it up and listen.*)
ME: By all means. Send Mr Eastwood in.
(*Marty looks worried. He sinks back in his chair. Clint enters.*)
EASTWOOD: Hope I'm not disturbing you.
ME: Not at all. You couldn't have arrived at a more opportune moment.
(*Rackin seems more deflated, more concerned.*)
ME: Have you read the new script?
EASTWOOD: Just got back in town. I'll read it tonight.
ME: I was about to tell Marty that we don't work the way he wants us to. For example (*pointing to paragraph on page 1*) read this.
(*Clint picks up the script and reads it, more or less to himself.*)
EASTWOOD: (*Holding script*) I don't see anything wrong with that.

I couldn't believe my ears. Clint had double-crossed me. Marty sat up straight in his chair, beaming with confidence. Clint walked away from the desk towards one of the windows. He slowly turned, facing us.

EASTWOOD: There's one way, Don, to handle a situation like this.
(*He rips the page out of the script, crumples it and throws it across the room. Marty turns green, now totally deflated.*)
EASTWOOD: Now we'll probably change every word in the damn script. Be seeing you, Don, Marty.

(He leaves quickly.)
RACKIN: *(Weakly)* Lose the battles – win the war.

*

The first shot in the picture was of a huge, hairy tarantula scurrying up a rocky hillside. The hoof of a horse, with startling speed, crushes it. The camera pans up to the rider, Hogan (Clint Eastwood), who is unshaven, hard-faced, tough looking. He is in the middle of an empty wasteland.

The Chapman Titan crane, with a 30-foot arm, moved towards Clint. The horse, fearful of this monster, bolted, almost throwing Clint, who had his hands full trying to control the frightened animal on the hillside. Holding tight to the reins, Clint jumped off the horse and hit it square on the jaw. I swear, the horse's legs buckled. I still don't understand how Clint didn't break his hand.

Of course, the horse had never seen anything looking like a crane and was extremely frightened. For that matter, so was Marty. In his ignorance, it never occurred to him the importance of 'movie-trained' horses. He was being educated under the fire of actual shooting. Thank God Clint, being a professional, got back on the horse and ultimately finished the scene. But it took time and was dangerous to do.

Hogan is riding up a rise of ground on top of which are large, scattered rocks. He hears something, which makes him slow his horse and then abruptly stop. From the other side of the rise comes a burst of raucous male laughter and an anguished cry from a woman.

Hogan moves into swift, silent action. He dismounts, slips his Winchester out of its scabbard. Unbuckling a saddlebag, he produces a cloth and wraps it around the mechanism of his rifle. Without any audible click, he pumps a shell into the breech. He reaches deeper into the saddlebag and extracts something from it. He slips it beneath the back of his belt. Then, he drops to his knees, slips a cigar between his lips and lights it. Quickly, he moves forward at a crouch to a spot between two rocks that are close together. He peers down.

A full-bodied woman is sitting on the ground surrounded by three men whose faces are on fire with sadistic glee and lust. She has been stripped to the waist and now wears only a last garment, a petticoat. Still in hiding, Hogan shoots two of the men, but the third grabs the woman so that her body shields him from Hogan. He shoves his revolver against her head. Suddenly, there is a sputtering sound and then a stick of dynamite, its fuse sparkling with fire, plops on to the earth a scant 12 feet from where he is holding the woman. The man is terrorized. He shoots twice at Hogan's position, then races for their horses. Hogan leaps up, revolver in hand, shooting the man three times in the back. Slowly, Hogan walks towards the sputtering dynamite. He reaches down, picks up the dynamite, holsters his pistol, draws his bowie knife and severs the fuse less than half an inch from the stick.

Later, when we wrapped, I told Clint that when he went to put out the sputtering fuse of dynamite, he was supposed to race down the hill. However, by doing it slowly, it created much greater tension. Whenever Clint comes up with a better idea, I call it a 'Clintus Shot'. If his ideas spark me to a better one, I call it a 'Siegelini Shot'.

I ran into Marty at the hotel. I told him that I was still keenly

27 *Two Mules for Sister Sara*: Sara (Shirley MacLaine) being used as a shield

disappointed in having three bandidos instead of American outlaws. I told him I hoped that the Mexicans' poor performances as Americans didn't get us off to such a bad start that we'd never recover. It's in very bad taste having Mexicans portraying American outlaws, particularly while shooting in their country.

The woman, who turns out to be a nun called Sister Sara (Shirley MacLaine, asks Hogan to let her accompany him as a detachment of French cavalry is searching for her at that moment because she has been involved in raising money for the Mexican army. Hogan reluctantly agrees and, at a gallop, they head for the Pantitlan Ruins nearby. At the ruins, Hogan suddenly reins them to a stop. He vaults off his horse and runs through one of the abandoned doorways. He quickly reappears and ties the mule's jaws together with the reins. As Sara starts leading the mule inside, there is a loud rattle.

SARA: (*Jumping back*) I can't. There's a rattlesnake in there.
HOGAN: Damn it! (*He pulls a knife from his boot, pushes Sara aside and starts carefully inside. The rattle sounds again.*)
HOGAN: (*Murmuring*) Keep singin', partner.

I decided to shoot a reverse on Shirley reacting to the coiling of the snake; Clint sticking the bottom of his boot towards the striking snake; Clint's foot stamping down just behind its head and his knife cutting off its head. The last thing I wanted to shoot was the actual snake, as we only had one. When I rehearsed with Shirley, her reactions were unbelievably unconcerned. I explained that she must show fear, revulsion, actually recoiling from what she is presumably seeing.

MACLAINE: I've killed rattlesnakes in my backyard. It's no big deal. Certainly it's nothing to be frightened of.
ME: But Shirley, in the part you're playing in the picture, you *are* frightened. Clint is the hero. In your eyes, what he is doing is extremely dangerous.
MACLAINE: Well, it isn't.
ME: Whether it is, or not, your character must *think* it is. So please, let's get on with it. I must have strong reactions to the killing of the rattlesnake.

I presume she tried; but I was not pleased with her performance. However, when I showed Clint's encounter with the rattlesnake, I heard her gasp, 'Must we kill it?' Unfortunately, her magnificent reaction was off scene. When Clint cut the head of the rattlesnake off, he stood up and handed it to her. Her face was green. She was shaking with fear and

327

28 *Two Mules for Sister Sara*: Sara (Shirley MacLaine) and the snake

revulsion. I uttered a crisp command, 'Don't drop it!' Trembling, she held on to the snake, which was still squirming. I yelled, 'Cut!' before she had a chance to faint.

HOGAN: Stay put. If we get split up, that snake'll make good eatin'.

Clint exited, fast. Although Shirley turned greener, she had the guts to hang on to the headless, squirming rattlesnake.

Early next morning, Hogan downs his hot coffee, puts out the fire and starts loading his packhorse. Sara is sitting up, sipping her coffee.

HOGAN: Get movin', Sister Sara. We're off.

We had a problem. Shirley was having great difficulty in riding the mule, a very stubborn animal. Unfortunately, the title *Two Mules for Sister Sara* and the various scripts all clearly indicate that Shirley rode the mule throughout the picture. I believed firmly in *not* asking permission from

Marty Rackin, or any of the bigwigs at the studio, for Shirley to ride a burro instead of the mule, because I expected the answer to be 'No.' So, without their knowledge, Shirley, Clint and I worked together to write a scene which would help not only Shirley, but the picture as well. The scene we wrote and shot, when seen by the studio executives in dailies, had two results. One: they liked it. Two: they were unaware of any change.

Sara and Hogan ride over a narrow, stone bridge which leads to a small village, Jantetelco. Hogan leads the way, his packhorse behind him, followed by Sara, on her mule, which is obviously limping. Hogan stops on the bridge, dismounts and walks over to Sara.

HOGAN: That limp's gettin' worse. (*Lifts mule's right front leg.*) Stone bruised. (*Puts leg down.*) Take a week for that to heal up. Well, maybe the people in this village will hide you out until this animal comes around.

SARA: Why couldn't I ride the packhorse?

HOGAN: (*Irritated*) 'Cause he carries my equipment, that's why, and I ain't about to miss bein' in Chihuahua on the fourteenth.

SARA: Please, Brother Hogan . . .

HOGAN: Look, I told you not to 'brother' me.

SARA: (*Getting off mule*) All right, Mr Mule. You know, you are as stubborn as my mule.
(*She leads the mule towards the village, as Hogan mounts his horse.*)

HOGAN: When we get up to that village, Sister, then I'll say adios. This is where we part company.
(*Sara is approaching a small, roadside shrine. Hogan takes a cigar out of his pocket. She crosses to the shrine and kneels before it, holding her cross with both hands.*)

HOGAN: Now what are you doin'?

SARA: I must say a prayer at this shrine.

HOGAN: You said your prayers last night and this mornin'. You're gonna wear 'em out.
(*Hogan, looking bored and annoyed, lights his cigar. He is sitting in a 'resting' position, with one foot out of the stirrup and the other leg dangling over his saddle.*)

SARA: It's a sin to pass a shrine without praying.

HOGAN: Not if you shut your eyes it ain't.

SARA: Please, Mr Hogan.

HOGAN: All right. It's a small shrine. Let's make it a small prayer.
(*A man, riding a small, laden burro, approaches Sara as she prays.*)

MAN: (*Raising his hat*) Buenos dias, Hermana.

(Sara does a double-take, her eyes opening wide. She looks up to heaven, quickly crosses herself, hurriedly grabs the mule's reins and rushes after the man. Hogan watches Sara and the man trade animals. The man leads the mule, now laden with what was on the burro, away towards the village. Hogan rides up to Sara.)

SARA: You see, Mr Hogan, what a little prayer can do? The Lord provided me with a kind gentleman, who accepted my mule in exchange for this creature of God. Now I can still be with you.

Hogan rides off. Sara climbs on a rock and attempts to mount the burro sidesaddle. She is immediately thrown off. Determinedly, she hauls the burro around, climbs the rock again and leaps on to the creature with legs spread apart, as the burro takes off in the same direction as Hogan. Sara's legs, gripping the burrow tightly, almost touch the ground. Her hand keeps striking his backside as he breaks into a slow trot.

*

Hogan is leading the way down a narrow gorge, wide enough for only one rider. Behind him is Sara on her burro and, behind her, the packhorse.

29 *Two Mules for Sister Sara*: Sara (Shirley MacLaine) on her burro

Hogan, with his right leg over the pommel of his saddle, has partially turned so that he can check on Sara and the packhorse. Suddenly, without warning, an arrow slams into his chest to the left of his heart. The impact is so powerful that he is knocked backwards off his horse.

Sara screams as a shout of joy peals out from a group of Yaqui Indians. There are about thirty of them lined up on their ponies. One of them, the youngest, is holding his bow aloft and shouting with joy. The others are smiling their approval at the youth. Sara has ridden her burro in front of Hogan's horse and is pulling her cross out of her pocket as she looks about. On every outcropping, silhouetted against the sky, are fierce, armed Yaquis. Hogan, dazed, in partial shock and in pain, is pushing himself up to a sitting position with his right hand. The tip of the arrowhead just protrudes beneath his left shoulder blade and the longest part of the shaft, ending with the feathers, is parallel to his face. There is a stream of blood on his shirt at both the entrance and exit points. Sara centres the glittering cross at the chief. As the reflection of the cross hits his eyes, a look of fear suddenly appears. The chief wheels his horse to the side and then kicks it into a gallop. Abruptly, the other Yaquis kick their horses into flight. They disappear into the gorge.

30   *Two Mules for Sister Sara*: Don Siegel with Clint Eastwood

Sara eventually succeeds in removing the arrow from Hogan by getting him drunk, and they set off for the gorge where they are going to blow up the French supply train. When they arrive, both stare at a railroad trestle that crosses a canyon about 70 yards wide. The canyon floor is about 50 feet below them. The trestle is constructed of wood and is supported by a network of closely knit crossbeams.

I had Al Whitlock come down from Universal Studios to help me plan how to shoot this scene.

WHITLOCK: Either you shoot the actual train, or you make a miniature and set it on the floor of the canyon, about a hundred feet in front of the real trestle. The miniature train and trestle will fall into the canyon after you have established the real train crossing the real trestle.

ME: Will the Mexicans be able to make a perfect duplicate in miniature of the real train and trestle?

31   *Two Mules for Sister Sara*: the derailing of the train

WHITLOCK: Frankly, Don, they'll do a better job than we could do –
and it will be a lot cheaper.
ME: Muchos gracious, Señor.

*

It is late afternoon on a curving path in hilly country. Hogan, as usual, leads the way, followed by his packhorse. Sara brings up the rear on her burro. On both sides of the path, there is high ground, covered with trees and boulders. Without warning, two thick ropes, studded with iron spikes, suddenly snap up in the path 5 yards in front of Hogan. One rope is about 3 feet off the ground, so it will catch a horse, the other is 6 feet off the ground. Only by stopping his horse sharply does Hogan avoid running into the spikes. A split second later, a similar one snaps up 20 feet behind Sara. Hogan's pistol is already in his hand. A Mexican voice speaks with authority.

VOICE: (*Offstage*) Put away your gun, gringo!
HOGAN: (*Holstering his pistol*) I'm Hogan! Beltran's waiting for me.
VOICE: (*Offstage*) It is *Colonel* Beltran!
HOGAN: Colonel . . . General . . . who cares. Just take me to him.

The barriers suddenly drop. An armed Juarista (Mexican guerilla) appears on a horse and gestures for Hogan and Sara to follow him. The Juarista leads them up a trail and around the face of a mountain. Watching them approach on the rim of a huge cave is Colonel Beltran (Manolo Fabregas). He is a fighter and a leader.

When Clint and Shirley dismounted, I had to stop the shooting. I kept the Colonel on the extreme left edge of the shot in the cave. I told Shirley to dismount the burro on the left side. By using my widest lens, I could keep everyone in frame. Also, by getting off the right side of the burro, Shirley was taking a chance she might fall, as the steep mountainside was on the burro's right.

I jumped down from the cave and slowly re-explained all this to her. Everything and everybody had to turn around, disappear down the narrow path and do it over again. Clint followed the Juarista and Shirley, on her burro, brought up the rear. The Colonel again made no mistake. Everything was perfect. Clint dismounted correctly; but to my dismay, Shirley got off the burro again on the right side, right out of my picture. I yelled 'Cut!'

ME: (*From the rim of the cave*) Shirley, didn't you understand that I
wanted you to dismount from the left side of the burro?
MACLAINE: (*Testily*) It is incorrect to get off the burro on the left side.

333

ME: Do you suppose the burro knows that?
MACLAINE: Don't get fresh with me.
ME: You do understand I can't hold you in the shot?
MACLAINE: I don't give a damn!
ME: Well, frankly Shirley, neither do I.

With that, Shirley not only left the set, with the *peón* and his open umbrella racing after her; but she left the location. Clint, although known as 'Mr Cool' 99 per cent of the time, can on occasion blow his fuse. He screamed after her departing figure what he thought of her unprofessional attitude. I grabbed him by the arm and begged him to stay out of the quarrel. I don't think he knew I had his arm firmly grasped. He just lifted me off my feet and continued his tirade.

Being an editor as well as a director, everyone expected me to shoot 'around' Shirley to complete our day's work. But I did some quick mental calculations. I figured I had shot more than half of the picture. I would probably share directorial credit. So, I thanked everyone, shook hands with my crew and not only left the set, I too left the location. On the way back to the hotel, I passed Marty going to the location. Our cars both stopped. We got out.

RACKIN: (*Surprised*) You finished already?

I couldn't believe his stupidity. He should have known that I had two more days and three more nights of shooting.

ME: I had a serious disagreement with Shirley. I'm afraid I was quite rude. When she left the location, I decided to quit too.
RACKIN: My God! This is serious. What does Clint think?
ME: He's not happy. (*Going to my car.*) See you at the hotel – if I'm still there.

That afternoon I received a call from Edd Henry, the executive in charge of the picture. He was known on the lot as 'Dr No', because he turned down every project offered to him with a firm 'No'. As most pictures were failures, he batted a solid 95 per cent success. I didn't like or trust him. However, to my astonishment, he was gracious, concerned and seemingly on my side.

HENRY: All I ask, Don, is that you continue to stay at Hotel Cocoyoc until I have a chance to clean up this mess. You will be hearing from me before nightfall.
ME: I hope so, as I've made arrangements to leave tomorrow.
HENRY: Please, just stay put, Don.

So I swam in the small private pool that was walled in behind my bottom-floor suite. I didn't feel sorry for myself. Directors are spoiled brats. I got dressed, which meant wearing shorts, thin sports shirt and Mexican sandles. There was a firm knock on the door. A lovely vision, Shirley, was paying me a call.

ME: Where's your 'umbrella man'?
MACLAINE: (*Laughing*) I slipped away. May I come in?
ME: Please. Can I fix you a drink?
MACLAINE: (*Entering, closing the door behind her*) No thanks. I'm talking.
ME: You might just as well have spoken in Spanish or Gaelic this morning, as I found your English incomprehensible. Sit on a hard chair, throw yourself on the couch, or recline on the pillows on the floor.
(*I remain standing.*)
MACLAINE: Are you going to join me on the floor?
ME: Not until I hear what you have to say.
MACLAINE: I'm truly sorry that I was such a fool.
ME: I appreciate your apology very much; but I'm going to level with you. You've driven my production staff right up the wall. If there's an eight o'clock shooting call, we're lucky if you show up ready by ten thirty. We can't keep you out of the sun. Those freckles on your nose look adorable. Unfortunately, your nose is peeling.
MACLAINE: Anything else?
ME: You haven't had enough rest and sleep during the night. Apparently you just don't go to bed. Consequently you're tired throughout the day. Also, you eat and drink wine, much too much.
MACLAINE: (*Getting angry*) I've done a few pictures. I think I know what I'm doing.
ME: Shirley, I've talked to every director you've ever worked with. They all say the same thing: 'You're very talented, but a pain in the ass.' And yet, don't ask me why, in spite of your being hoydenish, I can't help liking you.

Shirley bounded to her feet, tears steaming down her cheeks. She hugged and kissed me. From that moment on, she was a doll. When working, she was most co-operative. My major regret is that I never really sat down and found out what made her tick. But, thank God, we got along great.

*

When Hogan, Sara, Beltran and his men arrive at the French garrison,

335

they discover that the soldiers are not drunkenly celebrating their Independence Day. By blowing up the French supply train, Hogan and Sara have put the French on the alert. Without the element of surprise, the attack will fail. However, Sara does know how to provide this element of surprise. There is a tunnel leading into the garrison from the nearby residence of the Bishop. When Hogan enters the residence with Sara, he is in for an even bigger surprise.

HOGAN: Sister Sara, this is a cathouse.
SARA: (*Embracing the Madam*) No, Hogan, not a cathouse – the best whorehouse in town.

Marty was in charge of building the make-believe Bishop's residence/whorehouse. I never had a chance to see the set, or even plans of it, but Marty told me not to worry. He was overseeing it. I would like it.

I got to the set early in the morning to lay out my shots. Lo and behold, Marty was there. I walked around the set, with stairs leading down to it. There was a sizeable trapdoor leading to the tunnel. The main fault with the set was simple. It was much, much too large to be believable. It looked like the sitting room of a brand-new, spotless living room in Grand Rapids. Marty was seriously offended. At that precise moment, to my surprise, Clint showed up. He couldn't understand the obvious fact that it didn't look anything like a whorehouse in Mexico, or anywhere else, for that matter. He really ripped into Marty. Right in the middle of the one-sided argument, Miss Night Bird showed up. Shirley was unbroken in her continuous haranguing of Marty. Clint and Shirley were a formidable twosome to face. I began to fear that they weren't even going to attempt to shoot, so I opened my big mouth.

ME: May I have your attention!
   (*Shirley, Clint and Marty turned to me.*)
ME: I'm not saying it's going to turn this piece of trash into the Taj Mahal, and I wouldn't want it to, but . . .
MACLAINE: (*Shocked*) Don't you agree with Clint and me that it's . . . (*sputtering*) . . . terrible!
ME: I had it out with Marty before you both expressed your displeasure.
EASTWOOD: That's a nice, soft way to put it.
ME: I stole it from you. Seriously, the worst thing about the so-called whorehouse is that it's too large. My suggestion, which certainly is no cure-all, is to shoot everything tight, well inside of the wandering set. That way, I hope you won't be aware of the size of

the set, because you'll never see it. One last thought – if you don't think my idea will work – and you're probably right – let's shoot it when we return to Nevada, which is infested with whorehouses.

EASTWOOD: What do you think, Shirley?

MACLAINE: I can't think when I'm around such big, handsome men like you and Don.

ME: That's the sweetest remark – putting me on the same level as Clint. Let's stagger through a few rehearsals.

As I started to line up the set-up, off in the distance I faintly heard Marty's voice repeating a line he had memorized well.

RACKIN: (*Mumbling*) Lose the battles, win the war.

*

The first thing I did upon seeing the church and garrison was to check them out for practical shooting. The church was excellent. However, upon examination, I discovered that there wasn't one lock in the entire garrison. Even the gates had no strong boards resting on heavy wooden brackets. All one had to do to enter was to push open the gates. This had to be fixed immediately.

The battle between the Juaristas and the French soldiers, well trained and well equipped, is violent, brutal and ruthless. The Juaristas, despite their poor equipment, still have the advantage of fighting for their country. Although the French have no respect for the fighting qualities of the Mexican *peóns*, they are ultimately overwhelmed by the sheer ferocity of the Mexicans and the dynamite supplied by Hogan, plus his professional knowledge of warfare.

In order for a battle to have indubitable credibility, passion, hatred, fighting for a cause, etc., fear and bravery must be evident. A mother kissing her son goodbye, a father leaving his family, young lovers parting – all are part of what fighting means. Pain, blood and death must affect, excite or appal the viewer. In this battle, we must know the opponents: the French and the Juaristas. Why are they in mortal combat? For whom is the audience rooting? Unfortunately, we really only know Sister Sara and Hogan. I felt, as I was about to start shooting, that I was lacking the ingredients to make a truly great, moving ordeal of war. I decided to shoot it as realistically and as excitingly as possible. Each shot would be slightly tilted, less than 5 per cent, away from the preceding one. All cuts would be taut. There would be no fat. Hopefully, by doing the entire battle in staccato cuts, a pulsating, throbbing, exciting montage might be the result.

The breakdown of the battle into actual shots was difficult. Most shots

337

were under 5 feet; some were just flashes of film, twenty-four frames to the foot. Because of slightly tilting each shot in opposite directions, I had to shoot the battle in continuity. We were lucky – apart from scratches and burns, no one got hurt.

I don't recommend breaking down all the shots of a complicated battle; it's too time consuming and difficult. However, in this particular case, I thought it worthwhile.

32 *Two Mules for Sister Sara*: the attack on the garrison

338

Ennio Morricone composed and conducted the remarkable score of *Two Mules for Sister Sara*. The music is among the most original and unusual ever written for a film.

Marty and I went to see Morricone in Rome. He had read the script and his ideas were startling. The mule had special music, which sounded dramatic and amusing. The moment the viewing audience heard it, they burst into laughter and applause. A special litany was the theme for Sister Sara. The music had choral effects, which were enchanting. Hogan's character was well described musically to show action, strength and a great deal of humour.

However, a problem arose. Morricone insisted on scoring the film in Rome, using only Italian musicians. So that we would have some idea of what his music would sound like, he would send us cassette tapes of various parts of his score. Marty didn't know if the studio would agree. I pointed out that we had nothing to lose. If they didn't like the tapes, that would be the end of Morricone. As far as I was concerned, Morricone was a genius. In any event, the studio liked his music very much; but the music department was jealous. I still believe that the only reason Morricone was not nominated for an Academy Award was because of the envy and resentment of the music department.

*

Gabriel Figueroa had an international reputation as one of the greatest cinematographers in the world. He was a small, sprightly, pleasant man in his sixties, dedicated to his work. I noticed that when we made long shots from the church, shooting down past the garrison to the town beyond, he took a great deal of time to light it. I questioned my camera operator, Bruce Surtees, about this.

SURTEES: Figueroa is universally regarded as the greatest black-and-white cinematographer. Point out to him that the colour film he is now using is faster than the black-and-white film he used before.

I told this to Figueroa. From that moment on, he lost his fear of colour film and shot as quickly and as magnificently as he ever did with black-and-white film.

*

I'm sorry I didn't get along with my producer. Marty must have said hundreds of times, 'Lose the battles, win the war.' The war he won on *Two Mules for Sister Sara* was that he, not I, did the final editing. It's a limited victory, however, because if you cut the picture in the camera, shoot the minimum and get to do the first cut as Alfred Hitchcock or I do,

339

then there isn't that much leeway in editing, unless the producer orders more film shot.

The *Los Angeles Herald–Examiner* said: '*Two Mules for Sister Sara* is a solidly entertaining film that provides Clint Eastwood with his best, most substantial role to date; in it he is far better than he has ever been. In director Don Siegel, Eastwood has found what John Wayne found in John Ford and what Gary Cooper found in Frank Capra.'

31

The Beguiled

Universal 1971

Clint and I were having lunch in his trailer one day while shooting *Two Mules for Sister Sara*. I was intrigued by the amount of vitamin pills he took before each meal. He looked great: tan, full of vigour, a man who felt strong and fit. Apparently, he had no problems.

EASTWOOD: Don, I think I'm going crazy.
ME: (*Taken aback*) On your way to the bank, or —
EASTWOOD: (*Interrupting, serious*) I read a book last night that Jennings sent me. I couldn't put it down.
ME: What's upsetting you?
EASTWOOD: I've never read a book like it before. It's called *The Beguiled*, written by Thomas Cullinan. I don't know whether I hate it or like it, or even understand it. Would you . . .
ME: . . . read it. I'm intrigued out of my mind. I've never heard you talk this way before.
EASTWOOD: Put me out of my misery and puzzlement. (*Giving me the book.*) Tell me you hate it.

Early the next morning I stood outside Clint's trailer, singing in my inimitable voice the end of 'The Dove', a folksong of the Civil War period.

ME: (*Singing*)
Come all you pretty, fair maids
Come walk in the sun
And don't let your young man
Even carry a gun. . . .
(*The door flings open. Clint, half-dressed, looks at me in amazement.*)
EASTWOOD: (*Excited*) You've read the book!
ME: (*Holding the book*) I lived the Gothic, macabre book of an innocent thirteen-year-old child being kissed by a beguiler; of succulent nymphs caressing each other. I dreamed of a succubus,

341

head of a seminary, who had 'relations with her younger brother' and lesbian yearnings for her lovely, innocent assistant, while you kissed both of them. My nightmare ended with you showing an interest in a big, black housekeeper, who stated flatly that the only way you could have her would be if she were dead.

EASTWOOD: (*Falling into the mood*) My leg was cut off and I was poisoned by the 'innocent' child who prepared, for me only, toadstool soup, which killed me. It's a frightening book. No wonder I was crazy.

ME: Clintus, if the Black Tower bigwigs allow us to make this book into a film, it could be the best picture we've ever made.

EASTWOOD: (*Beckoning me in*) You mean you really like it?

ME: I love it.

EASTWOOD: I'll tell Jennings that you're crazy about the book.

ME: Good. Jennings will relish the fact that it will make a dirty flick. I think it's beautiful. Jennings will prognosticate that it's a frightening idea for a movie and worry about it making any money. The moment we finish *Two Mules*, I'll find out if he wants to make a 'pollyanna' version of this moody, troubled book.

EASTWOOD: Remember, Mr Negative, he gave me the book to do – so quit being crazy and play it cool.

ME: I thought you said you were going crazy.

EASTWOOD: Only about you, Siegelini. Adios.

*

Months later, at the studio, Jennings and Marshall Green, head of production, were both ebullient about my inspecting the Disney Ranch as the Southern location for *The Beguiled*. I told them that not only had I never seen the ranch, but I had spent very little time in our Southern States.

GREEN: There's a great Southern Mansion at Disney's.

LANG: Acres and acres of verdant grass and plenty of trees.

ME: I'll look at it carefully, but I need one vital favour: a production designer/sketch artist. Someone who knows the South.

LANG: Who do you want?

ME: Ted Haworth.

GREEN: Absolutely not. He's a troublemaker.

ME: He knows all the locations like no one else. He's enormously talented and it's ridiculous not to have me at least see the South.

LANG: OK. But the moment he steps out of line, kaput.

Ted Haworth, Claude Traverse, my associate producer, the location manager and two good assistant directors, Burt Astor and Brad Aronson, made up the group on our recce.

The Southern Mansion was scarcely a Southern plantation. It needed a great deal of work to make it believable and shootable. Where were the great magnolia trees which usually lined the main driveway to such houses? Where were the long strands of Spanish moss hanging in profusion from the magnolias? The trees that Jennings had mentioned were thin, scraggly, scrub oaks. Ted felt very strongly that the Disney Ranch was hopeless. He suggested that he go to Louisiana immediately to take photos of possible mansions, and was certain that when the studio saw what I liked, they would agree. Claude also pointed out that the Disney Southern Mansion had been used thousands of times and was familiar to millions of people.

We reported all of this to Jennings, who reluctantly agreed that Ted could leave immediately on his own. When Ted had left, I discussed whom we should use to write the screenplay. Jennings had one choice: Albert Maltz. This was fine with me, as I had just finished working with him on *Two Mules for Sister Sara*. I wanted to start with him as soon as possible. I would give him all my input, so that after reading what Maltz and I had come up with, Jennings would have a definite idea of what he liked or disliked.

The casting was going to be terribly important and difficult. I recommended to Jennings that we should get with the casting department for their suggestions, as we must get the best actresses possible. I felt that it was urgent to test the various girls as soon as we could.

LANG: The only casting that means anything is Clint.
ME: He may be many things, but he's not stupid. It's vital that the schoolmistress and her assistant be absolutely first rate, otherwise, the picture will suffer. They should get credit above the title with Clint.
LANG: (*Derisively*) I can just see Clint sharing credit above the title with anyone less than a star.
ME: Don't be so damn all-knowing. Clint wants this picture to be as well made as possible. He won't like it if you envision it as just another 'Spaghetti Western'. You're really strange. After all, you picked the property.
LANG: Yeah, and I'm growing less sure about it every day.
ME: (*Getting up, starting for the door*) That's mighty encouraging.

I left in a bit of a huff; but I felt certain he wouldn't dare do anything without taking it up with Clint.

*

343

Bruce Surtees was one of the best camera operators in the industry. I had a long talk with him in my office. I told him how much Clint and I liked his work, and I explained the interesting challenges that *The Beguiled* presented. In a certain sense, it was a *film noir*. It was macabre and Gothic. The lighting presented problems, as the interior night work was lit by candles. I was hoping Bruce could figure a way to shoot only with the light from the candles. I noticed him becoming increasingly uncomfortable. I wondered if I had made it clear that I wanted him to be the cinematographer.

ME: You realize that we want you to be our first cameraman?

Bruce's face became flushed, his breathing heavy. I thought he was about to have a heart attack. I poured him a glass of water and made him drink it. Tears appeared in his eyes and he spoke with great difficulty.

SURTEES: Don, I had no idea. I don't want you to get into trouble by
   hiring me.
ME: You idiot. You'll be doing Clint and me a great favour by doing
   the picture for us.
SURTEES: (*Pulling himself together*) I'd be very proud to be your
   cameraman. I won't let you down.
ME: Well, thank God, that's understood.

*

Ted Haworth came back from Louisiana loaded down with pictures galore of Southern mansions, layouts and sketches. They looked marvellous. The Disney Southern Mansion faded into obscurity compared to the Belle Hélène Plantation on the River Road, Baton Rouge. We took the material to show to Jennings and Marshall Green. To give Jennings his due, he was very impressed.

HAWORTH: The exteriors can be shot entirely at Baton Rouge. The
   interiors can be built and shot at Universal. In case of bad weather,
   we can shoot some of the smaller interiors in the plantation house
   in Baton Rouge.
GREEN: (*Pointing to the desk*) Have you any idea what this is going to
   cost?
HAWORTH: Until I have a complete script, it can only be a ball-park
   figure; but this much I promise you: we will save at least one
   hundred and fifty thousand by *not* shooting this picture at
   Disney's.
LANG: (*To me*) How are you getting along with Maltz on his
   screenplay?

344

ME: I'm not. I don't agree with his attack. I thought it best to let him go forward without my stopping his work by arguing. When he finishes his first draft, I'm going to need your advice on many aspects of the script. I'm not figuring on changing the structure of the story. The same sets will be used. It's what the characters have to say, what the picture's about, that I am at odds with.

LANG: (*Turning to Ted*) You've done a great job, Ted. Don, let me have the script, without fail, as soon as Maltz has finished it.

ME: I'm very happy you approve of Ted's work. (*Starting for the door.*) You'll get the script the moment I've finished reading it. Who knows — maybe the genius will double-cross me and write it the way I strongly feel it should be written. But I doubt it.

*

Albert Maltz, quiet and unassuming, wore his sixty years well. He had written *This Gun for Hire, The Man in Half Moon Street, Cloak and Dagger, Naked City,* and a number of other screenplays, besides *Two Mules for Sister Sara.* He was blacklisted for a while during the McCarthy era and he served time in prison for refusing to testify that anyone he knew was a Communist. He was polite, soft-spoken, small in stature, with a backbone of steel.

We discussed our points of view on the treatment he had just finished. He was about to start his screenplay. He wanted to write *The Beguiled* as a romantic love story. I saw it as strange and fierce, like the novellas of Ambrose Bierce. Albert disagreed completely. I countered with the names of writers that I was certain he admired: Edgar Allan Poe, who would see the story as Gothic and macabre, or Tennessee Williams, or Truman Capote.

MALTZ: (*Quietly*) I wish I had the talent of Bierce, Poe, Williams or Capote. Regardless, I can only write it the way I feel. These lovely children, taken in by this beguiler, distress me.

ME: (*With a bit more passion*) Pull off the mask of these innocent, virginal nymphs and you will reveal the dark, hidden secrets of wily manipulators.

MALTZ: I don't agree. I believe in people.

ME: But not all people. Surely you are aware of evil people you do *not* believe in.

MALTZ: I'm not writing about evil people.

ME: You've deliberately closed your mind to the exciting possibilities of the suspense and vicious plot complications which enrich this story. Why can't this very powerful subject be treated with

345

subtlety? Along with delicate plot twists, there are ambivalent characters and conflicting emotions.

MALTZ: I'm sorry, Don. I'm going into screenplay the way I feel the film should be made.

ME: At this point, all I can ask is that you try to write from a highly imaginative point of view. I intend to film it that way.

When I handed Jennings the script, he broke out in anger the minute he read 'Screenplay "Johnny McB" by Albert Maltz, undated, (133 pages)'.

LANG: Why no date?

ME: No idea.

LANG: (*Leafing through script*) What version is this one?

ME: As far as I know, it's·the first draft after his treatment, dated December fourth, 1968, ninety-two pages.

LANG: Why didn't you give me the script as soon as you had read it?

ME: Standing in front of you and looking square into your bovine eyes, I just finished reading the damn script.

LANG: You didn't like it?

ME: Read the script, then we will have a nice meeting in your office, laced with your superb martinis. My secretary sent a script off to Clint. I told him we wanted to hear from him, *au plus vite*. Damn curious to find out what you both think of 'Johnny McB'.

LANG: (*Starting to read*) So am I, Don.
 (*I leave quietly.*)

The next day, sipping on an ice-cold martini, I listened to Jennings as he ranted out his denunciation of Maltz: how did he have the gumption to pass it off as a script?

ME: Did you tell him all this?

LANG: To his face. I insisted on a complete rewrite that had a hell of a lot more to do with the book.

ME: You've hit the problem right on the nose. Go back to the book. It should be an ironic, humorous lethal love story, with a nice feeling for the grisly. Actually, it's Gothic and eventually horrific. When do you think you'll get the revised script?

LANG: Can you push and help him along?

ME: After my discussion with him on his treatment, I knew he was lost and scared. If I argue with him, all I can do is slow him down. I'm afraid he's your choice and you've got to live with him until you get the next script. I've got a thousand things to do without wasting my time with a very stubborn man.

Clint called from Yugoslavia, where he was filming *Kelley's Heroes* for MGM. He told me he didn't care for the script. I told him how Jennings had reacted, and promised to send him a copy of the next draft as soon as it was ready – which should be within a week.

Time flew by. I worked with Ted on his layouts and sketches. He was very enthusiastic about the book and thought Maltz's script was dull and unimaginative. Claude Traverse was full of ideas on how to fix the script, as was I. I had meetings with casting on their suggestions for various actresses.

My secretary, Ceil, informed me that Mr Lang was on the phone.

LANG: What did you think of the new script?

ME: Maltz refused to give me a copy. He apparently sent you several scripts.

LANG: Have you any idea what happened to scripts two and three? He only sent me a fourth draft titled *The Beguiled*, dated August first, 1969, a hundred and twenty-two pages.

ME: I was under the impression that he was sending you a revised script, draft two. Anyway, how is draft four?

LANG: We'll discuss it when you've read it. My secretary will be in your office in five minutes with two scripts. When you've read it, amble up to my office. I've an idea that you might like.

ME: It's not likely; but I'll be there.

I read Albert's work and, again, despite its being a fourth draft, I felt he had missed the boat by a wide margin. I honestly and frankly didn't think he could write the screenplay. A script, with a note explaining the status quo of Albert's latest version, was rushed off to Clint. I hastened off to Jennings's office.

Jennings thought the puzzling fourth draft showed little improvement, if any. I told him that the film, like the book, should be laced with allegorical and Freudian symbolism. In Albert's script every incident was either flattened out or not used.

LANG: Unfortunately, I agree. But I have a possible solution. I think this story should be written by a woman.

ME: You mean like William Shakespeare's *Taming of the Shrew* might have been better written by a woman?

LANG: (*Exasperated*) I know an excellent writer, Irene Kamp. A woman's point of view might prove to be very interesting. Helen Strauss [*an executive with Universal*] thought it a good idea.

ME: Could be. But I've never read, or seen, any of Kamp's work. In fact, I've never met her. On the other hand, any change is better than none.

Irene Kamp and I had a number of discussions concerning the book and what she intended to do with her screenplay. Her ideas were more original than Albert's; plus, she was more amenable. But she, too, insisted on a happy ending. She was simpatico with the nubile maidens, although she didn't like the inference that the children were nubile. Irene was obviously an experienced writer. She entitled her first draft screenplay 'Nest of Sparrows'; it was dated 6 October 1969 (129 pages). Her second draft, 'Nest of Sparrows', was dated 7 November 1969 (134 pages).

Neither Clint, Jennings nor myself liked the scripts. We felt, as the title indicated, that Irene was more interested in the children than in Clint. Her attempt at a compromising happy ending was uninteresting to us. She used no more of the book than Albert had. Anything that was macabre, or Gothic, she shied away from. She shilly-shallied from letting her 'girls' know too much about sensual matters.

Without discussing what we were going to do about the many writers who were being mentioned to rewrite the script, I decided to have a candid, tête-à-tête talk with Claude Traverse, the associate producer. I gave him all the material I had so that he could read it immediately. I wanted to know two things: did he like the material, and did he honestly feel that he could write it? I didn't tell him what I thought of the various scripts, or of the book itself. One thing I was certain about Claude. He would dead-level with me.

Claude showed up the next morning, slightly bleary-eyed from reading. To my amazement, we agreed on practically everything that had to be done to the proposed new script. He did not like Maltz's fourth draft, nor the two scripts by Irene Kamp.

ME: Claude, how long would it take you to write it?
TRAVERSE: Including all revisions, not more than three months. Maybe less, if the revisions aren't too complicated.
ME: How long would it take without revisions?
TRAVERSE: (*Smiling*) Less than a month.
ME: I'm going to set up a story conference with Jennings. Start working on a continuity as soon as possible.

A week later, I managed to set up an early-morning story conference with Jennings in his office. He looked glum and dispirited. As usual, he kicked off the proceedings.

LANG: Well, at least we all agree on one thing. We don't like any of the scripts.

ME: On *Coogan's Bluff* we started breaking down the various scripts, then getting Dean Riesner to correlate all of them. Finally, he wrote a very good script, giving us what we wanted.

LANG: We can't get Dean. He's totally tied up.

ME: I spoke to Clint the other day. He said if we can't come up with a good script, let's scrap the project and do a new Western.

LANG: (*A heavy sigh*) Well, what are we going to do?

ME: I know what I want in the script, subject to your approval and, of course, Clint's. I found a writer – Claude Traverse. He believes in a new script, based on the book. He could give us what we want. Without telling him what I liked or disliked, I gave him all the material I had. I also told him that it was critical that I had his thoughts, impressions and ideas as soon as possible. If he didn't think he could write it, I asked him to tell me so.

LANG: This is one hell of a build-up, or maybe a let-down.

ME: To my complete astonishment, when he showed up the next morning he told me what he wanted to do in screenplay form with the book, which he liked very much. Naturally, this met with my hearty agreement, as it was almost exactly what I wanted. Also, he didn't like any of the present scripts.

LANG: Could you be a bit more specific?

ME: I'm not sure I'm able to do it, but I'm going to give it a try. All I want is faith from you.

LANG: Good luck.

ME: Remember, I rehearsed diligently with the actual writer. He thought I did a pretty good job. Of course, he's prejudiced – it's his story.

*

The main titles for *The Beguiled* were made entirely of stills. The opening shot, in black and white, is of a group of Union soldiers gathered around Abraham Lincoln. A tom-tom is faintly heard, playing a dirge. Imperceptibly, the film becomes sepia. The camera dollies into a Matthew Brady print of a wounded Union soldier lying on a stretcher. It is the spitting image of Clint Eastwood. (Matthew Brady never made any action shots, so when I wanted battle scenes for the main titles I took blow-ups of old film and gave them the sepia grainy quality of a Brady picture. Ted Haworth found the print of the Eastwood look-alike and was a great help to us.) We continue with two Union soldiers standing behind a large cannon. The camera pans the length of the cannon to its mouth. There is the sound of an explosion and the still of a battlefield, the sound and still of Confederate muskets firing at Union cavalry, with the sound of frightened horses. Next is a close shot of a Union soldier yelling, mortally wounded. A puff of smoke comes from a firing cannon. The horse of a Union soldier rears at an attacking Confederate soldier. The Confederate soldier is killed by an exploding Union cannon. We focus on a line of dead Union soldiers in a trench. The sounds of battle have ceased. The tom-tom continues a dirge. The song of 'The Dove', a Civil War folksong, is heard being sung by Eastwood. In the far distance, the sounds of war continue. We see a dead Confederate soldier; dead Confederate soldiers lying near a fence; another Confederate soldier lying dead, his musket across his body; dead Confederate soldiers with a covered wagon in the background.

As the titles end, the dirge and tom-tom and the stills end. The camera pans down past the smoke of the recent battle. Exquisite music begins as we come to a girl of thirteen, picking mushrooms and putting them in a small basket. We are still in sepia. As she crosses to a large tree in the foreground, imperceptibly and very slowly, the film begins to take on colour. As she sees blood on the shoe of a soldier, we are in full colour. The girl falls over backwards to the ground, involuntarily whispering, 'Oh, my God.' The huge figure of a Union soldier collapses near her. His leg is bleeding badly and his face and hands are bloody and burnt. The girl helps the Blue belly, with great difficulty, to his feet. She reacts to the sound of horses and wagons approaching from a distance: 'Somebody coming.' Under the soldier's arm is a thick branch, which he uses with difficulty as a crutch. He nods towards a deep ditch along the other side of the road. The girl helps him move as quickly as possible and they slide into it, lying flat on their stomachs.

When the Confederate soldiers disappear down the road, the young girl, Amy (Pamelyn Ferdin), brings the injured Johnny McB (Clint Eastwood) back to a seminary for young ladies, run by headmistress Martha Farnsworth (Geraldine Page), her assistant, Edwina Dabney (Elizabeth Hartman) and a black slave and housekeeper, Hallie (Mae Mercer). Martha Farnsworth reluctantly takes in Johnny McB and, fearing that he might die on the way to prison, decides not to turn him in to a passing Southern patrol. Johnny McB slowly recovers and works hard at charming the school's women and six female students. He succeeds, hoping to escape when his leg has healed enough for him to walk without crutches. When a band of Southern soldiers almost captures him, he is protected by lies from the women.

One night, as he stands in the hall deciding whether to go to the bedroom of Martha or Edwina, both of whom anticipate his arrival, he is

33 *The Beguiled*: Johnny McB (Clint Eastwood) and the women

found by one of the students, Carol (JoAnn Harris), who convinces him to
come to her room. The noise they make in bed awakens Edwina, who,
finding Johnny McB in Carol's bed, becomes hysterical and pushes him
down the stairs. With his leg now badly broken, he is carried semi-
conscious to the dining room, where Martha vindictively amputates his
broken leg, claiming it is for the sake of his health. When Johnny McB
awakens to find that his leg is gone, his anger becomes uncontrollable. He
humiliates Martha before the girls by revealing that in the past she had
an affair with her brother. In his rage, he accidently kills Randolph,

351

Amy's pet turtle. Johnny McB announces that either he will stay and have his pick of the women, or he will turn them in to advancing Union soldiers. In spite of Martha's attempts to stop her, Edwina sympathetically goes to join him in his room.

That night, Johnny McB is invited down for dinner and he apologizes for his behaviour, explaining that he plans to marry Edwina. However, he realizes that he has been fed poisoned mushrooms, which Amy picked in the forest. He rises, staggers out and collapses to die in the hall, while the women finish their meal. The picture ends with the burying of Johnny McB's body out by the gates to the school.

The colour slowly becomes sepia, gradually turning into the black and white that began the film.

*

LANG: (*On phone to secretary*) Find out when I can talk to Mr Eastwood in Yugoslavia, as soon as possible. (*Hangs up; to me.*) Know what I'm going to tell him?

ME: How are the martinis in Yugoslavia?

LANG: Which reminds me . . . (*Picks up phone; to secretary.*) Where are the martinis?

(*He hangs up and gives me a long stare, a slow smile taking over.*)

LANG: Clint's going to hear a rave about the possibilities that exist in Claude's script. Don, I was very impressed.

(*The double martinis make their appearance. Jennings toasts Claude's work and my verbosity.*)

LANG: (*Picks up phone*) Get Claude Traverse in my office at three sharp.

ME: (*As Jennings hangs up*) Don't, for God's sake, play the agent and make the deal too sharp.

LANG: I guarantee he'll be pleased with the deal.

ME: If you're available, let's start casting tomorrow.

LANG: If I read you, you've already got it cast. (*He stands.*) How about meeting tomorrow morning at ten thirty? By the time you finish testing the girls, you'll be exhausted.

ME: I was born tired. Before I pass out, thanks for the kind words.

*

Two screenplays later, Claude turned out an excellent script, which we all liked. In the meantime, we started casting. I shot many tests of the girls, from which the jury of Clint, Jennings, Claude and, later, Lew Wasserman, made choices. I was very pleased with the girls who were picked. The leading roles of Martha and Edwina were also cast. My first choice for

352

Martha was the French star Jeanne Moreau. I felt she and Clint would make great chemistry. She had starred in at least thirty films and was very well known throughout the world; she was the Bette Davis of her time. I never understood why Wasserman turned her down. However, I was happy when he picked my second choice, Geraldine Page. In acting, Geraldine was second to none. Elizabeth Hartman was cast as Edwina.

34 *The Beguiled*: Geraldine Page and Clint Eastwood

*

Was it possible to show Clint front on with his trouser leg pinned up and, in the same shot, without cutting, see him from the rear? It didn't seem possible – for, after all, Clint was not minus a leg.

I figured out a way to do it. I had Clint on crutches coming down the cellar steps towards the camera, his trouser leg pinned up. I panned with him, as he passed a brick pillar, appearing with his back to the camera, as he made his way to a distant area of the cellar. We had a double for Clint, a real amputee, who waited behind the pillar for Clint to appear. Once Clint's body started to cross the pillar, the double took off, the camera continuing panning with him. It would be the perfect shot, totally believable.

Unfortunately, there was very little light in the cellar. Bruce Surtees, known to this day as the 'Prince of Darkness', failed to get the shot. Naturally, I was keenly disappointed. I was so downhearted and so pressed for time, I walked away from my pet concept. But to give Bruce his due, he'll try anything. I still think he is one of the most sensitive and imaginative cameramen in the business. He bought me a very expensive German finder, with accurate lenses. Ultimately, I gave it back to him to let him know I had forgiven him.

*

It was a time of great hardship for the young maidens in *The Beguiled*. The dresses they wore were home-spun, mainly burlap or potato sacks. Rarely did they wear any kind of foot-covering. Naturally, they wore no make-up whatsoever, or so I thought. I had made it very clear to these sweet children; no make-up of any kind. To my surprise and chagrin, I discovered that one of them was wearing nail polish; another, a touch of lipstick; a third, powder and rouge. In a scene that called for crying, I saw mascara running down the cheeks of Janie. I eliminated her part in the scene. Another, Carol, insisted on wearing nail polish. I was very angry and tough with her. She told Clint that I had made her cry. He spoke to me about it.

EASTWOOD: I hear you had a run-in with one of the girls – you got rough.

ME: Frankly, I don't think I was rough enough. Most of them sneak in their damnable make-up just before the screen is shot. We've gone to such pains to make this picture authentic, that it kills me that these little devils get away with their tricks. I'm going to cut the parts of those darlings who continue to use make-up. I may have to ask you to play one of their parts, because I know how much you hate make-up.

EASTWOOD: (*Smiled*) I'll keep my eyes open. If I catch any of them cheating, I'll spank their bottoms.

*

Mr Cool, known in the trade as the 'Man with No Name', was in a fury. He was extremely unhappy with the editing of *Kelley's Heroes*, the film he had starred in before *The Beguiled*. He had a phone in his trailer, and spent an entire day having torrid arguments with the head mogul of MGM, Jim Aubrey. Over the phone, Aubrey felt safe and was his usual stubborn self.

In the meantime, not only was I somehow supposed to film Clint, but other chores loomed up to plague me. For example, the *Herald Examiner* film critic, Bridget Byrne, was standing by that day, observing. To show her common politeness and keep her from being too aware of what was going on, I talked to her all day, giving her no hot story information. She wrote a long article for the *Examiner*, extolling the virtues of Mr Eastwood: how he worked, how pleasant he was (he never even noticed her on the set), and how he represented the best in American men. I was mentioned in the article: 'The director, Don Siegel, a small man who *never* stopped chattering. . . .'

At the end of the no-shooting day, to Clint's surprise and anger, notwithstanding his being surrounded in his trailer by agents, lawyers, accountants and other advisers, he made a huge discovery: he lost his battle with MGM. Actually, he won, but didn't, at this time, know it. His next picture, *Dirty Harry*, was made at Warner Brothers under the banner of Malpaso Company, which Clint owned lock, stock and barrel. No mogul could say 'Boo' to anything Clint wanted.

In the meantime, both he and I were sadly disillusioned by Universal's handling of *The Beguiled*.

It's always amazing to me that when a studio releases a picture badly – stupidly, if you will – they always blame the picture for not making money. The truth is, of course, that the picture doesn't make money as a direct result of their ineptitude. They released *The Beguiled* senselessly and the advertising was practically non-existent. What little there was of it was not only misleading, it was a lie.

Edward Gorey, a talented and well-known painter, saw my rough cut for *The Beguiled* and came up with priceless sketches of what the advertising of the picture should be. When I showed his ideas to Jennings, he flipped out. He personally took the drawings and text to handle the selling of it to the publicity people and studio heads. I never heard a word from him about what happened. Someone must have said 'No'. That was more than enough for our verbose, fearless leader. In the event, the

355

advertising portrayed it as a film in which Clint Eastwood single-handedly wins the Civil War.

In order for a film to qualify for prestigious film festivals such as Cannes or Venice, it cannot have been previously exhibited in any commercial theatre anywhere. It's difficult to believe, but Universal showed *The Beguiled* months before the qualifying period for the various film festivals. It was shown in, of all places, the home of the Spaghetti Western, Milan. The audience expected to see Clint in a film full of overt action – killing, fighting, blowing up adversaries with dynamite, etc. They not only didn't see what they came for and wanted; they simply didn't understand *The Beguiled* at all.

Throughout the world, the reviews were on the whole quite good; many were excellent. In France, the picture was considered a classic. Many distinguished critics said that if *The Beguiled* had been shown at the film festivals, it would have won.

Eastwood films are almost always released like a scatter-gun: play as many theatres as possible and the money pours in. Great. But it should have been recognized that a picture like *The Beguiled* needed to be handled differently. After winning a number of film festivals and acquiring some great quotes, it should have opened in a small theatre in New York. People would have been curious about what kind of an Eastwood picture, co-starring Geraldine Page and Elizabeth Hartman, was playing in one small theatre with such critical acclaim. It would have played for months, maybe a year. It wouldn't have been a blockbuster; but I guarantee that, at the very least, it would have grown slowly by word of mouth from a small start into a very successful film.

Showing the film first in Milan was a brilliant way of ensuring its failure. Not only did Universal lose money on it, but they ultimately lost for ever the services of the biggest star in the industry, Clint Eastwood. Jennings Lang's defence was as expected: 'Nobody went to see the picture.'

32

Dirty Harry

Warner Brothers 1971

I was working on a couple of projects that might get made when one day my secretary, Ceil, buzzed me on the phone. She told me Mr Eastwood was on the line. I pushed the button.

ME: What's up, Clintus?

EASTWOOD: I need a favour.

ME: What's the colour of her hair?

EASTWOOD: Seriously, I need your help on deciding which script I do.

ME: I don't like the terminology 'which' script.

EASTWOOD: I'll be right over.

ME: Nice of you to accept my invitation.
    (*Clint shows up carrying four scripts. I give him a hard stare. He starts explaining his problem.*)

EASTWOOD: Jennings Lang gave me an original screenplay titled *Dirty Harry*, which takes place in New York. After I read the script and said I would do it, Jennings lost the deal when he refused to pay the amount of money the agent was asking for the project.

ME: But why four scripts? One is bad enough.

EASTWOOD: The project was dead. Warners bought it and had three different writers writing three new scripts for Frank Sinatra, who agreed to do the film.

ME: Sinatra reminds me of you. I believe you both sing and I know you both fight.

EASTWOOD: Sinatra cut his hand and backed out of the film.

ME: Are you sure he didn't cut his throat?

EASTWOOD: (*Totally ignoring me*) Warners heard that I had said I would do the picture – so, they set me the fourth script. I read it and hated it. I told them so. They immediately sent me scripts one, two and three. I read them all and still only liked the original.

ME: Obviously, do the first script. Why muck my life up by making me read any of the scripts? Have you forgotten? I'm under contract exclusively to Universal.

EASTWOOD: Don, all I want is your advice on the four scripts.

ME: I've already told you – do the original.

EASTWOOD: (*Testily*) Seriously Don, I really need your advice.

ME: All right. But only if your secretary brings me one of your terrific health sandwiches to give me the strength to read. I'll do it while my own two projects go down the drain.

EASTWOOD: Carol will bring you two sandwiches and two brews.
(*I hold the scripts in my hand.*)

ME: They're too long. I'll call you as soon as I've read them, unless I fall asleep.
(*Clint leaves, beaming.*)

I finished the four scripts. My stomach growled from the sandwiches and brews. When I saw Clint, I figured I would tell him that the original script by Harry Julian Fink was the worst, the second was better, the third better yet and the fourth the best. Actually, the first was far and away the only worthwhile script. I dropped in on Clint, carrying my heavy load of scripts, with a sour expression. I chickened out when I started talking.

ME: It's true that the original Fink script is easily the best. However, you just finished *Coogan's Bluff* in New York. I'd suggest changing the locale to San Francisco. Also, a major rewrite is necessary and you'll need someone like Dean Riesner.

EASTWOOD: Don, I can't thank you enough. I just couldn't figure out why Warner Brothers used three new writers to spoil the first script.

ME: And I can't figure out why you get your jollies by making me waste my time.

EASTWOOD: How about producing and directing *Dirty Harry*?

ME: Wasserman will be so mad at you for leaving Universal that he'll never agree to let me go with you to Warners.

EASTWOOD: Just leave that to me. Give me a 'yes' or 'no'.

ME: I'm going to give you both. No, I don't want to stay at Universal. Yes, I very much would like to work with you.

EASTWOOD: God, you're difficult.

ME: (*Grinning*) All will be forgiven if I turn out a super job.

*

Clint and I kept our offices at Universal. I immediately started working with Dean on a new step outline. *Dirty Harry* was one of the few titles that was never questioned by anyone. In his office, Clint had a huge cardboard

35 Don Siegel: 'I threw a vicious right at Dirty Harry'

figure of himself playing Dirty Harry. Whenever we disagreed, I threw a vicious right at 'Dirty Harry', knocking it down. Clint was amused.

I went to San Francisco with Dean Riesner to find the actual locations, which would affect the step outline. It's peculiar and painstaking work finding locations which will help the picture. I've never understood why, but I have always had great luck finding superb locations. Of course, in one of the most beautiful cities in the world, no matter where the camera is placed, the set-up looks fantastic. San Francisco has six great hills, the bay, Alcatraz, the Golden Gate Bridge, the Ferry Building, the Embarcadero, etc. Nevertheless, we found locations that other motion-picture companies failed to use. Even the hardened veteran, Dean Riesner, grew excited. We rushed back to finish our step outline.

*

As *Dirty Harry* opens, from a nearby rooftop a sniper takes careful aim and slowly squeezes the trigger. A splash of scarlet spurts from a girl's shoulder and she sinks into a sundeck pool. The killer (Andy Robinson), who signs himself Scorpio, demands $100,000 from the police, threatening other deaths, including a priest, or a black. Harry Callahan (Clint Eastwood) of the San Francisco Police Department, is advised by Lieutenant Bressler (Harry Guardino) and the Mayor (John Veron) that they are going to pay off the killer extortionist. Even before he can begin on this case, Harry is wounded in the leg while foiling a bank robbery. Against his wishes, he is assigned a partner, Chico (Reni Santoni). He is young, bright and eager, and is amazed at what appears to be Harry's surly, negative attitude towards everybody and everything.

A police helicopter spots the sniper as he is gets another victim in his sights from another rooftop. The killer escapes. Harry and Chico, on patrol, follow a man they think may be the suspect, but Harry winds up peeking in a hooker's window and almost gets pounded to death by neighbourhood toughs. The police discover a young black shot to death by the sniper. On Harry's hunch that the killer's ego will bring him back to the same district, he and Chico stake out on a rooftop. They spot the killer on a distant roof; they open fire, he returns it, and in a blaze of shattered neon he again makes his escape.

Another note from the sniper advises the police that he has kidnapped a fourteen-year-old girl and that she is buried alive with a little bit of oxygen. He will let her die if he doesn't receive $200,000. Harry goes to deliver the ransom money. Although strictly forbidden to do so, Chico goes along with a walkie-talkie, keeping his distance, as Harry follows complex instructions before he is accosted by the sniper at the base of an enormous cross in Mount Davidson Park. The sniper, wearing a stocking mask, cracks Harry over the skull, viciously kicks him and says he is going to let the girl die. As he starts to do away with Harry, Chico emerges from the bushes and is wounded in the gun battle that follows. Harry manages to drive a switchblade into the killer's thigh.

Harry gets a clue from the doctor at an emergency hospital where the killer has sought help for his knife wound. The doctor believes that he lives in the keeper's quarters at Kezar Stadium. That's where Harry catches him, in the glare of lights in the middle of the deserted playing field. Harry not only shoots but also tortures the wounded killer. That's where he makes his mistake. The District Attorney (Josef Sommer) accuses him of torturing a suspect, denying medical attention and legal counsel. And the girl's buried body is found.

With the killer released, Harry begins harassing and tailing him day and night. In a warehouse one night, the killer pays a big brute $200 to beat him up. At the hospital, he accuses Harry of the brutal mauling. What Harry has been predicting now comes true. The killer is about to do it again. He beats and robs a liquor-store owner, taking a gun from him. Then he hijacks a school bus with a lady driver (Ruth Kobart) at the wheel and six kids in the back. He starts for the airport. He has called the police, demanding money and a fuelled and manned escape plane. As the bus nears the airport, Harry leaps from a railway trestle, landing on top of the bus. The driver faints, and the bus careens into the yard of a quarry company. Harry chases the killer through the plant, and when he seizes a young boy who is fishing, trying to use him for protection, Harry sends a bullet into the killer's shoulder, missing the boy's head by a quarter of an inch. Another blast from Harry's gun sends Scorpio spread-eagled into the muddy waters of a sump pit. As police sirens approach, he turns and walks down the road, a solitary figure, the man they call Dirty Harry.

*

We liked our story outline as a basis for a screenplay, and immediately gave it to Clint. After he read it and gave us his input, he sent out his challenge.

EASTWOOD: (*To Riesner*) Do you want to know something that surprised me? You're going to wind up with one hell of an exciting script. How long will it take you to write it and for Siegel to wreck it?

RIESNER: About two weeks.

ME: (*Angrily*) You're crazy. You remind me of a guy in a cafeteria – his eyes are bigger than his stomach. He orders everything and eats very little. It'll take you at least a month.

EASTWOOD: (*Indicating me*) The wrecker at work. (*To Riesner.*) Get moving, Dean. You're already behind schedule.

I got up with Dean, giving him a disgusted look of disbelief. As we left, I told Clint that I was only interested in a great script, as I know he and Dean were. We weren't competing in a track meet.

Dean worked day and night. I tried hard to be constructive, not destructive. Dean looked haggard and confessed to me that he was a damn fool to think he could transform a step outline into a finished script in two weeks.

ME: So you don't finish in two weeks. What are they going to do – fire you? As you would say, it's only words. Do the best you can and take the weekend off. Go to the races, rest and get plenty of sleep. I'll write the ending, which is only action. I'll turn it over to you Monday morning.

RIESNER: If I don't show up Monday, tell Clint to bury me in a pauper's grave. And, by the way, it's only two words, but they are important to me: bless you.

At 6.30 a.m. Saturday morning I was madly scribbling and enjoying it. I was writing the whole ending, which was full of action. I hoped Dean

361

would treat my work more kindly than I did his. When Ceil arrived at 9 a.m. she made coffee and took my scribbling to decipher and type. The hours sped by and, to my astonishment, suddenly I was on the last page. Before finishing it, I decided to read what I had written.

Exterior: Quarry – day
As the bus hits a pile of gravel, an enormous cloud of dust rises. Harry is seen flying through the air, disappearing. When the dust finally settles, he sees Scorpio, gun in hand, limping quickly towards a huge, swayback quarry building and disappearing inside. With the huge .44 magnum in hand, Harry rushes after him.

Interior: Quarry building – day
As Harry enters the huge building, the plant is in full operation. Conveyor belts are moving, jammed full of pieces of granite. A shot rings out from above. Harry throws himself flat on the conveyor belt moving towards housings of corrugated metal feeding into the rear of this strange, ramshackle-looking edifice.
Harry's point of view
Scorpio is on top of one of these housings, aiming for another shot. As he squeezes it off:
On Harry
Harry dives for cover and comes up firing at the corrugated metal housing. Blam! Blam!

Exterior: Small quarry building – day
Harry dashes up rickety stairs and throws himself inside a small quarry building. He peers off.
Harry's point of view
Far down the dark, narrow tunnel, with the conveyor belt bisecting it, Scorpio is frantically reloading his gun.
Angle on Harry
He suddenly springs up and charges down the tunnel. Scorpio fires. Harry throws himself flat on the moving conveyor belt as the shot skids past him. Harry fires.
Angle down tunnel
A whole section of piling rips away near Scorpio. He darts into a passageway and starts limping quickly down the tunnel towards daylight at the far end.
Angle on Harry
He starts sprinting towards a passageway and disappears.

Exterior: Small quarry building – close on Scorpio – day
Scorpio bursts out of the smaller building, where all the conveyor housings lead from it. He glances nervously around.

Exterior: Quarry sump – Scorpio's point of view – day
There is a big sump at the rear of the quarry. Fishing at the edge of the sump is a little, ten-year-old boy.
Angle on Scorpio
He fires back at Harry, hurtling down the tunnel. Suddenly, Scorpio slides down a stair bannister to the ground and runs desperately towards the sump. His limp is very evident.

Exterior: Small quarry building – close on Harry – day
Harry comes out of the small building and looks off towards the sump.

Exterior: Quarry sump – day
Scorpio runs up to the kid, grabs him in his left arm, presses the Luger against the kid's temple and turns to face Harry, smiling.

36 *Dirty Harry*: Scorpio (Andy Robinson) and the kid

Angle on small quarry building
Harry, magnum in hand, jumps off and starts running towards the killer.

SCORPIO: (*Matter of factly*) Drop your gun, or I'll blow his dumb brains right out the side of his head.

Wide angle
Harry stops. There is a beat, as the two men stare at each other. Scorpio continues to smile. Then, without warning, Harry snaps off a shot.
Angle on Scorpio
As Harry's shot takes Scorpio in the left shoulder, missing the kid's head by a quarter of an inch at most, Scorpio yells in surprise and pain. He spins to the ground, the Luger flying out of his hand.
Angle on kid
as he jumps to his feet and runs down the road.
Angle on Scorpio
as he sees his gun lying 2 feet away. He looks up at Harry. He doesn't know whether to try to reach for his gun or not.
Angle on Harry
advancing towards Scorpio.

HARRY: Now I know what you're thinkin'. Did he fire six shots, or only five? Well, to tell you the truth, in all this excitement (*apparently telling the truth*) I've kind of lost track myself. But being this is a forty-four magnum (*wryly*), the most powerful handgun in the world, and would blow your head clean off. (*Grins.*) You've got to ask yourself one question. Do I feel lucky? (*Wider grin.*) Well, do you *punk*?

Angle on Scorpio
His face contorts in anger. He hesitates for the briefest moment; then, in a blurring motion, he grabs for the gun and, in one movement, he starts to rise to his feet, bringing the gun up firing.
Another angle
Harry pulls the trigger, his .44 magnum blasts, the shot catches Scorpio right in the chest, spinning him around backwards. It's like the kick of a mule lifting Scorpio off his feet, sending him flying into the sump.
Angle on Harry
He crosses to the edge of the sump and looks down.
Harry's point of view
Scorpio is spread-eagled in the muddy waters of the sump. Blood is staining the muddy waters deep red.

Close on Harry

He stares down for a long moment. Now, he's really done it; disobeyed orders, endangering children, killing a man. There's bound to be hell to pay. He takes out his star from his pocket, wondering if it's worth the trouble of fighting to keep it. He hears, faintly at first, the distant sound of approaching police sirens. Grimly, he makes up his mind and throws the star as far as he can, skimming into the sump.

Suddenly, the buzzer rang. It was Ceil telling me Mr Eastwood was in the office and would appreciate seeing me. He couldn't have appeared at a worse time.

ME: (*Into the phone*) What the hell's he doing snooping around late on a Saturday afternoon? Show him in.
    (*Clint enters, apologizing for disturbing me.*)
ME: Wish I could say I was pleased to see you, but I'm awfully busy, Clint.
EASTWOOD: (*Crossing to desk*) What are you up to? Why isn't Dean around?
ME: I'm going to tell you something you're not going to like. Dean has been writing day and night. He was on the edge of a nervous collapse. I gave him the weekend off, told him to get plenty of sleep while I laid out the ending to give to him Monday morning.
    (*Clint looks over my shoulder and sees that the ending is almost finished.*)
EASTWOOD: (*Surprised*) You're on the last page.
ME: I don't know how Dean pushed himself so hard. Now, if you'll excuse me, I've got to finish. (*I continue writing while Clint waits.*)

Angle on Harry

He turns and starts back down the road in the direction he came.

Long shot

The camera shoots down past the bloodied figure floating in the sump. As the camera zooms imperceptibly back, the wail of sirens grows louder. Down the road, walking away from us, is a solitary figure growing smaller, the man known as Dirty Harry.

THE END

(I put down my pen and lean back in my chair.)
EASTWOOD: Can I please read it?
ME: I couldn't do that to Dean. It's his script and he must fix it up before you get it.

365

EASTWOOD: It's killing me, Don.

ME: How do you think Dean will feel? You'll get it on Monday, after Dean reads and works on it and before anyone else gets it, I promise.

EASTWOOD: You've never asked me for a favour and I've never asked you for one either. But I'm asking for one now. You have my word, I'll square it up with Dean.

ME: I give up. Take it and don't lose it.

Thanking me, Clint took the script and scooted out of the office. That night he called me at home. His voice showed emotion.

EASTWOOD: Don, it's the greatest. I'm so proud of you both.

ME: I'm walking on air. Now you can return the favour by calling Dean to thank him for the terrific job he did.

EASTWOOD: I'm already dialling. And again, many thanks, Don.

*

Dean and I were heroes. Everybody sang our praises over the script. Then about a week later, Clint appeared in my office. His face was set, he kept kicking the carpet like a stallion kicking turds. Finally, I broke the silence.

ME: What's bothering you? I've never seen you play an embarrassed cowboy before.

EASTWOOD: Don, I can't quit.

ME: You mean by walking off the picture? If you do, I can always get Sinatra.

EASTWOOD: I'm quitting my job when I throw away my badge at the end of the film.

ME: You're *not* quitting. You're rejecting the bureaucracy of the police department, which is characterized by adherence to fixed rules and a hierarchy of authority.

EASTWOOD: (*Kicking the carpet again*) I still feel I'm quitting by throwing away my badge.

ME: You're wrong, Clint. You're rejecting the stupidity of a system of administration, marked by officialdom and red tape.

Clint's face bristled in stubborn lines. I suddenly realized that if I had the audience by the last page, what major difference would it actually make if he didn't throw the badge away? So I gave in.

ME: It won't be as strong an ending, dramatically, but what if we did the ending another way? For example, Harry draws his arm back as if to throw the badge into the sump. Suddenly, he pauses, as he hears the faint distant wail of approaching police sirens before the audience hears it. Then, with something close to a sigh, he puts the badge back in his pocket and, turning, starts back down the road in the direction he came. The rest follows to the end, as written.

EASTWOOD: That's exactly what I wanted. Thanks, Don.

ME: I still don't think it's as meaningful as when you throw the badge away. And by the way, I'm sending you a bill for the damage you did to my rug.

Clint messed up my hair and left, a happy man.

*

John Calley, an amusing, likeable, erudite top executive, had a list of scenes that he (the word 'we' is used) felt were vastly better written in the early draft by Harry Julian Fink than in the Dean Riesner version. Also, he attached a comparison of scenes between the Fink and Riesner scripts. I called him immediately.

ME: John, I must confess that after reading your memo I'm not only surprised – I'm astounded.

CALLEY: Did you compare the two drafts?

ME: Yes, Mr Calley. And I flatly prefer the Riesner script.

CALLEY: You do?

ME: Indeed, I do. I'm not going through the scripts over the phone, but there are a few things I'm curious about. If you were so keen about the Fink script, which I like, when Sinatra and Kershner were involved and three different writers were hired to write three different scripts, why did you send Clint the fourth script – which obviously you thought was your best version? And when you discovered that Clint greatly preferred the Fink version, you hastily sent him the four scripts you had. Clint had me read all four. We agreed the only possible script was the Fink version.

CALLEY: I admit that it was a careless mistake.

ME: One other point that amused me and made me wary of your story perception: you (we) say that 'All references to Harry's past are out of a different movie'. In the *entire* film, when Clint is walking down the fire exit from the sunroof with Chico's wife, concealed frequently from the camera by brick posts, there is one exposition scene, when he briefly mentions his wife was senselessly killed by a drunk driver.

CALLEY: I don't recall that scene.

ME: John, let me tell you something. I work quickly and I work loose. Everything I do, or that Dean does, we get Clint's input and approval. Every time you run down Dean, you are maligning Eastwood and Siegel.

CALLEY: I certainly had no intention of doing that.

ME: John, I've made up my mind. I realize this will have to be a verbal agreement at this time. I disagree with all your thoughts and, effective immediately, I am no longer on *Dirty Harry*. I wish you well with the project.

CALLEY: But Don, surely —

ME: (*Interrupting*) Sorry, John.

I hung up, somewhat stunned; but I felt I was right. I wanted no part of Calley's ideas. I started to pack my briefcase, clear my desk, etc. A few minutes later, Clint appeared in my office.

EASTWOOD: Calley just called. He said you quit the picture.

ME: Did you read his 'Comparison of Scripts', plus his long list of what he preferred in the Fink draft over the Riesner draft? I just disagreed with all his ideas and, as far as I knew, you didn't agree either.

EASTWOOD: Just give me five minutes to talk to Calley. I'll be back shortly.

(*Clint dashes off. About five minutes later, the phone rings. Before Ceil can answer it, I pick it up. It is John.*)

CALLEY: Well, Don, I sure learned a lesson. Never again will I write a story memo. It was very stupid of me not to have a personal talk with you.

(*The door opens and Clint enters.*)

ME: My position is exactly the same.

CALLEY: Don, please forget what happened and shoot it the way you and Clint think best.

ME: (*Speaking for Clint's benefit*) Now, let me have a very clear understanding with you. Is it clearly understood that I am *not* going to pay any attention to your memos?

CALLEY: Of course.

ME: It's easy to say 'of course'; but I mean specifically that you are not to interfere in any manner, shape or form with the way I shoot or with the content of the picture?

CALLEY: Absolutely.

ME: Then under the aegis of Mr Clint Eastwood, I am very happy to continue directing *Dirty Harry*.

(*Clint smiles.*)

CALLEY: Thank God.

ME: And bless you for not being stubborn.
  (*I hang up. Clint shakes my hand.*)
EASTWOOD: I wish you'd quit stalling and get back to work. How about a brew in my office?

I strolled back with Clint to his bungalow, aware that I had not won the battle. Clint had.

*

Finding ourselves with time to spare, we had a small room in the homicide squad quarters dressed as a hospital emergency room. Having no time to cast the role of the black intern, we hired our second assistant director, Charles Washburn, who had no previous acting experience.

It is night in the San Francisco General Hospital Emergency Room. We close in on a young, black intern.

INTERN: (*Mock serious*) Well, Harry, I think we can save that leg.
  (*Camera pulls back. Harry is seated on a table. The intern has one of Harry's trouser legs rolled up. Harry indicates his lower thigh.*)
HARRY: I really appreciate this, Steve.
INTERN: That's OK. We Russian Hill boys, we've got to stick together.
  (*Pauses.*) Did you ever consider another line of work?
HARRY: All I want from you, Steve, is a little xylocaine and a quick tweezer job.
INTERN: Do I come down to the station and tell you how to beat confessions out of prisoners?
HARRY: Come on, Steve, I haven't got all night. (*Indicates thigh.*) Couple up here, too.
  (*The intern has turned away and is looking through a drawer. Harry's face is set. He looks at the intern for a moment, then indicates the scissors, which the intern now holds in his hand.*)
HARRY: What are those for?
INTERN: I've got to cut your pants off.
HARRY: Oh no. Pull 'em off.
INTERN: It'll hurt.
HARRY: For twenty-nine fifty, let it hurt.
  (*As the intern starts to pull the trousers off Harry's legs . . .*)

Several of the top executives at Warner Brothers insisted on omitting the intern scene. I thought they were dead wrong in not allowing me to shoot it. For one thing, the script was not long. (Clint told these meddlers that they didn't know how taut and tight I shot.) But the most important reason was to show our audience that Harry was *not* a bigot. We needed a

369

scene which showed that he and the black intern were the best of friends, brought up in the same neighbourhood, Russian Hill. I had to let the audience know that Harry killed the bank robbers because they were bank robbers, *not* because they were black.

We shot a scene in which Harry and his new partner, Chico Gonzales, are in the Communications Room of the Hall of Justice. Tape recorders are spinning, slowly taking down car calls; a loudspeaker on the wall is broadcasting a pebbly-voiced report from the helicopter. There is a wall map broken into districts, each with a red, green and yellow light denoting the condition of that district's police-car unit. There is also a large architectural scale model of San Francisco. Harry and Chico move towards it. As Harry stops, checking a message, a stocky plainclothesman, Frank DiGeorgio (John Mitchum), stands by the teletype. DiGeorgio looks over.

DIGEORGIO: Hey, Harry. Nice work yesterday.
HARRY: Thanks, fatso.
    (*We move with Harry to the relief map, where Chico is standing.*)
CHICO: Why do they call you Dirty Harry?
    (*Harry just looks at Chico for a long moment. DiGeorgio comes up, grinning.*)
DIGEORGIO: One thing about Harry, he plays no favourites. Harry hates everybody – Limies, Micks, Hebes, fat Dagoes, Niggers, Hunkies, Chinks – name it.
CHICO: (*Standing between Harry and DiGeorgio*) What about Mexicans?
HARRY: Especially Spics.
    (*Harry crosses by Chico and as he passes DiGeorgio he winks at him.*)

I had Harry wink at DiGeorgio after he said that because otherwise the audience would definitely think Harry a bigot instead of a tease.

*

The first time the audience fully sees Scorpio, hiding on a roof, he is wearing highly polished parachute shoes with white laces going up the sides. He is rubbing first one shoe, then the other, against his dirty, tan dungaree pants. On his belt is a large, lopsided peace symbol. No verbal exposition is ever given, but to those who might have questioned his strange attire, it is possible that in his tilted fashion he could have returned from Vietnam bearing a crazed grudge.

*

An enormous amount of preparation, both in lighting and in special effects, went into my attempt to shoot in one direction with seven cameras during the rooftop shoot-out between Harry, Chico and Scorpio. We were on roof 4, shooting past the revolving 'Jesus Saves' sign, past roof 3, where Scorpio has been previously established, lurking Washington Park and a Catholic church. Washington Square is very visible to Scorpio, who has sworn to kill a Catholic priest. The laying of cables all this distance was extremely difficult, but if it worked it would save considerable shooting time.

Minor accidents occurred at night when cars brushed against each other, possibly blinded by our lights. I was worried about what would happen to our main protagonists when the revolving 'Jesus Saves' sign was alternately bathed in pink and green, with special effects simulating Scorpio's shots smashing into the sign. The neon tubes shatter. Wires are shorting. Electricity is cascading out of the sign. Part of the neon tubing pulls loose and starts to fall. Harry and Chico are under the sign, as it crashes to the rooftop, just missing them. This was a very dangerous shot and it was my responsibility to go over it with Bruce Surtees and special effects many, many times to ensure that no one would get hurt.

Endless complaints poured in. People wanted to sleep. The lights, the noise, the firing of shots – all were legitimate complaints. Some people had to go to work early; others were ill. The police, who were magnificent, were at their wits' end.

It was after midnight and the pressure was mounting. Clint, who had been sleeping in his trailer, made a yawning appearance. He yelled at the special-effects men on roof 3 to quit stalling and get the hell on with the shot! I rushed over to him.

ME: Clint! They know what they're doing.
EASTWOOD: Then why the hell are they taking so long?
(*Everybody backs away from us, wanting no involvement with a director having a dispute with the star and boss of his company, who are making the picture.*)
ME: The shots are dangerous and I'll be damned if I'm going to rush it and hurt someone. Clint, please go back to your trailer. I'll call you the instant we're ready.
(*I turn away to join Bruce. He speaks to me, close to tears.*)
SURTEES: Don, I can't work under tension.
ME: Come on Bruce, let's do everything we can to help special effects. Will the generators stand up to the heavy load? It looks like miles of cables out there.
SURTEES: It is. I've tested and retested. It's the biggest shot I've ever tried to make.

A figure bent over me and gave my cheek a gentle kiss. As I slowly turned around, I caught a glimpse of Clint's back, headed quickly for the exit doors to the street. I'll never forget his consideration and kindness.

*

When you're in trouble, possibly being mugged, raped, robbed, threatened with a knife, a pistol – the list is a long one – who do you call for

37 *Dirty Harry*: 'Dirty Harry is a hard-nosed cop'

help? If there's not a policeman nearby, save your breath. Without
hesitation, all members of the police department will risk their lives trying
to save yours. Who else will move a muscle?

If I do a film about a murderer, it doesn't mean I condone murder. If I do
a film about a hard-nosed cop, of course it doesn't mean I condone all his
actions. I find it very difficult to explain my reasons for making a film like
Dirty Harry, other than that I'm a firm believer in entertainment, hoping
that every picture I make will be a commercial success. Not once
throughout *Dirty Harry* did Clint and I have a political discussion. We
were only interested in making the film a successful one, both as
entertainment and at the box office. I can't understand why, when a film is
made purely for entertainment, it should be criticized on a political basis.
The response from my many friends – members of the 'Siegel cult', some
of them left wing or Communists, others conservative Republicans or
Fascists – has not surprised me.

*

38   *Dirty Harry*: Harry (Clint Eastwood) leaps . . .

39 *Dirty Harry*: . . . and lands on the stolen bus

We shot the sequence in which Scorpio hijacks the school bus on Sir
Francis Drake Boulevard. The bus comes towards us, down the off ramp,
swinging right to merge into the road. There is no sound of children
singing. As the bus approaches the boulevard, it has to brake for a slow
Volkswagen. The Volkswagen precedes the bus as they approach a
railroad trestle, which crosses over Sir Francis Drake Boulevard. Inside the
bus, Scorpio is somewhat nettled at the slow-moving car ahead. His eyes
widen in apprehension, as he stares fixedly. Then we have Scorpio's point
of view, shooting forward through the windshield as the bus approaches
the trestle. Harry stands on top of the trestle, directly over the path of the
oncoming bus.

   We had to stop to prepare properly what was going to be a series of
extremely dangerous shots. Clint insisted on jumping on to the bus. His
double, Buddy Van Horn, insisted on trying it first. He made the jump
and, when the bus swerved, he was able to save himself by clinging to one

of the parallel metal strips which run along the top of the bus fore and aft.

We would make shots of the children screaming in terror when the camera was inside the bus. However, when we were outside the bus, we used midgets in place of the children. We had to set squibs on the roof of the bus, which would go off near Clint. This would intercut with Andy Robinson firing from inside the moving bus. The most difficult shot was when the bus wipes out the chain-link fencing, with Clint riding on top. The bus barrels towards an enormous pile of gravel. As it hits the pile, an enormous cloud of dust rises. The figure of Clint is seen flying through the air, disappearing.

When I was tied down on top of the bus near the front, I asked the grips where a real director would be. They answered, 'Where you should be, sitting in a director's chair, with a script open on your lap.'

*

The ending of *Dirty Harry* remained as written, with Harry finally killing Scorpio at the sump. However, while preparing to shoot the very last scene, where we had agreed that Harry would keep his badge and walk down the dirt road, Clint came up to me.

EASTWOOD: Don, I've changed my mind. I'd like to throw away my badge as you originally had it.
ME: When you made up your mind not to throw your badge away, I only ordered one badge. I can't lose it. You can't just throw it away now. Anyway, the chances are that we'll never get it in one take.
EASTWOOD: Can I throw it left-handed?
ME: Clint, you can do it standing on your head if you want to. If I had an inkling that you were going to change your mind, I would have ordered at least twenty more.

I told Clint to practise with Bruce by throwing stones the same size as his badge into the sump. We laid a large, black cloth in the bottom of the sump, in the hope that we might recover it. Clint, cool and confident, with no nerves, took his one left-handed throw. Naturally, it was perfectly executed. He thanked me. I couldn't resist giving him a huge smile.

33

Charley Varrick

Universal 1972

Howard Rodman wrote the first draft of a screenplay entitled 'The Looters', based on the novel of the same title by John Reese. However, the studio simply didn't like his script and he was long gone. I worked differently with the second writer, Dean Riesner. I had already found most of the locations and explained to Dean that we would leave shortly for Genoa, Nevada, and would be staying at a new dude ranch, Sierra Shadows Lodge. I would show each location to Dean and he would the write the script, now entitled 'Last of the Independents'. For example, the small, sparsely populated town of Tres Cruces in our script would be shot in Genoa. The town's old, small two-storey museum would be the exterior location of the Tres Cruces Western Fidelity Bank.

ME: After you've finished writing the first sequence, we'll go over the second sequence. While you're writing that, I'll write down my suggestions on the first sequence. After rewriting the first sequence, you'll now have a third draft, instead of a first draft. However, we'll only refer to it as first draft. We'll work this way throughout the picture.

Dean worked easily and quickly. The front office liked his script and we were ready to start shooting the first of next week.

The leading character, Charley Varrick (Walter Matthau), is an independent crop-duster, a former stunt pilot in an air circus. However, what he really does is rob banks – small banks, in small, isolated towns. The take is small; but so is the risk. He doesn't want to hurt anyone, or to get hurt. Then one day he robs a bank in the little town of Tres Cruces, where the Mafia have temporarily deposited a quarter of a million dollars. When Charley realizes that he has inadvertently stolen the Mafia's money, for the first time in his life he has to think cerebrally. He must come up with the perfect crime. He must completely lose his identity. Someone must be dead who is thought to be Charley Varrick. He carefully lays his plan, but a Mafia hit-man, Molly (Joe Don Baker), is soon on his heels. The pair do battle on the crop-dusters' airstrip, Charley in his biplane, Molly at the wheel of his car, but in the end Varrick's perfect crime is executed.

Walter Matthau was set to star and he was the only person I knew who did not like the script. He sent me a cassette of his criticisms the moment he finished reading it. The tape is much too long to include here, but selections from it will give an idea of what a director is up against.

The two cops, Sanchez and Steele, may be superfluous. I don't believe them in the first place. I don't believe that Nadine would have a car running in front of a bank and Charley, with a cast on his foot, would go in and cash a cheque. I believe that the woman would naturally go in and cash a cheque if her husband had broken his ankle. Why wouldn't she do it? This also would serve the purpose of eliminating the two cops at the beginning; because, as I said, they're comic-opera buffoons. I mean, you start off with a very tough premise to swallow at the very beginning.

I think that there should be a device which explains what is happening. Since I have read it three times, and am of slightly better than average intelligence – 120 IQ – I still don't quite understand what's going on. Well, I really do understand what's going on, but only because it was explained to me. There's no way to explain to people sitting in the theatre what they're seeing; so why don't we explain it? Why don't we have a device?

For example, you show at the beginning of the picture a man telling this story to a story editor in a motion-picture company about what actually happened to him many years ago. That would be Charley Varrick, perhaps ten years after the picture starts, or maybe twenty. How old do you want to play him? Or you could have Charley on a psychiatrist's couch in Argentina – London would be better, because then he would be speaking English, in which he has to get this story of what happened to him out of his system – so that before each of the things happen, they are explained: his motives are explained, his reasons are explained, the things he's going to do are explained. They are so outlandish that if they're explained and then done, there will be a certain thrill, a certain satisfaction, a certain fulfilment for the audience . . .

The above small portion of Walter's recorded notes is typical. Walter wants to see the banana *before* he slips on it. I don't want everything explained and then see it. I want to see the banana *after* I slip on it.

*

Michael Butler, our young cameraman, who looked like a film star, was preparing to test his camera equipment before the first day of filming. He suggested to me that, while testing, it might be a good idea to shoot something for the main titles. I thought that made excellent sense. We shot a quiet, sleepy little town, yawning its way into the start of a new day.

We shot at dawn, starting with Walter's twelve-year-old son, Charles Matthau. He tried to put a saddle on an uncooperative burro. It was a draw. Kit, my younger daughter, aged seven and a half, ran through sprinkler heads as they were suddenly turned on. Anne, my elder daughter, aged thirteen, pushed a lawnmower with surprising strength. Nowell, my elder son, fourteen and a half, lurked in a wagon, whistling at passing girls. We found an eleven-year-old boy who owned a miniature racing car. He looked great fishtailing around a dirt lot. An older boy was sweeping leaves off the sidewalk. An elderly man opened his small post office by hanging an American flag in front of the entrance. Groups of kids, including my six-year-old son Jack, chased each other. There were other shots of the beautiful, serene countryside.

We shot without a script clerk. None of the shots was listed. Instead of marking the can of film 'Opening Main Titles', it was simply marked 'Camera Tests'. Consequently, my film editor, Frank Morriss, found it by accident only weeks later. When we finally saw the dailies, they looked great. It was a terrific lead into the start of the picture. After the tranquillity of the peaceful little town awakening, violence erupts outside and inside the bank.

*

At the Sierra Shadows Lodge, I had the only telephone in my room. Our first day of filming was to begin early in the morning. It was 1.35 a.m. when the phone rang. I picked it up, hoping it wasn't a drunk calling. It was Larry Butler, Michael's father and one of my best friends. He was a brilliant expert in optics. His voice sounded strained.

LARRY BUTLER: I've got bad news, Don. Mary just died. It was hopeless; my lovely wife suffering from cancer. Would you be kind enough to call Michael to the phone?
ME: I'm so terribly sorry, Larry. Hold on. I'll be right back with him. (*I rush over to Michael's room and knock loudly.*)
MICHAEL BUTLER: Who is it?
ME: Don.
(*He looks very sleepy when he opens the door.*)
ME: Your dad is on the phone. (*Hesitating.*) Your dear mother just passed away.

378

Tears welled up in his eyes, as they did in mine. We walked together back to my room. I put my arm around him. No one knew on the company, but I was Michael's godfather. I told him I would wait outside and I closed the door. I thought of his mother, half-English, half-Spanish. She was a very beautiful, spirited woman. She had a great sense of fun and was a devoted Catholic. I admired her energy and the respect and love she received from her three sons. Michael came out. He was crying quite freely.

ME: (*Trying to be strong*) How did your dad take it?
BUTLER: He's tough. He knew for many months that she was dying. He never told me.
ME: Michael, you can fly back tomorrow. After the funeral, we will start shooting.
BUTLER: No. I loved my mother deeply. She would want me to start the picture this morning.
ME: There's no problem. I can push the picture back three days. I could use the time to work on the script.
BUTLER: (*Hugging me*) Don, my father, my mother and I want me to work. I'll see you at breakfast.

He left. I'm afraid neither of us slept much before seeing each other at breakfast.

*

The first scene in the film is the robbery of the Western Fidelity Bank in the small town of Tres Cruces. Charley Varrick and his accomplice Harman (Andy Robinson) rush out of the bank, throw their sacks of money into a waiting car and get in. Charley's wife Nadine (Jacqueline Scott), who has been sitting behind the wheel, now rams it into drive.

At this point, Michael Butler and I had a meeting with the stunt co-ordinator, Paul Baxley, who was to wear a blonde wig and Nadine's clothes (the reason for her high-necked blouse and long sleeves), and Whitey McMahon, head of special effects. I explained slowly and deliberately what I wanted. Varrick's car, a Continental, slams into a deputy sheriff's car. The hood on the deputy's car springs open. The hood of the Continental is tied down firmly, so the Continental slides off into the parking lot and careens on to the highway, skidding out of the shot. Varrick and Harman were doubled by stuntmen. The special-effects men went to work on the cars. Michael and I set up five cameras, ranging from close shot, rear wheel of Continental, which pans with the car throughout the scene until it disappears down the highway; medium close shot, shooting down on the impact of the Continental smashing into the deputy's car; fuller shot of the Continental and deputy's car throughout

40   *Charley Varrick*: Walter Matthau

the shot with an Army Iron 16 mm camera hidden on the front of the
Continental, possibly to be used as shock effect as the cars collide. We
were ready. Michael re-checked all the cameras. He nodded to me that
everything was OK. I had a bullhorn in my hand.

ME: (*Into bullhorn*) After speed, Michael will check with each camera to find out if they have reached speed. Pay no attention to that. The only time you start the shot is when I yell 'Action!' Any questions?

The silence was deafening. The cameras rolled, Michael checked the speed on each camera. He gave me the OK, I yelled 'Action!' and the Continental lurched forward and smashed into the deputy's car. The engine hood did *not* spring open. The hood of the Continental sprung straight up, completely blocking Nadine's view. The scar skidded into the parking lot and started for the highway when I yelled, in disgust, 'Cut, cut, cut!' The Continental's engine was turned off. We checked if anyone in the cars was hurt. Everybody was OK. I got hold of Paul and Whitey.

ME: What the hell happened?
BAXLEY: (*Looking at Whitey*) Damned if I know.
WHITEY: I could have sworn the Continental's hood would never open. And the deputy's car's hood would spring open.
ME: (*To Michael*) How did the shot look to you before I yelled cut?
BUTLER: Great – except that they can't drive the Continental with the hood up.
BAXLEY: Shall we start repairing the cars?
ME: Don't touch them. You'll drive the Continental with the hood up. Start with a skid into the parking lot and, driving blind, careen on to the highway and down it. We will make a short exit.
BUTLER: That's hairier than what we planned.
ME: (*To Whitey and Paul*) All carefully planned by you two geniuses. At least now we don't have to waste time repairing the cars.

We made the shot of Paul, driving blind with the hood up, exiting short from the highway. Then I made a reverse of the real Nadine, her eyes showing nothing. I made a reverse close shot of Charley, showing concern. Behind him, Harman is yelling in fear. Nadine's point of view of the inside of the upright hood shows nothing but the hood.

I got alone with Paul and Whitey and explained that Paul had to hit the sheriff's car, driven by a stunt double, broadside. I didn't care what happened to the sheriff's car; but the Continental had to lose its hood, or it couldn't continue on its escape up the side dirt street that the sheriff's car has just appeared from. It would be nice if the sheriff's car overturned into the vegetables piled high in front of the small grocery. Sheriff Horton (William Schallert) was doubled by a stuntman, as was Horton's young deputy. I walked through the sequence with Michael, Paul and Whitey. As usual, no one saw any problems. We were ready to shoot. Again, I told Whitey over the bullhorn that I didn't care what happened; but lose the hood of the Continental *after* hitting the sheriff's car. I gave everyone my usual instructions about no one getting hurt. I spent quite a bit of time with Michael on laying out the shots. I asked Paul if it was safe to use a camera operator to film the sequence in the grocery store behind the vegetables. He nodded, 'Yes.' I turned to Michael and said, 'No way. Shoot it wild. I don't trust anyone.'

On 'Action!' the Continental, hood up, swayed from one side of the highway to the other. The sheriff's car came flying down the side street, siren blaring and red lights flashing. The Continental hit the sheriff's car broadside, overturning it into the grocery store, where, according to Paul, it was safe to position a camera operator. The Continental went slithering down the highway, still with the hood up. Paul spun the car vigorously and, finally, the damned hood fell off. Paul turned sharply right up the dirt road that the sheriff's car had come down. I screamed through the bullhorn, 'Cut! Cut! Cut! Check the sheriff's car!' No one was hurt, thank God, in either car. I yelled to Michael to see if the cameras were OK. He reported back that everything was perfect.

I had a meeting with our production manager, Dick McWhorter, and Michael, Paul and Whitey.

ME: Thanks to Paul's spinning the Continental, we got rid of the hood. Whitey, your work is unsatisfactory. I suggest you work closer with Paul and Michael. Dick, I'd like to suggest we stick with the Continental until we finish with it. Is that all right with you?

MCWHORTER: I think it's a good idea.

ME: Please set it up on the dirt road leading to the upper highway for tomorrow's work. We will need the doubles for our principals and the van fully dressed. Thanks for a lucky first day.

*

Naturally, we were a happy group. I was a mite short of being a genius. Someone brought up the question of titles. I asked them why they thought the title 'Last of the Independents' was changed to *Charley Varrick*. No one had the foggiest idea. I explained that at least twenty people at Universal thought I was nuts changing the title. They all reacted the same way when I told them that I hadn't changed the title – Lew Wasserman had. An abrupt change occurred as they sputtered in embarrassment: 'Well, I can understand – Varrick is a very uncommon name.' They all hastened away from me.

We were doing something on this picture that I've never seen before. We started with the burning of the name 'Charley Varrick' as the first title of the main titles; and the exact same shot would be used as the last shot of the end titles. In using the title 'Last of the Independents', it had been my intention to burn 'Last of the Independents' as the first and last title of the picture. However, Wasserman didn't like the title, so I gladly accepted *Charley Varrick* so that I wouldn't lose, what I fear, was a gimmick. I thought the title 'Last of the Independents' made sense. Charley was the last of the independent crop-dusters; but, more importantly, the last of the independent bank robbers. In my opinion, a great picture makes a great title. A great title doesn't make a great picture.

*

The Continental, minus hood, laboured up the ruts of the road, Nadine driving, slewing and sun-fishing. Charley and Harman hung on in the jouncing, bumping car. Their point of view (through the windshield) up ahead was a locked chain-link fence across the road, barring their way. Varrick yelled to Nadine to 'Bust into it!' and she stepped on the gas – and slipped through it like butter. I yelled, 'Cut it! Cut!'

41 *Charley Varrick*: the Continental smashing through the fence

I ran up to Whitey and yelled for Paul, who was driving the Continental.

ME: (*To Whitey*) I have a pretty good idea of what you must think of directors. I spent seven years in special effects at Warners and, without a doubt, you are the most incompetent head special-effects man I've ever had the displeasure of working with.
(*Paul comes running over, followed by Michael.*)
ME: I want that fence to hold and scratch and damage the car as it fights its way through it. (*To Paul.*) Paul, see to it that this fence, made out of the softest lead in America, is strengthened. Use anything that's strong. (*To Michael.*) We'll re-do the shot. Leave the cameras where they are and help on this fence.

We reshot the Continental smashing through the fence. It was better than our first effort, but could have been improved. I decided to push on with our filming.

*

The manager of the Tres Cruces bank, Harold Young (Woodrow Parfrey), sits nervously in his car at the Travel-on-Inn Motel. Maynard Boyle (John Vernon), President of Western Fidelity, appears and gets into Young's car.

YOUNG: I've got to talk to you.
BOYLE: (*Fingers to lips*) Not now, Harold.

Young drives out of the parking lot and down a highway, which leads to the countryside. Young starts to say something, but again Boyle insists on silence.
    The car comes up past a farm with silos and barns. Young veers off the blacktop on to the shoulder, past a fenced pasture with a herd of Holsteins grazing. He stops. The two men get out. It is late afternoon. The two car doors slamming has a feeling of openness and echo. They walk away from the car. Young waits for Boyle to speak first. The camera moves with them as they walk alongside the fence.

BOYLE: I don't suppose they could get a bug into my motel room or your car this fast; but it never hurts to be careful.
YOUNG: They'd have to get a court order to install a listening device.
(*They have come to the end of the fence and move down to the white pasture gate, the camera always following them. Boyle looks off at the emerald expanse of pasture with the entire valley beyond. He stares at the Holsteins.*)

BOYLE: I never thought I'd be willing to trade places with a cow.

YOUNG: A cow?

BOYLE: They *are* cows, aren't they?

YOUNG: I don't understand the thrust of your comment.

BOYLE: What's the worst thing that can happen to them? A short circuit in the electric milker? Compared to what I'm facing, that's child's play.

YOUNG: Are you talking about the Las Vegas people?

BOYLE: (*Nods*) They're going to ask me why did I pick this *particular* bank – and believe me, from where they sit, it looks damned peculiar.

YOUNG: Surely they don't suspect you?

BOYLE: Harold, you and I are the only ones who knew all the money was going to be in the bank.

YOUNG: Then they suspect me too . . .
(*Boyle nods his head.*)

YOUNG: Good God, Maynard, *you* don't think I had anything to do with it?

BOYLE: Of course not. I believe you, Harold. I just hope they do when the time comes. They're going to ask questions. The one time we really load up – bang, this little horseshit bank, a million miles from nowhere, gets hit by four professionals. Now they're going to think that's peculiar . . .

YOUNG: Well, admittedly it's —

BOYLE: (*Talking through*) They're going to think it's odd that you just trotted right over and opened the vault.

YOUNG: I had a gun at my head. Don't you understand?

BOYLE: I understand perfectly. It's our Mafia friends – they'll want to know why you took them directly to the vault with the money in it, rather than the empty vault in the rear. And frankly – why did you do that?

YOUNG: Surely you know what would have happened if I had taken those people to an empty vault?

BOYLE: The money would have been saved and there'd be no question of an inside job.

YOUNG: Inside job?

BOYLE: That's the way their diseased minds work. A bank gets hit. They look for a double cross.
(*Young turns away, close to breaking.*)

YOUNG: I don't know what to do. I don't know what to do.

BOYLE: You need a rest. A trip to another country. Another name.

42 *Charley Varrick*: Maynard Boyle (John Vernon) comforts Harold Young
(Woodrow Parfrey)

YOUNG: (*Turns back to Boyle*) I can't start my life again.
BOYLE: They'll try to make you tell where the money is. They'll strip
    you naked and go to work with a pair of pliers and a blow torch.
YOUNG: Oh, my God.
BOYLE: If it's a matter of money, Harold, I can help.
    (*Young puts his face in his hands. Boyle puts his arm around him
    and leads him back towards his car.*)

This sequence, shot in its entirety from a Titan boom, is one of the most
difficult I've ever attempted. The sun is setting slowly behind us.
Throughout the valley, a shadow is crossing, matching the setting sun. I
had to time the length of the scene with the time it took for the sun to set.
The actors had to be letter-perfect. It was a difficult scene to play and to
stage. My first effort ended in failure. I simply ran out of sunlight. The
second attempt, late the next afternoon, failed because I started shooting
too soon. I finished the scene just as the shadows started to appear. My

third try, the third afternoon, proved successful due to luck, the wonderful acting of John Vernon and Woodrow Parfrey and the superb work of Michael Butler and his magnificent crew.

*

It was about 7 a.m. when I arrived at the location of Charley Varrick's hangar to begin shooting Charley's confrontation with the hit-man, Molly. Larry Butler, Michael's father, was with me: he was going to help special effects and Michael rig up a Steerman biplane on a large, flat truck bed so that I could shoot close-ups of Varrick apparently flying the plane. The moment we got out of the car, I knew something was wrong. We were surrounded by the entire production staff, Michael and his crew, the special-effects men and the stuntmen, including Frank Tallman, the stunt pilot of the biplane. No one was working. All were trying to talk at once.

ME: Whoa! One at a time, please!

PRODUCTION ASSISTANT: The owner of the junkyard (*pointing*), over there, refuses to let us shoot.

MICHAEL BUTLER: He's got a big new trailer parked right where we can't miss seeing it.

BAXLEY: (*Pointing*) There's the owner of the junkyard, his two brothers and a lawyer.

ME: Where is Dick McWhorter?

PRODUCTION ASSISTANT: He hasn't shown up yet.

ME: Get him on the phone, or send one of the cars searching for him. In the meantime, I'd like Michael, Larry, Paul and anyone from production to accompany me to find out what's wrong.
(*Our group meets with the group standing resolutely in front of the trailer. I introduce myself as the producer/director. I make it clear that as the producer, I have no authority to make deals. The angry owner breaks in.*)

OWNER: You'll have to make a deal, or you ain't shootin' my yard. What happened to the bald-headed son of a bitch who lied to us about what you were going to do to my yard?

ME: Mr McWhorter will be here in a few minutes. I want to know what was done that was wrong.

LAWYER: My client had no knowledge that his yard was going to be so messed up that he couldn't find the parts that buyers were looking for. It put him out of business.

ME: The yard is a junkyard. What losses have you incurred?

LAYWER: It's cost him a hundred thousand dollars. It's a salvage yard, not a junk yard.

387

ME: That certainly strikes me as exorbitant. The company I work for, Universal Pictures, won't stand still to be blackmailed. Why did you wait until we were ready to film before letting us know that you were breaking a signed deal?

LAWYER: That's what we want and that is what we're going to get.

ME: Universal can play very rough. (*McWhorter approaches.*) My advice to you, sir, is to come way down in your demands, or you'll wind up being sued for certain. Instead of getting money, you'll be paying it out.

(*A very angry McWhorter arrives.*)

ME: Dick, get this settled. In the meantime, I'll work out what I can shoot without this salvage yard.

(*As we walk back to the hangar to have our production meeting, we hear McWhorter screaming at the four men.*)

ME: Get a long table, chairs, coffee and doughnuts and put it in the hangar. We'll work out a new schedule. Also, get me Marshall Green on the phone.

(*The hangar is soon filled with our crew. I grab a styrofoam cup of black coffee and finally get Marshall on the phone. I explain everything to him.*)

GREEN'S VOICE: Don, you can shoot at a local junkyard near the studio.

ME: It's a salvage yard. I want to give McWhorter a little more time. He still might win. Anyway, we have plenty to do. We're about to make out a new schedule of shots I can definitely make without shooting towards the salvage yard. I need you to come to the location immediately.

GREEN'S VOICE: (*After a long pause*) OK, Don. Let me talk to McWhorter.

ME: I'll have him call you as soon as he's free. I hope, by that time, you'll be on your way here. I'm putting on our transportation captain. He'll give you the flight schedules and will arrange to pick you up. Here's transportation.

(*I hand the phone to the transportation captain and go back to the table to discuss what we can shoot without the salvage yard.*)

ME: Speak up, anyone, if you don't agree with me, or if you have other ideas. First, we can shoot the hangar with the Steerman biplane, its wheels in chocks, facing towards Reno. Nothing else in this shot. Second, we can shoot Charley's phone conversation with Sybil Fort (Felicia Farr) inside the hangar. Then he puts overalls on over his new outfit. His wristwatch is missing. His wedding ring is missing and he's only wearing Nadine's ring on his left pinky. Third, Charley fastens the hangar doors, goes to the biplane, removes the chocks from under the wheels and climbs into the cockpit. He puts on his goggles and crash helmet. He starts the motor, which is apparently warm, releases the brakes and takes off down the airstrip, past the long line of telephone poles. The biplane slowly lifts in the air towards Reno. Fourth, the biplane arrives at Reno airport. Fifth, the biplane leaves Reno on its way back to the airstrip. Now, let's set up the first shot. Larry, get with Whitey and work out the rig for shooting the biplane on the truck bed. We'll shoot close-ups of Matthau on the ground and in the air. Get with me when you're ready.

TRANSPORTATION CAPTAIN: I'm picking up Marshall Green at ten thirty a.m. Should be here by eleven.

ME: Thanks.

(*McWhorter appears, his face still red with anger.*)

ME: Call Marshall. You might just catch him. He'll be at the location by eleven.

Somebody, I know it wasn't me, came up with a brilliant idea. There were two junkyards buttressed against the salvage yard. Our boys planned to move yard 3 and place it in front of yard 1. That way, we wouldn't be bothered with what we might see in yard 1. It's very unlikely we'd see anything but a blur of junk. They would also move the hangar about 100 feet down the airstrip and nobody would be the wiser. We would have total control. It would mean working night and day – an enormous amount of hard work. The cost would be small, as we would replace all the cars back on yard 3 when we were completely finished.

Several hours later, Marshall showed up at the location with McWhorter in tow. Marshall still thought we could finish the picture within a reasonable distance of the studio. I flatly disagreed. Marshall was told about moving the salvage yard in front of the junkyards and when it was explained that no one would be able to tell we had moved the hangar approximately 100 feet from where it now stood, he gave in. I called Larry and Whitey over.

ME: Show Marshall what you've got planned.

(*Larry quickly draws a large flatbed. He fastens a simple round gimbal to the bed of the truck and runs a pipe to the biplane, which will hold the biplane in any position we want, within reason.*)

GREEN: (*To Whitey*) Will Butler's plan work?

WHITEY: (*Nodding*) But it will cost a lot of money.
ME: What kind of money are you talking about?
WHITEY: About three hundred dollars.
   (*I didn't even look at Marshall. I immediately order Whitey to build it.*)
ME: Marshall, this will give me plenty of shots to make while our boys fix up the salvage yard.

I thanked Larry for helping us out. I told Marshall to take care of Larry's expenses – no salary – as I didn't want him to lay out a dime of his own money. Again, Marshall agreed, at last thanking Larry for his kindness in helping Universal.

   I had lunch with Marshall alone in my trailer. What bothered him most was McWhorter's being late on the set in the morning.

ME: To the best of my knowledge McWhorter has always been on the set before anyone else.
GREEN: Could you get along without him?
ME: Dick is a hard worker and most knowledgeable. If there was any weakness, in this instance this morning, McWhorter, being Scotch, felt that once a deal was signed, that was it. I felt that perhaps he was being too stubborn in not trying to make a new deal. Maybe giving those crooks, say, five thousand dollars might have settled the whole issue. But I still hate the thought of working without him. If you insist, I'll go reluctantly with whatever you want me to do. At least Mr Wasserman will feel that you've taken care of the mess. (*Getting up.*) When they've moved the hangar and all the junk cars, I can finish every shot with the biplane, the Chrysler and the characters of Varrick, Boyle and Molly.
GREEN: That means you'll complete the ending.
ME: Keep it our secret. Many thanks for coming up. I really appreciate it. I'm going to juggle the schedule so that the boys will have plenty of time, without overtime.

After seeing the Steerman biplane disappear in the sky towards Reno, I said goodbyes to Marshall Green and Dick McWhorter. Then I spoke to the rest of the production department, Larry Butler, Michael Butler and his crew, propmen and Paul Baxley. We were gathered again in the hangar.

ME: I've fixed the schedule so that Paul and his boys won't have to kill themselves changing the yards. Get anything you may need to move the hangar whatever distance is necessary. Paul, work out

390

with Frank Tallman, when he returns, how deep and wide he needs the new yard to be to flip his biplane. As for everyone else, we will shoot all the Reno sequences, both day and night scenes. If we do this, it will give Paul enough time to get ready for us. Considering what we've gone through, we had a good day, thanks to all of you. Now, we've got to move fast. Any questions?

BAXLEY: How much time do we have?

ME: At least three full days. Be sure to talk things over with Tallman and stay with Whitey to be sure it's ready. Production staff, be sure our cast is notified. Check out the super apartment I picked to shoot the scenes with Walter and Farr. Good luck.

*

A car drives up to the crop-dusters' airstrip. It stops by the hangar in the early morning. The door opens. Boyle gets out and looks around. The camera pans around the area, past the hangar, past the empty field, past the junkyards. Boyle starts walking towards the middle of the airstrip. Charley Varrick, in the cockpit of his biplane, flies towards the airstrip. Boyle now stands about a quarter of a mile from the hangar. He hears the sound of the biplane's motor. He looks off and, at last, finds a speck in the sky. The camera zooms in. The speck becomes Charley's biplane.

Charley drops down, looking left and right. He sees Boyle in the middle of the strip. Now he looks ahead at the salvage yard. He flies past Boyle and drops low over the junkyard, just skimming over the first car in the yard. Charley barely sees the maroon Chrysler that Molly drives, somewhat hidden by the debris. The camera zooms in as Molly is hunched down; there is just a fleeting glimpse of him. Close on Charley in cockpit (this and other close shots of Charley in the plane were shot on a gimbal of the plane on a flat bed). Charley begins to smile. His perfect crime is beginning to work.

The biplane banks left as he returns to Boyle, then touches down. Charley taxis to Boyle, blowing dust, gunning his engine and applying his brakes. Molly leans forwards, peering through the windshield. He sees the biplane come to a stop, the propeller idling. Charley gets out of the plane, jumps off the wing, hurrying towards Boyle; he is jubilant. He has taken off his helmet and goggles. Charley runs up to Boyle, in a close shot, and hugs him, dancing with joy.

VARRICK: We did it! We pulled it off! Put on my helmet and goggles.

At the same time, Boyle is trying, unsuccessfully, to avoid Charley's ebullience.

391

BOYLE: What are you talking about, you crazy bastard? Take your
   hands off me!

Close shot of Molly's face, his worst suspicions about Boyle confirmed.
He releases the brake of the Chrysler and guns out. The car leaps
forwards and careens through the alley of wrecked cars on to the
airstrip. He sees Charley and Boyle still wrestling around. Charley and
Boyle look at the Chrysler hurtling towards them; there is a frozen
moment. Then Charley bolts for the biplane. Boyle runs away from it.
Molly veers off towards the running Boyle, who looks over his shoulder
and sees Molly coming after him. Boyle stops, facing the pursuing car.
As the speeding car nears, Boyle feints to his left. Molly goes for the
feint, swinging the wheel, as Boyle dives in the opposite direction. As the
Chrysler's nose goes past Boyle, Molly grins and swings into a deliberate
skid. The rear end of the Chrysler whips around and hits Boyle, sending
his body cartwheeling 100 feet. Molly stops and sees that Boyle's
crushed body is dead.

   I spoke with Paul Baxley and Frank Tallman. I told them they could
choreograph the Chrysler's pursuit of the biplane anywhere on the
airstrip, across the endless fields and anywhere near and in the junkyard.

ME: I'd like it to be as exciting as possible. Do as much damage as
   makes sense, but remember, nobody gets hurt. You are on your
   own, excepting I don't want to overturn the biplane in this shot.
   I'll have one wide angle that will hold the Chrysler and the
   biplane. A second, closer camera will follow the Chrysler wherever
   it goes. A third camera will follow the biplane close, wherever it
   goes. I'll have two cameras with close-up lenses that will follow
   the Chrysler and biplane. On the Chrysler, I'll hide an Army Iron
   .16 camera. I'll do the same with the biplane.

Michael and I watched the areas that Paul and Frank covered. Michael
suggested that we shoot at different heights. I found myself safely
ensconced on a 10-foot parallel. My camera followed the biplane. Finally,
we were ready to go – Tallman, of course, in the biplane, Baxley in the
Chrysler. I yelled 'Action' and Paul tore after the biplane. Tallman got
away, time after time; but he never left the ground. Actually Paul, on
occasions, obviously had to slow up, or he would have smashed the
biplane. I realized something was wrong and yelled 'Cut' into a powerful
bullhorn. In my disappointment, I jumped off the parallel and on to the
field. The biplane and Chrysler surrounded me. I shouted for the engines
to be turned off, then I asked what happened.

TALLMAN: I did my best to get away from the Chrysler, but it was too fast for me.

BAXLEY: I tried to make it look real, Don, but I didn't want to seriously damage the biplane.

ME: Did either one of you ever read the script?

TALLMAN/BAXLEY: Of course.

ME: (*Opening up my script*) I'll read just part of page twenty-nine. It looks like goodbye Charley, when suddenly the airplane gives a little spavined *jump* into the sky. The Chrysler shoots right under the biplane. The biplane staggers *up in the air* again at just the precise moment of projected impact. The Chrysler shoots *under the plane. The plane settles back to the ground*, the Chrysler swings back to ram again, *the plane rises weakly in the air again* at the very last moment, etc., etc.

TALLMAN: This airstrip, the whole countryside, has an altitude of four thousand five hundred feet. It's all I can do with a long run to get it up in the air for flying.

ME: Then why in the hell didn't you tell me? You're supposed to let me know if you can't give me what the script calls for. (*Turning to Paul.*) And Paul, what about you? Surely *you*, my brilliant stunt co-ordinator, knew that you were at an altitude of four thousand five hundred feet. I can't believe that you two prized idiots never thought to tell me that you couldn't give me what the script calls for.

BAXLEY: I thought you knew.

ME: What you mean to say is that you didn't know a goddamn thing. Well, let's get our three stupid heads together and figure our way out of this mess. I'm bitterly disappointed with both of you.

TALLMAN: The only way I can get the plane to bounce over the car is to be in the air. When I hit the ground, Paul will have to time it so that when I hit the ground, his car will be in the right place for me to bounce over it.

BAXLEY: That'll work.

ME: Thank God. It's going to add to our schedule, so keep your mouths shut. We are trying to make an exciting sequence, not shoot a schedule. Start practising. Our cameras are ready for everything. Paul, you might also, at a later date, build a ramp which can show you going over the plane while it is moving on the ground. Good luck. Don't panic into anything that might get you hurt.

At this moment of failure, the timing was perfect. I was notified – not asked, but told – that George Roy Hill, an excellent director, was coming out to see me shoot the biplane attached to the gimbal on the large flatbed truck. That's all I needed: to have a director watch me shoot when, as had just happened, I might fail. Also, I didn't like being told: I insist on being asked. Later George Roy Hill wrote me a nasty letter about the lack of co-operation between directors. I answered that if I were going to visit his set, I would at least have sense enough to ask the director for permission. I ended by noticing that his letter was belligerent. That was OK with me, as I was kind of feisty too. Months passed before we made up. He understood why I didn't want him on my set. Later, when he made *The Great Waldo Pepper*, he used the rig that Larry Butler had invented and I had used successfully on *Charley Varrick*. Hill used it a great deal, as his picture was all about flying. So all's well that ends well.

In talking to Michael, he felt that we already had many shots that could be gainfully used in putting the sequence together. In fact, he bet me that we didn't need to re-shoot it. What we needed now were specially planned short shots, such as the biplane bouncing over the Chrysler, plus a shot or two of the Chrysler zooming over the biplane. So, even though the necessary extra shots were difficult and time-consuming, we might not do too badly. One thing did bother him. How could Paul be so careless in using a very heavy Chrysler? He should have used a Mercedes 190 SL, which would fly through the air with the greatest of ease.

We started shooting with the biplane circling overhead. Below the plane, in the Chrysler, was Paul, ready to speed to the point where the biplane hit the ground and bounced. As the biplane descended, Paul judged how fast he had to go to be at the exact place where the biplane was to bounce over his car. I crossed my fingers for luck. The biplane bounced over the racing Chrysler with what looked like inches to spare. I yelled 'Cut' and our entire crew applauded. They did three more shots in different areas, all done the same way, all very hairy indeed.

I got together with Tallman and Paul, accompanied by Michael, and shook their hands in congratulations. I suggested we made two shots of the Chrysler zooming over the biplane, then called it a lucky day.

ME: Paul, you need practice without the plane to find out if you can get that heavy Chrysler over the plane. If you feel it won't work, forget it. We will put the biplane on the gimbal and make close-ups of Matthau to cover all the sequences on the ground and in the air. (*Speaking through bullhorn to the entire crew.*) It's a wrap! All labourers and grips, check with Paul Baxley. He needs your help

394

and is in charge. (*Turning to Tallman, lowering bullhorn.*) Frank, I think you should be with Paul, so there are no surprises for you. If you feel uncomfortable, we won't make the shots tomorrow morning.

*

Paul had built a ramp at either end of the field. Frank was in his plane when Paul showed me, at high speed, how high he could go up in the air when he hit the ramp. I called them both over to me.

ME: How do you feel about it, Frank?

TALLMAN: There's not much room for a margin of error. I'll swing sharply left if I think Paul's not going to make it.

BAXLEY: And I'll swing sharply right if I feel I'm going to hit him.

ME: OK. Go ahead and make it. Can you crank that Chrysler any faster, Paul? It's supposed to be able to go a hundred and forty miles per hour. Frankly, you looked like you were driving a heavy truck.

BAXLEY: If the son-of-a-bitch can do a hundred and forty, that's what I'll be doing.

ME: Of course, I want and we need the shot. But if you're not certain you can clear Frank's biplane, veer off. Nobody's going to get hurt in our ball game. Is that clear?

Both men nodded. They warmed up their engines and each signalled me that he was ready. I crossed my fingers, my legs, my arms, and through the bullhorn I yelled to the soundman to let me know when he had 'speed' (that means that the film is rolling through the various cameras twenty-four frames a foot). He confirmed, and I yelled, through the bullhorn, 'Whenever you're ready, take your own "Action"!'

After an eternity, Paul sounded his horn so Tallman would know he was about to take off. I watched the Chrysler, although my camera was on the vibrating biplane. Paul floored the Chrysler from the very start, which caused him to skid and slide. He quickly had it under control and, at full speed, went straight at the camouflaged ramp. He hit it hard and took off through the air. Frank perfectly timed his plane and got through by maybe an inch. I screamed 'Cut!' Everyone cheered.

Paul and Frank slowly wheeled their vehicles to us and turned their engines off. As they got out, I rushed over to them.

BAXLEY: A cup of tea.

TALLMAN: I threw up. He outweighed me by several tons.

ME: Both of you did splendidly.

395

43   *Charley Varrick*: the stunt with the biplane and the Chrysler

BAXLEY: Thank you. Shall we get ready to shoot the second ramp?
ME: No. That's the last ramp for the two of you. I know now I
   shouldn't have shot it. Never again. We are all damn lucky. Let's
   walk away from it. Larry, Michael, Whitey, Frank and Paul, let's
   rig the Steerman biplane on to the gimbal. We'll spend at least the
   rest of the day proving what a magnificent pilot Mr Matthau is.
   Hop to it and many thanks.
   (*Walter and his son, Charlie, come up to me. Walter is
   uncharacteristically excited.*)
MATTHAU: Gee whiz, that was some shot.
ME: Do you realize that's the first kind thing you've said to me about
   any shot in the film?
MATTHAU: It's the first thing I've seen that I like.
CHARLIE: Mr Siegel is a great director.
MATTHAU: Charlie, I've told Mr Siegel if he ever shot a decent script,
   he would be the greatest director extant.
ME: Unfortunately, I can't continue this absurd conversation. I have to
   oversee the preparation of you actually in the cockpit, in the air
   and travelling on the ground. Please excuse me; particularly you,
   Charlie. As for you, Mr Matthau, I find you a joy to work with;

but what you have to say about the script I find particularly stupid.

I left in a hurry to see if the biplane was already attached to the gimbal. Tallman was climbing into the cockpit. Under the direction of Larry, they dipped the wing precariously to the left, to the right, up and down. Michael was setting up three cameras. I looked through them: a close-up of Frank, a close shot of Frank and a fuller shot of the plane, showing Frank looking over the sides, the tilting wings showing in the shot. The cameras were fastened to the bed of the truck. It looked real to me and I complimented Larry on his rig. I whispered to Michael.

ME: You've got quite a dad.

MICHAEL BUTLER: He's the best. So is my godfather.

ME: That'll be the day. (*To Tallman.*) What do you think, Frank?

TALLMAN: I've been flying these crates longer than Michael has years. It's the best rig I've ever seen.

ME: Larry, what are you going to pull it with?

LARRY BUTLER: The small generator. It will take less rigging. If we ruin any dialogue, and there's not much of it, we'll loop it.

ME: When will you be ready?

LARRY BUTLER: It's up to Michael when he gets it lit. All the lights have to be fastened on the flatbed and all the lights tied into the generator.

MICHAEL BUTLER: I need about thirty minutes. Can I have Matthau dressed and in the cockpit?
(*Three production men, one make-up man, one wardrobe man and one hairdresser speed to Walter's trailer. I go with them. Walter greets us.*)

MATTHAU: Do you realize, gentlemen, that I shall actually fly this fragile biplane off to the blue horizon?

ME: Why aren't you ready to fly, with six parachutes strapped on and a football crash helmet?

MATTHAU: I find your concern for my well-being touching.

ME: For the ground stuff, Baxley will pursue you on all sides. We will try to make it as similar as the shot we made yesterday, where he chased the plane all over the field.
(*The make-up and wardrobe men pay no attention to us, but attack Walter with speed and finesse.*)

The moment of truth arrived. I told Walter to give me all his standard reactions of fear, low cunning, pleasure, alarm and a feeling of success.

397

Given that Walter Matthau is world famous as the most mobile face in the industry, he had no trouble at all.

I asked Paul if he had communication with the driver of the generator. Paul had radio communications with him, as there would be a great deal of noise. On Paul's single shots, I would shoot at twenty frames a foot, so that he would appear to be going faster. He liked that. He told me that the driver knew the route he wanted to travel. Paul was going to try to cover the same shots as in his first attempt the previous day.

ME: Need I add, watch yourself and the biplane. I don't want you, or the plane, to get damaged.
BAXLEY: What about Matthau?
ME: He's indestructible. Good luck.

They took off at a snail's pace; but as they progressed they went faster and faster. Not only did Matthau run the gamut of emotion, but Paul did more near misses than I thought was possible. The biplane took a beating, but survived in one shaky piece. Michael worked the dipping and lifting of the wings, which was sheer ballet.

We printed the take and decided to rearrange our cameras for the simulated flights in the air. I decided to make more shots of Matthau on the ground, where he looks back. With cameras behind Matthau, we made shots of him glancing behind him at the pursuing Chrysler. By now he was rehearsed, and was amazed at how real the shots looked. When I printed take 1, part of the Siegel/Eastwood credo, I told Walter that he was more realistic than Frank. He was not one to let an opportunity for sarcasm pass.

MATTHAU: I don't consider that a compliment. How dare you compare me to a man with one leg? Of course I'm more realistic than Tallman. I'm frozen stiff with fright.

Our next flight was with Tallman, descending over the landing strip with cameras on the actual flying biplane. We were shooting past him in flying helmet, goggles and overalls as he flies over the junkyard, getting as close as possible to the Chrysler surrounded with wrecked cars, with Joe Don Baker, as Molly, almost hidden. I asked Tallman if he thought he might have had a glimpse of Joe Don in the car. He said it was impossible, although the flying shots must have looked good.

I got hold of Michael and explained that there was more than one way to skin a cat.

ME: How about stripping an Arriflex sixteen millimetre camera of its sound covering and attaching it in its skeleton form to the top of a Titan crane, with a fifteen-foot extension? You operate it. We'll attach a long, heavy rope to the top. We'll get grips and labourers to pull it down as hard as they can. As it sweeps past Joe Don Baker, hiding in the car, it will look like the biplane swooped down on it. God knows what will happen to you if you hit the ground; but talk to your Dad and your grip and find out what they think.

Michael was off like a shot, confident it would work. It would cut in great with the biplane starting to dive at the Chrysler. We made three passes at swooping down on the Chrysler. Michael was certain he saw Joe Don Baker looking up on the third take. I printed the three takes. Tomorrow, we would have Paul forcing the biplane into the junkyard.

*

When we shot Baxley forcing Tallman to enter the junkyard, he did it by hitting the biplane with the Chrysler. I was afraid that the plane was going to crack up, as was Tallman. It certainly appeared that Tallman had to crash into the junkyard. To our audience's surprise, the biplane goes right into the yard. But we see, as part of the perfect crime, that the biplane is going down on a pre-cleared path in the yard. The implacable Chrysler is right on the plane's tail. Without warning, Tallman attempts to flip the plane on its back. Up it goes, totters a moment, then falls back upright on all three wheels. I yelled 'Cut!' Tallman was carefully examining his plane, and all was well.

TALLMAN: I thought I had enough speed to flip the plane. (*To Paul.*) You had me worried, Paul. The plane felt like it was disintegrating.
BAXLEY: As soon as the Chrysler touches you, Frank, I jam on my brakes, or veer off. Let's pack down the cleared entrance so you can go faster.
ME: It was a damn good try, Frank. As soon as you and Paul are ready, we'll shoot. I still don't understand how you can tip the plane over on its back without getting hurt.
TALLMAN: Believe me, Don, I'm nice and cosy. Quit worrying.

After repairing any structural weaknesses in the biplane, Frank and Paul yelled out that they were ready. The plan was to start farther away from the entrance to the junkyard, so that Frank would have more distance to gain speed to flip his plane. On 'Action', the biplane started, first with the

Chrysler coming in on the side and literally hitting the biplane forward. When Frank's biplane did a nose dive, the plane lifted up in the air, nose on the ground, hesitated at the top and, in slow motion, slowly fell forward on its back upside down. It hit hard in a cloud of dust. Frank hung upside down, his goggles and helmet in place. He was motionless in his harness. Pulling up in the background and stopping was Paul. I screamed, 'First aid! First aid!' I forgot to yell 'Cut!' Frank slowly lifted his arm free and circled his thumb against his forefinger, signalling that he was OK. We all let out a loud cheer. The stillman took several polaroids of Frank's position, so Walter could duplicate it. Frank was carefully lifted out of the biplane, got to his feet and smiled at Paul.

TALLMAN: Just a cup of tea.

Special effects carefully drained out the small amount of gasoline still in the tank of the plane. No smoking was the order of the day. I put my arm around Tallman.

ME: I've got a confession to make to you. I wasn't going for a third try.
TALLMAN: I wasn't either.

*

Joe Don Baker and Matthau met me in my trailer. We started talking about what they faced in the coming scene.

ME: Naturally, we'll go over the lines and what I want you to do, Joe, so Walter won't have to hang upside down any longer than absolutely necessary. And by the way, can you hang upside down without fainting?
MATTHAU: My dear Don, I've been hung from trees with a rope around my neck. I've hung from my heels, held by a Mafia gorilla, out of a window, until I agreed to pay my usual gambling debt. I was born upside down. I think and make love upside down.

We went over the dialogue a number of times; both of them knew it perfectly. I showed them the logistics of where the money was hidden, what happened when Molly tried to get it and where Charley's escape car was. They were ready. All I had to do was to get with Michael and lay out the shots.

I had to have a cut-away to Molly, after the biplane is flipped over on its back. Molly, in his maroon Chrysler, skids to a bruising stop near the overturned plane. He gets out of his car, then he slowly smiles. His point-of-view shot shows a helpless Charley, imprisoned in the flipped biplane, hanging upside down. We dolly with Molly, his expression now benign, as he takes out a pipe and leans down against the plane, studying Charley, who is bleeding out of the side of his mouth. Charley's point of view of Molly is that he is upside down. Molly takes off Charley's helmet and goggles. His face is bloody.

VARRICK: (*Weakly*) I'll make a deal with you.
MOLLY: (*Sniffing*) Smell that gasoline. I'll bet this thing would burn in a hurry. (*Taps his pipe against the fuselage.*)
VARRICK: I know where the money is. You'll never find it without my help.
MOLLY: And your end is what?
VARRICK: Just help me out of here and let me go.
MOLLY: (*Lighting pipe*) Where's the money?
VARRICK: We got a deal?
(*Molly smiles. There is a pause, then Charley comes to a decision.*)
VARRICK: In my right coat pocket, there's car keys.
(*Molly puts his hand into the pocket and retrieves the car keys.*)
VARRICK: That green Essex over there. In the trunk.
(*Molly looks off and sees an old, green wreck.*)
VARRICK: I'm trusting you.
MOLLY: I'll be back.

Molly smiles and pats Charley's upside down cheek. He moves off towards the green car. The car is in the foreground, the upside-down aircraft in the background. Charley watches as Molly stops at the trunk of the car, looks off at Charley, then puts the key into the trunk lock. As Molly lifts the lid of the trunk, the trunk light goes on. Sitting in the trunk is the dead body of Harman. He is dressed in Charley's clothes. The two canvas and leather bags, with 'Tres Cruces Bank' stencilled on them, are in his folded arms. All this is taken in a flash, zooming in to Harman's left hand and wrist. He is wearing Charley's wristwatch and wedding ring. There is a close shot of Molly, in shock. He snaps a quick look at Charley, who is hopelessly ensnarled in his safety straps.

The car trunk suddenly blows up. Molly and the car are blown to hell. The burst of flame and smoke obscures the screen.

Charley, with surprising ease, frees himself. The Essex is burning fiercely in the background. Charley quickly drops out of the upside-down biplane. He gains his feet and reaches back up into the cockpit and hauls out two green plastic garbage bags full of money. We dolly with him as he passes the blazing car, carrying his plastic bags, crossing to a blue 1960 Chevrolet with a white roof. He opens the trunk of this car and tosses the green plastic bags in.

44 *Charley Varrick*: the perfect crime goes into action

The flaming Essex draws his attention. He reaches into one of the green bags and comes out with a healthy double handful of money. He crosses back to the blazing car and flutters the money around the fire; some of it falls safely to the ground. He quickly strips off his overalls and throws them into the fire. He hurries back to the Chevrolet, slams down the lid on the trunk, moves quickly around to the driver's side and gets in behind the wheel. Charlie puts the key in the ignition and turns it. The car won't start. He puts a couple of sticks of gum in his mouth and starts chewing vigorously. Trying to be calm, he tries to start the car again. Again, it won't start. Now really worried, he tries the engine for the third time. It *finally* catches. Relief floods his face.

On a boom and zoom, the camera starts pulling back and up. As he drives past the junkyard, he sees a dead, soiled Molly outstretched on the roof of a wrecked car. He continues past the airstrip and on to the highway, heading east. The boom holds as he disappears on the highway, then starts to move slowly back and down towards the burning car. The boom moves in to where Charley threw his overalls. They are almost burned away, except some of the writing on the back. The zoom continues in until the writing, though burning, is legible. All that's left is 'Charley Varrick'. The exact same burning letters made the first shot of the picture. We hold on the letters at the end, until they crumble into ashes.

*

When I saw the first cut of the classic pursuit of the Steerman biplane by the vengeful, ruthless Chrysler, I liked the constant peril that Charley was in. There was no question that Frank Morriss had done a miraculous job of editing. But taken as a whole, it seemed to run out of juice; the malignity of the excitement was missing. I told Frank how I felt. He was astounded.

ME: The oldest bromide in the movie industry is *not* to mix constant loud sound effects with music.
MORRISS: It's true, Don. You wind up with a free-for-all fight between sound and music, with neither side winning, spoiling the end product.

I told Frank to set up an early running with Lalo Schifrin to see the car–plane sequence with us, but asked Frank not to let on why. Lalo Schifrin is one of the most talented composers in the film industry. He is a prominent conductor and a brilliant pianist, and he is very knowledgeable about films. In addition, he is a 'Siegel buff'. We are the best of friends.

We ran the entire pursuit sequence, including the end of the film. When the lights went up, Lalo was staring straight ahead, thinking about what he had just seen. Finally, he stood up and faced us.

SCHIFRIN: It's an extraordinary piece of film. As usual, Don, your work is exciting and novel. (*To Frank.*) Your editing is faultless. (*To both of us.*) I'm only sorry that, correctly, I have nothing musical to contribute.
ME: Lalo, I need your help, your imagination, your improvisation vitally. I don't like the sequence as it now stands. It's empty and dull. I don't care if you pan the ivories, vamp, tweedle, fiddle, etc. I'm fully aware that loud sound effects *usually* don't work with music. Come up with something that will make the sequence excite me.
SCHIFRIN: (*A long pause*) This is a wild idea. I've never tried anything like it before. If it's no good, you still will have a good sequence. (*Fixing his eyes on mine.*) I have perfect pitch. What if the music

45   Don Siegel with composer Lalo Schifrin

that plays for the Chrysler is in the exact pitch of the Chrysler's
motor? And what if the music that plays for the biplane is in the
exact pitch of the plane's motor? When the car and the plane are
together, the music will sound exactly like the two of them. But,
when the camera swings off the car to the biplane, the music will
show it as surely as we hear the sound of the car changing to the
sound of the plane and vice versa, all in perfect pitch. I can play
games and experiment. I can lose the sound of the plane and only
use the sound of the music and vice versa.

ME: You're a genius. Now all you've got to do is to write the music. At
least it will be original. I have a very strong hunch that I'll like it.
Anyway, thanks for the effort.

When we heard the sequence with the music and sound effects, we loved
it. Frank couldn't believe the improvement the music brought. Its energy
and intensity made the sequence. Most people who saw the picture were
unaware that music was used at all.

*

When Jules Stein, Chairman of the Board of MCA, which owned many properties including Universal Studios, complimented me on my work on *Charley Varrick*, it was high praise indeed. But there was one point that bothered him. Why would a man who had done such meticulous planning deliberately throw good money into a fire so that it was totally lost? It struck him as senseless and stupid. Stein, one of the wealthiest men in the world, plus one of the most charitable – his donations include the Stein Eye Institute to the University of California at Los Angeles – looked accusingly at me.

ME: In order for Charley Varrick to emerge victorious, he had to come up with a perfect crime. Unless his intricate plan was perfect, the Mafia would never give up. He threw the money in the trunk and scattered the rest on the ground, hoping that the money on the ground would be found by the Mafia. This was another link that held the perfect crime together. I appreciate your criticism and hope that my rebuttal satisfies you.

Stein now understood. It had been done so naturally that it fooled him.

*

Walter Matthau is addicted to gambling and knows it only too well. He compounds his illness by actually *not* wanting to win. His excitement and enjoyment in gambling come from losing.

I lost a bet with Walter that a picture he had completed some months before *Charley Varrick* would earn more money than our film. I bet him $1,200 that he was wrong. I wrote out a cheque and sent it off to him. While working on this book, I found the returned cheque, totally voided. I'm returning the exact cheque back to him. This will make him idiotically happy.

I didn't realize that throughout its making Walter told every reviewer that he neither liked the picture nor understood it. I felt his attitude seriously hurt the profits. Yet he won many awards and accolades for his superb performance, including the British Film Academy Award as 'Best Actor of the Year'. I still feel he deserved all his awards and excellent reviews. Unfortunately, because of his negative attitude, he was, to a large extent, responsible for the studio's lack of interest in *Charley Varrick*. If a studio doesn't get behind the selling of a picture, you might as well not make it.

Dec. 25, 74

Dear Donsie,
the results
are not in yet.
You must wait
at least 5 years
to get an accurate
picture. I'm
returning your
cheque.
But your memo
puzzles me. Why
will I need money?
Was Earthquake the
ruination of me?
I owe.
Falta.

**walter
matthau**

34

The Black Windmill

Universal 1974

I was working with two producers, Richard Zanuck and David Brown, on a book they owned entitled *Seven Days to a Killing*, written by Clive Egleton. What made this project unusual was the fact that the producers were intelligent, downright erudite and eager to do their best work. In addition, they were pleasant and fun. They both recognized that, fine writer as Clive Egleton is, his novel presented difficulties when it came to transforming it into a viable, entertaining and exciting screenplay.

We struck out with three writers at an early stage, when they verbally 'winged' their ideas for a screenplay. When an unknown, at least to me, English writer, Leigh Vance, appeared, he came prepared. His ideas made a great deal of sense. We had several story sessions with him and we all agreed, enthusiastically, to hire him. So far, so good.

Leigh Vance was the most disciplined writer I had ever worked with. In addition, he worked quickly and, most importantly, well. Dick and David enthused over his work. I suggested that Leigh and I pick the English locations, so that he could incorporate them in the screenplay that I would be shooting. The fact that Leigh was English and that I had lived in London for a number of years as a student at the Royal Academy of Dramatic Art should make our task easier. However, God, in his infinite wisdom, works strangely. The day after Leigh turned in his script, entitled 'Drabble', the Screen Writers' Guild went out on strike. Leigh, a former President of the International Screen Writers' Guild, went on strike too, picketing Universal. I carried a tray of coffee and doughnuts out to the writers, who were walking up and down in front of the main gate. I was roundly booed. I asked Leigh if he was leaving with me to go to England. He was shocked. He would not even discuss that possibility during the strike.

Richard Zanuck felt that the strike would soon be over. I had a trillion things to do to get this picture made.

ME: How do I go about making the many script changes I'm considering?

ZANUCK: Until the strike's over, perhaps you can find a good writer in England.

ME: I'll try; but I've heard that they are co-operating with our Writers' Guild.

ZANUCK: (*Smiling*) You're a director/*auteur*. You won't be in any trouble.

So I took off on my own for merry England. An attractive lady, Eva Monley ('e.m.'), turned out to be my production manager. She was most efficient. I interviewed casting directors and wound up, naturally, with a female casting director. I interviewed propmen, special-effects men (worst idiots I ever worked with), art directors, cameramen, wardrobe and costume designers, and on, and on, and on. I saw an old friend, Carl Foreman, who was President of the English Writers' Guild. He was extremely cordial until I asked if I could hire an English writer. He froze instantly. Other than to say 'Absolutely not', he refused to utter a word concerning my plight.

I shrugged off the indisputable evidence that I was impossibly busy; that I had never read a script that didn't need work, such as changes to fit new locations, stars wanting scenes rewritten, etc. Indubitably, I was tired. Not only could I not think clearly, but my ego was so inflated that I didn't face up to the fact that, in addition to producing and directing, it was much too much to expect that I was up to rewriting the script. What I should have done, if I'd been sane, was to state firmly that as soon as the strike was over I would start working with Vance and continue to shoot the film. I would have been happy to rest, play golf, eat my fill of hamburgers, see movies, enjoy a book, a play, or be with my friends. I deserved all my troubles. God, or the Devil, has a way of getting even with those of us who can't look in the mirror and see the truth.

*

The White Elephant is a private dining club. I was in the middle of a delectable grilled Dover sole when a phone was brought to my table. I was told that Mr Wasserman was calling from California.

WASSERMAN'S VOICE: (*Coming directly to the point*) It is absolutely imperative that you see *Day of the Jackal* at two o'clock, your time, at Pinewood Studios.

ME: My God! It's just past one.

WASSERMAN'S VOICE: (*Ignoring what I have said*) I want to know what you think of Edward Fox to play the lead in 'Drabble'. The picture is being run by Sir John Woolf. Then it will immediately be shipped to me. If you miss the running, you'll have to fly here to run it.

ME: I'm off. I'll call you at the studio after I see it, or I'll be at Universal tomorrow.

I hung up and dashed to my chauffeur, standing beside his car – a Rolls-Royce, of course. We immediately left for Pinewood Studios.

In the theatre, Fred Zinnemann, the director, rushed up to me. We embraced. I wished him luck. He told me he knew all about Wasserman's instructions for me to see his film. He whispered in my ear.

ZINNEMANN: Even if you don't like the picture, say something nice about it.

ME: Fred, I read the book and you're the perfect director to make it.

He introduced me to Edward Fox, who looked surprisingly slight of build, about my height. He appeared most pleasant and nervous, as I wished him well. Sir John Woolf and his entourage entered the projection room. I was introduced to the group. As all took their seats, I discreetly sat in the back of the theatre. Just before the lights went out, per my instructions, my driver entered and sat near the exit door.

The picture was very well made. It was exciting and held my interest throughout. It was professionally produced and brilliantly directed. The décor had just the right look. The cast was exceptional, except for Mr Fox. Physically, I didn't believe that he was the only man in the world capable of playing this difficult role; I felt that a physically larger man would have fit the part better. However, I thought that the picture would do very well at the box office. I complimented everyone. I thanked Sir John Woolf for letting me see his picture.

When I got back to my office, I called Lew and told him more or less what I had told the others. He then asked how I liked Fox.

ME: Physically, I thought he was wrong for the part.

WASSERMAN: Do you think he can play the lead in 'Drabble'?

ME: I much prefer Michael Caine, who has read the script and wants to do it.

WASSERMAN: Get him. Make a deal.

ME: Thank you, sir.

WASSERMAN: What else did you think of the film?

ME: As I told you, I really liked it. Like most films, it needs a certain amount of honing. There are a few spots where it slows down.

But, I'd like to add this: you've got a blockbuster. Congratulations.

I made three calls. The first was to Michael Caine. He was extremely happy and funny, as usual. I then called his agent, Dennis Sallinger, and told him about Wasserman okaying Michael. I told Dennis *not* to make the deal too tough. I then called Dick Zanuck. I filled him in on all the details and asked him, if he approved, to handle Sallinger. I also told him to see *The Day of the Jackal* and find out for himself what he thought of Fox for the lead.

*

Naturally, I started shooting out of continuity. Little did I realize that continuity was the least of my worries. We got permission to use part of a new motorway, which was undergoing construction. A Land Rover, with two stuntmen in it, is supposed to be travelling in a straight line when suddenly it disintegrates. Riding safely behind and ahead of the Land Rover are several cars, driven by stuntmen. On the opposite side of a small barrier are several cars approaching the Land Rover – all the drivers are stuntmen.

We used a medium-sized boom, which embraced the whole area from a high angle. A second camera panned closely with the Land Rover. A third camera was in the car that followed the Land Rover. The fourth camera, on a high-hat (on the ground), with a wide-angle lens, covered the action featuring the Land Rover. The fifth camera panned with the approaching cars, which included the Land Rover exploding.

After several rehearsals, obviously with no explosives in the Land Rover, all the stuntmen knew what the speed would be and where to position their cars. For no reason, other than a hunch, I shot the rehearsals with all the cameras. The two stuntmen in the Land Rover got out of the car. All the movement and explosion was to be controlled by radio. On 'Action', all the cars would start moving, which would be the cue for the Land Rover to start. The special-effects men knew exactly when the car was to explode.

When we finally shot it, all the cars moved, *including* the Land Rover. Then the side door fell off. It looked like a Mack Sennett film. I yelled through the bullhorn 'Cut! Cut! Cut!', but to no avail. Instead of the Land Rover going in a straight line, it circled to its right towards the small barrier, with cars approaching. As it bounced over the barrier, it exploded, the whole car falling apart. There was no point talking to special effects, as obviously we didn't speak the same language. Actually, I was just grateful that, miraculously, no one got hurt. I couldn't look at 'e.m.'. I told her I wanted next to shoot the sequence with McKee (John Vernon) and Ceil Burrows (Delphine Seyrig) in their van, with Delphine driving. A small radio remote-control device was to be in the glove compartment.

ME: (*To Monley, still unable to look at her*) Be *sure* that the activating button doesn't work!

'e.m.' smiled wanly and sped off. Soon she returned. She had found a private road. John and Delphine were getting made up and were wearing their correct wardrobe. Unfortunately, I found out that Delphine had never driven on the 'wrong side' of the road; in addition, she had never driven a stick shift before. 'e.m.' was close to tears.

ME: (*Putting my arm around her*) We've got the rest of the day to teach her. I'm going to get with my cinematographer [*Ousama Rawi*] on the private road. I'd appreciate it if the cast joined me as soon as possible.

MONLEY: I'm terribly sorry about what happened. We're getting another Land Rover.

ME: Don't. I think I can put the sequence together without re-shooting. I'll know definitely when I view the dailies. Remember, I had five cameras on the débâcle. Also, get me the stunt co-ordinator. Hopefully he can teach Delphine how to drive.

Delphine really looked frightened. John Vernon wasn't too happy about being in the car with her.

ME: (*To Delphine*) Our first shot will be your double driving the van down the road with John bravely sitting beside the double. So far, so good?

SEYRIG: You're a darling.

ME: Delphine, it's only the beginning. After we've made the first shot, we will put you in a straitjacket and pull the van, with fearless you at the wheel. We will make a two-shot and two singles. Next, we'll make an insert of John pressing the activating button that causes the Land Rover to explode. That will be the end of you both, if the English special-effects man gets his hands on it. The last shot will be your double, driving the car down the road with nervous John sitting beside her.

VERNON: You've saved my life, Don.

ME: And one more thing. When the difficult French dialogue is being spoken, your director will be wrapped around a platform in front of the van. This will give you confidence; for if there is an accident, at least I'll be dead. (*Turning to Rawi.*) How do you want to shoot? The two exteriors, or the four interiors, including the insert?

RAWI: The two exteriors.

ME: (*To John and Delphine*) OK. Rehearse your lines.

When we shot the interiors of the van, Burrows, apparently driving, looked at McKee.

BURROWS: Can we trust those two men not to talk?
   (*McKee takes a small radio remote-control device from the glove compartment and presses the activating button.*)
MCKEE: We can now.

This is what was supposed to happen. On the motorway, several cars are going in opposite directions. The Land Rover is about 30 yards behind another car as it suddenly explodes into a million fragments.

*

On the second day, two small boys, about ten years old, were to fly a miniature aeroplane by a radio remote-control device. Actually their device was not real. A special-effects man had the only control of the plane, although it would appear that the taller lad, David Tarrant (Paul Moss), was actually flying the plane. His smaller friend, James Stroud (Mark Praid), was agog with excitement. They were both dressed in public-school clothes, with a school emblem on their blazers.

   I couldn't believe my eyes. The special-effects man was flying the miniature plane, out of control, at about 70 miles per hour. I yelled for him to stop.

ME: Are you crazy? If that plane hits one of the boys, it will tear his head off!
SPECIAL-EFFECTS MAN: I'll have it under control in just a minute.

We watched him from a safe vantage point – the kids, Monley and a frightened director, huddled in a truck. It appeared to me that the nut was deliberately swooping and diving the plane at the truck.

ME: Eva, fire that insane man before he not only wrecks the plane, but kills all of us.

I turned to the kids and indicated that they should follow me with their plane. I decided, out of desperation, to shoot the scene entirely differently. I placed the two boys on the other side of the fence and handed Paul (playing David) the miniature plane. I had them stay out of sight until my 'Action' and then, as I started close on the wire fence, David's head pops up, casing the area. It is an abandoned, run-down, World War II airfield, with a rusty, dilapidated hangar in the distance. There isn't a soul in sight. David climbs the fence, then turns to James, who hands him the miniature plane. James starts to climb the fence as David, holding the plane aloft, throws it through the air like a javelin thrower. It glides smoothly and settles on the ground – a perfect three-point landing.

*

John Tarrant (Michael Caine), an agent in the government's Subversive Warfare Department, receives a distraught phone call from his estranged wife Alex (Janet Suzman), saying that something has happened to their son, David. Tarrant soon learns that his son has been kidnapped at the airfield by a man, McKee, calling himself Drabble (John Vernon), who demands that Tarrant's boss Harper (Donald Pleasence) pay a ransom of £517,057 in uncut diamonds – exactly the amount that Harper has in his possession to pay for his undercover activities. If Harper fails to deliver the diamonds in twenty-four hours, McKee will kill Tarrant's son.

What disturbs Harper is not the ransom demand, but that Drabble knows the exact amount Harper has on hand to pay his agents. In consultation with Sir Edward Julyan (Joseph O'Conor), the Chairman of the Intelligence Committee, Harper decides to place Tarrant under surveillance as the person most likely to be involved in the plot. In the meantime, they decide to stall for time.

As a way of implicating Tarrant in the plot, Drabble breaks into Tarrant's flat with Ceil Burrows and takes a nude photograph of her on Tarrant's bed; he then plants it, along with some other incriminating evidence, into one of Tarrant's desk drawers. Tarrant, meanwhile, has returned to his wife, Alex, where they try to help each other cope with the pain they are experiencing.

Tarrant receives a communication from Drabble informing him that he has to go to Paris with the diamonds. He prepares to leave, equipped with a booby-trapped briefcase. However, he suspects that Harper will not want to sacrifice the diamonds for the life of a young boy, so he decides to take matters into his own hands and successfully removes the diamonds from the bank where they are being held.

By the time Harper realizes that the diamonds are gone, Tarrant is already in Paris, where he is met by Ceil, who brings him to Drabble. Tarrant discloses that the briefcase with the diamonds also contains a pound of explosives and that he will detonate them if he is not reunited with his son. Drabble tricks Tarrant into thinking that his son is in the wine cellar. As Tarrant passes him, Drabble kicks Tarrant forward, causing the briefcase to explode and rendering Tarrant unconscious. As a result of the blast, red wine gushes out of its flagons, engulfing Tarrant, who lies spread-eagled, unconscious, totally covered by the torrent of wine. Drabble, Ceil and the others in the gang rush in and lift him up

46 *The Black Windmill*: John Tarrant (Michael Caine) comforts his distraught wife (Janet Suzman)

before he literally drowns. Drabble slashes the leather of the briefcase and extracts the diamonds. Tarrant's body is carried out of the wine cellar.

Tarrant wakes up in a French hospital, only to find Harper accusing him of being involved in the plot to steal the diamonds. He had been found unconscious in Ceil's bedroom; she had been found dead, strangled with the chain of Tarrant's briefcase – supposedly in a lovers' quarrel. Harper is convinced that Tarrant is in league with Drabble and his gang.

47   *The Black Windmill*: Tarrant (Michael Caine) awash in wine

As he is being taken away in Harper's custody. Drabble attempts to kill Tarrant, who manages to escape this attempt on his life and also to elude Harper's men. Back in London, he makes contact with Alex and tells her that Drabble has revealed that David is being held in a farmhouse with two unusual windmills. Alex finds the location in a National Trust reference book and conveys the information to Tarrant.

Convinced that an intelligence leak in the department has supplied Drabble with the information about the diamonds, Tarrant devises a plot of his own which unmasks Sir Edward Julyan as Drabble's accomplice. There is a violent confrontation between Tarrant and Julyan.

Before we started to shoot, Joseph O'Conor, playing Julyan, took me aside, in the darkness, to explain that he was a jujitsu expert. He thought if he used it, a most interesting fight between Michael Caine and himself would occur. I told him that his part called for an elderly man showing no physical or mental strength. O'Conor seemed nettled by my reaction. I told him that Caine was in his trailer. If he approved, I would go along with the idea – although it made little sense to me. Apparently Michael turned him down.

Tarrant subdues Julyan and forces him to reveal that his son is in the second windmill. As he attempts to reach David, Tarrant meets with violent resistance, but he is more than equal to the task and succeeds in shooting Drabble, who tumbles down the steep steps of the windmill, landing still and dead.

The English stuntmen were not well trained, but they were very brave. The stuntman, Terry Plummer, should have hit the side wall, bounced off

48   *The Black Windmill*: the final shoot-out

the bannister and then hit the bottom of the stairs. This would have decreased the speed of his fall. Instead, he just let himself fall straight down. He had a neck as wide as my shoulders. For a moment, I thought he had concussion. It's a miracle he didn't.

Tarrant races through the windmill, finally reaching his son, whom he carries out past the twin mills on his way back home to Alex.

*

There is no black windmill in the film. The windmills in the story are known as the Twin Mills. The people who were responsible for what the picture is titled – the head of the studio, the head of publicity, the head of the exhibitors, etc. – had very little idea of how to sell it. They were not interested in asking the maker of the film, who produced and directed it.

My idea of how to sell 'Drabble' (which means 'to become wet and muddy') properly would be to excite interest in Drabble. For example: Who is Drabble? How many Drabbles are there? Why is Drabble? Do people have Drabble as their surname? (Yes). What is Drabble?

The executive producers liked the title 'Drabble' very much, but the studio said no. Finally, in desperation, David Brown came up with the title *The Black Windmill*. The proof is in the pudding. As a title, *The Black Windmill* did nothing for the picture. It certainly had nothing to do with the Dutch Reformation. It certainly had nothing to do with the success of the picture, as the picture was not a success.

So disillusioned was I by the lack of support from the studio that after the release of *The Black Windmill* I wrote to Sid Scheinberg at Universal:

February 8, 1975

Dear Sid,

As a director auteur, I welcome constructive criticism. However, I do feel there's an area of 'instant coffee' making of films at Universal. For example, "Charley Varrick" received rave reviews; yet, the studio let it flounder and that's the end of that film.

During pre-production on "Black Windmill", there was a Writers' Strike. As the Producer/Director, I was enormously busy and should not have been asked to rewrite the script. Again, "Black Windmill" received minimal publicity and backing.

I'm sorry to point out to you that I'm not particularly happy about being under contract to Universal. I'm only interested in making a picture as well as it can be made and to bring it in under budget. But if the studio doesn't get behind my films, there's no point in my working for Universal. If you feel the same way about me, I would greatly appreciate your abrogating my contract.

Thank you.   Sincerely,

Don Siegel

The Shootist
1976

The Black Windmill was released in 1974. Two years later, *The Shootist* was released. The story of this film is out of continuity because I felt that it was better for you to know me as a seasoned director at the beginning of my autobiography. Then, when the story flashes back to my beginnings as a film librarian in 1934, you have already made the acquaintance of the experienced director I was to become.

35

Telefon

MGM 1977

The difficulties in making a motion picture seem endless. One point alone: getting a script that the various executives, the production department, the cast and the studio committees agree on, is almost impossible.

Paul Kohner, Charles Bronson's agent, submitted *Telefon* for me to consider directing for MGM. The screenplay, written by Peter Hyams, was based on the novel *Telefon* by Walter Wager. Peter's script was much too complicated and long. Marty Elfan, the executive producer and a close friend of Hyams, had him do a complete rewrite. Richard Shepherd, the head of MGM's Motion Picture Division, was furious with the carelessness of Peter's revised script, as was Marty.

Another writer, Scott Hale, was hired. No one liked his script. Then Stirling Silliphant was brought in to do another version. Stirling is a very experienced writer and immediately, after reading all the previous material, went to work.

I was called in for a private meeting with Richard Shepherd. He told me that Marty Elfan was leaving the picture for a top executive position with Warner Brothers. He suggested bringing in another producer, Jim Harris, who had worked for Stanley Kubrick. I told Dick, in my inimitable sweet manner, that I had produced more pictures than both of them put together and I didn't need a new producer. What I did need was a good script, without the help of his helpless studio committee. I had never heard of directing a film by committee; nor had I ever read a decent script written by a committee. Dick prevailed upon me at least to talk to Jim Harris. I surprised him by saying 'Yes.'

Jim Harris showed up at my office. He was quite thin, about 5 foot 8, and was on his way to becoming bald. He was a soft-spoken, serious-looking man. I asked him what he thought of the various scripts. He answered directly and immediately.

HARRIS: I don't like them at all.
ME: (*Shaking his hand*) You've got the job.

It turned out that he was knowledgeable and very helpful with the script. I liked him.

The members of the MGM committee were Dick Shepherd; Ray Wagner, a top executive; Leo Greenfield, head of publicity; Lew Rachmil, head of production; and Sherry Lansing, who I think was head of the story department. At one of the numerous committee meetings, I sat on Dick's left, as I was the target of their story suggestions. Ray Wagner usually had nothing to say, which sounded good to my ears. However, I remember well two words which Leo Greenfield frequently used: ambience and panache.

Sherry Lansing was a most attractive girl in her late twenties. She was very enthusiastic about a sequence in one of the earlier scripts, which took place in the lady's restroom at a train station. The scene showed our leading lady combing her hair. While looking in the mirror, she notices one of the toilet doors slowly opening, revealing a filthy derelict holding a knife. As he tries to rape our leading lady, she badly beats him up.

ME: It's difficult to shoot leading ladies in any type of physical encounter. Bronson could and should take care of all the physical encounters. I know he'll want to. Also, we don't need the scene.

LANSING: (*Voice filled with emotion*) When she is attacked by this bum and fights him off, the audience will stand up and cheer!

ME: Sherry, the script is very long now and this scene should be the first to be cut out.

LANSING: I feel very strongly that it should be left in.

ME: When it comes to rape, you unquestionably know more than I do. I'm also quite sure that in karate you are much better than I. (*Very businesslike, standing up.*) Perhaps the committee might like to witness what would happen if I tried to rape you – without a knife, of course. (*Walking towards her.*) I think you should get to your feet with your back towards me. Don't worry about hurting me.

Her face turned beet-red. She was glued to her chair. Having made my point, Dick asked me to take my seat. Sherry's face no longer looked flushed. Hatred filled it instead.

What amazed me, with all the verbal and written criticisms of the committee, was that no one ever mentioned that the *catalyst* of the story was impossible to believe.

The audience was expected to accept the preposterous notion that, by using drug-induced hypnosis, people can be triggered into committing acts of extreme violence. This was accomplished in the story by lamely

49 *Telefon*: Carol Rydall and Don Siegel

telling these people, in person or by telephone, part of poem. Idiotically, it didn't matter how many years had elapsed between their being hypnotized and their hearing the poem. My only hope was to shoot these sequences so realistically that the audience would be swept into accepting this ridiculous premise. At best, it was a long shot. At least I tried.

*

MOSCOW
10 January
0657 Hours

Through the diffused falling snow a group of KGB agents enters an imposing building. They reach an apartment door on the first floor. At the door, the KGB men aim their guns. The door is kicked in and the KGB men rush in. It is empty. Dalchimsky (Donald Pleasence), the man they are looking for, is gone.

A small garage with the lettering 'BASCOM'S AUTO REPAIR'. As the phone rings, Harry Bascom (John Mitchum) rolls out from under a car. He picks up the receiver.

MAN'S VOICE: (*Filtered*) Is this Harry Bascom?
BASCOM: Yeah, this is Harry.
MAN'S VOICE: (*Filtered*)

> The woods are lovely, dark and deep.
> But we have promises to keep.
> And miles to go before we sleep . . .
> Remember, Nikulin, miles to go . . .
> before we sleep.

Throughout this, all expression has vanished from Bascom's face. His eyes glaze over.

BASCOM: Remember, Nikulin, miles to go . . . before we sleep . . .

A click is heard from the other end, as the man hangs up. Bascom, eyes blank, hangs up, goes upstairs and gets a heavy metal box. Putting a gun under his belt, he carries the box downstairs. Bascom gets into his truck and drives to the nearby US Army Department of Chemical Research. Shooting the military policeman stationed at the gates, Bascom accelerates through the barrier. There is a large, military brick building about 1,000 yards ahead. Bascom races towards it, pursued by a military jeep. Bascom is 500 yards from the building and doing 60 m.p.h. The jeep skids to a stop when the truck is gaining speed, 100 yards from the building. When the truck hits the building, a huge yellow-orange flash turns into raging balls of fire as the entire building collapses, followed by a series of explosions. Soldiers rush towards the explosion. A parked station wagon is on the road leading to the base. We dolly in close to a bald man wearing dark glasses. The reflection of the burning, exploding building is visible in the glasses.

The building we blew up was the old Central Avenue High School in Great Falls, Montana. We hired demolition experts to rig an implosion, which causes a building to collapse inwards. Larry Butler, in charge of the special-effects men, was responsible for the explosions and fire. These men had to work closely together. The building was about a square block long and three storeys high. It was an extremely dangerous shot to make and they knew they had one chance at it. Michael Butler and his crew strategically set up seven cameras for the shot. Prior to the explosion, Paul Baxley, our stunt co-ordinator, drove the tow truck into the building. The moment he disappeared, all cameras were stopped. With great care, Baxley and the special-effects men removed the iron 35mm stripped-down Mitchell camera attached to the front bumper and the sound equipment. When the building was empty of all personnel, the cameras rolled again. The demolition experts frightened me during the count-down. The boss told me he had never dropped a building in conjunction with explosions and fire before. He didn't know what was going to happen and was mighty uneasy about it. When the building exploded, I choked up with emotion – a first for me. But, more importantly, no one got hurt.

*

An aerial view in the hills features an eight-storey building, covering more than 100 acres. It is ugly–functional, but its sheer bulk is impressive. Over this shot, computerized letters rattle:

LANGLEY, VIRGINIA

CIA HEADQUARTERS

18 January

0943 Hours

Inside the computer centre, officials discover that Bascom died twenty-two years earlier.

Who died in the explosion then?

APALACHICOLA, FLORIDA

20 January

1116 Hours

Carl Hassler receives a phone call which triggers off the hypnotic mechanism. As he gets into his helicopter, he is watched at a distance by a man with fair hair, whose face is covered by large binoculars. He lowers his glasses with a pleased expression.

At a nearby Naval Communications Center, Hassler attempts to crash his helicopter into the base. In defence, a rocket is launched, exploding the helicopter into a thousand pieces.

Next, Mark Peters blows up himself and an ammunitions dump outside Akron, Ohio.

It is a bitterly cold day behind the Iron Curtain. On the busy street are some telephone booths with the word 'Telefon' painted on them in the Cyrillic alphabet. Over shot, computerized letters appear:

50 *Telefon*: Carol Rydall and Don Siegel on set with Charles Bronson

MOSCOW
24 January
1454 Hours

In an office in the KGB building, Colonel Malchenko (Alan Badel) is having a meeting with Major Grigori Borzov (Charles Bronson). Borzov has a face that gives no clue to what he's thinking. He has a moustache, deep-set eyes and moves like a cat. The two of them are alone, a mood of utter privacy and isolation. Malchenko reveals to Borzov that years ago the KGB initiated a deep-cover operation code-named Telefon in which agents were infiltrated into America to retaliate against American military or strategic targets in the event of a nuclear war. They were each to be launched on suicide missions by a trigger phrase which could be activated by a telephone call.

The man for whom the KGB are hunting, Dalchimsky, intent on destroying both Soviet and American society, is known to be in the

424

USA with a list of the programmed agents. Three are now dead; fifty-one remain. Borzov is to find Dalchimsky and leaves for North America.

A jet airliner, landing gear down, prepares to land. Over shot, computer letters flash:

CALGARY, CANADA

26 January

1215 Hours

I felt that inasmuch as Bronson wore a heavy moustache in Russia, it would help his disguise if he had no moustache when he arrives in Canada. However, he didn't want to shave it off.

BRONSON: (*Smiling*) The reason I want to keep the moustache is that without it I never earned any money.
ME: With it, you're a multi-millionaire. You can afford to shave it off to help your credibility for one film.
BRONSON: (*A bigger smile*) No moustache – no Bronson.
ME: I've known you, Buchinsky, for many years. I don't buy your reasoning. What's more, I don't believe it. But if you don't care, just remember that I do.

We rehearsed the shot where Borzov, carrying a valise and a briefcase, exits from the crowded air terminal. He sees a lovely girl, his American contact Barbara (Lee Remick), waving to him from a waiting car. He crosses to her, throws his valise in the back and tells her to continue driving as he gets in the car. She smiles at him as he glances around and they take off. When they had done the scene, I suggested to Bronson that he embrace Lee, as though she were his wife. He refused.

BRONSON: When my wife meets me at an airport, we never kiss.
ME: But Bronson, you want anyone observing you to realize that the lovely lady is your wife.

Bronson felt it wasn't necessary and left the car to go back to the terminal.

ME: Lee, when Bronson gets into the car, embrace him.
REMICK: But Don, I don't dare. He's liable to hit me.
ME: Always trust your director. I promise you, he'll like it. I know I would.

I left her to get the shot ready.

Borzov, carrying his valise and briefcase, notices the horn blowing and Barbara waving at him with a big smile. He crosses to the car, throws his

425

51 *Telefon*: Don Siegel with Charles Bronson and Lee Remick

valise in the back, tells Barbara to continue driving and gets into the car. Barbara embraces him with fervour, which Borzov returns. Barbara drives off smiling as Borzov scans the area.

From this point on, the script refers to Borzov by his American name, Gregg. (Apparently he has only one name, for reasons I was never told.)

*

Wide shot at night of a snow-covered park. A large sedan, with lights on, follows two figures walking through the park, illuminating them. Computerized letters appear:

MOSCOW

29 January

1015 Hours

General Strelsky (Patrick Magee) and Colonel Malchenko, wrapped in heavy coats and topped with fur hats, are walking along the snowy path, both puffing Havana cigars. Their breath, in the bitter cold, gives as much smoke as the cigars.

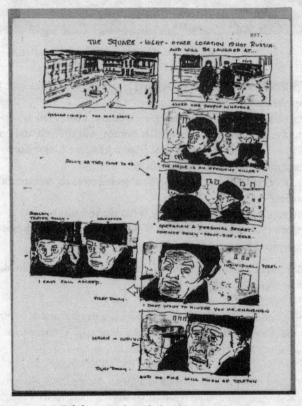

52   *Telefon*: storyboards for the Moscow scene

53   *Telefon*: The Moscow scene

STRELSKY: I have nightmares of having to confess that we kept this
    operation our personal secret.
MALCHENKO: I wish I could have nightmares. I can't fall asleep.
STRELSKY: I continue to believe that Borzov will succeed and no one
    will ever know about Telefon. (*Pause.*) Except Major Borzov.
MALCHENKO: Surely he can be trusted.
STRELSKY: He does not have to be subjected to such insupportable
    stress.
MALCHENKO: (*Suddenly alarmed*) What do you mean?
STRELSKY: His American contact will eliminate him the moment he
    completes his mission.

Strelsky looks pleased with his private arrangement. Malchenko looks
horrified and betrayed.

Morning aerial view, shooting down on a home, its grounds covered with
vivid red flowers, the whole area mountainous. Computerized letters
over:

CAMBRIDGE, NEW MEXICO
29 January
0810 Hours
Marie Willis (Sheree North) is the next agent to be activated by

428

Dalchimsky. She goes into the local hills, not realizing that the mountain range is full of rocket-launching pads. She detonates an explosive device, destroying the launching pads, then takes a suicide capsule and is dead before her head hits the ground.

We shot this sequence at Rocketdyne. As usual, we got into a bit of trouble. We were riding on the Titan crane, waiting for permission to shoot our fake explosions. Rocketdyne were ready to test one of their real launch pads. The officials ordered us to wait at the lower gates until the test was over and we heard from them. While we were waiting, we shot some footage of their test, which to us didn't amount to much. When they learned about it, they demanded that we immediately turn over the negative and all the developed film we had shot of their test and refused to allow us to continue filming at their plant. Realizing our unfortunate error, we immediately turned over all footage and the negative. Lewis Rachmil wrote a letter of apology. Fortunately, they kindly allowed us to finish filming our sequence at Rocketdyne.

*

Gregg and Barbara walk through the Los Angeles Music Center trying to figure out the pattern governing Dalchimsky's actions. They realize that the home towns of the victims spell out Dalchimsky's name.

> *Denver* (Bascom)
> *Apalachicola* (Hassler; but because Hassler failed in his attempt, Dalchimsky needed another *A*)
> *Akron* (Peters)
> *Los Angeles* (Father Diller)
> *Cambridge* (Willis)
> *H* (is next)

Gregg checks his memory for the names and addresses of the victims and realizes that there are two possibilities:

> *Halderville* (Doug Stark – but he's gone fishing)
> *Houston* (Martin Callender)

Day shot of Houston, Texas, shooting down from the top of a skyscraper to the street below. Over shot, computerized letters appear.

HOUSTON, TEXAS

30 January

1145 Hours

We had planned to shoot this sequence at the new Bonaventure Hotel in Los Angeles, representing the Hyatt Regency in Houston. However, we were *personae non gratae* at the Bonaventure due to too many explosions, too much smoke and too much violence in the sequence. I decided to use the Hyatt Regency in San Francisco instead. It was closer to Los Angeles, but, more importantly, my contacts in San Francisco with the Mayor and the police department were much better.

On our first day's shooting in San Francisco, I ran into Bronson early in the morning. He was wondering why we weren't shooting this sequence in Los Angeles or Houston. I explained why, which sent him off about the filth of Market Street, the San Francisco bums, etc.

ME: Well, at least the food's excellent.
BRONSON: (*Hitting his stomach*) I don't eat.

He had evidently gotten out of bed on the wrong side, because when I marked in black tape where he should get off the escalator so that the extraordinary beautiful glass elevators going up and down were in the shot, he exploded in senseless sarcasm.

BRONSON: You don't have to show off by telling me how to get off an escalator.
ME: Let's take a walk.
   (*Bronson follows me until we are out of sight of the crew.*)
ME: I've known and worked with you since your name was Buchinsky. I don't remember our ever having a quarrel before. I suggest we go back, make the shot and forget the whole incident.
BRONSON: I thought you were making fun of me.
ME: You were wrong – and if we don't get along immediately, I'm going to do something very wrong, like leaving the show.
   (*Bronson sticks his hand out. I shake it, in pain. We walk back to the escalator.*)
ME: How in the hell can I argue with you when you can shatter my hand as easily as I can squash a mosquito?

*

Barbara is at the wheel of their rented car with Gregg about to get out. They are parked in front of the hotel. She touches his arm and warns him to be careful. He smiles confidently at her. He enters the huge hotel lobby by taking the escalator. He pauses at the top; the elevators are busy going up and down. He crosses to the reception desk and finds out that Callender is having lunch on the top floor. He gets in one of the glass elevators and goes to the top floor.

This day was my day not only to lose my temper, but to fire some of my production staff. The foyer, leading to the top-floor restaurant, was walled entirely in glass. The dining area revolved slowly, so that one had a magnificent panoramic view of the city. It was impossible to shoot Bronson getting off the elevator without the camera seeing itself in the mirrors, in addition to seeing members of our crew, including me, flat on the floor. When we checked this location prior to shooting, I gave strict instructions to my first assistant director to make sure we had a 'wild' mirror, the same size as one of the many mirrors in the foyer. The reason for this was simple. By tilting the 'wild', or 'extra', mirror, we could see the reflections in that mirror, which did not reveal the camera or our crew in the shot. Both my assistant and the production department forgot the mirror. To complicate matters, we had only a few hours to shoot the whole sequence before lunch was served in the restaurant. I screamed that they get the mirror immediately. I'll say one thing for production: they came up with the proper mirror within thirty minutes. At the end of the day, I fired my first assistant. It had been his sole responsibility to have the mirror there.

*

On the upper floor, a group of people, including Gregg, waits impatiently for an elevator. It arrives. He pushes in. The doors close. Gregg presses his face against the plexiglass, looking down. He sees Callender walking with singular intensity on to a descending escalator. Gregg's elevator arrives on the ground floor. He roughly pushes out and runs for the descending escalator.

To give the sequence as much excitement as possible, we put our camera operator in a wheelchair. As soon as Gregg moved through the elevator door, we spun the wheelchair in a complete circle, picking up Bronson running. I've never seen that shot before or since. It worked beautifully.

Gregg pursues Callender on the different descending escalators, always behind by a floor, pushing people aside. Callender disappears into the underground garage.

As Barbara is about to get into her car, she freezes. She sees Dalchimsky across the street, waiting in his station wagon.

In the large underground garage, Callender is loading a heavy black box on to the back floor of his new yellow Continental. He closes the door, then gets into the car. Gregg runs into the underground garage, filled with parked cars. The camera pans and dollies with Gregg as he moves past rows of cars. He hears an engine start. Failing to make the turn out of his parking space, Callender smashes the right front fender. He backs up, this time making the turn. As the Continental squeals down an aisle and skids right into another aisle leading towards the exit, Gregg, with great agility, leaps on to the hood of a parked car, pulls his gun and aims. Suddenly, a blue Cadillac pulls out in front of Callender. There is an enormous crash, as both cars catch fire. The impact sweeps Gregg back against the windshield. Gregg gets to his feet and sees Callender in a dazed condition behind the wheel. He aims and fires point-blank at Callender, blowing him away. As Gregg runs towards the exit away from billows of smoke and fire, the Continental erupts in a huge explosion, caused by the explosives in the black box.

Dalchimsky stares at the billows of black smoke pouring out of the exit ramp. In frustration, he starts his engine. Barbara, reacting to the sound, switches on her ignition. When Dalchimsky pulls his car into the street, Barbara deliberately swings her car across the traffic lane to block Dalchimsky, smashing into his left rear fender. Dalchimsky curses at her in Russian, backs his car off and speeds down the street. Barbara slumps over the wheel of her car.

Gregg emerges from the smoke-filled grarage. He sees Barbara in the car, apparently unconscious. He rushes to her.

In the rehearsal, Bronson grabbed Lee right after she lifted her head. I asked her to touch him on his face, showing concern for him.

REMICK: I don't dare. He'll bite me.
ME: Remember, always trust your director. Lift your head as he
    approaches you. Touch him gently on his face. This is the
    beginning of your love for him.

Barbara raised her head, then reached out and touched Gregg's face with her fingertips.

GREGG: (*Concerned*) You all right?
BARBARA: I am now. I was worried about you. I tried to stop
    Dalchimsky, but he got away.
GREGG: Damn it! We have to get to Halderville before he does.

When Gregg and Barbara arrive at Doug Stark's place, in Halderville, Texas, Gregg activates Stark (Roy Jensen), then tells him to abort his mission. However, because of the strength of the trance, Stark is incapable of responding to anything. In desperation, Gregg garrottes Stark with Barbara's silk scarf.

Just as Gregg is covering Stark's body, Dalchimsky appears. Gregg pretends to be Stark, assuming a glazed look. Before Gregg can attack Dalchimsky, two patrolmen arrive looking for Stark. By the way Gregg reacts, Dalchimsky knows instantly that he is not Stark. Using the protective presence of the patrolmen, Dalchimsky goes to a phone to activate the next agent. Gregg pushes open the door to the telephone booth as Dalchimsky tries to get out the last words of the trigger phrase. Gregg's arm moves swiftly, striking Dalchimsky's trachea. In seconds, Dalchimsky is unconscious. Holding him upright, Gregg quickly takes the black book of agents' names and numbers from Dalchimsky's pocket. He pushes a green capsule between Dalchimsky's teeth and forces the teeth to break the capsule. Gregg then picks up the receiver and sets Dalchimsky's ear against it, propping his body against the booth.

Early the next morning Barbara calls her boss, Sandburg (Frank Marth), to tell him that she has no intention of killing Gregg now that the mission is over. They simply want to be left alone, and if Sandburg or the KGB try to find them, they'll use Dalchimsky's black book to activate all the other agents. As they drive off, Barbara turns to Gregg.

BARBARA: You wouldn't really do that, would you?
GREGG: Do what?
BARBARA: Make those telephone calls.
GREGG: No, I wouldn't. But as long as they don't know that, we'll be
    safe.

They smile at each other. He starts the car and they drive off down the highway.

The last sequence of the film was shot in three types of weather. It was snowing in the morning. We started shooting, but then a heavy rain stopped us. We started to shoot in the rain, then the sun came out. We started all over again in bright sunlight, this time completing the sequence.

36

Das Boot

1978

Early in 1978, producer Ken Hyman, a 'bear of a man', submitted an idea
for a film based on the book *Das Boot* by Lothar-Günther Buchheim. The
story was about the lives of a captain, his officers and the men of a German
submarine during World War II, as told by a journalist stationed aboard
their U-boat. I recommended Dean Riesner to write the screenplay. Ken
enthusiastically agreed. The three of us flew to Munich for a meeting with
the executives of Bavaria Studios – Dr Helmut Jedele, Dr Harald Junge,
Herr Lutz Hengst, Dr Helmut Krapp and Herr Rolf Zehetbauer. However, the main purpose of this trip was to meet the author, Lothar-
Günther Buchheim. Our trip was successful. Everyone agreed to let Dean
write the screenplay, entitled 'The Old Man'.

In the beginning, Dean sent me pages, which I worked on, mostly
steering a course by means of editing which would bring the script in at a
reasonable length. At first everything seemed secure and pleasant. However, as time went by, I noted that the pages I was sent gradually dwindled
in number, until I was receiving no pages. But I trusted Dean, having
worked on a number of projects with him in the past. I talked to him by
telephone several times and what he was writing sounded exciting. I
figured I would soon get the pages from him, work on them with him and,
when we were satisfied, give them to Ken, who was a very knowledgeable
and pleasant man. We'd make any changes he suggested, then send the
total screenplay to Bavaria Studios.

After a number of days, I again enquired about the pages, but Dean
seemed evasive. He was friendly, but no pages appeared. I decided to drive
to his house with my associate Carol Rydall. I left her in the car and rang
the bell. Dean, looking well tanned, greeted me effusively. When I asked to
see the pages, he replied that when he had finished the screenplay he would
give them to me. This had never happened between us before. I strained to
keep my temper; I didn't want Carol to learn that I was seething inside. I
asked Dean how far he had to go. He replied that he was practically
finished.

ME: Why are you not giving me the pages you have now?

RIESNER: (*Uncomfortable*) I promised my wife we would fly to New York when I finished. If you go over the pages, it will delay our trip.

ME: You don't feel embarrassed that you're deliberately changing the way we've always worked together?

(*He says nothing.*)

ME: Will I at least see the pages before anyone else reads them?

RIESNER: I'm sorry, Don, but it will be quicker my way.

I turned and left. When I reached the car, Carol asked where the pages were. I told her, holding back my anger, 'I wish I knew.'

When I got home, the room spun around and I fell to the floor. For the next two weeks, whenever I tried to get out of bed, I had to hang on for dear life. My ear doctor, the famous Victor Goodhill, guaranteed that my middle ear wasn't causing the problem. He knew, of course, what had happened. By holding back my temper, he felt sure that one of the capillaries had been pinched, cutting off the blood going to my brain. I went to a famed neurologist, who put me in the UCLA Hospital for tests. He agreed with Dr Goodhill that a small capillary had been pinched by strain. He felt certain that if I didn't lose my temper I would be cured and it wouldn't occur again. It hasn't happened again.

As for *Das Boot*, it was delayed due to a severe illness of one of the top executives at Bavaria Studios. In the meantime, I became involved with another project, *Escape from Alcatraz*.

37

Escape from Alcatraz

Paramount 1979

On 29 March 1978, my William Morris agent, Lenny Hirshan, tele-phoned me that a young writer by the name of Richard Tuggle wished to submit to me a prison story he had written, *Escape from Alcatraz*. I asked Lenny if he had read it. As usual, he mumbled that he had glanced through it and thought it was quite good. He sent the script to me by special messenger. The next day I read it and liked it very much. However, I was currently involved with *Das Boot* and was scheduled to catch a plane for Munich the next day to discuss making the film with Bavaria Studios. I had Carol Rydall send Tuggle's script back to Lenny with a note that I thought the script had great potential and that I wanted him to read it immediately.

On 2 April I returned from Munich. The next morning, I phoned Lenny to find out what he thought of the script. He felt it was a sure winner. I told him that the lead character, Frank Morris, was perfect for his client, Clint Eastwood. Lenny agreed and said he'd send it to Bob Daley, Clint's executive producer. I told Lenny simply to give the script to Clint. However, for reasons which annoyed me, he gave it to Bob first. Daley also liked the script and gave it to Clint to read. I now heard that Clint was very interested and wanted to do it with me. I balled Lenny out for not having given it directly to Clint. I told him that in the future, if I had a property that I thought Clint might be interested in, I would deal directly with him.

Clint finally called to tell me how much he thought of the project; he felt that, together, we could make a great picture. He asked if there was any chance that the German picture I was working on could be postponed, as he wanted to go ahead with *Alcatraz* immediately. By then I was able to tell him that the logistics of making *Das Boot* that year were almost impossible. By good luck, the executives from Bavaria Studios were due to arrive in Los Angeles around the end of May and I would talk with Ken Hyman about the possibility of postponing the film. We then discussed the fact that *Alcatraz* would need a lot of work. I told Clint that I had such belief in the picture that I would be more than willing to put up the money for the script. I also told Lenny this. I realized that Clint was shooting another *Dirty Harry* sequel, but I thought we should have a meeting to discuss the script and terms of our deal. I never heard from him.

On 5 May I telephoned Tuggle to obtain another copy of his script, as Clint had my only copy. I suggested that he bring it over to my house, as we had never met. We could then have our first real discussion about the picture. I invited him to stay for dinner, which he did. We discussed the strong possibility of my doing the film with Clint and were both enthusiastic. After dinner, Tuggle told me that he had submitted the script to me because in 1964 I had been sent the book *Escape from Alcatraz* by the author, J. Campbell Bruce. I had written back to Mr Bruce that I liked the book very much, but I felt it needed a lot of work. Bruce had showed my letter to Tuggle, and Tuggle wanted me to direct this film not only because of my original interest in the book, but also because he was aware that I had directed *Riot in Cell Block 11*, the best prison film he had ever seen.

I decided, after meeting with Tuggle, that I wanted to buy his script and, whichever studio I made the picture for, he would do the rewrite. Whatever small percentage of the picture he wanted, he could work out a deal with Bruce. Naturally, Tuggle would be paid for the rewrite. I wanted to hear sensible figures from his agent on the deal the next morning. We shook hands. We were in business and we liked each other. One thing I wanted to know: where had his script been submitted? Tuggle smiled: 'Everywhere.'

The next morning, Tuggle's agent called me and we agreed on terms. I told him my personal cheque would be in the mail. He was very pleased with the whole set-up and wished me well. He would draft a simple agreement and get Tuggle's and Bruce's signatures.

Not having heard from Clint, I decided to give Michael Eisner, the President of Paramount Studios, a call. I reminded him that I had previously been wooed by Paramount to make films for them and that I now had an excellent script, which I owned. I was told by Eisner that someone in their story department had previously read a synopsis of *Alcatraz* and turned it down. I told him that Warner Brothers wanted to make the picture with Clint Eastwood and myself. On *Dirty Harry* I had had many problems with Warner Brothers and, consequently, I wanted to know as quickly as possible if Paramount wanted to make it with me. I gave Eisner my last copy and suggested we have lunch the next day if he was interested in talking an immediate deal. His answer was direct and short: 'Be in my office at half past twelve.'

At lunch the next day, Eisner and his Vice-president, Don Simpson, were all smiles.

EISNER: It's a great script.
SIMPSON: We've already fired the reader.

During lunch, we discussed the script, the kind of deal I wanted and how soon I thought I could start shooting. Eisner asked if I could get Eastwood.

ME: Clint and I are the best of friends. I see no reason why he can't work here at Paramount, as well as at Warners.

With our glasses of white wine, we toasted the picture, Tuggle, Eastwood and ourselves.

EISNER: I'll send you a cheque to cover every dime you spent on the script.
ME: Make it out in dollars. It's an awful lot of dimes. Plus, my percentage must recognize that not only do I own the script, but it's 'A Siegel Film' and I'm producing and directing the picture.
SIMPSON: Where the hell is your agent? It's Lenny Hirshan, isn't it?
ME: After we work out the deal, we'll let him copy it . . . for a measly ten per cent.

*

In 1954 Walter Wanger had taken me on an inspection tour of three maximum security prisons – Alcatraz, San Quentin and Folsom – looking for a location for *Riot in Cell Block 11*. I was very depressed by what I saw at Alcatraz. It was impregnable and totally escape proof. All the prisoners had single cells and most of them should have been in an insane asylum. At that time, it was hopeless even to think of shooting there. In 1978 I checked out Alcatraz again. It was now run by the Department of Parks and Recreation Commission. It needed extensive refurbishing, but it was shootable.

Richard Tuggle, Carol Rydall and I worked hard on the rewrite. I though it was in good enough shape to show to Clint. I still hadn't heard from him, which was somewhat strange. I decided, with the blessing and encouragement of Eisner, to send him the script and a note asking to sit down with him to discuss it and his playing Frank Morris, if he was still interested. If he wasn't, which frankly would surprise me as he was born for the part, I would go ahead without him, which would keenly disappoint me.

Clint called me the next day. He asked me to drop by his office to share a tuna sandwich and a brew. At that time, we could discuss and hopefully settle all our problems.

438

ME: Are there any problems?

EASTWOOD: Frankly, I was a bit unsettled at your not setting up a deal at Warner Brothers.

ME: And I was nettled at the way they totally ignored *Dirty Harry* for the Academy Awards nominations. I felt strongly that they should have supported the film.

EASTWOOD: I can't fault you for that, Don. I felt the same way.

ME: Clintus, let's get your deal settled. I need your input on the script.

EASTWOOD: I'll get Lenny on it immediately. If we can work out our deals with Paramount, we should be there within a week.

ME: There's only one thing bothering me. Could I have another brew?

The next week, Clint and his entourage of Robert Daley, the executive producer, and Fritz Manes, the associate producer, moved in. We had a meeting in Eisner's office. Eisner and Simpson were ecstatic. They wanted to know when we were going to nail down Alcatraz. I told them as soon as Clint had a script meeting with the writing team of Tuggle, Rydall and Siegel.

EASTWOOD: Would tomorrow be too soon?

SIMPSON: After you finish making your changes, we have a creative group that works on all our properties.

ME: Let's see how Clint's ideas mesh with the present script. (*Turning to Clint.*) Frankly, we don't believe that committees make pictures.

EISNER: (*Getting up*) I can't tell you, Clint, how happy I am that you're aboard. Good luck.

We all left in good spirits. The meeting with Clint took place the next day in my dumpy, dirty Paramount office. He appeared in shock at the lack of decent office space provided by Paramount, but soon all our thoughts were on his ideas. Some of them we didn't buy, many of them were excellent and most of his suggested changes were incorporated into the revised script. He was very pleased and the script was much improved.

ME: That makes my day. The creative group has read the revised script. They have four pages of notes. I thought that Daley and I should have a meeting with Simpson. If they have anything useful to suggest, I'll let you know. But my gut feeling is that what we now like, they'll dislike. I'll infer that you don't want the script changed. If when we're shooting we get an idea, we'll make the changes ourselves.

EASTWOOD: (*Smiling*) You've taken the words right out of my mouth.

At the meeting in Simpson's office, I listened to his suggestions. He had the four pages of exposition notes in front of him. He felt that we should know all about Morris's criminal history, what kind of person he was and, especially, why he had chosen a life of crime. *Dirty Harry*, in his hands, would have had girl friends, he would have been in the car when his wife was killed, etc. I pointed out to Simpson that the more you describe, analyse and *explain* a character, the less real he becomes. The trick is to *suggest*, to try to leave holes, problems, questions that the viewer's imagination will fill in a much more satisfying way than we could ever do. I suggested that we call it a day and leave well enough alone. Bob Daley and I left him staring at his notes.

*

We left for San Francisco to scout Alcatraz. Clint, Bob, Carol, Fritz and Allen Smith, our art director, were all 'mothered' by me through the interiors and exteriors of the island. Clint climbed everywhere, excited like the kid he truly is. I told Smith I wanted sketches, models and blueprints of all the interiors we had to build or fix up. I wanted them as soon as possible with a 'ball-park' figure of what his work would cost.

We then met the various members of the Parks and Recreation Commission – mostly women. They warned us that every half-hour a boatload of tourists would wander all over Alcatraz, inside and out. My eyes found Clint's, spelling out that I needed help. The women, who were somewhat hard and negative, turned to putty before the Eastwood charm. Without Clint's handling of the female members of the Commission, I don't believe *Escape from Alcatraz* would ever have been made. We left San Francisco with a feeling of success.

However, the shooting of the picture was indeed greatly determined by the presence of the tourists, who arrived daily on the island. They were allowed by the Parks and Recreation Commission to go anywhere on the island. They watched us filming, frequently talking during the actual shooting. At this point, Clint's help was invaluable. He would call out to the crowds of spectators, 'Let me lay out the scene with my director and then I'll sign autographs and let you take pictures.' The situation became so impossible that we were forced to change the schedule and shoot a great many sequences at night, since the tourists were not allowed on the island after the sun had set.

We also had to paint over the graffiti that had been written on the walls by the Indians who had seized and camped on the island. This had to be done with water-soluble paint, so that we didn't damage the graffiti, which was seen by the Parks and Recreation Commission as part of the history of the island. We then had to wash the paint off before we left.

Altogether Paramount spent a fortune refurbishing the island. For example, all the wiring was corroded. There was no heat on the island. In the cold weather, and with the large amount of night shooting, it's a miracle no one came down with pneumonia, or pleurisy, or both. Mark Twain was right when he said, 'The coldest winter I ever spent was a summer in San Francisco.'

*

54 Escape from Alcatraz: Clint Eastwood and Don Siegel

55   *Escape from Alcatraz*: Clint Eastwood

The night is foul, with numbing rain and gusts of cold, whirling wind. A
small boat is making its way across San Francisco Bay towards Alcatraz.
On it is Frank Morris (Clint Eastwood). He is staring straight ahead, his

face dripping wet. He sees, with no reaction, the island through the buffeting rain. As the boat approaches the dock, the rain is coming down in sheets. Morris, who is shackled, is pushed into a bus. A searchlight ferrets him out, always blinding him. The bus goes through an archway, losing the searchlight as it veers off, revealing the constant downfall of rain. The bus climbs a steep, narrow cobbled road to a huge cell block. Two guards help the shackled Morris out of the bus and up the steps to the steel door.

We were not allowed to use salt water for our rain effects because of erosion. We used large barges filled with thousands of gallons of fresh water. On the first night of shooting, I was sopping wet, wearing what I thought would keep me dry. The second night, I wore yellow slickers and boots. I was warm as toast and also dry.

*

Morris is first taken to an examination room, and then escorted, stark naked, down the corridor to his cell. The Warden feels a man loses his dignity when forced to walk naked before gaping prisoners and guards; but Morris's face remains impassive, his eyes staring straight ahead. They stop in front of Cell 109, the silence broken only by the sound of pelting rain, distant thunder and the sharp crackle of lighting. As Morris enters the cell, the door shuts with a clang of finality, which echoes throughout the cell house. On the cell door is a nameplate: MORRIS AZ1441.

GUARD: Welcome to Alcatraz.

The guards leave. Lightning flashes reveal the naked Morris staring through the bars.

Morris has made several earlier escape attempts from an Atlanta jail. Now the Warden (Patrick McGoohan) warns him that no one ever has, or will, escape from Alcatraz. After a fight with a brutish prisoner, Wolf (Bruce M. Fischer), in the showers – for which Morris is thrown into solitary – he slowly begins to adapt himself to life at Alcatraz, becoming friendly with Doc (Roberts Blossom), who has painting privileges. When the Warden discovers Doc's mocking portrait of him, he withdraws his painting privileges. In despair, Doc hacks off his fingers and dies. In response, Morris decides to escape, and works out a plan with two new arrivals from Atlanta, the Anglin brothers (Jack Thibeau and Fred Ward), and the inmate of the next cell, Charley Butts (Larry Hankin). Using makeshift tools, they slowly dig their way out into the prison's utility corridor shafts. They also devise dummies to place on their cots and fashion a raft out of raincoats.

The escape attempt is jeopardized by an attempt by Wolf – who has just

443

56 *Escape from Alcatraz*: Don Siegel directing the fight scene

57 *Escape from Alcatraz*: the fight scene

been released from solitary – to get his revenge on Morris, but Wolf is circumvented by inmates sympathetic to Morris. The Warden, meanwhile, becomes suspicious and is determined to move Morris from his cell the next morning. That night Morris and the Anglin brothers set off. Charley Butts develops cold feet and by the time he decides to join them they have disappeared, leaving him stranded.

A massive search the next morning reveals nothing except a chrysanthemum – a flower associated with Doc's paintings – on the rocks. Refusing to believe the evidence before him, the Warden concludes that they must have drowned.

Alcatraz was closed less than a year later.

38

Rough Cut

Paramount 1980

I was shooting interior sequences on *Escape from Alcatraz* at Paramount when Lenny Hirshan appeared with a distinguished producer of Broadway plays, David Merrick, and introduced him to me. Merrick wanted me to direct a picture for him, entitled *Rough Cut*, starring Burt Reynolds. He handed me a script by one of the best writers in Hollywood, Larry Gelbart. Merrick was slightly corpulent and well dressed. He was polite, assured and comfortably seated in a director's chair. The propman gave him a cup of coffee.

Clint Eastwood sauntered by and, upon being introduced, Merrick had an attack of nerves. He jumped to his feet, his hand shaking so badly that he spilled coffee over his smart attire. When Clint left us, Merrick calmed down. Strange.

I explained that I had to get back to my set. I asked if he would possibly be free for dinner. He enthusiastically accepted my invitation.

ME: I'll be finished shooting at seven. There's a charming little restaurant, Adagio, three blocks from Paramount. Carol Rydall will be my companion and I'll have her make the reservations.

MERRICK: I'll be by myself. We'll get to know each other and will have time to discuss the story.

ME: Obviously, I won't have time to read the script before dinner. Looking forward to this evening.

We shook hands. I like a man who doesn't waste time.

That evening we had an excellent dinner and pleasant conversation.

MERRICK: I make no pretence of knowing how to make pictures. That's your job, Don. You'll have final cut, seventeen per cent of the net, plus your usual fee for directing.

ME: As soon as Carol and I read the script, we'll meet with Burt. If all goes well, we will let you know immediately.

RYDALL: I'm certain the script is great. Larry Gelbart has no peer in Hollywood.

MERRICK: (*His face darkening*) Actually, I don't particularly care for the script. I'd like you to come up with a list of writers.

ME: Until we read the script and meet with Burt, the status quo remains as is. We certainly will do our utmost to please you. However, your start date doesn't give me much time to prepare. But I'm like you – I won't waste time.

(*We say our goodbyes. Merrick, in a chauffeured limo, leaves for the Beverly Hills Hotel, Carol and I for my home overlooking Beverly Glen.*)

ME: Notwithstanding numerous malicious remarks people have made about Merrick, I found him charming and generous.

RYDALL: I agree. Giving you final cut before you have a chance to ask for it. I believe in judging people by how they treat you.

ME: I'm anxious to read the script. That was the only negative comment he made.

RYDALL: Let's keep our fingers crossed.

*

We met with Burt Reynolds over the weekend at his lovely Hombly Hills home. Dick Clayton, Burt's agent, let us into the beautifully furnished house and apologized for Burt's tardiness, explaining that he would be right down. I remembered that I had met Burt once, just long enough to be introduced by Clint, as we parted in opposite directions. At that time, he was somewhat stocky, very well built and about my height. He had a gracious smile, which women swooned over. Now we stood and waited for him to descend the stairs. A slim figure, completely dressed in black, slowly made his entrance. Dick introduced us. Carol, in high heels, was well over 6 feet. Burt was at least 6 foot 4 inches tall. I felt like I was talking to Clint, as I looked up into his eyes. We sat down in easy chairs facing each other. Carol and I smiled; Burt didn't. He immediately went into a mild tirade against his doing this picture. I felt like 'Testing... one, two, three . . .'

ME: Burt, if I may use your first name, why are you asking me why are you doing this film?

REYNOLDS: Well, you're here to do the picture, aren't you?

ME: Not unless you like the project. Carol and I had absolutely nothing to do with the script. If you don't like it, I suggest we start all over again, maybe on a rainy day, when you're more in the mood to discuss the project.

(*Burt looks at me hard.*)

REYNOLDS: What did you think of Larry Gelbart's script?

ME: I finished reading it half an hour ago. I've never had the pleasure of meeting Mr Gelbart, but he is one of the best comedy writers in the business. His script undoubtedly needs editing. Obviously, there are certain areas that can be improved. When the rainy day becomes a torrent, and you're in the mood, perhaps we can discuss what you think of it.

Reynolds got up, explained that he had a migraine headache, and went back up the stairs, slowly. Dick saw us to our car. I told him I didn't understand Burt at all. Dick explained that Burt had arrived from Florida only hours before and had jet fatigue. I told Dick that I suffer from picture fatigue, so that made us even.

Merrick called. He wanted to know how Burt and I had got along.

ME: We didn't. He didn't smile once. He appeared to blame me for his having to do the picture. He was suffering from a migraine headache and jet fatigue and I was suffering from boredom.

MERRICK: How did you like the Gelbart script?

ME: I had just finished reading it. He is a very funny man. Like all scripts, it needs editing. Certain areas need rewriting. If we're to make the picture, I want to read all versions and rewrites.

MERRICK: I'll send you everything I've got. What do you think of your *Alcatraz* writer doing a version?

ME: He'll have to tell me, after reading all the material.

MERRICK: Don't get discouraged. Burt is a bit peculiar, but I know for a definite fact he wants you as his director.

ME: Let me read everything before I make up my mind if I want to direct him. We'll keep in touch. Carol sends her best.

*

Numerous screenplays, some undated, arrived from Merrick. The first one I read, entitled 'Diamonds in the Rough', by Thomas McGuane, abruptly ended on page 70. The second script, by David Rayfiel, had one major fault: 154 pages of increasing dullness. The third script, by William Hamilton, was 98 pages of confusion. The attempt at humour was forced. I had a funny feeling – the only one, I might add – that Merrick had worked closely with this writer. Another version was a revised step outline by Larry Gelbart. It was a good outline for the script but had no ending. A first draft screenplay by Larry Gelbart had many moments of great fun. It needed editing and a new ending. The last was a revised final screenplay by

Larry Gelbart. This script had class, with a lot of laughs and I felt the ending finally worked.

I called Richard Tuggle in and explained that Merrick had suggested giving him a crack at a screenplay. I suggested he read all the material. If he felt he could write the script, the job was his. Tuggle was hesitant.

TUGGLE: I've never written a comedy.
ME: You've never written anything but *Escape from Alcatraz*.
TUGGLE: I've heard strange stories about David Merrick.
ME: So far, he's been decent and considerate. What have you got to lose? After you've read all the scripts, if you don't think you can do it, forget it.
TUGGLE: How many scripts are there?
ME: (*Handing him scripts*) At least six. See me tomorrow afternoon.
TUGGLE: (*Taking scripts*) I won't be able to. I'll be sound asleep.

He looked tired as he left.

After reading all the material, Tuggle liked the Gelbart script best. As a matter of fact, he thought it was damn good and told Merrick that. Merrick, on his way to London to set up the company for us to begin filming there, immediately hired Tuggle with one admonition – make the ending different.

*

While Carol and I worked with Tuggle at Paramount on his script, entitled 'Two of a Kind', we were also working on Gelbart's script. I called Burt to tell him that Merrick had hired Tuggle. With Merrick in England, it would be a wonderful time for him, Carol and me to get together and start talking script. We would send Burt our notes on Gelbart's script by messenger. He agreed to see us the next afternoon at his home.

Burt looked fit and wore his famous photogenic smile. He was equally famous for his embraces. He wrapped his arms around Carol, but something was amiss: they were both 6 feet tall. When he embraced me, in true Mexican style, he was two inches taller than I.

REYNOLDS: The changes you made in the opening sequence of cutting out Inspector Willis at the party are sensational.
ME: I didn't tell Larry about our changes. I like working directly with my star, and actually what we've done is nothing. Larry inspired us and will improve the script. Knowing Larry, do you think he'll be annoyed at us for not showing our suggested changes to him first?
REYNOLDS: I really don't, Don. How's Tuggle coming along?

ME: As soon as I get some sequences from him, I'll send them to you. (*Rising*.) Let's get out of here, Carol, while we're still ahead. We'll have some more pages for you soon.

REYNOLDS: Thanks and keep up the good work.

He embraced us both and, for the moment, we were heroes.

Carol and I continued to work hard on the continuity of Larry's script and I felt we were progressing well. I sent Burt ten more pages. We attempted to edit the script, which moved the picture along at a much faster pace. We hoped Burt, Larry and Merrick would agree.

Several days later, Burt met us in his kitchen, now wearing tennis shoes. He had a wonderful smile as he embraced Carol; but this time, he was not as tall as she. When he embraced me, we were the same height.

Burt raved about our changes. We loved his reaction and were growing extremely fond of him. Typically Hollywood, but that's how we felt. He had great charisma, a keen wit and a lot of knowledge about making pictures. I suppose if he hadn't liked our work, we would have been thrown out of his house, or we would have quit. I only hoped that his pleasantness continued.

Tempus fugit, and we now had about fifty pages. I decided this was a good time to call Larry. He was working on several projects at the same time.

ME: (*On phone*) While Merrick's in England setting up shop, Carol, Burt and I have put together fifty pages for you to read and consider rewriting.

GELBART: I'll take a look at them, but I don't like rewrites.

ME: Larry, let me make this crystal clear. Carol, Burt and I are *not* writers. Obviously we don't want, or deserve, any credit. We simply hope you can make good use of what we've done. If you can't use any of it, burn it!

GELBART: OK, *auteur*.

ME: OK, author.

Carol and I delivered the pages to Larry at his Beverly Hills home. We wished him luck and quickly left. While waiting to hear from Larry, we worked with Tuggle on his script, which was turning out to be much better than we had expected. However, his main weakness was the ending, which I was certain Merrick would not accept.

We showed Tuggle's script to Burt, who had some very funny ideas. He surprised me by liking Tuggle's script on the whole. Merrick was due back shortly and we worked doubly hard with Tuggle so that Merrick could read his script when he returned.

Larry called to say he was working hard on our suggestions and, on the whole, he liked our ideas. He wanted to meet with us at his home at our earliest convenience.

ME: How about this afternoon?
GELBART: You're merciless.

He greeted us cordially, complimented us and hoped we liked his 'rewrite'. He handed us a stack of pages and insisted we read it immediately in his library.

ME: You're merciless.

Carol and I read the pages very quickly, made notes, then returned to his office.

RYDALL: Hope we aren't disturbing you.
GELBART: Depends on what you think of the revised script.
ME/RYDALL: Absolutely wonderful. Very funny.
GELBART: My exact reaction. With Burt feeling the same way, let Merrick burn the pages. Do you want any changes?
ME: Let's wait for Merrick's reaction.
GELBART: His only remark will be, 'Where's the ending?'
RYDALL: I'll get these pages xeroxed and sent back to you.
GELBART: Many thanks to you both. It's damn good, if I say so myself.
ME: Carol, we're off. After we run the *Alcatraz* answer print, onward to London. You'll be hearing from us, Larry.
GELBART: I can hear the telephone ringing now. 'Help!'

*

When Merrick returned from London, we had lunch with him and his associate, Alan DeLynn. After ordering lunch, we started the question period.

MERRICK: (*Smiling*) My idea of using Tuggle was a failure.
ME: As were the other scripts. Seriously, David, there were many funny sequences in Tuggle's script. However, I knew you wouldn't like the ending.
MERRICK: The ending was the beginning of disaster. When are you and Carol leaving for London?
ME: Legally, I can't leave until I give my approval to the *Alcatraz* answer print. Unfortunately, there have been a series of lab

451

failures, which has delayed my seeing the print. It should be ready by the end of the week.

RYDALL: Is everything set up in London?

MERRICK: We're setting up offices at Pinewood Studios.

ME: I do have some good news. Burt, Carol and I worked very hard on Gelbart's script. We gave our ideas to him to fix it up with his marvellous dialogue. We now have fifty-five pages, ending at Wimbledon, which we love. But we have to continue in continuity so we'll know where we are. I'll give you the pages at my office when we finish our lunch.

DELYNN: Do you think Larry can write the ending?

ME: Alan, there's only one person who can answer that question and that's David.

MERRICK: So far, I don't like his endings at all.

ME: For goodness sake, don't sell Larry a bill of goods that he can't write it. All I know is that we think he's perfect casting for the picture. Encourage him, or we'll wind up behind the eight ball.

MERRICK: I really don't like anything he's written.

ME: You have *not* read what I'm about to give you. What you're saying makes no sense. Carol and I will fix up a script of new pages, new continuity, and new dialogue for you to read. If you both don't like it, I see no reason for Carol and I to go to London. (*Getting up*.) See you in my office. Let's go, Carol.

I told the café owner to charge the bill to me and we left.

Carol gave Merrick two sets of new pages. She told him I was busy. Actually, I was on the phone to Tuggle.

ME: Richard, he said very little; but he didn't like your ending, period.

TUGGLE: I wasn't crazy about it either.

ME: I'll tell you who liked the entire script – Burt. He thought it had many funny sequences. Anyway, thanks for trying. I wish I were in your shoes. At least you're off the picture.

The next day, Merrick called. He thought the Gelbart script was vastly improved. The only thing he didn't like, or understand, was opening the picture on a 50-foot balloon.

ME: We can always cut it out, but I think it makes for an exciting opening.

MERRICK: I told Larry how much I liked his script.

ME: Thanks, David. Keep the faith. You'll get your ending. Carol and I are running the *Alcatraz* answer print Thursday. Hopefully, we should be in London on Monday. I'm very happy you liked Larry's revised final. See you soon.

On Thursday, Carol and I sat alone in a projection room running *Escape from Alcatraz*. When the lights went on, Carol turned to me.

RYDALL: Congratulations! It's a terrific film.
ME: I agree. Everybody's excellent, particularly Clint. Let's start packing.

*

Carol and I arrived in London the following Monday and went straight to Claridge's Hotel with my English secretary, Francine Taylor, with whom I had worked on my last English picture, *The Black Windmill*. Francine had ordered a bowl of fresh fruit, liquor and lots of good English ale. We thanked her. She wanted to know if we were going to my offices at Pinewood Studios before unpacking. Carol groaned.

ME: Why not set up a list of crew members that I can start interviewing tomorrow. Round up a crackerjack assistant director, try and get the sound crew I had on *Black Windmill* and get the best people you can find. OK?
TAYLOR: I also have various houses for you to look at and have set up interviews for housekeepers and cooks.
ME: What type of car do I have?
TAYLOR: A chauffeured Mercedes, subject to your approval.
ME: Approved. (*Calling out to Carol.*) Is ten o'clock all right with you to be picked up tomorrow?
RYDALL: Up to you, darling.
ME: That's it, Francine. Certainly glad you're on the sinking ship with us.
(*Carol comes in with our precious fifty-two pages. She hands them to Francine.*)
RYDALL: Could you please have these pages xeroxed, about fifty copies with covers?
TAYLOR: Certainly. Be seeing you tomorrow.
(*As soon as she has left, I turn to Carol.*)
ME: I need a shower and a shave. We'll have lunch at the White Elephant. The afternoon is yours. We'll rest up, or go on a shopping spree.

*

The next day at Pinewood Studios was one of my busiest days ever. I had to meet my first assistant director and his staff, my director of photography and his crew, various production designers, script supervisors, costume designers, etc., etc.

Over the next few days, I went location scouting with our location manager (Jim Brennan), my production designer (Ted Haworth), my cinematographer (Freddie Young) and Carol to locate an English manor for the opening sequence. We spent several days looking at manors of every size and appearance. We found one that particularly fitted our story: a huge estate, West Wycombe Park, West Wycombe, run by the National Trust. The house was four storeys, with large balconies running across the entire front. It was beautifully furnished, and it was also very expensive to rent. That I left for Merrick, who was expected to arrive in London later in the week. I was introduced to Sir Dash, the owner of the estate. I thought his name·fit the manor, as he slowly sauntered about his lonely house.

I hired a casting director, Irene Lamb. She was very knowledgeable and pleasant. Francine gave her our fifty-two pages of script. She was wonderful in her job until near the end of shooting, when she quit, totally exhausted and frustrated.

Merrick arrived in what was becoming his usual mood: disagreeable. I was at Pinewood Studios selecting cars for our actors – a beautiful, brand new convertible Camargue Rolls-Royce for Burt and a new Aston Martin for Lesley-Anne Down. I didn't understand why Miss Down needed such a grand car, but that's what Merrick wanted for her. I was looking at the Aston Martin when Merrick walked up and snarled at me. He thought the car was too cheap looking. I asked the mechanic how much it cost.

MECHANIC: Forty thousand.
ME: Dollars or pounds?
MECHANIC: Pounds.
  (*I walk back to Merrick.*)
ME: Have you any idea what this 'cheap' car sells for?
MERRICK: I don't care. It doesn't look like much of a car.
ME: They make possibly one car a day. The cost, forty thousand
  pounds. You told me when you hired me that you knew nothing
  about making pictures. You forgot to mention that, in addition,
  you know nothing about cars.

I called Merrick the next day.

ME: It's absolutely essential that you look at the manor estate for the
  exterior and interior opening party sequence. You'll either like it

454

or hate it. If you don't make a deal soon, we won't be able to start the picture.

MERRICK: Of course, I'll see it tomorrow. Is there only one choice?

ME: There's only one that fits the action of the script. By all means, look at them all. I suggest you go with your production manager, Peter Price, Ted Haworth and the location manager, Jim Brennan.

MERRICK: Will you be with us?

ME: I'm sorry, I can't spare the time. In addition to interviewing various crew members, I'm also attempting to cast the picture and am preparing a list with Irene Lamb for your approval and suggestions.

MERRICK: There are marvellous actors in England.

ME: Couldn't agree more. And there are many other locations I have to pick. Do you realize we have only fifty-two pages of script to shoot? What are you doing about the rest of the script, including the ending?

MERRICK: We must have a meeting.

ME: After you've seen the various manors. Call me when you get back.

Several days later, a tired Merrick visited my office. Irene was with me, finishing up the cast list.

MERRICK: Do you mind if I have a few minutes alone with Mr Siegel?

LAMB: I'll be upstairs with Carol, if you wish to go over the cast list. (*She leaves, carrying bulky books on casting, etc.*)

MERRICK: I hate the opening balloon shot.

ME: What did you think of the manors?

MERRICK: The only one that fit the script is the one you liked. It's expensive. Why not rewrite the script?

ME: Because it's a wonderful opening to the story. Burt, Larry, Carol and I like it very much. And although you don't realize it, when you see it cut together, you'll like it too.

MERRICK: Sir Dash's manor won't be ready to shoot for weeks. They are having a big party for the Mother Queen.

ME: We will have to pick all the locations we need up to the date we can shoot the manor. In addition, we'll have to finish the script. This delay will help us. Would you care to go over the cast list?

MERRICK: (*Getting up to leave*) Send it to my office. I'll study it.

In Merrick's office he, Irene and I had a casting meeting. The only name he didn't like was David Niven for the role of Chief Inspector Willis.

LAMB: I must confess, I'm surprised.

ME: Me too. Is he too expensive?

MERRICK: No. I don't think he's a good actor.

LAMB: What about the rest of the list?

MERRICK: It seems satisfactory.

LAMB: I'll come up with other names for the Chief Inspector.

MERRICK: (*Standing up*) Thank you for your efforts.

LAMB: As soon as I have at least five names, I'll give them to you. (*She leaves.*)

ME: I would appreciate your making up your mind on Sir Dash's manor.

MERRICK: I should know in a couple of days.

ME: I've got to hustle on the locations and script. (*Standing up.*) I'll keep in touch, though I must get my crew signed and delivered. Wish me luck.

The only member of the crew that Merrick seemed interested in was the production manager, Peter Price. Merrick had hired him and, naturally, he proved to be a very weak link. Perhaps I should count my blessings, as Merrick approved all my suggestions. He evidently believed in giving the director enough rope to hang himself. My team included:

Director of photography: Freddie Young (won Academy Awards for *Lawrence of Arabia* and *Doctor Zhivago*; worked mainly for David Lean)

Production designer: Ted Haworth (won Academy Award for *Sayonara*, in addition to many nominations)

Associate to Mr Siegel, writer and dialogue director: Carol Rydall

First assistant director: David Tringham

Costume designer: Anthony Mendelson

*

Merrick told me that although Sir Dash's manor was very expensive and we could not begin shooting there until 2 August, with rehearsal scheduled for 31 July, he would rent it. I thanked him. I thought his decision was the proper one. Among a thousand other things to do, I was going out there with Freddie Young and his gaffer (head electrician) to make sure that we had the necessary equipment.

MERRICK: What do you shoot until the manor is available?

ME: I'm going to try to shoot in continuity until I reach the day of the rehearsal. That way, we'll have a better understanding of what we're doing.

MERRICK: I'll always hate the balloon.

ME: Maybe I'll use a dirigible. Bye for now.

Freddie, his gaffer (Johnny Tythe), his key grip (Richard Lee), Ted Haworth and the location manager took a ride out with me to see the manor. After we walked through the exteriors and interiors, Freddie made an excellent suggestion.

YOUNG: If you and I could be here for the Queen Mother's party, it would be educational for me to see how they light the areas we plan to shoot. At the same time, you'll learn how the guests dress, how they behave, etc.

ME: Freddie, I'm glad I thought of your splendid idea. I'll try to find Sir Dash.

I asked the housekeeper if Sir Dash could see me for a moment. He appeared a few minutes later. I explained Freddie's idea to him.

SIR DASH: Will there just be the two of you? Security will be very strict.

ME: Yes.

SIR DASH: Then I think we can arrange it. I'll have my secretary get in touch with you.

ME: That's most kind of you. Again, many thanks.

Ted was waiting for me, talking to Francine in my outer office.

ME: You're just the man I was about to call.

TAYLOR: Miss Lamb has some good news for you.

ME: (*Entering my office*) Remind me to call her.
(*Ted follows me into my office. I sit behind my desk, indicating that Ted sit down.*)

ME: What's the bad news?

HAWORTH: I've instructions from Merrick to start building sets immediately.

ME: That's extraordinary. I need to shoot Rhodes's apartment, including the elevator and corridor, *before* anything else.
(*Ted starts scribbling on his pad.*)

HAWORTH: Keep talking.

ME: I need the exterior of Gillian's mews. Next, I must have a wild wall of the interior of the mews when Gillian telephones Willis. You'll undoubtedly build that set. We still haven't cast Willis.

HAWORTH: I found a marvellous exterior mews.

ME: I'm at your beck and call every minute, night or day. Let me know

457

if you run into money problems. At least Merrick has one important asset – money. There won't be any problems.

HAWORTH: Great

ME: Then, we'll need Inspector Willis's office, interior. Perhaps you can use Scotland Yard, or for that matter any office in any building. I'll also need to shoot the 'New Scotland Yard' sign. Remember, we will be shooting in continuity as much as possible until the party rehearsal on July thirty-first.

HAWORTH: I'll try to find as many locations as I can where I don't have to build sets, as I've got all I can handle now. Are you sure this is all you want?

ME: Yes, until I receive more script. I shall be eternally grateful.
(*He leaves quickly. Francine enters, laying cast photographs on my desk.*)

TAYLOR: Should I call Miss Lamb?

ME: Yes, but no more calls after that. I've got to get home.
(*A few minutes later, the phone buzzes. I pick up the receiver. It is Irene.*)

ME: Sorry to be so late, but I've been working on a new schedule with Ted Haworth. I'll send you a copy. No one, other than Ted, knows a thing about it – so mum's the word.

LAMB: Thanks. I need that information in working out the various deals for the cast. (*Her voice grows excited.*) I think I've got hopeful news. I showed Mr Merrick six alternative actors for the part of Chief Inspector Willis. After a long pause, he asked if the six actors were any good. He was unfamiliar with all of them. I told him they were all excellent, experienced actors. He then asked if I had my choice, who would I pick? I replied, 'David Niven', without question. He asked me to check on his availability and salary. I think we've got a chance of getting him.

ME: Even if we fail, I'm thrilled. Irene, you're the best. Many thanks and keep me posted.

I hung up. I had had quite a day. Maybe this sick picture would get well. Maybe.

*

The story of *Rough Cut* begins with an extremely large evening party in celebration of the first wedding anniversary of the elderly Lord Palmer (Roland Culver) and his young bride. The verdant lawn is filled with laughing guests holding aloft their glasses of champagne as Lady Palmer (Cassandra Harris) breaks a bottle of champagne on the edge of the gondola of a huge, 50-foot balloon with the inscription 'Happy Anniversary'. The balloon takes off, while the guests raise their glasses in a toast.

A solitary figure is watching. He is Jack Rhodes (Burt Reynolds), an attractive man in his late thirties. His eyes are now riveted on a beautiful woman, Gillian Bromley (Lesley-Anne Down), who is returning from the crowded grounds and is entering the huge manor. Rhodes follows her. She glances in his direction, then crosses the hall and goes up the stairway to the first floor. Rhodes hurries after her, noticing that the first door down the hall is closing. He tries to open it. It is locked. He tries other doors, all locked. He goes up the back stairway to the second floor. Outside the window is a flagpole. He climbs out of the window, grabs the pole and slides down it, landing on a large balcony below.

He crosses to a window where he sees, in the moonlight, the vision he has been pursuing. She is riffling through a drawer and finds a black, velvet box. She quickly opens the box, reaches into her black bag and removes a gold cigarette case. She swiftly takes a pair of diamond earrings from the box, dropping them into the cigarette case. She then puts the gold case in her bag and replaces the jewellery box. Then, hearing someone knock on a door, she picks up her bag and hides it under a cushion. Rhodes has seen it all. She crosses to the bathroom. Outside the bathroom

58 *Rough Cut*: Burt Reynolds

door, a man (Stephen Reynolds) pleads to get in. Gillian returns to the bedroom, picks up her bag, crosses to the door, unlocks it and goes out.

Rhodes slides down the flagpole and walks back towards the front door. He enters and crosses the busy hall to the foot of the stairs. Gillian enters at the top of the staircase, carrying a black feathered boa, and starts down the wide staircase. As she passes Rhodes, he reaches into his inside jacket pocket and takes out a cigarette case – the same one Gillian put the stolen diamonds in. She can't believe her eyes. She opens her bag. The case is gone. Rhodes flicks the case open. It is filled with cigarettes. Gillian turns away from him, bids him good night and leaves the manor.

Rhodes returns home, but as he is entering his flat he suddenly hears a noise upstairs. He moves quickly and noiselessly up the brass, spiral stairs to the open double doors of the bedroom. There he discovers Gillian in his closet trying to rob him. He produces the cigarette case and asks if that's what she was looking for. She opens the case, but it contains only cigarettes. When she asks what happened to the diamond earrings, he tells her that he returned them to their rightful place in the manor. Although he has outwitted her, Rhodes is intrigued by Gillian. When he asks her what her game is, she admits to being a kleptomaniac. Rhodes is interested enough to make a date with her for lunch and, as a parting shot, she returns his wallet to him. Rhodes looks after her admiringly.

When Gillian returns home, she telephones Chief Inspector Willis (David Niven), who seems to be very pleased with Rhodes's fascination with Gillian. Her looks, style and wit will provide the perfect bait with which Willis can ensnare Rhodes.

After lunch, Gillian takes Rhodes for a drive in the country. Rhodes soon realizes that Gillian not only doesn't have a licence, but has in fact stolen the car they're riding in. She is driving at a reckless speed and suddenly a police car is in hot pursuit. Trying to escape the police, she narrowly avoids an accident with a large truck. With the police still in pursuit, they skid into a factory yard, where Rhodes climbs into a dump truck and causes the truck to bury the car under tons of textile waste. They continue the journey home by taxi, sharing a bottle of champagne on the way. Although Gillian allows Rhodes to carry her to the door of her cottage, she refuses to allow him to enter.

Over the next few days, they date constantly and gradually fall in love. Gillian learns nothing about Rhodes's past, but she reveals that her father is a senior official in the government. One night, when Rhodes returns her to her cottage, Gillian says that she is available for him every night but one. Rhodes is intrigued. She explains that a friend of hers, Maxwell Levy (Douglas Wilmer), is the senior partner in a diamond firm. Several times a year, he sends up to £1,000,000 in rough stones to Antwerp. The shipment is always kept secret; but he always phones her the night before a shipment is due and considers sleeping with her good luck. When Rhodes seems disturbed and somewhat envious at the prospect of Gillian sleeping with Levy, she promises that this time she won't actually sleep with him. In any case Rhodes agrees with her that it's a long, boring story.

The following day, Willis appears at Gillian's cottage to learn how Rhodes reacted to the story about the diamond shipment. Although Gillian is convinced that Rhodes couldn't have cared less, Willis is sure that his reaction is exactly what was to be expected, since if Rhodes had acted enthusiastically, he would have been admitting that he was a diamond thief. In fact, not only is Rhodes a gifted thief, he also knows how to fence gems successfully. Willis is convinced that Rhodes will ask whether Gillian has heard from Maxwell Levy. But now that Gillian has fed Rhodes the bait, she wants to extricate herself from the conspiracy. However, Willis blackmails her into staying in the game.

The next day, as Rhodes and Gillian are sharing strawberries and champagne at Wimbledon, they encounter a friend of Rhodes, Ronnie Taylor (Julian Holloway), who introduces them to his companion, Maxwell Levy. Later, when Gillian is speaking about Maxwell Levy as they are driving away from Wimbledon, she realizes that Rhodes has tricked her. He was not the real Levy, but an actor Rhodes hired to determine whether Gillian was telling the truth. She then confesses to Rhodes about Willis and how Willis blackmailed her into meeting him at a party. However, stealing the diamond earrings was her idea. Although she has deceived him, Gillian tells him that her feelings for him are honest. Rhodes finds this difficult to believe, especially after the way in which she helped set him up.

When they return to her cottage, he asks if her refusal to go to bed with him was also part of Willis's plan. She replies exactly the opposite – she didn't want to be another one of his conquests. However, she didn't want him to be as clever and as attractive as he obviously is and, all things considered, perhaps he'd better come in. Smiling, Rhodes follows her into the cottage.

A trail of discarded clothing – shirt, trousers, shoes, dress, slip, stockings and two empty champagne glasses – leads to the bathroom, where Rhodes and Gillian are lying in a tub filled with bubbles. Rhodes decides to beat Inspector Willis at his own game. He admits to being interested in the Antwerp diamond shipment, but had never taken a run at it because he never knew the date. Now all he has to do is ask Scotland Yard. Or, rather, Gillian can ask Scotland Yard. Gillian says she won't be

59 *Rough Cut*: David Niven and Lesley-Anne Down

party to something that will put him away for ever; but Rhodes entices her
by reminding her that if stealing diamond earrings gave her a charge, just
imagine what $30,000,000 worth of diamonds would do to her.

The next day, when Gillian appears in Inspector Willis's office, he
knows at once from the mutinous expression on her face that Rhodes has
asked about the diamond shipment. When Willis threatens her with the
rigour and discomforts of prison, Gillian relents and agrees to pass on the
actual date.

While he is waiting for the date, Rhodes and his cohort, Nigel Lawton
(Timothy West), plan the robbery. Rhodes then flies to Germany to recruit
his old friend Ernst Mueller (Patrick Magee), to pilot the jet across the
channel. After their meeting, Rhodes telephones Gillian, who tells him
that Willis has given her the date: the 28th. Rhodes replies that the fact
that it is in one week's time seems to be a vote of confidence on Willis's
part. Rhodes then asks her to join him in Paris. They meet that evening at a

French discotheque, where Rhodes recruits a black singer and piano player, Ferguson (Al Matthews), to employ his skills as a radio-man on their diamond venture. For 10 per cent of $30,000,000, it's hard for him to say no.

The next step is to find a driver in the Red Light District of Amsterdam. His name is De Gooyer (Wolf Kahler). After a brief conversation, in which De Gooyer volunteers his services to make people disappear, either temporarily or permanently, Rhodes decides that he doesn't want to be involved with him. When De Gooyer tries to prevent them from leaving and suggests that Gillian can work for him as a hooker, Rhodes knees him in the groin and they hurry out over his prostrate body.

The next morning, Willis comes face to face with a catastrophe. The directors of Diamond House have received an anonymous phone call warning them that there will be trouble on the 28th. They therefore decide to postpone the shipment until the 10th of next month. Willis uses the authority of his office to assure the directors that the shipment will be protected. He himself will stay with the shipment until it's on its way to Luton Airport and will then fly ahead to Antwerp to cover its arrival there. If the directors cancel the date, from that moment on their timetable will be dictated by tipsters.

An hour later, the directors phone Willis: the 28th it is. But who was the anonymous tipster? Willis admits to Detective Sergeant Pilbrow (Andrew Ray) that it was he. How else could he ensure the massive security that is needed? Willis is determined to bag Rhodes before he retires. Willis knows that Rhodes has contacted an ex-pilot and an ex-air traffic controller; but he doesn't know where Rhodes is going to steal the diamonds – in London or in Antwerp? He tells Pilbrow that perhaps Gillian knows.

While Willis is busy interrogating Gillian in her cottage, they are interrupted by the arrival of Rhodes. In the course of their bantering, Willis reveals that he is about to retire on a modest pension; but that before he goes, there is room for just one more head on the wall.

The gang, now including Gillian as the driver, rendezvous at the airfield the day before the shipment to finalize all the arrangements. That night, Rhodes and Gillian pass through customs at Antwerp, dressed in Muslim robes, while being observed by two Belgian plainclothesmen (Michael Sheard, Geoffrey Larder). Rhodes carries two suitcases. When they reach the restrooms, he hands the smaller case to Gillian, who then goes into the Ladies' Room. Rhodes goes into the Gents. A short time later, the two Muslim-robed figures emerge from the restrooms. The plainclothesmen follow them. Rhodes and Gillian, now dressed casually, emerge from the restrooms and head for the flight to Amsterdam.

In Amsterdam they get an airport security car, identical to the airport security police cars in Antwerp. They also obtain all needed equipment. In London, Mueller and Ferguson paint and put identical decals on the engine cowling of jet no. 2, to match the paint and decals of jet no. 1, which will be carrying the diamond shipment.

In London, Willis has arranged for many identical armoured vans to follow the armoured van carrying the diamond shipment from Hatton Garden to Luton Airport – the shipment to be put on jet no. 1 going to Antwerp. If Rhodes is going to try anything in London, he'd be hopelessly confused. Willis is then to meet Belgian Inspector Vanderveld (Joss Ackland) at the Antwerp Airport.

The armoured van carries the two blue Securicor sacks from Hatton Garden to Luton Airport. Jet no. 1 takes off with the diamond shipment. From a nearby airport, jet no. 2, with Mueller piloting and Ferguson on radio, takes off at exactly the same time as jet no. 1. En route, jet no. 2 follows jet no. 1. As the two jets approach the air space above the border between the two countries, neither the pilots nor the towers of either country can transmit to each other. At this point, Ferguson radios jet no. 1 to divert to Amsterdam Airport due to an emergency. Jet no. 2, carrying fake quartz stones, flies on to Antwerp Airport. Both jets will land at the same time.

At Amsterdam Airport, Rhodes and Gillian, dressed as police security and wearing gas masks, overpower the crew by spraying tear gas, knocking them out. They grab the two blue Securicor sacks which hold the real diamonds and make their escape, while being pursued through the streets of Amsterdam by numerous security police cars. Rhodes and Gillian arrive at a pre-planned, isolated airstrip, where Mueller and Ferguson, prepared for take-off, are waiting. Rhodes and Gillian speed down the tarmac to jet no. 2, grab the Securicor sacks and leap aboard. As jet no. 2 takes off, several security police cars try in vain to catch the jet, which lifts off to freedom.

The next day, the headlines read: 'CHIEF INSPECTOR WILLIS RETIRES IN DISGRACE'; 'MULTI-MILLION DOLLAR DIAMOND THEFT'. An unkempt, unshaven Willis sits in the living room of his home, as Mrs Willis (Isabel Dean) enters with her suitcase in hand, having decided to leave him because of his disgrace. As she departs, the postman delivers a registered letter to Willis. On the back of the envelope is a Jack of Diamonds. He rips the envelope open. Slow dissolve to:

Tag Ending 1

On a tropical beach, Rhodes and Gillian are embracing beneath a waterfall. Gillian is wearing a large, impressive diamond around her neck. Rhodes yanks it off the chain and tosses it into the water. It's not a diamond, it's only quartz. Gillian knows, but asks Rhodes that if the stones in Antwerp were quartz and if the stones in Amsterdam were quartz, where are the real diamonds?

Before Rhodes can answer, Willis makes his appearance on the beach in a white suit and a panama hat. Willis explains to Gillian that he and Rhodes made a deal shortly after they met at her cottage. The plan was that Willis would steal the diamonds and replace them with quartz and Rhodes would fence the stolen gems.

As the three of them walk along the beach, Rhodes suggests that perhaps they should take a trip to India. At the Taj Mahal, there is a diamond big enough to live in. But perhaps they should discuss it after dinner. As they all laugh, the camera freezes on the three of them.

Tag Ending 2

Rhodes and Gillian are sitting at a table on the balcony of a tropical restaurant, sipping champagne. When Rhodes notices Gillian admiring the diamond she is wearing around her neck, he yanks it off and tosses it over the balcony. When she reacts with angry surprise, Rhodes informs her that the diamond is actually quartz. He then explains that the stones in Antwerp were quartz and that the stones in Amsterdam were quartz. Gillian asks where are the real diamonds?

Before he can answer, he sees Willis, dressed in an impeccable white suit and carrying a long, cool drink, approaching them. Willis admits to Gillian that he is the one who stole the diamonds. However, Rhodes points out to him that he needs someone to fence them for him. Willis and Rhodes bargain about the amount Willis wants for the diamonds. They come to an agreement, when Rhodes offers much more than Willis was demanding. Rhodes then suggests that they might take a trip to India. At the Taj Mahal, there is a diamond big enough to live in. But perhaps they should discuss it after dinner. They all laugh.

Tag Ending 3

This is the same as ending 2, with the exception that the scene takes place on a yacht.

Each morning, on my way to work, I would stop at the tailor's for a few minutes to have my dinner jacket fitted for the Queen Mother's party. It and the accoutrements cost a small fortune. No English gentleman ever pays his tailor for years. Unfortunately, being an American and not a gentleman, I paid the bill immediately. I'm still in shock.

One day, Merrick burst into my office, his face flushed and familiarly angry.

MERRICK: I've decided not to shoot Sir Dash's manor. It's too damn expensive.
ME: Have you found another place to shoot?
MERRICK: Everyone's looking, with the exception of you.
ME: Do you want me to stop shooting and start looking?
MERRICK: We'll find a manor that will work.
ME: It better work, or it will cost you more in lost time. By the way, Freddie and I were going to the party, so he would know how to light it and I would learn how royalty dresses, etc. Of course now, under the false pretence of shooting the manor, we can't go – although I spent a fortune buying my evening clothes.
MERRICK: Well, that's just too bad.
ME: It's also too bad that you apparently don't realize that the film looks great.

He stalked out in a fury.

We continued to use the manor.

*

Lesley-Anne Down could not drive a stick-shift car. In addition, the cars that Merrick chose for her to drive were a Ferrari, a Maserati, a Lotus and a Porsche. All were much too powerful for her. At the time, Lesley was in fact just learning to drive. I noticed a white 190SEL Mercedes with an automatic shift; it belonged to Lesley's stunt double. I made a deal with her to use the car and for her to teach Lesley to drive.

While Lesley, Burt and I were having lunch inside an inn, Merrick came over to our table, ecstatic over our selecting the Mercedes. He thought it was perfect. This was the man who hated every car because it was too cheap. When Merrick left, we all collapsed in laughter.

*

Merrick wanted me to shoot the discotheque sequence in Paris or Stockholm. I pointed out to him that Ted Haworth had shown me a discotheque in London called Dingwals. If we shot there, it would save thousands of dollars.

The actor portraying Ferguson, who was black, claimed to be an

466

excellent dancer. In the scene he was to play the piano and sing an original song he had written. He also wanted to dance in the sequence. I had him bring his female partner to Pinewood Studios to show us how well he could dance. He had two left feet – absolutely hopeless. In talking to the girl, who was a wonderful dancer, she told me she had a super partner. In rehearsal, when I saw them dance together, I immediately decided to use them.

The discotheque was the noisiest building I had ever been in. All the 'pots' were wide open. My eardrums ached for days.

*

'Jack of Diamonds' was the unanimous choice of the studio, Gelbart, Reynolds, Rydall and Siegel as title for the film. Everyone preferred it to *Rough Cut*. Burt even gave the crew gifts of expensive jackets with 'JACK OF DIAMONDS' on them.

At first, Merrick liked the title. But when everyone else liked it, he quickly went back to *Rough Cut*.

*

Unbeknownst to me, my associate, dialogue coach, bit actress, expert typist and story consultant – my wife, Carol Rydall – kept a diary of what went on behind the scenes during the filming of *Rough Cut*. I read her diary for the first time in June 1987 when I was writing about this film for my memoirs. I found the diary fascinating, truthful and full of incidents that I had long forgotten.

Carol Rydall's Diary

When we started filming on 16 July 1979, David Merrick had approved only the first fifty pages of Larry Gelbart's revised screenplay. Normally, one has a complete script to work with. Merrick hated the rest of the story, particulary the ending. His concealed idea was to duplicate the twists and turns in the plot of *Sleuth*: he secretly hired Anthony Schaffer, who wrote the play and screenplay of *Sleuth*, to rewrite the second half of *Rough Cut*. Merrick's attitude throughout filming was that he hated any original ideas coming from Don Siegel and Burt Reynolds. However, after viewing dailies, he would then change his mind and became enthusiastic. His perverse attitude caused great dissension, day after day.

I began keeping a diary on 11 August, the last night of filming the opening party sequence.

AUGUST 11 At approximately 4.30 a.m. Saturday, we completed filming the opening party sequence (night shooting) at the West Wycombe

467

mansion. Peter Price, the production manager, made a poor deal with the owner of the mansion and if we hadn't finished this sequence in the allotted number of days, the company would lose approximately £10,000 per day. However, Don *did* finish this difficult sequence a day under schedule, thereby saving the company a lot of money. David Merrick was at the location most of the night, which was extremely unusual. Normally, he has made his appearance and then left. I soon found out why he stayed so long this particular evening.

After completing the last shot, Don walked up to Merrick to shake hands and inform him that he had finished a day under schedule. Merrick handed him an envelope and told Don he was sorry he had to do this. The envelope contained a letter of dismissal.

I was in Don's trailer with Freddie Young and Chic Anstiss, our camera operator, when Don came in. He handed the letter to Freddie. Then I read it. We were all in a state of shock. Freddie was ready to quit, but Don talked him out of it by saying that his crew needed to work and Freddie's quitting would affect them. David Tringham, our first assistant director, came to the trailer. He was stunned when he heard the news.

Shortly after David left, Peter Price interrupted us. He told Don he was surprised and sorry to hear of Don's dismissal. He also stated that he was just told the news and that he didn't have any knowledge of who the new director was. Everything Price said was a lie. We found out the following:

The last time Merrick viewed dailies with us was August 5. After that day, he started looking at dailies on Sundays, which cost double to have the projectionist and others work on that day. Also, our editor, Doug Stewart, was requested not to be there on Sunday. His English assistant, Michael Duthie, would run with Merrick.

Peter Hunt was hired weeks ago to replace Don.

Peter Hunt secretly travelled to Antwerp and Amsterdam to look at the locations picked by Don and had also secretly checked our sets at Pinewood, all without Don's knowledge that this was taking place.

Peter Hunt never contacted Don to tell him that Merrick hired him as the new director.

Prior to being fired, Don was given Monday's shooting schedule. A scouting trip planned for Sunday, August 12, with our second unit at Luton Airport, was immediately cancelled. Both Burt Reynolds and Lesley-Anne Down had left the location prior to Don's firing.

Upon arriving home, Lee Stevens, a New York William Morris agent representing Merrick, telephoned Don. He told him that Michael Eisner, President of Paramount Studios, upon learning of Don's dismissal, tried to buy out David Merrick's interest in the film. Merrick refused, telling Eisner that *Rough Cut* is going to make a lot of money.

At 6.30 a.m., Don phoned his attorney, Arnold Burk, who was visiting in London at the time. He informed Mr Burk of his dismissal. Don then made calls to Burt Reynolds, who was extremely upset, Lesley-Anne Down, Freddie Young, Anthony Mendelson and Doug Stewart. All were in a state of depression. He told the crew not to quit and to continue on. He also instructed Stewart to ship all the film to the Paramount executives, who had not seen a foot of film. Later that evening, we had dinner with Irene Lamb. Don insisted that she should continue working also.

AUGUST 12   Don and I met with Burt Reynolds and Lesley-Anne Down at Burt's flat. Burt called Barry Diller, Chairman of Paramount Pictures. Burt and Don both spoke with him. Don informed Diller that he was under schedule and under budget at the time he was fired. He also told Diller that Merrick had been secretly running the film on Sundays with Peter Hunt. Lesley told Don that Peter Hunt's art director was seen looking over the sets at Pinewood within the past two weeks. Burt and Don then called Robert Aldrich, who was the past President of the Directors' Guild. Don explained everything that had happened. Aldrich particularly wanted to know if Peter Hunt had communicated with Don as to his replacing him. Don told Aldrich that up to this moment, he hadn't heard a word from Peter Hunt.

AUGUST 15   Today, the company was shooting at Luton Airport with Hunt. Ted Haworth called. He was told by Peter Price that there were changes in the script. Also, the whole ending was being changed. Amsterdam was out and the discotheque location was to be changed to Paris. Merrick was also changing the location of the tag ending to Rio de Janeiro. Lesley-Anne Down jokingly suggested to Merrick that the tag ending should take place in India. Merrick loved that idea also. All script changes are being made by Merrick without verbal, or written communication with Siegel.

Don Simpson, Vice-president of Paramount, and Lenny Hirshan arrived in London, along with Dick Zimbart, a top Paramount attorney. Don and I were convinced to stay in London for one week, per Burt's request.

Don Simpson and Dick Zimbart viewed all the film at Paramount before they left for London. Lenny Hirshan and Lee Stevens were not allowed to see the film. After viewing the film, Simpson called Siegel to tell him how much he liked the opening sequence. However, neither Simpson nor Zimbart has been to see Don since they got here. Zimbart and Simpson had dinner with Merrick.

AUGUST 17   Hirshan left town. We had a dinner date with Burt at the Connaught Hotel. Burt called and wanted us to come over to his flat prior to dinner. He told us he had arranged for Blake Edwards to fly in from Switzerland. Edwards and Merrick had a meeting this morning to discuss the possibility of Edwards taking over the film, since everyone, including Merrick, according to Burt, was dissatisfied with Peter Hunt. However, the deal with Edwards blew up. Burt told us that Merrick just called and said he wanted Don back on the film.

A meeting was arranged for Saturday, August 18th, at Reynolds's flat.

AUGUST 18   Merrick arrived with Lee Stevens at Burt's house. Reynolds and Stevens left Don and Merrick alone. Merrick apologized to Don privately and told Don he wanted him back on the picture. It was a gentlemen's agreement. Don was to start work Monday, August 20. Merrick told Don he was sending a letter to Peter Hunt at his hotel tomorrow, August 19th, firing him. After meeting for an hour, Reynolds, Stevens and Dick Clayton (Burt's agent) returned to Burt's flat to discuss Don being rehired. Siegel insisted that Peter Price also be fired as production manager. Merrick agreed, as this was an integral part of the new deal between Merrick and Siegel. Reynolds, Stevens and Clayton were all witnesses to Merrick's agreement to fire Peter Price. However, Merrick went completely back on his word.

Don arrived home and telephoned Arnold Burk regarding his being rehired. Burk told Siegel he would discuss the situation with Hirshan when he returned to Los Angeles.

AUGUST 20   Don and I went back to work, shooting a sequence in Rhodes' apartment.

This evening, Don received a call from Arnold Burk. Merrick had refused to sign a written agreement drawn up by Arnold stating that Merrick would not be able to fire Don again and that Merrick would not sue Don for anything prior to Don being rehired as the director. Don then phoned Reynolds to explain the situation. He then phoned Merrick and Alan DeLynn. Both were out. Don left a message to have them call him.

AUGUST 21   At 6 a.m., Arnold Burk phoned, indicating to Don that Merrick could be suing him. Arnold then dictated a letter for me to type up. Don was to give Merrick the letter at the studio.

We drove to the studio with Reynolds and explained the conversation with Arnold Burk and read him the dictated letter. When we arrived at the studio, Burt called Bob Aldrich regarding the situation. The letter to Merrick was immediately delivered to his office by Francine Taylor. Merrick and DeLynn arrived on the set at 10.30 a.m. Don directly asked Merrick why he was suing him. Merrick replied that he was not suing him. Don then told Merrick that his representatives gave him this information. Merrick emphatically denied this.

While Merrick was still on the set, I ran up to his office and secured Don's unopened letter while the secretary was in another room. No one knew I took it.

That evening, Arnold Burk called. Siegel told Burk that Merrick emphatically denied that he was suing Don and that Don would try and continue working on the film without the demands set forth in that letter.

At 8 p.m., Bob Aldrich called. Aldrich told Don he thought he made the right decision and that Merrick, after firing Don and then rehiring him, had no basis for a lawsuit.

Lenny Hirshan then called Don to tell him he just spoke with Merrick. Merrick told Hirshan that everything was great.

SEPTEMBER 1 At 2 p.m., a production meeting was held at our home.

Merrick wanted to re-shoot the Wimbledon sequence at Ascot. Burt agreed, since he was unhappy with the actor who portrayed Maxwell Levy and he also felt he could do better in the sequence.

During the course of the meeting, Don and Merrick got into a verbal argument over Peter Price, who is still working on the film as Merrick's production supervisor. After the meeting was over, Lee Stevens called from New York. He had just received a call from Merrick, complaining about Don bringing up the Peter Price situation at the meeting and saying that Merrick was upset about it.

We saw dailies after the production meeting. The film looked great. Don hasn't slept well and had a terrible sore throat.

SEPTEMBER 2 Don stayed in bed with a cold. Doug Twiddy called telling Don that Merrick just phoned him. Merrick told Doug, 'I sign all the checks and there will be no whorehouse, "Red Light District" sequence in *my* film and whose side are you on?'

Sally Fields then called. She said the phone rang until 3 a.m., with Merrick going crazy making phone calls to stir up trouble. Merrick was still upset about Don bringing up the Peter Price situation at the meeting. Sally was concerned about Burt, who is very ill and she is thinking about

471

putting him in a hospital. Don told Sally to tell Burt that everything was fine and Don apologized for his recent fight with Merrick.

SEPTEMBER 3   Don is quite ill with 100° temperature. Burt is equally ill, having difficulty in breathing. Both men saw the studio doctor.

SEPTEMBER 4   Today, we found out that we cannot shoot at Blackbush Airport tomorrow because the production department can't get the jet we need by Wednesday. We have nothing else we can shoot, because all scenes with Willis are being rewritten by Schaffer. Also, Merrick has a deal with David Niven that if Niven starts working earlier than his start date, it will cost the company money.

Alan DeLynn came to our trailer during the lunch break. He told us that Anthony Schaffer had given Merrick his new ending and that Merrick, evidently depressed by the new ending, flew to New York with the pages. Again, nothing was shown to Siegel because Merrick had the pages with him.

SEPTEMBER 6   Merrick is still in New York with Schaffer's new pages. We failed to reach Schaffer by phone.

SEPTEMBER 7   We completed filming at Blackbush. We called Alan DeLynn to come out to the location. When DeLynn arrived, Don pointed out to him that, again, we've run out of work because we haven't received the new pages. DeLynn promised Don he would receive some pages that afternoon. He then told us about Merrick's idea of having Willis steal the diamonds after they are loaded on jet no. 1, then taking off on a private jet to Antwerp. We both hate the idea. DeLynn said that Merrick is returning to London Saturday and will call and meet with Don that afternoon.

We received some pages at the location this afternoon. We were extremely disappointed with these new scenes, written by Schaffer. Several hours later, we received blue pages, which included the new scene of Willis stealing the diamonds from jet no. 1.

SEPTEMBER 8   Ted Haworth called and wanted to know if he could strike Rhodes' apartment set. He then told Don that Merrick wanted the complete set crated and shipped to his address in New York. [We later found out that Merrick did the same thing with Gillian's mews set, without Paramount even having knowledge of this.]

David Niven called. He was due to arrive in London this evening. Merrick had phoned Niven earlier. Don had planned on shooting Niven's last scene, where he has a beard and has let his hair grow long. Then David could shave and cut his hair for all the other sequences. Niven has not shaved or cut his hair for two weeks. Merrick told Niven that his last scene was out and to shave and cut his hair. Of course, Niven was extremely upset. Merrick then told David that he would receive new scenes at his hotel on Sunday. No call from Merrick.

SEPTEMBER 9   Still no call from Merrick.

SEPTEMBER 11   Don called Burt this evening regarding Burt's directing the second unit's balcony sequence with the stuntmen at Pinewood Studios. He also told Burt that he asked Merrick to fire the script clerk and that Merrick said he would let her go. Burt previously asked Merrick to fire the script clerk. However, Merrick did not fire her, as she was part of Merrick's group.

SEPTEMBER 13   I worked with Lesley-Anne Down today to help reorganize the Willis/Gillian sequences, incorporating her ideas. That night, Don, Lesley and I met with David Niven to discuss the rewritten sequences. David couldn't understand the changes unless he reread the whole script. We all agreed to sort out the changes tomorrow, when Schaffer will be with us.

SEPTEMBER 18   I stayed home with the flu. Don shot the Willis bedroom scene today. We are still running out of work because the ending is being held up by Merrick.

SEPTEMBER 20   Went to work today. We shot the Willis kitchen sequence at a home close to Pinewood. Merrick spoke to Don after dailies and told him he could shoot the Willis tag sequence at the house on Friday.
   Burt met with Hal Needham all day. Burt suggested that Needham could direct the Amsterdam chase sequence, while Don finished all the other work remaining in England.
   Don and I went out to dinner. When we returned home at 10 p.m., we received Schaffer's new pages of the Willis tag scene we are scheduled to shoot tomorrow. The phone rang. Anthony Schaffer called to explain the new tag sequence and to tell Don about Merrick's idea of having a mini car drive out of the ambulance at the end of the heist. This whole ending is being written by Schaffer without Merrick even mentioning his new idea to Don.

SEPTEMBER 21 We arrived at the location early and immediately met with David Niven and Isabel Dean to discuss the new dialogue for the tag ending. During our meeting in Don's trailer, Merrick and DeLynn arrived and opened the trailer door without knocking, interrupting our meeting. Don abruptly asked if he could finish talking to the actors first. Merrick closed the door. After our meeting, Merrick and DeLynn entered the trailer.

Merrick wanted the tag ending shot two ways: (a) with a package of diamonds being delivered; (b) with a registered letter being delivered. In the envelope would be a brochure of Rio de Janeiro. The location we would shoot at would be Mexico instead of Rio.

After leaving the trailer, Merrick told Doug Twiddy and David Tringham that the sequence we were filming at the house today must be finished in one day. Both men told Merrick it was impossible. Merrick told them to do it. Tringham then informed Don what Merrick had just told them. Don was extremely upset. He wanted to be replaced. On top of all this, it started raining and it was too dark to shoot inside, so we shot the postman arriving. Don called Arnold Burk, but could not reach him due to it being a holiday.

Around 4 in the afternoon, Merrick came back to the location and spoke to me. He confessed he knew it was impossible to finish the sequence in one day, especially because of the weather, and said we could complete this sequence next week, or the week after. Earlier that morning, Merrick told me that he didn't like this tag sequence and didn't feel it was necessary because of the new ending. I replied that we haven't seen the new ending! Merrick told me he decided to let Don have his way and film it, even though it won't be in the final cut of the film. Merrick thought we could re-shoot the drive from Wimbledon on Monday. He promised the pages late today.

SEPTEMBER 24 We were promised the new ending last Friday and still no pages today. We shot the sequence with Gillian and Willis at her mews house. Merrick visited the set this morning for five minutes and was surprisingly pleasant for a change. Lee Stevens, Stan Kamen and another William Morris agent visited the set also. They were in London to meet with Merrick regarding CBS's lawsuit with Merrick for a million dollars pertaining to a project Merrick was doing with CBS. William Friedkin was set to direct.

SEPTEMBER 26 Don called Burt at 10 a.m. Burt loves the new pages of the mews sequence that Lesley and I have worked on. When Merrick arrived on the set, Don showed him the new scene. Anthony Schaffer had written his version and Merrick wanted to compare the two.

After reading our version, Merrick insisted on keeping Schaffer's dialogue on why Willis was unhappy about retiring. He then told Don that Burt liked Schaffer's version of this sequence. Don told him that Burt liked our edited version better. Merrick said he didn't care and that we would shoot Schaffer's version and that was it. Don then blew up at Merrick's demand. When Don started towards Merrick, I physically intervened, fearing that Don would punch him out. The last thing we needed now was for Merrick to again threaten to sue Don. I told Don to cool off and go back to the set.

I tried to calmly talk to Merrick and told him it was unfair to Don and the actors in not giving the new ending to them. How were we supposed to know how this sequence fit into Schaffer's new plot ending? I told Merrick to call Schaffer and have him come immediately to the set and we would all sit down and rationally discuss the situation. Unbeknownst to me, Lesley-Anne Down overheard the whole argument.

I was still talking to Merrick when Burt arrived. Burt told Merrick he was tired of receiving new pages from Schaffer the night before shooting a scene, or the next morning on the set, and that he hated everything Schaffer has written. Merrick countered that he hated everything we've shot so far and he thought it was garbage. Burt flipped. He slammed his briefcase on the ground, ruining everything in it, and said, 'You're telling me that the first hundred pages we've shot so far is shit?' At this point, I was rooting for Burt to punch Merrick out. However, Merrick immediately backed down and replied, 'No. We like the first hundred pages.' Their heated argument lasted approximately half an hour. Burt ended the argument by telling Merrick that he wouldn't use Schaffer's dialogue and that no actor could make that dialogue work. Burt immediately left the set for our office.

Merrick continued talking to me for the next forty-five minutes, raving about Schaffer's new ending. I again implored that we must immediately have the pages. Merrick then admitted to me that he purposely had been holding back the pages so that he could improve it to perfection before handing them over. He then promised me we would receive the new ending this afternoon. He also explained that he has never complained about spending money on the film. For example, Ted Haworth wanted to rent antique German planes for the exterior shot of the air museum and that renting the planes cost quite a bit of money. However, I pointed out to him that Don saved a tremendous amount of money by shooting this sequence at the deserted airfield in London, instead of shooting it in

Vienna, which Merrick wanted to do. Merrick also pointed out to me that we were slow because Don and Freddie Young were slow. I countered that if Don was slow, it was due to the fact that we had to slow down because we were always waiting for new pages and the new ending. Because we ran out of work, Don decided to take more time with a scene than was necessary, rather than finishing a scene and have the crew not working the next day, waiting for more scenes to shoot.

SEPTEMBER 27 Today Don shot the drive from Wimbledon. After arriving at the location early this morning, Don told Ted Haworth that he wanted to use the bedroom set of Gillian's mews for the ending of the Rhodes/Gillian/Willis scene he was scheduled to shoot tomorrow. Ted informed Don that Merrick had already struck the set. Don was not told this and he was furious. A producer cannot strike a set without the director's approval. Anyway, Ted immediately went to work putting the set back together, re-renting the furnishings, etc. Several hours later, Ted came back to the location and told Don that Merrick heard about Ted reconstructing the set and emphatically told Ted not to put the bedroom set back together. We'll see what happens tomorrow.

Don finished shooting the Wimbledon drive sequence, except for Lesley's close-up. The sun was setting and there were shadows on her face. Don told David Tringham that tomorrow morning everyone would have an early call. We'd look at the dailies of the Wimbledon sequence and, if he needed to re-shoot Lesley's close-up, weather permitting, we'd come back early tomorrow morning, finish her close-up, then move to the studio and shoot the Rhodes/Gillian/Willis sequence.

Doug Twiddy then told Merrick what Don wanted to do. Merrick told Twiddy that we would go directly to the set tomorrow morning.

Don and I left the location and went back to the office to pick up the new ending Schaffer had promised. When we arrived, there were still *no* pages. I called Merrick's office and spoke to Sherry, his secretary. She told me that the pages were being xeroxed and that we would receive them in ten minutes. We waited for an hour. No pages. I called again and Sherry told me that the xerox machine broke down and the pages were not numbered, etc. More stalling. Since it was quite late, Don decided to leave and get some rest. We went out to dinner and when we arrived home, I called Merrick at the Savoy Hotel. He wasn't in, as usual. I left a message: 'We have not received the pages, as promised. When will we receive them?' Arnold Burk then called and informed Don that Barry Diller or Mike Eisner would be calling in a half-hour to discuss the situation of the constant and never-ending battle between Don and Merrick.

SEPTEMBER 28   Merrick and DeLynn arrived at the set around 11 a.m. Merrick told me that we could not mention Amsterdam, according to Schaffer's new ending. I told him that it was ridiculous to keep stalling. He left.

We broke for lunch before making the first shot. Don and I viewed dailies of the Wimbledon drive. Don decided that the shadows definitely ruined her close-up and that he had to reshoot it.

During lunch, *we finally received the new ending.* Ted came to our office and told Don that Merrick had changed his mind and that it was OK to put the bedroom back together for the scene Don was about to shoot. He also said that Merrick also changed his mind about Lesley's close-up and it was OK to re-shoot it.

After we read the new ending, Don and I were both confused and we didn't like many things. We went back to the set. Merrick arrived and admitted that the ending needed further polishing. Don was depressed about the new pages and told Merrick that he should find someone to take over. Merrick suggested that Don read it again over the weekend and they would discuss the pages then.

SEPTEMBER 28   Don shot the mews sequence two ways for protection: mentioning Amsterdam in the dialogue and not mentioning Amsterdam. Don then threw a party for the cast and crew after work. Everyone seemed to be happy and many of the crew members thanked Don for the party. During the party, Lesley suggested that we all meet to discuss the new pages. Burt was against this idea and suggested that Don meet alone with Merrick.

SEPTEMBER 29   Don had lunch with Merrick to discuss the new ending. Don told Merrick that Burt is the star of the film and we are selling a Burt Reynolds picture. In Larry's script, Rhodes is the greatest and most successful diamond thief in the world. If Willis actually steals the jewels, then the original plot of Rhodes getting away with the heist is ruined. The story was built on Rhodes stealing the jewels. Merrick agreed to go back to Gelbart's ending of Rhodes and Gillian stealing the jewels.

After arriving home, Don called Burt and told him the good news. Burt was extremely happy. Later that afternoon, Merrick called Don. Don told him he had told Burt about the excellent meeting they had and that Burt was extremely happy about going back to Larry Gelbart's ending.

OCTOBER 16   At lunch, we met with Burt, Hal and other production people involved with the second unit. They were to fly to Amsterdam and meet with Schiphol Airport officials and convince them to let us use their airport for this sequence. The airport officials were extremely concerned about showing a lack of security at their airport.

OCTOBER 17 Doug Twiddy called Don and told him that Merrick was halting the second-unit work to be done in Amsterdam. Burt then called us from Amsterdam and told Don that everything was going well with the airport officials.

Don then told Burt about Merrick cancelling the second unit because Peter Price told Merrick that it would cost $300,000 more. Merrick stated that he was already into the end money and that he couldn't raise the additional $300,000.

Burt then phoned Barry Diller from Amsterdam. Diller told Burt that Paramount would put up the extra money, only if Merrick promised to pay them back, without interest. Burt called Don back and told him what Diller was offering.

Don then called Merrick, who, of course, was not in at 10 p.m. He left a message saying, 'IMPORTANT'. Don called Merrick again at 11 p.m. and his line was busy. It turned out that Merrick was talking to Dick Zimbart, who is in London. Merrick never called back.

OCTOBER 18 Don didn't sleep at all. He called Merrick at 7 a.m. and told him that Diller said Paramount would put up the money if Merrick promised to pay it back, without interest. Merrick said he spoke to Dick Zimbart last night and Zimbart mentioned nothing about Diller. He said he would call Zimbart again this morning.

At Stansted Airport, we filmed jet no. 2 arriving and the unloading of the diamonds, with Willis and Vanderveld supervising. Merrick showed up at the location and told Don that Zimbart denied that Diller gave any instructions for Merrick to receive any further money for the chase sequence. Don challenged this as being impossible. Diller spoke to Burt and told him this. Merrick said they refused to put up the money. We felt that Merrick was again lying and, furthermore, Don felt that Merrick would not agree to pay Paramount back.

At 2.30 p.m., Hal Needham called Don at Stansted Airport. He said that Burt was flying back to London at this moment. Burt told Hal to call Merrick, which he did. Merrick told Needham that he only received our version of the chase two days ago and that the second-unit work on the chase would cost half a million more to shoot. He then told Hal that he liked the ambulance sequence better than the security-car version. He also stated that Burt and Don were taking over the show and that Hal had better call Don.

Hal then told Don that he was here to help with the show by shooting an exciting chase and that if we shoot the ambulance with a few security cars chasing it, we don't need him to do that. He then asked Don to call him back later in the evening and let him know what the decision was.

After our last shot, Don called Burt at his flat. He spoke to Tom Ellingwood, his make-up man. Tom told Don that Burt couldn't work tomorrow because he is quite ill.

Dr Sacks, head of the motion-picture doctors in England, called Don this evening and told him that Burt is indeed quite ill. He gave him injections and medications and said that it is quite serious. Burt cannot work tomorrow.

Don then called Hal in Amsterdam and told him that Burt is very ill and that he couldn't reason with Merrick. Don talked Hal out of flying to LA and, instead, talked him into flying to London to see Burt before he leaves. We are all very worried and concerned about Burt.

OCTOBER 19   Burt did not work today.

While shooting at Luton, Doug Twiddy arrived at the location and told Don that Merrick had again changed his mind and that we could go ahead with the security-car ending and the second-unit work with Needham in Amsterdam. Don immediately phoned Burt. He couldn't speak to him because the doctor was examining him. Don spoke with Tom Ellingwood and told him the good news and asked him to relay it to Burt. Twiddy had a lot of work to do, arranging the shipment of crews and equipment to Amsterdam, so that they will be prepared to start shooting Monday morning.

OCTOBER 21   Don had lunch with Merrick today. He brought back Merrick's new tag ending for me to read. I read it and almost vomited. Burt called. He told Don that he was putting up the money for the security-car chase by giving up his end salary of $100,000 per week for three weeks. At lunch, Merrick told Don that he had raised the money, but he didn't tell Don from whom. In order to shoot the chase, Burt had to finance it, which I'm sure pleased Merrick greatly.

OCTOBER 22   Today we shot the Maria Montez/Turhan Bey scene at Stansted Airport. Burt was very shaky and pale. Merrick showed up at the location and immediately sat in Burt's director's chair. Burt did

60   *Rough Cut*: the Turhan Bey scene

everything he could to hold back from punching Merrick out. Insult on top of everything else. Needham began filming in Amsterdam.

OCTOBER 23   We shot the interior of the German Air Museum at Pinewood Studios. We discussed the tag ending with Burt, then showed him Merrick's version. We all vomited together.

OCTOBER 24   We filmed the process shots of the Mercedes with Burt and Lesley. Burt and the script clerk, who has yet to be fired by Merrick, got into a verbal argument on the set. It seems that she was giving acting directions to Lesley-Anne Down, which not only angered Don, but also Burt. Burt and Don talked me into playing the role of the hooker in the window in the Red Light District sequence.

OCTOBER 28   Today I packed for our trip to Amsterdam. Don called Merrick. Merrick never returned his call. Burt called and he sounded good. Everything is going well in Amsterdam. They are waiting for permission to dump two security cars in a canal.

OCTOBER 31 At 4 p.m. we started shooting the Red Light District exterior shots, including the lighted bridge and the walk down the street, and finished shooting around 2 a.m. Burt again was not feeling well. He wants to work this Sunday, so that we can leave Amsterdam on Monday. Freddie Young and his crew refused to work Sunday. Part of the reason is that Freddie was upset upon learning that he and his crew are not going to Hawaii to shoot the tag ending and that an American camera crew will be hired.

NOVEMBER 1 We slept late, had breakfast, then went to look at the set at the Amsterdam studio. Freddie Young finally agreed to work Sunday.

NOVEMBER 4 We finished the Red Light District. Luckily, we were shooting again on the set because it's pouring rain today. Merrick finally threw a cast and crew party. However, the attendance was poor because everyone, including Don and myself, was packing after work to leave tomorrow.

NOVEMBER 5 We flew to London. We then connected with a flight to Los Angeles, which Burt, Lesley and Tom Ellingwood were on. During the flight, Burt told us he was meeting with Larry Gelbart tonight in hope of his improving our tag ending.

NOVEMBER 6 All day I unpacked. Burt dropped by and gave us the tag ending that he and Larry had worked on.

NOVEMBER 8 Burt and Tom flew with us to Hawaii. We discussed Gelbart's tag ending during the flight.

NOVEMBER 9 On the island of Oahu, we had a meeting at 9.30 a.m. in Burt's hotel room and met part of our new crew: Michael Butler, our cameraman; Marty, the location manager; Peter Bogart, the assistant director; plus Haworth, Don, myself and Merrick. I handed Gelbart's ending to Merrick and everyone else attending. Merrick made no comment, but asked me if Burt wrote it. I told him that it was my understanding that Gelbart wrote it.

That afternoon, a group of us flew to the island of Kauai to look for the location for the tag ending. We found a beautiful spot with a waterfall and a huge cave, which is an ideal tropical setting. However, the only way to reach the area is by helicopter. All cast, crew and equipment would have to be flown in.

When we returned to Oahu, we heard through the production department that Merrick refuses to allow us to shoot on Kauai because it is too expensive and also because he hates Gelbart's new ending. Don phoned Arnold Burk about the possibility of Merrick firing him again when they get into a fight. Then Hirshan called and told Don that Merrick just called him in Los Angeles and he suggested that Don call Merrick and discuss the latest disagreement between them. Throughout this film, Merrick has never called Don directly. He always calls agents, lawyers, etc., and has them call Don requesting that Don call Merrick.

NOVEMBER 10   Don had a meeting with Merrick this morning. He told him it was OK to now shoot Gelbart's tag ending, but he demanded that Don also shoot his tag ending. Don finally agreed, under great duress.

NOVEMBER 11   We flew to Kauai and had a production meeting at 6 p.m. with the rest of our new American crew. Merrick seemed somewhat pleasant for a change.

NOVEMBER 12   We had a beautiful day and shot the first part of the waterfall sequence. All equipment, cast and crew were flown to the area by helicopter. We met with Burt, Lesley and David and made some minor alterations to Gelbart's version.

NOVEMBER 13   Today we ran into bad weather. It was raining and was quite windy. We just barely managed to finish the last shot, pack our equipment and escape by helicopter. An hour later, due to the increasing winds, it would have been too dangerous for the helicopter to fly and we all would have been stuck there overnight.

NOVEMBER 14   Today we filmed Merrick's version at the hotel. I had edited this sequence the day before and there was time for the actors to learn their lines of pages and pages of dialogue. Of course, Merrick had to approve my edited version before he allowed me to hand out the pages. Burt, Lesley and David used cue cards to finish this sequence.

We completed our work and had lunch with David Niven. Then, David and the rest of us flew back to Oahu on a chartered flight at 3 p.m. in order to shoot an added vault scene, where we show that Willis had access to the diamond shipment. Don came up with this idea as protection for a confused ending. We had to finish this scene today, as Niven had to make the last flight out in order to fly to India, where he is to start work on another film. However, we did have our problems.

First, we couldn't obtain the raincoat made for David in England, and the wardrobe people had to scout around Hawaii for an English raincoat. Then, Niven's wardrobe was lost on the chartered flight from Kauai to Oahu and we were delayed until they found his wardrobe and sent it out to the location. After finishing the shot, we said our tearful goodbyes to David. *Last day of shooting.*

[NOVEMBER 15–19 Don and I flew to the island of Hawaii for a vacation after finishing principal photography. One day, while having a massage, the masseur noticed a lump below the latissimus muscle on Don's chest. Since it had been raining ever since we arrived, we decided to fly home and see Don's doctor. Dr Hoytt ran some tests and diagnosed the lump as a cyst.]

[NOVEMBER 20–29 We set up our offices at Paramount Studios. I was off payroll as of the last day of filming, November 14. However, money was still due me and I had to fight for it. Merrick informed Paramount that Don could not hire a secretary during post-production. Paramount agreed to pay the secretary's salary. Don began coughing more frequently and was steadily losing weight.]

DECEMBER 5 Lenny called Don about Merrick being allowed to see the cut footage of the chase. Don replied that *he* hadn't even seen the cut footage and after he had viewed it, Merrick could see it. At 2 p.m., Don met with Lenny and Arnold Burk in his office. After the meeting, Don decided to let Merrick view the chase before he saw it. Merrick saw the footage today.

DECEMBER 6 Don viewed the aerial footage, which arrived from England today. He also viewed the cut footage of the chase sequence. This was the first time he had a chance to see it.

DECEMBER 11 Merrick phoned Don and wanted to have a drink with him after work at the Beverly Hills Hotel, where Merrick is staying. Don wants Hank Mancini to score the film, which Merrick agreed to.
Merrick requested, through Don, that I issue a final script, which includes Gelbart's and Merrick's tag endings. Of course, I am no longer on salary, as of the last day of filming; but all the post-production work I have done on the film was for Don. [Little did I realize that at a later date, Merrick would have the title page retyped, putting Anthony Schaffer's name as sole writer.]

MARCH 24   Don and I were in a projection room running Don's cut, when Merrick called. Several days ago, Don ran the film for Larry Gelbart. Larry suggested shooting an insert, which Larry would write. Don mentioned this to Merrick and he said OK. Don then told Merrick that he was going into the hospital on March 25th for some tests.

Merrick called Don this evening. He freaked out. Evidently, he just read an article in the *New York Times*, written by Gelbart, putting down the film. Merrick is furious. He told Don that both Burt and Larry were detrimental to the film and that Burt threw away the dialogue of Merrick's tag ending. He then told Don that he is working on getting Reynolds, Niven and Down together to shoot a new tag ending that Merrick wants. Merrick then started shouting obscenities, such as 'You're full of shit', etc. Don told Merrick that he is tired and weak and he would not continue to argue. Don hung up.

[While Don was in the hospital, the doctors discovered that the so-called cyst was in fact a malignant tumour and that Don had lymphoma, a cancer that spreads quite rapidly through the body. We both credit Don's oncologist, Dr Van-Scoy Mosher, in saving his life through chemotherapy.]

While Don was in the hospital, Merrick took over. When Henry Mancini realized that Merrick wanted various Duke Ellington songs incorporated into the score, he decided to quit and Merrick hired Nelson Riddle instead.

Merrick then forced Burt Reynolds, Lesley-Anne Down and David Niven to shoot a new tag ending, which was filmed in Florida by a new director Merrick had hired. Don glanced at the pages for the new ending, but he never saw the finished film.

After extensive chemotherapy treatment, Don has recovered and has been in total remission. However, we all still bear the scars from David Merrick.

*

Once during filming *Rough Cut* I was working alone with Burt on the forever changing script. We discussed the senselessness of Merrick. I was bitter and upbraided Burt, declaring that it was actually his fault. He smiled and thanked me for being so gracious. I pointed out to him that if he hadn't given up all his rights of control on the picture, we could have made a film we truly were proud of. God, what fun we could have had.

Burt got up, a peculiar smile on his face, and crossed to his desk. He picked up a letter and returned, handing it to me. He thought it strange and hoped that I could explain it to him. It read:

Dear Bert,
Do you suppose Clint isn't *really* a friend of yours?
    David

It certainly was strange. Typically Merrick. Maybe Clint spoke highly of my work to do Burt in. Or maybe a thousand other ugly, tilted thoughts. I asked if I could keep the letter. Burt nodded his head.

39

Jinxed

United Artists 1982

The producer Herb Jaffe was in partnership with United Artists in a project based on a screenplay entitled 'The Edge', written by Frank D. Gilroy. Gilroy also wrote a revised screenplay, 'Jackpot'. When I met Jaffe for the first time in his office at United Artists, he handed me the latest script, 'Jackpot'. He wanted a quick read. Jaffe looked fit, in his middle fifties; a genial, pleasant man. He suggested that I immediately read the script in the next office, which was empty.

ME: When I'm making up my mind on whether to accept a project, if I feel it has a chance, I read slowly. (*Smiling*.) I just shoot fast. Who's set to star?

JAFFE: Bette Midler, one of the most promising stars today.

ME: I've never seen her.

JAFFE: She was nominated for an Oscar in *The Rose*. Surely you've heard her sing?

ME: I believe so. As I recall, she has a somewhat coarse voice.

JAFFE: Several weeks ago Bette came to my office, laid down a sheet of paper with six directors' names written on it. They were all excellent directors. I asked her who she wanted. She replied, 'None of them. I want Don Siegel.'

ME: Well, I've got to admit, she has good taste. I'll read the script today and let you know what I think of it tomorrow morning. What time do you get in?

JAFFE: I play tennis every morning and I'm usually at the office by ten.

ME: (*Getting up, shaking his hand*) Tennis is a wonderful game. It's exciting to lose by love. Be waiting for you tomorrow morning.

The next morning I was waiting, script in hand, for Herb to arrive in his office. He showed up full of vigour.

JAFFE: Sorry to keep you waiting.
  (*I look at my watch and grin*.)

ME: A lot can happen in a period of waiting five minutes, but you're forgiven.

JAFFE: Well, what do you think of the script?

ME: For one thing, it's the third version of *The Postman Always Rings Twice*. The first one, shot in 1945, starred John Garfield and Lana Turner. It is easily the best. The second, starring Jack Nicolson and Jessica Lange, made in 1981, used the same title. The third one is written by Frank D. Gilroy, presumably titled 'The Edge'.

JAFFE: I know all this.

ME: Well, Herb, it puzzles me. The first one made money. The second one bombed out. All three screenplays have basically the same plot. An older man is in love with a younger girl. A young man falls in love with the girl and they have an affair. She convinces her new lover into helping her murder the older man.

JAFFE: (*No smile*) I know that too.

ME: Gilroy's background to the story is gambling. However, many similarities exist. Why make the story a third time?

JAFFE: Don't you feel the script is well written?

ME: I admit that Mr Gilroy writes well, while blithely indulging in plagiarism. I also admit he camouflages his work with a flair for reality.

JAFFE: Miss Midler is vacationing in Mexico and wants to call you tonight. Do you mind listening to what she has to say?

ME: Herb, it might be difficult talking to her. I don't want to jeopardize your project.

JAFFE: I have complete faith in you. I'm just sorry you aren't keen about the project.
(*I get up to leave, taking the script with me.*)

ME: Who knows? Maybe I'll fall in love with Bette and make a beautiful love story out of 'The Postman Refuses to Ring'.
(*I leave before he has a chance to reply.*)

*

At around 9 that evening, the phone rang. I lifted the receiver. A cheery voice spoke over the phone.

MIDLER: Mr Siegel, this is Bette Midler.

ME: It's my pleasure.

MIDLER: Mr Siegel . . .

ME: (*Interrupting*) The name's Don, if I may call you Bette.

MIDLER: Of course. What did you think of the script?

ME: It's very difficult discussing a script over the phone. Why don't we have a meeting when you return?

MIDLER: (*Her voice now strident*) I would simply like to know if you like it or not.

ME: There are some things that interest me. Gilroy is undoubtedly an experienced writer . . . but he sort of zigs when he should zag.

MIDLER: Well, I hate it.

ME: You may have a legitimate point there. It's like horse racing. People usually differ in their opinions.

MIDLER: I'm only interested in what I feel. I'll be returning on Monday. Why don't you drop by my house around seven thirty in the evening? My secretary, Bonnie, will call you and give you my address.

ME: OK. I'll give the script another read. Can my wife Carol come along with me? She's pretty sharp on script.

MIDLER: Anything you want.

ME: Thank you. I'm looking forward to meeting you.

Carol and I met Bette and her entourage: her secretary Bonnie Bruckheimer, in her late twenties, and her skit writer, Jerry Blatt. Miss Midler, surprisingly small in stature, was somewhat Napoleonic in strength of character and temper. She was bright, energetic, hypersensitive, witty, with a great sense of fun and occasionally full of hate. She rented a lovely old house, with beamed ceilings, off Coldwater Canyon. Richard Chamberlain was her landlord.

We sat around a large dining table. Bette and Jerry were impatient to get to work. They sat at opposite ends of the table. Carol and I sat on either side of Bette. Bonnie discreetly disappeared. Bette, chewing on a yellow pencil, a yellow pad before her, took over.

MIDLER: (*A bit rough*) Let's get on with it. We've got a long way to go.

ME: Before the charge of our 'brigade', I have a question I would appreciate asking you.

M'DLER: Fire away.

ME: You mentioned, quite definitely, that you hated Gilroy's script.

MIDLER: An understatement.

ME: Why did you accept the assignment?

MIDLER: I haven't signed any papers, as of this moment. And, more importantly, I refuse to sing the title song, or any other songs in the picture. How do you like that, Mr Siegel?

ME: Well, frankly, I couldn't care less.

MIDLER: I take it you don't like my singing?

ME: Isn't it perfect that I agree with you not to sing in this picture? What if I said, 'You have to sing in the picture'? I made six different pictures with singers and they all felt exactly like you – they didn't want to sing and they didn't.

MIDLER: All right, let's mush on. Do you believe that a man can have the whammy on one particular dealer and never lose?

RYDALL: Why not? The man is the dealer's Jonah.

ME: That's true. Even the Bible's on our side.

BLATT: Throw doubt out of the window and have faith in yourself. After all, you're seeing it actually happen again and again. You've gotta believe.

After several hours of discussing the script, Carol and I got up, explaining we had an 8.30 appointment in the morning. We all agreed that in order to make the film the story had to be rewritten. We all felt good and friendly. In saying our goodnights, I told Bette that I would work on a much shortened version of the story. It would take less effort to rip it apart.

*

What transpired is actually the story of how *not* to make a motion picture. The next screenplay, revised God only knows how many times, was entitled 'Jackpot', written by Bette Midler, Jerry Blatt, Carol Rydall and Don Siegel, dated 27 January 1981. Frank Gilroy had disappeared, only to reappear in the main titles under the pseudonym of Bert Blessing, for story and screenplay. I'm assuming that the world 'Blessing' was his gratitude for not having to take the blame by using his real name. I can't say that I blame him.

On 6 March 1981, another revised script, entitled 'Hot Streak', made a startling appearance, written by Jerry Blatt, based on 'The Edge'. It was my hunch that 'Hot Streak' was largely written by Miss Midler.

Bette Midler had enormous energy and drive. She worked on every script and revision. Each time we finished a script, I thought this was it. And I was wrong. She made many changes I knew nothing about. The last person she talked to, be it Dustin Hoffman, Anthea Sylbert, Robert Towne, members of her entourage, or the janitor sweeping up the stage – she was wide open to their ideas. However, on this last revised script, 'Hot Streak', she showed genuine enthusiasm; so I took off. A great deal of the script was undoubtedly hers, plus her writer's name was on it.

There is so much to do in pre-production that it is literally scary getting ready for the starting date of shooting. I had great need to go on a location

489

trip with Vilmos Zsigmond, director of photography, Ted Haworth, production designer, Carol Rydall, associate producer, Mario Iscovich, location manager, Luigi Alfano, first assistant director, Larry Whitehead, gaffer, Robbie Banks, best boy, and Dick Deats, key grip.

In Nevada, I laid out to the crew how I intended to shoot the script. Things were progressing well when I received a message to call Herb Jaffe immediately. I hopped in a car and rushed down the hilly mountain road to a pay phone several miles away. I got Jaffe on the phone.

JAFFE: How are you doing, laying out the story to the crew?
ME: Not badly.
JAFFE: I just spoke to Bette and she hates the script.
ME: Yesterday she definitely told me she liked it and thought we finally had a shooting script.
JAFFE: Well, today she hates it.
ME: So do I. There's no point in wasting time laying it out for the crew. I give up. I'm returning at once, with the crew. See you when I get back.

The next morning I met with Jaffe, who commiserated with me. I told him I wished he had let me leave to do a film with Paramount before contractually signing me to do the UA picture. He didn't blame me. As a matter of fact, he wished he had left with me.

I made an 11.30 appointment with Stephen Bach, Vice-president in charge of production at UA. I entered his office and thanked him for seeing me.

BACH: I take it there is trouble.
ME: We are all in trouble. It is impossible to make a picture when the star and the director both hate the script. In my opinion, there is only one way to proceed. Cancel the picture before you wind up losing every cent you will have invested in it.
BACH: Thanks for your advice, but we will proceed with the picture.

*

Bette said she wanted to play opposite Ken Wahl and her entourage thought it was a smashing idea – especially her agent, Arnold Stiefel, who also represented Ken Wahl. I thought that Bette was joking. Ken was around twenty-five, tall, sexy and a surprisingly good actor; but much too young to play opposite Bette. However, she stuck to her guns until the studio said 'OK'. Then she beat a hasty retreat. I met with Ken and liked him. He thought that it made no difference if he was younger than her. Stephen Bach arranged a casting meeting in his office. Invited were Bette,

Bonnie Bruckheimer, Arnold Stiefel, Herbe Jaffe, Carol Rydall and Don Siegel.

BACH: It's the studio's right to assign anyone we want to play opposite you. You initially suggested Ken for the role. However, I'm going to leave it up to all of us to vote on this matter and abide by the decision of the majority. All against Ken Wahl, raise your hands. (*Bette immediately raises her arm, followed by Carol and yours truly.*)

BACH: All those in favour, raise your hands.

Bach, Jaffe, Stiefel and Bruckheimer all raised their hands. Of course, Mr Stiefel was to gain another 10 per cent if Ken got the role. I looked at Bette. Her chin quivered. She was spitting mad. She got up quickly and stormed out of the room. I felt sorry for her. I must confess I felt sorry for Ken, too. When we were making the film, they hated each other.

*

One great bit of casting that we totally agreed on was Rip Torn for the part of Harold, the gambler that Willie (Wahl) could never beat. In addition to being a great actor, Rip is an excellent director, mainly on the stage. In addition, he is one tough hombre. When Rip arrived at Harrah's Casino in Lake Tahoe, he was refused a room at the hotel. He had just gotten back from a two-week fishing trip and looked it: they couldn't believe he was one of the stars of the picture. Rip walked across the street to the Blue Jay Motel, where some of the crew were staying. The only room available was our editing room. At that time, the room was empty because the editing facilities had yet to be set up. So Rip took the room, happy to be out of Harrah's. Approximately one week later, Doug Stewart, the editor, and Tony Spano, his assistant, arrived to set up the editing room. They were embarrassed to find Rip Torn in the room, sound asleep. They explained their predicament to Rip. By this time, the manager liked Rip, who supplied him with fish. He quickly got him another room. During the entire shooting, Rip lived with the crew at the motel. There was nothing 'fancy' about our co-star.

In one of Harold's scenes with Bonita (Bette Midler), she is driving the GMC pulling their trailer into Reno. Harold is concentrating on an anagram in a book of crossword puzzles. He asks her for help. The answer to the anagram is the word 'pistol'. In the script, Harold comes up with the word. Bette decided to change the dialogue so that Bonita comes up with the word. She did this without permission. When Rip read the changed line, he came to me, quite upset, and wanted to know why I had changed it. I told him that I knew nothing about it until I read it on a revised page.

TORN: Don't you make the changes?
ME: I have on every picture until this one.
TORN: Did Bette make the change?
ME: I can't think of anyone else rude enough to do it but her.
TORN: Do you mind if I do something about it?
ME: Be my guest.

Rumour hath it that Rip and Bette had a verbal battle over who was going to say 'pistol'. It wound up with Rip threatening to quit the picture and copious tears from an angry Bette. Rip won the battle of words, plus the respect of Bette. They not only became good friends, but they helped each other greatly in their scenes together.

Ken Wahl presented constant problems for Bette. When she attempted to change many of the scenes between them, if Ken disagreed, he would tell her so. He could be very stubborn. I would try to steer a middle course so we could continue shooting. I was occasionally able to help them patch up their differences; but it was tough sledding.

Now that Bette, in real life, is happily married and has a beautiful child whom she adores, I wish I had had the opportunity of knowing her when she was radiant in her happiness. One thing is certain. I would have been happier. Without question, the picture would have been much, much better.

61   *Jinxed*: Don Siegel and Bette Midler

40

A Confession

In reading this manuscript from beginning to end, looking for errors and changes to be made, I had an uncomfortable thought. I felt I had 'bitched' my way through the entire autobiography. It's extremely unlikely that everyone is out of step but me.

The reason I'm so feisty is because I enjoy it. All pictures, if you care, are very difficult to make. But the truth is, 'it's all a game'. It's 'make-believe' time and I had fun playing the game. If I am picked on by 'authority', I respond with sarcasm. Generally, the people in charge of the studios are so self-conscious of their position that they can't take sarcasm or teasing. Teasing is my bread and butter. Of course, I overdo sometimes. I frequently lose the argument or the quarrel; but I'm tricky.

Wonderful people like Bogart and Cagney are out of my class. They can cut you down to size in the blink of an eye. Walter Huston can spin a tale that leaves me speechless. Michael Caine's laughter is so contagious that I am helpless, caught in my hysterical joviality. The difficulty in naming names is the enormous number of people who should be mentioned. Nevertheless, I can't leave out my dear talented friends – Clint Eastwood, Hank Fonda, Dick Widmark, Peter Lorre, Sidney Greenstreet, Walter Matthau, Geraldine Page, Sheree North, Elizabeth Hartman (God bless them). My love to all the rest of the marvellous actors and actresses, and cameramen like Bud Thackery, Robert Burks, Sam Leavitt, Michael Butler, Bruce Surtees, Freddie Young, Vilmos Zsigmond . . . and so many, many others.

41

Clintus and Siegelini

Clint Eastwood and I worked together on five films: *Coogan's Bluff* (1969), *Two Mules for Sister Sara* (1970), *The Beguiled* (1971), *Dirty Harry* (1971) and *Escape from Alcatraz* (1979). In 1971 I signed his Director's Card and he directed me as a bartender in his first directorial effort. The picture, *Play Misty for Me*, turned out very well indeed. The bartender, a good-luck charm, is my best piece of acting.

I think what has made our relationship work is the respect we have for each other. I think that Clint is most knowledgeable about film, acting and modern music. He's become the biggest (I'm not referring to his 6-foot 4-inch frame) star in the industry.

The millions of people watching Clint in one of his movies can be misled. He doesn't go in for the histrionics of some actors. To the uneducated eye, he appears not to be acting – which is one of the most difficult feats an actor can perform. Most of the time his voice and mannerisms are low key; the actors playing opposite him sometimes appear to be over-acting. Clint couldn't care less for his 'image'. Other actors, at times, strain for their faces to be seen by the camera, but Clint will frequently play part of a scene with his back to the camera, which can be startlingly effective.

In choosing his projects and in acting, Clint goes strictly by his instinct. His batting average is very, very high. He comes on the set prepared. He works loose, which is the way I prefer to work.

Men not only like him; they are somewhat in awe of him. Women, of all ages, fall into an easier category: they love him. He is pleasant, affable, easy-going and has a wonderful sense of humour. But when he's working, he's all business. He likes the scenes to be shot quickly. Not carelessly: he insists on the best from his staff and crew. Although Clint is 'Mr Cool', he is not someone to fool around with on the rare occasions when he loses his temper. If you can't pull your weight, he'll fire you on the spot. He won't put up with nonsense, nor with waste of time. I can't remember the exact set of circumstances, but I can vividly recall him once saying, 'I may be many things . . . but I'm not stupid.' I got the message.

Clint is very loyal to his old friends; in my opinion, sometimes too loyal. Whenever he asks a question, I give him a straight answer. He does the same with me. It's remarkable that in the confusion of making films, we've never had a quarrel. Disagreements, yes. Differences of opinion, yes. Perhaps that's because he might look up to me as a surrogate father. If that is the case, it makes me very proud.

He's a great believer in his instinct. Why not? He's rarely wrong. Maybe we get along so well because we're so different. He's a Republican, I'm a Liberal. Would you believe we've never discussed politics? He's cool and calm. He thinks things out. I'm feisty and hot-headed. My decisions are dictated by my emotions.

I know I'm a better person because of our friendship. When Clint grins at my teasing, I'm happy. He doesn't say much, but what he has to say makes sense.

His foreword to my memoirs touched me deeply.

God Bless.

APPENDIX
Television Work

Dictated to Stuart Kaminsky

I must say that most of my peers are phoney when it comes to directing for television. They were in television for the same reason I was: to make money. I can't see any other reason to do it. You have less time to work, less time to prepare and absolutely no post-production time. So I don't understand when they start talking 'artsy-craftsy' about what they do on television. Most of the work done on television is poor, particularly as far as directing is concerned. If you're going to be in television, be a producer, because a director is not important. On a series, you have a regular producer, cameraman, crew and cast. When a stranger steps in – the director – he doesn't wield much authority.

When I have done television shows, I have kept the right to do the first cut. Most directors can't afford that. They do a three-day show and rush away to do another one for someone else the following week. Most television directors don't even have time to look at the footage they've shot each day. The directors of television usually direct traffic. When they do a good job, they deserve a lot of credit; but good television direction is rare, because it is so incredibly difficult. The preparation time is ludicrous. Many busy directors read the script for the first time on the way to the set. Now that is not true about television pilots. There you have time and money. The only important thing is that you have to make it so good that someone will surely buy it. It's actually dishonest, for when the sponsors or networks buy it, they don't realize that the series will bear little resemblance to the pilot. The pilot for a one-hour show will have a big budget, a good director and a shooting schedule of several weeks. When the series starts, the budget will be small and the director will have a week to complete the shooting .

Select TV Credits

1953   I co-wrote an original story entitled 'The Bogeyman' for the United States *Steel Hour*. The show was directed by Alex Segal. In addition to his last name being wrongly spelled, I didn't like his direction. Years later, I ran into him at Universal Studios. I told him of my displeasure at the way the story was directed. He nodded his agreement and pointed out that the show was shot live with three cameras. Moments before the show went on the air, one of the cameramen fainted. They had to improvise using only two cameras. In my embarrassment, I apologized. I told him I thought he did a hell of a good job.

1954   The very first television show I did was on a series entitled *The Doctors*. I directed three half-hour shows. Two of them took three days apiece to shoot. The last one took two days, and Lee Marvin co-starred with Dorothy Malone. The alternate director (who was also the production manager and had directed many more shows than I did) was Robert Aldrich. I quit after the third show.

1954   I directed the half-hour pilot *The Lineup* for CBS. It starred Warner Anderson, Tom Tully and Charles Bronson (then Charles Buchinsky). I shot two-thirds of it on tape; we finished the last third on film. The Screen Directors' Guild was about to fine me $1,000 for working with non-Guild members in San Francisco. When I explained that the San Francisco shooting was all on tape, the Board of Directors looked into my bovine eyes and let me go free. Actually, in those days they had no jurisdiction over tape. I've loved tape ever since.

1961   I directed 'Paper Gunman', the first episode of the series *Frontier* for producer Worthington Miner.

1961   I directed the pilot *Code Three* for Hal Roach, Jr, which was sold as a series.

1963   Roy Huggins, a Twentieth Century Fox TV producer, wanted me to direct the pilot of *Bus Stop*. I turned it down unless I could use the original William Inge script. The screenplay was adapted by Robert Blees. The photographer was J. Peverell Marley. The cast included Tuesday Weld, Gary Lockwood, Buddy Ebsen, Joseph Cotten, Marilyn Maxwell and Rhodes Reason. The pilot was sold and made into a series. I thought the pilot was good, but the series was terrible; which is about par for the course. Roy made thirteen pilots for Twentieth during that year. Only one sold: *Bus Stop*.

1963   Richard Collins, the producer of *Breaking Point* for Bing Crosby

497

Productions, asked me to direct the first episode, entitled 'There Are the Hip and There Are the Square', written by Mark Rodgers; executive producer, George Lefferts; photographed by Robert Houser. The cast of the fifty-minute show included John Cassavetes, Carl Lawrence, Paul Richards, Arthur Franz, Woodrow Parfrey, Virginia Gregg, Seymour Cassel and J. Pat O'Malley. The series ran for several years.

1964   I directed two half-hour episodes of *The Twilight Zone*, both of which were narrated by Rod Serling. 'Uncle Simon' starred Sir Cedric Harwicke, Constance Ford and Ian Wolfe. I was shocked when I saw Sir Cedric. I put my arm around him. He was terribly thin. He said to me in a weak voice, 'I'm not the man I was.' I pooh-poohed the idea that he was sick. He played a robot named Uncle Simon. His acting, as usual, was superb. Unfortunately he couldn't remember his lines. The most I could shoot would be a sentence or two. I kept repeating this way of working throughout the show. Yet, when it was all cut together, no one was aware of how it was shot, due to the consummate artistry of Sir Cedric. When shooting him, I stationed myself right next to the camera, just out of its range. I was prepared to catch him if he started to fall. Somehow, we got through the show. I believe it was the last time he worked. He was a dear friend. I miss him.

The second *Twilight Zone* episode was entitled 'Self Improvement of Salvadore Ross', starring Don Gordon. Frankly, and it's about time I admitted it, I have only the faintest recollection of the episode.

1964   I directed one episode of *The Lloyd Bridges Show*, starring Lloyd Bridges and Glynis Johns. It took three days to shoot and I needed every minute. Glynis Johns, who is a wonderful, imaginative actress, went blank. She had a terrible time remembering her lines. It could have been the script. Anyway, I suffered with her.

1965   I directed a one-hour colour pilot entitled *Johnny I Hardly Knew You*, which sold as a series known as *Destry*, made for Universal. The pilot was produced by Roy Huggins, photographed by Bud Thackery. The cast for the pilot included John Gavin, Tammy Grimes, Broderick Crawford and Neville Brand. I don't believe the series ran for more than a year. I not only didn't like it – I didn't care for the pilot.

1965   I directed and produced the fifty-minute black-and-white pilot *Convoy*, which sold as a series. The cast included John Gavin, John Larch, Linden Chiles, Gia Scala. It was photographed by Bud Thackery. The executive producer, Frank Price, was very enthused about this sea project, about two captains (John Gavin and John Larch) of two separate ships. He felt it would be as successful as the Western series *Wagon Train*, which ran for eleven years. This made no sense to me, as it proved impossible to work out the story that in World War II these two ships and their captains could be together to play scenes: they were on separate ships and different assignments.

I told Sid Sheinberg, who at that time was the head of TV at Universal, that I didn't like the show and wanted out. He told me that it was up to Frank Price. Frank was as smooth as glass. I had written him a rather nasty letter, hoping that, in his anger, he would let me go. I saw him the day after I sent the letter, which was conspicuous on his desk. Frank never mentioned it. All he talked about was his strong belief that *Convoy* would become the *Wagon Train* of the seas. When I told him that was stupid reasoning, he totally ignored me.

Convoy was a difficult show to shoot. It took hours to move the equipment. One time I was shooting the wheelhouse (or pilothouse). I decided to stay there until I had completed several sequences. The unit manager, a famous former child star, Wesley Barry (Freckles), stuck his head in the wheelhouse.

BARRY: Don, break your set up. We're going to shoot the crew
    escaping the fire, jumping off the bottom deck.
ME: You must be crazy. I'm staying in this wheelhouse until I finish.
BARRY: I've got everything set for the fire sequence.
ME: By the time the equipment is moved to the bottom deck, it will be
    dark. We won't be able to make a single shot.
BARRY: I'm calling Paul Donnelly, who, as head of production, will
    order you to do as I say.
ME: Get your ass out of this wheelhouse and put me on report.

Barry left in a rage. I continued to shoot. It seemed like only a few minutes when, through the ship's intercom, a voice bellowed out.

VOICE: Mr Siegel, report on the double to the radio room.

I rushed down to the radio room. Barry was talking on the radio to Paul. He was in the midst of telling him that I had refused to move out of the wheelhouse to shoot the fire sequence. I grabbed the speaker, pushed the button and started talking.

ME: Sorry to break in, Paul, but the only way I can get off this ship is
    to finish each sequence. Over.

DONNELLY: How long will it take you to shoot the fire sequence? Over.

ME: About a day. I suggest that I finish the wheelhouse, finish the fire sequence and shoot everything else at the studio. Over.

DONNELLY: Put Barry on. Over.

BARRY: Barry speaking. Over.

DONNELLY: Get Mr Siegel off the ship as soon as possible. Let him finish the wheelhouse; then the fire sequence; then back to the studio to finish the picture. Over and out.

I thought Barry was going to have a heart attack, or start crying. If I had stayed on the ship, it would have taken me weeks of further shooting. Every word we uttered over the radio was heard throughout the ship. As I entered the wheelhouse, I was greeted with applause. In three days, we were back at the studio. All the necessary sets were miraculously ready.

Convoy sold. It lasted a year as a series. It cost Universal a fortune. Frank Price's insistence that *Convoy* would be the *Wagon Train* of the seas proved one thing: the *Wagon Train* concept sank as soon as it hit the seas. It never resurfaced.

1966 I produced and directed the half-hour pilot *The Legend of Jesse James* for Twentieth Century Fox. The screenplay was by W. R. Burnett. It was based on Nunnally Johnson's script for *Jesse James*, which was directed, in colour, by Henry King in 1939.

Naturally, all the stock footage was in colour. I was dumbfounded when Bill Self, head of TV at Twentieth, decided to shoot the pilot and series in black and white. That decision killed any chance for the series' success, as the networks all agreed to release only colour television the following year. I didn't direct any of the series. I was the 'line producer' – a thankless job of coming up with stories, writers, directors, finding locations, casting each segment, editing and all post-production work. I will always be grateful to Bill Self for killing the series. I hated it.

The pilot was photographed by George T. Clemens. It starred Christopher Jones (a disturbed young man), Allen Case (a pleasant young man), John Marley, Woodrow Parfrey, Don Haggerty and Ann Doran. I produced thirty-four episodes in the series. David Weisbart was the executive producer.

Although I subsequently made three two-hour shows for TV: *The Killers*, *The Hanged Man* and *Stranger on the Run*, they were released as features. So *The Legend of Jesse James* was the last TV show I produced or directed.